The Running Times Guide to

Breakthrough Running

Running Times

Gordon Bakoulis, Editor-in-Chief

Candace Karu, Editorial Director

Human Kinetics

Library of Congress Cataloging-in-Publication Data

The Running times guide to breakthrough running.
    p. cm.
   ISBN 0-7360-0217-0
   1. Running. 2. Running--Training. I. Title: Breakthrough running. II. Running times.
GV1061. R8415 2000
613.7'172--dc21

00-027146

ISBN: 0-7360-0217-0

Acquisitions Editor: Martin Barnard; **Developmental Editor:** Julie Rhoda; **Assistant Editors:** Susan Hagan and Carla Zych; **Copyeditor:** Bob Replinger; **Proofreader:** Julie A. Marx; **Indexer:** Nan N. Badgett; **Permission Manager:** Cheri Banks; **Graphic Designer:** Nancy Rasmus; **Graphic Artist and Illustrator:** Kimberly Maxey; **Photo Editor:** Clark Brooks; **Cover Designer:** Jack W. Davis; **Photographer (cover):** Photo Run; **Photographers (interior):** Photo on p. x © David Madison/Bruce Colman Inc.; photos on pp. 19-22 courtesy of Roy Benson; photos on pp. 109, 111-120, and 128-132 © Michelle Bolduc; photos on pp. 306-307 and 312-314 © Doug Peck; photos on pp. 53, 127, 176, 182, 205, 209, 231, 243, 261, and 274 © Tom Roberts/Human Kinetics; and photo on p. 288 © R. Walker/H. Armstrong Roberts. All other photo sources noted beside photo; **Printer:** United Graphics

Human Kinetics books are available at special discounts for bulk purchase. Special editions or book excerpts can also be created to specification. For details, contact the Special Sales Manager at Human Kinetics.

Printed in the United States of America   10 9 8 7 6 5 4 3 2 1

Human Kinetics
Web site: http://www.humankinetics.com

United States: Human Kinetics
P.O. Box 5076
Champaign, IL 61825-5076
1-800-747-4457
e-mail: humank@hkusa.com

Canada: Human Kinetics
475 Devonshire Road Unit 100
Windsor, ON N8Y 2L5
1-800-465-7301 (in Canada only)
e-mail: humank@hkcanada.com

Europe: Human Kinetics, P.O. Box IW14
Leeds LS16 6TR, United Kingdom
+44 (0)113-278 1708
e-mail: humank@hkeurope.com

Australia: Human Kinetics
57A Price Avenue
Lower Mitcham, South Australia 5062
(08) 82771555
e-mail: liahka@senet.com.au

New Zealand: Human Kinetics
P.O. Box 105-231, Auckland Central
09-523-3462
e-mail: humank@hknewz.com

Running Times
Web site: http://www.runningtimes.com

Corporate office: Running Times
213 Danbury Road
Wilton, CT 06897
203-761-1113
203-761-9933 fax

Subscription orders and inquiries:
Running Times
P.O. Box 50016
Boulder, CO 80322-0016
800-816-4735
303-604-1464 in Colorado and
    outside the U.S.

*This book is dedicated to every runner
with the courage to strive for a
breakthrough performance.*

Contents

Acknowledgments

We gratefully acknowledge the wisdom and dedication of the contributors to this book. It has been an honor to work with such an extraordinarily talented group of writers and runners.

This book would not have been possible without the diligent work and well-timed advice and counsel of acquisitions editor Martin Barnard, developmental editor Julie Rhoda, and assistant editor Carla Zych of Human Kinetics, along with their committed and resourceful staff. In addition, the constant encouragement and guidance of *Running Times* publisher Carol Lasseter Rice and senior marketing/promotions director Jeff Darman have been invaluable in making this project a reality.

And finally, we would like to thank our families for their love and support.

—Gordon Bakoulis and Candace Karu

Introduction

Breakthrough: "A sudden advance in knowledge or technique." In running terms, we often think of a breakthrough as it relates to speed. These milestones—our own and those at the highest levels, such as national and world records—are reported in the press as fast as they are made. A record-breaking performance represents a breakthrough for both the athlete who achieves it and the sport as a whole.

We at *Running Times* believe that the definition of breakthrough running applies to all runners, not just elite athletes. We created this book because we know that every runner can have a breakthrough in his or her running, at any performance and fitness level. Like the individual runner, each breakthrough is unique. We define it as taking your performance to the next level—whatever that is for you.

It could mean running two miles for the first time without stopping to walk.

It could mean entering a 5K race after years of solitary running at one easy pace.

It could mean getting through six months without a flare-up of plantar fasciitis.

It could mean training without pain for the first time, thanks to a new stretching program.

It could mean finishing a marathon—or deciding to train for one.

It could mean finally getting a treadmill after a dozen winters spent slipping on snow and ice.

It could mean committing to racing less often or allowing yourself to take a day off each week.

It could mean attending a group workout for the first time or seeking sound training or racing advice.

It could mean deciding to work with a coach to plan your training and racing schedule.

This book will help you achieve these kinds of breakthroughs and more. It will guide you in the pursuit of that next level. We have gathered the sport's leading experts to show you how. The new ideas and creative and innovative thinking in these pages may challenge your concept of what running is all about. That's good! Breakthrough running should challenge the existing structure of your running. It should make you examine what is working for you and what you need to change.

To help you make these changes, we have kept these chapters practical and hands-on. Besides cutting-edge ideas and running philosophy, you'll find easy-to-follow guidelines to apply to your existing program as well as new (but proven) training and racing programs to invest in. Included are customized training programs for various distances, several types of speed workouts, injury-prevention strategies, guidelines for nutrition and hydration, shoe and apparel information, advice on rest and recovery, and much more.

This book is divided into three parts: training, racing, and recovery. Each section begins with an overarching philosophy, which draws on the wisdom and experience of the experts who wrote the chapters. Within each section, the chapters cover questions and concerns that runners are likely to have about specific issues. These take a variety of formats, including question-and-answer sessions, interviews with experts, lists, charts, tables, and first-person accounts. Training, racing, and recovery all are related in the performance-oriented runner. These three aspects of running work toward the same breakthrough goals—becoming the best runner you can be and gaining the greatest fulfillment you can from your running—whatever that means for you.

The Running Times Guide to Breakthrough Running is the definitive book of its kind. It is for the regular runner who is committed to running as a sport, a fitness outlet, and a lifestyle. It is for the runner seeking to advance that commitment to the next level. Your breakthrough may be a sudden and dramatic improvement in performance, or it may be something more subtle. You may find a renewed commitment to the running lifestyle or a deeper understanding of all the factors that contribute to a great racing career.

To bring you this book, the editors of *Running Times* have drawn upon a wealth of running experience, along with years spent gathering, organizing, and defining the best information and advice available to the running community. We hope that *The Running Times Guide to Breakthrough Running* will provide you with the information and impetus you need for a lifetime of running breakthroughs.

PART I

Breakthough Training

In distance running, perhaps more than in any other sport, an athlete's training constitutes the basis of any breakthrough in performance. Of course, the importance of raw talent as an ingredient of success should not be discounted, nor should the mastery of racing tactics and skills (the focus of part II of this book) and the careful observance of health-promoting practices that enable the body to recover from the stresses of training and competition (the focus of part III). But without a solid, well-conceived, progressive training program, one carefully crafted to condition the body to run long and hard, all else is beside the point for a distance runner wishing to reach the next level.

Our strong belief in the importance of training for distance runners is why we have designed this first part of *The Running Times Guide to Breakthrough Running* as a comprehensive, progressive training guide. Each of the chapters instructs the reader in mastering an essential aspect of training, from building a base to choosing the right gear to maintaining strength and flexibility to choosing the proper training diet. Although each chapter, written by an expert in the field, is individually valuable, we believe that taken as a whole they provide an even greater benefit as a complete performance-maximizing program.

As runners, we know that everything you do to enhance your performance in and enjoyment of running is interconnected. Although each expert has his or her own perspective on how you can be the best runner you can possibly be—and you'll find as you read through the section that these views aren't always in perfect agreement—they all share our opinion that a comprehensive, holistic approach to running and all that supports it is of greatest benefit. Here is what you can expect in the pages ahead.

Chapter 1, written by *Running Times* editor-in-chief Gordon Bakoulis and editorial director Candace Karu, looks at what it is that differentiates training—that is, running with a purpose other than recreation and health—from ordinary running. It is our hope that this opening chapter will get you to look within yourself for what motivates you to be the best runner you can be, and to think about what *best* means for you. For some, it may mean winning the New York City Marathon or the neighborhood 5K. For others, it may mean running without injury or pain, learning to fuel properly for workouts, or successfully integrating running into a comprehensive fitness program.

The chapter also covers goal setting, which for many runners is the first and most important step toward a breakthrough. It reminds you that you have what it takes to be the best runner you can be. In distance running, no matter what your level and how serious you wish to become, you will find that the more you put into running, the more you will get back from it. Bakoulis is a former world-class runner who has placed in the top 10 in the New York City, Twin Cities, Grandma's, and other marathons; qualified for the U.S. Olympic Marathon Trials four times; and edited *Running Times* since 1997. Karu, who takes a less competitive approach to running, considers her daily runs along the Maine coastline as much a spiritual exercise as a physical one. She cherishes the deep and lasting friendships she has formed and nurtured through her years "on the run." The combined perspectives of these writers will help you to tap into what your personal running breakthrough entails.

In chapter 2, renowned coach and self-described amateur exercise scientist Roy Benson examines running biomechanics—that is, how the body moves while running. According to Benson, most runners misdirect the energy of their bodies when they run. If you don't believe that, Benson says, just see for yourself by having someone videotape you while you run. A critical look at your running form from the front, back, and side, and from jogging pace to 5K race-pace effort isn't designed to discourage or humiliate but to illuminate basic biomechanical problems that you can correct with simple drills. Benson outlines the two most common form faults, excessive upper-body rotation and overstriding, and shows how any runner can identify and permanently correct these problems.

Chapter 3 looks at the all-important question of what to wear (above the ankle) while running. It's written for every runner who has ever had a perfectly good training run ruined by an inappropriately chosen garment or by the failure to don one particular apparel item or another. Teresa Gibreal, a long-time member of the running-apparel sales industry, presents crucial information and advice on dressing for the cold, heat, wind, rain, snow, and whatever else Mother Nature may dish out. Gibreal bases her advice on the premise that thanks to an explosion in the development of high-tech fabrics designed to keep outdoor exercisers comfortable and safe just about anywhere and anytime, there's almost never an excuse to miss a run because of bad weather. The chapter includes a glossary of high-tech terms to take the intimidation factor out of shopping and a windchill conversion chart to eliminate the guesswork from running on days ranging from chilly to frostbite inducing.

In chapter 4, we look at training footwear, courtesy of shoe experts Kirk Rosenbach and Gregory Sheats. Shoes are said to be a runner's most important piece of equipment. Indeed, the revolution in shoe materials and construction over the past 25 years has drawn millions of people into the sport on the noncompetitive side and helped those at the elite level train longer and harder than was ever possible with the footwear of yesteryear. the mystery out of finding and purchasing a shoe that's right for you, based on your foot's function or unique biomechanical profile. Also included are dozens of helpful tips for buying, caring for, and replacing training shoes. With the constant procession of new shoes reaching the market and the ever-increasing hype about shoe performance, this chapter is a must read even for those who are happy with their current training shoes and think they know how to stay that way.

Chapters 5 through 9 delve into the meat of designing and executing training programs to maximize running performance. Because this task is part art and part science, we've called upon a group of experts who are both artists and scientists to present the information and guidelines.

Chapter 5, by Tudor O. Bompa, PhD, and Michael Carrera, outlines the principles of periodization—the scientific method of varying the timing, duration, and intensity of your workouts. Bompa is the world's foremost expert on periodization, a concept that he pioneered in 1963. This chapter lays out the crucial importance of training with a plan that allows the body to build fitness gradually, sharpen speed and race readiness, perform at peak levels, and then rest and recover before beginning the cycle again. It explains the science behind this method in terms that make sense to the nonscientist and includes examples of appropriate workouts for runners aiming to peak at distances ranging from 1,500 meters up to the marathon. This chapter gives an overview needed to integrate the elements of training described in the following chapters, 6 through 9.

In chapter 6, renowned collegiate coach and former U.S. Olympic Marathon team member Mark Conover presents the basics of base training, which involves building a foundation of aerobic fitness upon which all other elements of a successful performance-enhancing training program can be erected. This chapter is required reading for any runner who believes in shortcuts to great performances. Conover, drawing on his experience as an athlete and a coach, as well as proven principles of exercise science, shows how a program of aerobic running strengthens the cardiovascular system as well as the muscles, bones, and connective tissue to prepare for the rigors of more-intense training and racing. The chapter includes sample training programs and mileage guidelines for runners training for distances from 1,500 meters to the marathon.

Chapter 7 looks at training for distances from the marathon on up—the realm of ultradistance running. Few know more about this than accomplished ultrarunner and *Marathon & Beyond* editor Rich Benyo. After describing our natural human capacity to run for longer distances than perhaps any other species, Benyo outlines how ordinary mortals can train to complete—on a competitive basis, if they wish—distances ranging from 26.2 miles to six days of continuous running. Included are tips on event-specific fueling and hydration, developing an ultradistance mindset, and such practical matters as adapting to running on trails (where many ultra events are contested). There's plenty to learn here even for those who swear they would not run a marathon (much less a longer event!) if their lives depended on it.

In chapter 8, we draw upon the expertise of one of the most respected names in distance running, Pete Pfitzinger, MS, coach, exercise physiologist, and two-time Olympic marathoner. In this chapter, Pfitzinger, author of *Road Racing for Serious Runners*, examines lactate-threshold (LT) training, perhaps the single most important ingredient in a performance-maximizing training program for distance runners. LT training involves raising the level at which the body can meet its energy needs by burning oxygen—in relative comfort and without having to tap into other, less efficient energy systems. Pfitzinger carefully and clearly explains what the lactate threshold is, why raising it is crucial to success in distance running, and—most important—how to train to bring one's lactate threshold to the highest possible level. Sample workouts are included for distances ranging from 1,500 meters to the marathon.

Chapter 9 builds on chapter 8 by outlining the various ways to condition the body to run faster. Coach Brooks Johnson, who has guided dozens of U.S. athletes to Olympic glory, is adamant about the need for speed in a training program, whether your goal is the 100 meters or the marathon. This chapter explains how speed-oriented training prepares the heart and lungs, the working muscles, the biomechanical frame, and the mind to cover ground quickly. Johnson includes sample training weeks to show how speedwork fits into an overall distance-training program, as well as biomechanical drills designed to turn the body into a smoothly functioning speed-producing machine.

Chapters 10 through 12 encompass three aspects of distance running that are sometimes deemed peripheral to successful participation in the activity, but which we view as essential components, no matter what your level of commitment.

In chapter 10, personal trainer and 2:35 marathon runner Stephen Anderson describes what a solid strength-training program can do to enhance a distance-running regimen. Strength training with free weights, weight machines, and the body's own resistance can reduce injury risk and promote a balance of strength between pairs of muscles that work together in the body. Anderson provides a complete toe-to-head strength-training routine that can be performed in 20 to 30 minutes, several times per week. It's revealing to note that many of the world's top elite distance runners engage in some type of strength training. They know that staying injury free and balancing the strengths of the muscle groups of the body are essential if a breakthrough is to occur.

Preventing injury is also a major focus of chapter 11, on flexibility. For distance runners, staying flexible means maintaining the body's capacity to move freely by preventing the shortening and tightening of the muscles and connective tissue that running can induce. Freelance running writer Heather C. Liston draws upon the research and observations of the world's leading experts on flexibility, addressing the essential question, "Must I stretch?" Besides stretching (yes, you probably should do it), the chapter covers yoga, chiropractic, massage, and other roads to improved flexibility.

Not all runners cross-train, but those who don't often admit that they probably should. In chapter 12, *Running Times* editor-in-chief Gordon Bakoulis explains why cross-training in some fashion can be the key to a breakthrough in distance running. Quite simply, the pounding of running is a stress for even the most well-adapted body, and cross-training— substituting other aerobic activities for running on a consistent, programmed basis—can reduce the injury risk incurred by all those miles while actually improving overall fitness. The chapter includes a discussion of the most popular and beneficial cross-training activities for runners and gives several sample training programs that use various cross-training activities in a range of proportions in a running-based program.

Eating and drinking to fuel a training program are perhaps more important to distance runners than to athletes in any other sport or fitness activity. In short, a runner who is not properly and adequately fueled cannot reach his or her performance capacity. In chapter 13, sports nutritionist and former elite distance runner Suzanne Girard Eberle, MS, RD, explains the importance of proper fueling for a distance runner, then outlines how to eat and drink to set the stage for a breakthrough. Eberle's advice centers on commonsense principles and solid science. Rather than promoting so-called wonder foods and gimmicky nutritional supplements, the chapter focuses on the overall diet and gives advice every runner can live with.

Finally, in chapter 14, exercise physiologist and former U.S. Olympic Marathon team member Pete Pfitzinger, MS, looks at the practice of training at high altitude to gain a performance edge in distance running. Altitude training is popular among elite runners all over the world, yet science has not definitively linked it to improved performances in races run at sea level. Pfitzinger looks at the science behind the hype. In particular he examines the new practice of high-low training, doing recovery running at high altitudes and speed sessions at lower elevations.

In sum, although distance running has been called the simplest of sports, its training can be complex and interconnected. Part I helps unravel the mysteries and spells out a straightforward training program in a way that makes sense to runners at all levels. Most important, it points the way toward the training goal of all committed runners, a breakthrough performance.

1

Creating Your Training Mindset

GORDON BAKOULIS
Editor-in-chief of *Running Times*, coach, and
four-time U.S. Olympic Marathon Trials qualifier

CANDACE KARU
Editorial director of *Running Times*

The difference between running and training is that we train with the goal of improving a performance standard.

You're a runner. It's been quite a while since you used the *J* word to describe your regularly scheduled, heart-rate-raising, sweat-inducing efforts on the roads, track, or trails. Running is part of your lifestyle, including your social life, and it's a healthy outlet for your competitive urges.

Often you use another word interchangeably with *running* to describe what you do. That word is *training*.

When exactly did *training* creep into your vocabulary as a way of describing your running efforts? If your base of experience is from running competitively in high school or college, perhaps you have always thought of your running as training and described it that way to others. If you've come to a committed running lifestyle as an adult, it's more likely that you started running recreationally, in a low-key fashion, running at first for fun, fitness, health, and camaraderie.

Put simply, the difference between running and training is that we train with the goal of improving a performance standard. This book is for you runners who, no matter what your current level, would like to raise the bar. Although many runners who train rather than run use competition (races) as a way to measure their improvement, racing is not a prerequisite for training. Nor, as you shall see, is "getting faster" the only yardstick for measuring the improvements that can result from training.

From Running to Training

Throughout your running career you may find that you cycle through phases of running and training depending on your goals or objectives. The transition from running to training is one you can make at various times, back and forth, throughout your life's experience in running. If you were a serious high school and college runner, you might decide after your last competitive scholastic season to quit competing for a few years following graduation as you concentrate on your career and settle into the real world. If you continue to run, it's strictly for fun and stress relief. Then one day you see a flyer for an upcoming local road race and say to yourself, why not? You decide to step up your running to "train" for it. You increase your mileage, take more care to eat well, arrange to get enough sleep. You stretch, keep yourself hydrated, and perhaps even join in a few group speed workouts with a local running club.

After the race, you may go back to being a fun-and-fitness runner. Then, a year later, the marathon bug bites you, and you map out a training program for a 26.2-miler that's six months down the road. So it goes through your adult years: sometimes you train with a purpose, sometimes you run strictly for the fun and health of it, sometimes you even move away from the sport for months at a time. Through all the changes, running remains a part of your life, although consistent, uninterrupted training may not.

Running Versus Training

What exactly is the difference between running and training? The meanings of the terms overlap. Do you know anyone who runs purely to meet competitive goals, never once running for the sole purpose of stretching the legs, gossiping with a friend, or recovering sanity after a hectic day at the office, in classes, or with the kids? Do you know a runner who resides at the other end of the spectrum—one who has never, ever been tempted to push the pace just a little when passed by someone wearing baggy shorts, black socks, and headphones? Does a runner exist who has never stood on the starting line and felt the pulse jump just a bit at the thought of putting the

Most of us run for fun and camaraderie as well as to meet our competitive goals.

© Greg Crisp/SportsChrome USA

recent mileage to the test? Quite likely, runners and trainers alike experience this surge of adrenaline; it's just part of doing something that is physically challenging. In that sense, the universe of the trainer and runner overlap, although the jangle of nerves is probably somewhat louder among the more competitive athletes.

That said, we can also make a few distinctions between running and training. In the most general sense, running is an end in and of itself, while training is done in pursuit of a specific goal. Although excelling in competition is often the intent, reaching health or fitness standards can also be a goal.

Most of us run, of course, because we love the experience of moving our bodies through space under our own physical power. We love using our muscles and joints and lungs and heart to propel us forward, feeling nature around us, being alone with our thoughts, or sharing the fellowship of friends. We'd probably do it even if it didn't promote better health and fitness and give us more energy for everything else we do.

We train, on the other hand, because we seek to perform well, to test ourselves against our limits or rise to the standards set by others—beating a rival, qualifying for a team, reaching a challenging time goal. Running provides us with an endless assortment of ways to test ourselves physically, mentally, and emotionally. Through running we discover and learn how to tap into resources we never knew we possessed.

Doing Our Best

In our experience, runners who race regularly—at any level—tend to think of most or all of their running as training. This is true even if their racing performance is not the supreme focus of their running, and it's true during fallow periods, such as between racing seasons.

Does a runner exist who has never stood on the starting line and felt the pulse jump just a bit at the thought of putting the recent mileage to the test?

Joan Benoit Samuelson, the 1984 Olympic gold medalist and American record holder in the marathon, has certainly done her share of hard, put-it-all-on-the-line racing over the years. Although still competitive, Joan no longer races with the do-or-die mentality of seasons gone by. In fact, she says she would be perfectly happy never to run another race. She claims, however, that if she couldn't run, she would probably explode!

Few who have seen Joan zipping along the roads and trails on even a casual run would describe what she does as mere running rather than training. That's because, like most of us, when she pins on a number and lines up at a race, Joan's goal is to do her best. Therefore, she gives her best effort to every training session. As you will see in part III, the goal of some training sessions is rest and recovery, so it may sometimes *look* like an athlete is just taking it easy. The point is, however, that every workout done by a runner in training to reach a competitive goal is geared toward that goal, which will be attempted somewhere down the road.

Three-time world cross country champion Lynn Jennings has spoken of "just letting my body be" for a month or longer after a grueling race season or championship event. During this recovery period, she'll run when she feels like it (which for her still ends up being almost every day), but she will let her mood, her schedule, and her body's feedback dictate the distance, terrain, and pace. Although this is low-key running, it's still a form of training for Jennings, who uses this type of active rest to recover, physically and mentally, from her season, and to lay the groundwork or base training for her next big effort. (See chapter 27 for more on active rest and chapter 6 for more on base training.)

You can, of course, call your running whatever you wish. Let's assume, though, that if you are a regular racer (or in some other way, you periodically test your running fitness and performance), the miles and hours you put in are your training for that performance.

Identifying What Motivates You

Training, although itself rewarding, requires work. To put in that effort, you'll greatly benefit from identifying your motivations. Don't assume that you're motivated solely or even primarily by the desire to get faster, the most often mentioned motivating factor among runners in training. Rather, look within yourself and ask what will get *you* out the door for your training runs—even when it's raining, snowing, blustery, or dark, or you feel tired or overwhelmed by the commitments and stresses in your life. Performance aspirations may factor into your motivations—achieving a time goal in your next race, beating your rival, or simply completing a challenging distance—but you should also consider motivations such as improved physical and mental health, energy enhancement, or simply the sense of well-being that envelops you after a run. Learn to tap into your motivations during the times (and we all experience them) when it's hard to take those first few steps.

> Look within yourself and ask what will get *you* out the door for your training runs.

Setting Goals

Do you remember the first goal you set as a runner? It may well have had nothing to do with holding a particular pace or beating certain other athletes. More likely your early goal was simply to complete a certain distance, such as running around the block without stopping to walk. From that moment you were training because you were setting goals—aiming to accomplish something with your running. And reaching your goal, no matter how humble it may seem to you now, was your first running breakthrough.

By setting specific goals and training to reach them, you can attain any number of breakthroughs as a runner. Remember, you can set training goals, racing goals, or both. It's perfectly acceptable to train throughout your entire running career without ever setting competitive (racing) goals, and it's fine to move in and out of setting racing goals as your lifestyle and motivations change over the years. Once you achieved your first goal, you no doubt set and then worked toward others—running around the block twice, running a mile, running two miles, completing a 5K race, aiming to complete your next 5K in under 30 minutes, and so on.

Once you set your goal, you will greatly increase your chances of achieving it (or at least giving it your best effort) by writing it down and drawing up a written plan for working toward it. If your goal is performance driven (that is, achieving a certain racing standard or covering a particular distance), you might want to consider enlisting a coach or advisor to help you get there.

Writing it down. Seeing your goal in black and white makes it real; it's not as easy to hide from what you would like to attain. Post your written goal in places where you will see it frequently—in your training log, on the bathroom mirror, on your work bulletin board, even on your car dashboard.

Drawing up a plan. You need to figure out, both generally and specifically, how you will get from where you are now to where you wish to be. The chapters in part I give you the tools to do this. They show you the various components of training and outline the best ways to combine them so you get the most out of your hard work, avoiding injury and overtraining. If your goal relates to a specific event such as a race, your plan will be time limited and will probably focus on a weekly schedule with interim goals along the way. If your goal is open-ended and less measurable ("reducing stress," for example), it will help if you can come up with ways of measuring your progress (say, reducing the amount of yelling and snapping you do at other people) and some sort of timetable.

Teaming up with a coach or advisor. The value of a coach is objectivity and a second, more informed perspective. You can learn a lot from reading books like this as well as magazine articles and information gleaned from the Internet, but the information will not be specifically tailored to you. A coach can help you evaluate your goals, tell you honestly if they are realistic, and outline your plan to meet them. The best coach-runner relationships are interactive, in which advisor and athlete have equal input and frequent contact to fine-tune both training schedules and goals.

Working Toward Your Goals

Setting challenging but achievable goals and making a plan to work toward achieving them is the foundation of any distance-training program. Part I of *The Running Times Guide to Breakthrough Running* focuses on providing you with the training tools to work toward achieving your breakthrough— better biomechanics, proper gear, training programs, and proper nutrition. Each section suggests schedules, drills, and other strategies that help you organize a particular aspect of your training with an eye toward reaching the specific goals you set for yourself.

Let's look briefly at a how you can set one simple goal as a runner, then draw up an overall plan that allows you to work toward achieving it.

Goal: Cutting 30 Seconds From Your 5K Time

This is an excellent goal for a runner who is relatively new to competition and therefore is still seeing improvement from one race to the next. Of course, any competitive runner would be thrilled to set a 30-second PR. Such a goal is probably not realistic for someone who has been competing for a few years or longer and has seen race times plateau to the point where improvements come in 2- or 3-second intervals, if at all.

Basic plan

First, select a race that's convenient for you, far enough in the future to allow you adequate time to prepare, and one that you want to do. Next, determine your current level of fitness. Are you fit enough to complete the distance based on your training right now? Your past achievements and all the desire in the world won't get rid of those 30 seconds if the answer is no. If you have the endurance base, improving your time is a matter of increasing your lactate threshold and working on your speed (see chapter 8 regarding lactate-threshold training and chapter 9 on speed training). Even if your training tells you that you are fit enough to run close to your goal time, you may still need to brush up on racing tactics. Chapter 22 can help you work on those skills.

Finally, you should sit down with a calendar, mark the race date, and outline your training between now and then. A coach or advisor can help you with this process, or you can do it on your own, using the guidelines in this book as references. Use part I, "Breakthrough Training," to review your running form (biomechanics); make sure your shoes and apparel are up to the task; set up a progressive program that allows you to train hard without breaking down along the way and to be in the best possible shape at the precise time of your competition; work on your flexibility and muscular strength; and make sure you're properly fueled through it all. Your schedule doesn't have to be exact, and it may well change along the way. Indeed, it *should* be flexible to account for schedule changes, necessary adjustments in your training, and factors you can't control, such as the weather. The idea of setting a schedule is to give yourself a blueprint to follow—a pathway leading toward your goal.

You Have What It Takes

One of the most important, yet often overlooked, aspects of training as a distance runner is believing in yourself. Believing is not everything—you still have to do the challenging work of training! Still, without a belief that you can get from where you are to where you want to be (your goal) through hard, smart, organized training, you may as well not bother.

The remaining chapters in part I of *The Running Times Guide to Breakthrough Running* are designed to help you realize your potential by training in a sensible, intelligent, informed, and progressive fashion toward your running goals. You have it within you to reach any reasonable running goal you set for yourself. You may be frustrated along the way by injury, illness, or other interruptions due to complications or stresses in other parts of your life (family, job, etc.). Or you may choose to step off the path leading toward your goal, then return to it later. The key is to know that your goals are always there and that you don't lose the capacity to go after them. Beyond that, it's a simple (though not always easy!) matter of organizing your life so you can put in the training you need, constantly observing and fine-tuning your progress along the way.

Running is a lifetime sport—a simple activity that just about anyone can master. You don't have to pay dues, join clubs, or buy a lot of special equipment to train as a distance runner. Start setting your goals now; then let's start training toward them.

2

Improving Your Biomechanics

ROY BENSON
Coach of Roy Benson's Nike Running Camps and
Marist High School track and cross country teams in Atlanta,
contributing editor of *Running Times*

You may be able to make significant performance breakthroughs by identifying form faults and making simple adjustments that allow you to run with greater efficiency of motion.

Humor me a bit by assuming that I can compare a runner's cardiorespiratory system to an automobile engine. Then let's take the analogy a step further and compare the runner's musculoskeletal system to the transmission and wheels of an automobile. In this chapter, instead of viewing runners and the process of running from the physiological, biochemical, or psychological perspective, let's look at them as biomechanical specimens and systems.

If we must train physiological systems to use oxygen economically, then it's also fair to assume that we must fine-tune biomechanical systems to assure efficient movement. This chapter will show you how to accomplish this fine-tuning.

Economy of motion refers to the amount of energy required by working muscles to run at a given pace. Efficiency of motion is all about minimizing the energy that is wasted at that pace by form faults, which are imperfections in a runner's movements, such as overstriding. A runner's efficiency of motion can affect how economically he or she runs. A runner with serious form faults, such as excessive upper-body rotation, is inefficient because he or she is wasting energy on movements that impede forward progress. (Of course, an efficient runner, one who has good form, can be uneconomical if he or she is in poor shape, because the person must recruit more muscle fibers to do the job.)

By correcting faults in your form, you can become a more efficient runner. If you've been training and racing for several years, chances are you are no longer improving much because you have honed your physiological systems to perform at or close to their maximal level. But you may be able to make significant performance breakthroughs by identifying form faults and making simple adjustments that allow you to run with greater efficiency of motion. I have analyzed the running form of more than fifteen thousand runners over the past 27 years, from novices to elite competitors, and helped many improve their form (and thus their performances) by making just a few small changes.

In this chapter we'll look at the two form faults that are by far the most common ones I see. Nearly half the runners I've seen over the years suffer from these form faults. Runners can easily correct these biomechanical mistakes by performing several simple drills. The result is a more efficient runner who uses less oxygen and energy to run at the same pace, thus becoming more economical.

Analyzing Your Form

Taking a close look at your running form starts with capturing yourself on film as you run. You can do this in two ways. One, you can pay big bucks to be filmed and analyzed by a high-rent professional coach who knows biomechanics, or two, you can get a friend with a video camera to film you, then do the analysis yourself by following a few simple instructions. Trust me, it's not that hard because the two common form faults are glaringly easy to identify.

Capturing your running form on film will help you analyze and correct your running faults.

Start by going to a track or other open, flat, traffic-free spot with someone who can operate the zoom on a video camera without cutting off your feet. An asphalt or track surface is better than grass or dirt because the paved surface allows you to get a good view of your footstrike. As you would before a workout, jog at least a mile, stretch, and run a few strides before filming. After all, you wouldn't want the camera to record you sustaining a serious hamstring or calf-muscle injury, would you?

The camera operator will film you from three views—front, rear, and side. See how easy this is?

A more efficient runner uses less oxygen and energy to run at the same pace, thus becoming more economical.

© Tony Demin/International Stock

Front and Rear Views

1. Station the camera operator in a middle lane of the track about halfway down the straightaway. Stand facing the camera about 50 yards up the track. Have the operator zoom in on you for a close-up view of your whole body.

2. On command, run at your 5K race pace down the middle lane toward the camera. As you run, have the camera operator back off the zoom to keep as much of you in full frame as possible.

3. When you get too close to be in full frame, have the camera operator focus on the upper half of your body, particularly your arm and shoulder motion.

4. Stop directly in front of the camera and turn around while the camera operator keeps a close-up focus on your back, shoulders, and head.

5. On command, run back to the starting point at 5K race pace. Again, the camera operator should first focus on your upper body, then your entire height as you move fully into view.

At this point, have the camera operator rewind the film and play it back to check the results in the viewfinder. On more than one occasion I have failed to notice that the camera was already on when I pressed the record button. This, of course, meant that I had turned the camera off when I wanted it on and on when I wanted it off. A quick double-check now will save time and energy if your camera operator has made the same mistake. You can also repeat the filming at this point if you are not happy with the quality.

Side View

1. Station the camera operator on the infield about 10 to 15 yards from the inside edge of the track. You will be doing a series of 50-yard runs down the straightaway; position the camera at the midway point.
2. Stand in the middle lane so the curb on the inner edge of the track won't block the view of your footstrike.
3. Make three round-trips back and forth over this 50-yard distance at the following paces:
   * Jogging
   * 5K race pace
   * Close to an all-out sprint

   These three round-trips will provide views of both your left and right sides at various paces.
4. Make sure the camera operator zooms in on your full height at the start of each run. As you draw closer, the operator should back off the zoom to keep you in full view. It's OK if the operator lops off your head, but your feet must be in the picture so you can analyze your footstrike.

Again, review the tape and repeat the process if the quality is poor, especially when you are closest to the camera. Those three to four strides as you run directly in front of the camera are crucial.

Correcting Common Form Faults

The filming is the easy part of this exercise. Now comes the hard part—analyzing yourself on film. You will probably be surprised to find that you do not look as graceful as Suzy Favor-Hamilton or as powerful as Michael Johnson. I hope this dose of reality won't be too difficult to absorb as you watch your video, looking for the form faults illustrated in the accompanying pictures. (Slow-motion playback on your VCR will greatly magnify slight faults, so don't despair if you think you look awful.)

Fault: Excessive Upper-Body Rotation

Excessive upper-body rotation wastes energy as the top half twists above the hips much like a washing machine agitator swishing back and forth. The upper body turns in partial circles (rotary motion) instead of following the lower half along the straight line (linear motion) that the runner is trying to run. As you can see in figure 2.1a, this form-faulted runner lets the right wrist fly away from his side, probably in a flawed attempt to "relax" the arms and shoulders. He swings his right elbow around behind his back, pulling his right shoulder back along with it. This much rotary force causes the opposite hand and arm to cross over the runner's front midline (the imaginary line down the center of the trunk from nose to navel), pulling that shoulder forward and adding to the rotary twist (figure 2.1b).

Consequently, to maintain a straight course instead of veering off in the direction the upper body is pointing, the forward leg must compensate by crossing over the midline. This extra motion not only wastes valuable energy that the runner could use to move forward but also can cause the hip and leg to hyperextend unnecessarily. This, in turn, strains the iliotibial tendon, which runs over the hip joint and along the outside of the leg to where it attaches below the knee.

Figure 2.1a Excessive upper-body rotation: back view.

Figure 2.1b Excessive upper-body rotation: front view.

Correction: Reducing Arm and Shoulder Swing

Most runners with excessive upper-body rotation can eliminate or minimize it by using the simple drills described below and incorporating the changes into their running.

The goal of the drills is to keep your entire body moving in the direction you're running, like the fine-looking runner in figure 2.1c. Do this by keeping your arms close to your sides every time you run.

Drill 1: Standing still, slowly swing your arms as you would while running. Do this first in front of a mirror to match visually what you are doing with how it feels. Concentrate on lightly brushing the inside of your wrists against your shirt just below your ribcage. The arm motion should be relaxed and on a slight diagonal crossing in front of the sides of the ribs. Your hands should not cross the midline of your body. On the backswing, let your hand swing all the way back until it's even with your hip. As you keep your wrist in contact with your shirt, you'll notice that your elbow—but not your whole arm—swings back and away from your side. You should feel as if you are elbowing someone next to you and slightly behind you in the stomach or chest.

Once you've gotten the hang of this new arm and shoulder motion, take a test run to try out your new form. Remember to keep brushing your inner wrist against your shirt.

Drill 2: Here's another drill that helps most runners. Stand in front of a mirror and let your arms hang at your sides with your shoulders relaxed. Then pretend that you are in a Western and are going to draw your six-shooters. Bend your arms at the elbows, raising your forearms until they're perpendicular to the ground. Next, make a fist and point your thumbs straight up. Finally, rotate your right wrist slightly until your thumb is pointing to ten o'clock. Do the opposite with the left wrist, rotating your forearm enough to point your thumb to two o'clock. The rotation of your wrists is crucial to this drill because it allows your forearms to swing naturally back and forth while your shoulder muscles stay completely relaxed.

You should find that your arms, not your shoulders, are alternately swinging back and forth, hand to hip and elbow to hip, in

Figure 2.1c Keeping arms close to your shirt reduces excessive upper-body rotation.

rhythm with your stride. Practice in front of the mirror; then, when it feels natural, try it on a training run. Keep practicing and have someone film you occasionally to check your progress.

Fault: Overstriding

The most common biomechanical mistake made by runners is overstriding. This wastes energy because it actually puts on the brakes with each footstrike. See figure 2.2a for a good view of an overstrider in action. Let's analyze how runners make this biomechanical error.

Gross overstriding occurs when the foot strikes the ground heel first, far in front of the runner's center of gravity, with the leg straight and the knee locked. At the moment of contact, the leg has to absorb one and a half to four times the weight of the body, depending on the pace. The greater the speed and the longer the runner is airborne, the greater the impact. For example, a 150-pound runner traveling at a 5:00-per-mile pace strikes the ground with 450 to 600 pounds of force. Because of physical law, the impact creates an equal and opposite force.

These impact forces go straight back up the leg, directly opposite the direction the runner is trying to travel. Not surprisingly, this slows the runner's pace. It also creates stresses all the way up the leg, through the ankle, knee, and hip joints as the body tries to absorb the impact forces. As you might expect, injury risk increases as a result. Ironically, as injury risk increases, so do sales of shoes specifically designed (but not completely able) to cushion this unnecessary impact.

Correction: Becoming a Flat-Heel Striker

Instead of absorbing this punishment to the body and pocketbook, overstriders need to make a simple adjustment in their biomechanics to eliminate the problem. Here's how: they can become flat-heel strikers and stop landing on the back edge of their heels. Figure 2.2b shows a runner about to land with

Figure 2.2a Overstriding is the most common biomechanical error runners make.

his leg bent and his foot almost flat. By landing closer to flat footed, with just an inch or two of daylight under the toes instead of the five or six inches you see in figure 2.2a, the runner can avoid overstriding.

The trick is to make a conscious effort to relax the shin muscles, allowing the toes to drop toward the ground while the foot in still in the air. This lifts the heel, thereby creating more space for the leg to swing back under the bending knee. In effect, you shorten your leg length by raising the heel to keep it from striking the ground too soon and too far in front of you.

I use a simple drill to teach runners how to make the switch from being an overstriding heel hitter to a smooth, efficient flat-heel striker. You can find out if the lesson applies to you by checking the heels of your running shoes. If they are severely worn down along the middle of the back edge and the rest of the heel shows little evidence of wear, you may be an overstrider. (Note that normal footstrike at slow paces usually occurs more on the outside corner of the heel, so wear in that area may not indicate a tendency to overstride.)

Next, analyze the videotape of the front view and note how much daylight there is under the toe of your shoe at the moment of heel contact. Then, from the rear view, look to see if you are hitting the back corner of your heels on impact. If several inches of daylight appear under the toe at contact, look at your knees from the side view. Are they locked (leg straight) at the moment of impact? Usually this effect will become more obvious and dramatic as speed increases.

Figure 2.2b To avoid overstriding, become a flat-heel striker and stop landing on the back edge of the heel.

If the evidence causes you to suspect you're overstriding, try this drill. First, jog in place. This will show you how it feels to get off your heels because no one can comfortably run in place landing heel first. You should feel as if you're running like a sprinter. Don't try to imitate Michael Johnson by landing on your toes or the balls of your feet; rather, just try to get the feel of landing flat heeled. Continue the drill by starting to run with this exaggerated flat-foot strike. As you continue at a comfortable pace, somewhat faster than jogging, you will come down off your toes and begin landing on the balls of your feet. After a few steps you'll probably be running flat footed, and finally you'll be back on the edge of your heels. That's OK; it takes time to make the adjustment permanently.

Repeat this drill several times, concentrating on the sequence of ball-of-foot striking to flat-foot striking to heel striking. You should start to develop a kinesthetic feel for which part of your foot is striking the ground first. By doing this drill regularly at the end of your runs, you will gradually gain the coordination and strength you need to change your stride mechanics permanently. Eventually, you will no longer regress to running on your heels. Making this adjustment is not difficult once you feel the differences in how your feet strike the ground—and how the rest of your body feels—in these various positions.

Biomechanical form faults rob runners of energy by making them work harder than necessary. Fortunately, you can reverse this loss of economy caused by inefficiency. Think about it this way: changing your form to become a more efficient runner means you'll get faster without having to get in better shape. It's like free money!

So invest in making changes in your form if you need them. It will pay big dividends.

3

Gearing Up for Training

TERESA GIBREAL
Assistant manager of Phidippides Running Store in Atlanta

When it comes to performance running, a garment's functional aspects, should take precedence over fashion.

When you're trying to make a breakthrough in your training, the last thing you should have to worry about is being too warm, too cold, or too wet. Thanks to today's athletic-wear fabrics and constructions, many of the discomforts runners used to suffer routinely—cold, soggy sweat suits, chafing cotton gym shorts—have gone the way of Popsicle sticks in finish-line chutes. Sure, the wind still blows, the rain falls, and the summer sun beats down, but today's technical garments go a long way toward controlling those elements, freeing you to focus not on the weather but on taking your running to your highest possible level.

Improvements in gear leave you freer than ever to train when, where, and as long as you choose; bad weather is no longer an excuse. (That may occasionally be more a curse than a blessing for some runners!) On utterly awful days—ice, blinding snow, thunderstorms, extreme heat and humidity—the treadmill or indoor cross-training options are always available.

Although no one can deny that fashion plays a role in apparel choices, when it comes to performance running a garment's functional aspects should take precedence. Remember too that because we all come in different shapes and sizes, apparel should fit your particular body type and needs.

What to Wear to Keep Warm and Dry

What's considered a cool or cold day for a runner? Tolerances for the cold vary, of course—what may seem tropical paradise to one person can feel like a step into Antarctica for another. Therefore, our definition of cool or cold weather—a day when you need to give thought to keeping warm rather than cooling off—is when you are no longer comfortable running in shorts. For many runners, that happens around 40 degrees (4 degrees Celsius). A good rule to use is that if your legs are cold to the touch, your muscles may tighten up, which can increase your risk of injury. In addition, under such conditions you will need to expend extra energy just to keep warm.

For running in temperatures in the no-shorts zone, you can choose from a variety of technical garments that will enhance comfort and performance. You'll find a growing and changing array of fibers and fabrics in today's running garments that provide the feel of natural fabrics while offering superior moisture management, breathability, wind resistance, waterproofness, and durability.

Included here are lists of the most common high-tech fabrics used in today's base-layer and outerwear running garments. Rely on your local running specialty shop to keep you up to date on the latest and greatest of the performance garments and fabrications available. Running and multisport magazines frequently review garments, providing an excellent shopping resource. You can also learn a lot by carefully reading running-gear catalogs, which often include glossaries of the latest high-tech terms.

High-Tech Fabrics and What They Can Do for You

Most fabrics used in today's technical garments are varieties of polyester and nylon or combinations of the two. Probably the biggest advantage of these fabrics is that they are *hydrophobic,* or water hating. Worn next to the skin, they keep skin dry by drawing moisture (both perspiration and rainwater) from the skin surface outward, where it can evaporate. In contrast, cotton holds on to moisture.

Use the two lists below as guides to the basic types of products available.

The lists are not all inclusive nor do they offer a recommendation of any specific product or brand. Many more fabrics with similar characteristics are available besides those listed, and manufacturers introduce new fabrics and technologies every season.

Base-Layer Fabrics

These fabrics are worn next to the skin to provide warmth (under a protective outer layer) and dryness. Most are used in tops, tights, briefs, and bras, and may be found in jacket liners, gloves, caps, shorts, and pants. The heavier weight base-layer garments are constructed of two layers in a "moisture-management" system. A layer next to the skin surface pulls moisture away from the skin and transfers it to an outer layer that spreads the moisture over a larger area for easier evaporation. Lighter constructions are worn alone in warm conditions to provide quick evaporation of perspiration. All the fabrics below have moisture-transfer properties; additional features are noted.

Capilene (Patagonia)

ClimaLite (adidas)

CoolMax (DuPont)—A polyester weave that retains 14 times less water than cotton. Depending on construction, it can be used in cool or warm conditions.

Dri-FIT (Nike)

DriLayer (Moving Comfort)—A brushed-back moisture-transfer fabric.

DryLete (Hind)—Excellent for cold weather. A lighter-weight version is known as DryLite.

Dryline (Milliken)—Contains Lycra for stretchability.

Hydrator (Hind/DuPont)—A finely spun version of CoolMax that offers a very soft feel.

MicroMattique (DuPont)

PolarTec PowerDry (Malden Mills)—A mesh polyester with a light fleeced backing.

Polypropylene—One of the first lightweight, moisture-transfer fabrics used; a recent version, Polyolefin (Innova), is treated to eliminate odor-causing bacteria.

ProCore (Hind)—This three-component fabric contains rayon for warmth and a soft, cottonlike feel; polyester for moisture transfer; and Lycra for stretchability.

Supplex (DuPont)—A brushed nylon fabric known for its soft feel.

Technifine (Sugoi)

Why Pick on Cotton?

Whether your goal is to keep warm or cool during training, you want to avoid garments made with cotton. What, no cotton? What about all your favorite race T-shirts and your alma mater sweatshirt?

Unfortunately, cotton has a fundamental weakness as a performance fabric—it loves moisture. When it comes in contact with water, cotton refuses to let go. That means you get wet and stay wet throughout your run. If it's cold, you feel colder, especially if it's windy. If it's hot, you can easily become overheated because the cotton absorbs sweat and is slow to allow moisture to evaporate. This reduces the breathability of the fabric (which is low to begin with), making the heat buildup even greater. Wet cotton is also abrasive, causing chafing and blisters, and can become heavy.

For these reasons, all-cotton garments should not be part of your technical wardrobe. Save your cotton T-shirts for looking sharp *after* training and racing. Wear your sweats when curling up in front of the fire with a good book or rooting for the home team from the sidelines.

Thanks to today's high-tech fabrics and constructions, there's almost never a weather-related excuse to skip an outdoor workout.

© Warren Morgan/H. Armstrong Roberts

Outerwear Fabrics

The challenge of outerwear garments is to enhance warmth and provide protection against rain, snow, and wind yet still allow the fabric to breathe. The higher-end waterproof fabrics included here do this by using a laminated material that allows smaller water-vapor molecules to pass to the outside while blocking larger water molecules from reaching the inside. Keep in mind that as a fabric becomes more water and wind resistant, it becomes less breathable. Unless otherwise noted, all fabrics listed here are treated laminates.

Many outerwear fabrics are made of microfiber, a broad classification of materials that can serve as a single, untreated layer under dry to moderately wet conditions or as the basis of a water-resistant treated layer to keep out moisture. The fibers are tightly woven nylon or polyester that enhance breathability and dry quickly. Many of today's fleece fabrics are made of microfibers. Worn alone, fleece provides lightweight warmth without water and wind resistance.

Activent (W.L. Gore)—The latest protective outerwear fabric from the makers of Gore-Tex.

Clima-FIT (Nike)

Climashell (adidas)—A polyester microfiber with a Teflon coating.

Climawarm (adidas)—A microfleece fabric.

Gelanots (Tomen Corp.)

Gore-Tex (W.L. Gore)—Considered the original water-resistant, windproof outerwear laminate, it's now considered insufficiently breathable by some.

HTF Microfiber (ASICS)

Microfine (Sugoi)

Therma-FIT (Nike)—A lightweight microfiber fleece.

Versatech (Burlington Industries)—A polyester microfiber treated with Durepel for water repellency.

Now that you know something about the fabrics to choose, the next step is to know how to layer these garments to keep yourself warm and dry.

Avoid Overdressing

I see many runners overdressing for cold weather when they go out for their training runs. It's normal to bundle up on a chilly day, but you should remember that running is a natural heating mechanism. This means that if you feel toasty at the start of a run, you'll probably be sweltering a mile or so later. Here's a good rule: Add 20 degrees (11 degrees Celsius) to the air

Apparent Windchill

	45	40	35	30	25	20	15	10	5	0	-5	-10	-15	-20	-25	-30	-35	-40
4mph	45	40	35	30	25	20	15	10	5	0	-5	-10	-15	-20	-25	-30	-35	-40
5mph	43	37	32	27	22	16	11	6	0	-5	-10	-15	-21	-26	-31	-36	-42	-47
10mph	34	28	22	16	10	3	-3	-9	-15	-22	-27	-34	-40	-46	-52	-58	-64	-71
15mph	29	23	16	9	2	-5	-11	-18	-25	-31	-38	-45	-51	-58	-65	-72	-78	-85
20mph	26	19	12	4	-3	-10	-17	-24	-31	-39	-46	-53	-60	-67	-74	-81	-88	-95
25mph	23	16	8	1	-7	-15	-22	-29	-36	-44	-51	-59	-66	-74	-81	-88	-96	-103
30mph	21	13	6	-2	-10	-18	-25	-33	-41	-49	-56	-64	-71	-79	-86	-93	-101	-109
35mph	20	12	4	-4	-12	-20	-27	-35	-43	-52	-58	-67	-74	-82	-89	-97	-105	-113
40mph	19	11	3	-5	-13	-21	-29	-37	-45	-53	-60	-69	-76	-84	-92	-100	-107	-115
45mph	18	10	2	-6	-14	-22	-30	-38	-45	-54	-62	-70	-78	-85	-93	-102	-109	-117

Unpleasant   Frostbite likely. Outdoor   Exposed flesh will freeze within half
                 activity dangerous.   a minute for the average person.

temperature (taking the windchill factor into account; see chart above), then dress accordingly. If it's 40 degrees (4 degrees Celsius) without a windchill, for example, dress as you would for a stroll in 60-degree (16-degree Celsius) weather. This will help prevent you from overdressing. Besides the added bulk, overdressing can cause overheating, which leads to increased sweating and the chance of subsequent chilling if you stop, slow down, run into the wind, or experience a sudden drop in temperature.

When running in cold weather, follow the old rule of dressing in several lightweight layers rather than one heavy garment. Layers trap warm air as insulation and allow you to adjust to changing conditions (or your perception of them) as you run.

Now that you understand the importance of dressing properly for the cold, let's look at some clothing options.

Base Layer

Your choice of clothing on days colder than 40 degrees (4 degrees Celsius) should start with what is commonly referred to as a base layer. This consists of a long- or short-sleeve top and tights in a single-layer wicking fabric. The base layer should be fairly form fitting (to reduce wind drag if worn alone and allow for overlayering if worn under other garments), lightweight, moisture wicking, and breathable to prevent the buildup of moisture. Good fabric choices for your base layer include Supplex, Thinsulate, Polypropylene, and Thermax, depending on the temperature and windchill.

The main requirement for the base layer is to wick moisture away from the skin to the outer surface of the garment for rapid evaporation. The base layer may be the only layer you wear on moderate days with little wind and no precipitation. When temperatures drop, winds pick up, or rain or snow falls, it is ideal as the garment next to your skin.

Start with a base layer on cold days. This layer will wick moisture from the skin to keep you dry.

Tops

Consider two types of weaves when selecting a short- or long-sleeve top for your base layer. A breathable mesh construction is recommended for those who tend to sweat excessively or overheat. A closed-weave garment, on the other hand, provides more warmth. You can layer garments, of course, as the temperature drops; on extremely cold days, medium- to heavyweight tops, vests, or jackets are the recommendation. You should also consider the softness of the fabric (known as the *hand)* and the form of the neck (crew, mock turtleneck, or half zip). *Cut* refers to how the shape of the garment matches your body type. For example, larger women and men don't do well with a princess cut or more form-fitting designs. Also, you might choose garments constructed so that fabric lies between your skin and the zipper instead of those that place the zipper right next to your skin.

Some bras made especially for very cold weather include DryLete, Dryline, and Dri-FIT fabrics, to name a few of the most popular ones. Even with a warm bra, though, it's crucial to make sure that you protect your entire upper body from cold and wind.

Tights

Most runners wear tights as their base layer on the bottom half when temperatures drop below 40 degrees (4 degrees Celsius). Tights are form fitting and stretchable for ease of movement and minimal drag. They provide a thin "second skin" of protection from cold and wind.

As with tops, the biggest differences among tights are the tightness of the weave and the softness of the fabric. A running tight with a tighter weave offers more warmth and wind protection than looser-weave tights of the same weight. A softer tight simply feels better to some runners. (See list on page 27 for fabric choices.)

What if you're just not the tight-wearing type? Loose-fitting tights, known as track pants, are made of technical fabrics. They are a little bulkier than tights, but sleeker than sweatpants, and have the advantage (for some) of leaving a little more of your anatomy to the imagination.

Men may want to look for briefs made from Windstopper or a similar cold- and wind-protective fabric, due to the limited wind-resistive capability of tights. Alternatively, they can wear wind-resistant pants.

Thermal Layer

You'll need more than a base layer when the temperature drops. A medium-to heavyweight tight and top will add warmth and enhance your outfit's moisture-wicking capabilities. Combined with a base layer, a thermal layer is suitable on cold days with or without heavy precipitation or strong winds. Thermal-layer fabrics can be divided into three layers. Mesh short- and long-sleeve tops for running are the lightest level; a medium level consists of single-layered garments made of CoolMax, Dryline, light Capilene, or the like and would correspond to the lightest outdoor garments; the heaviest level for running, consisting of fleece-type garments, has nothing close to the bulk and weight of the heaviest outdoor garments. The fabrics may be similar but the weight and thickness are not. (Note that the fabrics used in medium- to heavyweight running attire are still lightweight compared with what's found in the outdoor garment industry, although there is some overlap.)

A medium- to heavyweight running tight or top will be double layered and therefore highly effective at keeping moisture away from the skin. In most double-layer garments, the layer next to the skin draws the moisture from the skin surface to the outer layer, which in turn invites the moisture outward and spreads it over a wide surface area for quick evaporation. The double layer also has the ability to trap heat without moisture for insulating warmth.

On extremely cold days, microfiber fleece has moisture-wicking capability as well as added warmth. Fleece is available in some thermal-layer garments as well as outerwear items. Microfiber fleece is recommended for runners because it can provide warmth without excessive bulk.

Outer Layer

You'll need one more layer on cold days when it's raining or snowing heavily or when a significant wind is blowing (see windchill guidelines and use your judgment based on your tolerance and previous experience). Wind can really spice up your run. A 15 mile-per-hour wind can make a 30-degree (–1-degree Celsius) day feel like 9 degrees (–13 degrees Celsius). Add rain or snow, and your run can become a disaster if you aren't prepared. See the windchill chart on page 30.

On such days your running attire should include a wind-resistant and water-resistant or waterproof shell (jacket or vest). Thanks to an array of new fabrics and constructions, this protective outer garment can block the wind, keep out most of the water, and still be breathable.

The fabric most commonly used for outerwear garments is microfiber. Besides being lightweight and relatively quiet while moving, the tight weave of microfiber allows the small molecules of heat vapor to escape while providing moderate protection from the larger water molecules.

Outer-shell garments are available in three basic levels, appropriate for a range of conditions:

Level 1. A vented, unlined microfiber jacket or vest is the most versatile outerwear garment for most climates. It's appropriate for a wide temperature range. Lightweight, breathable, and wind and water resistant, it's also the most moderately priced outer-layer option.

Level 2. A jacket with a laminated layer or a protective application that enhances wind blockage and water resistance may be necessary if you live in an area where the wind howls and the rain falls. Keep in mind that as you increase the water and wind resistance of a garment, you reduce its breathability. These garments are priced somewhat higher than level 1 options.

Level 3. A waterproof jacket or suit is probably your best protection on extremely cold days or in moderate cold with heavy rain or snow. What is meant by *waterproof*? The term is defined as seam-sealed and able to withstand rain at 100 pounds per square inch. With excellent waterproof and wind-resistant high-tech fabrics available, you would think every runner should own such a garment, right? Maybe not. Before buying one, honestly consider your environment and running habits. A waterproof, wind-resistant jacket is *not* ideal when it's 45 to 50 degrees (7 to 10 degrees Celsius) and raining lightly. Under such conditions you need something much more breathable unless you want to give your sweat glands a better workout than you do your muscles. You'll end up as wet on the inside of the jacket as it is on the outside. In most moderate temperature ranges, you'd train better with a level 1 jacket and a water-resistant cap.

A waterproof, wind-resistant jacket and pants are best worn in temperatures below 20 degrees (–7 degrees Celsius) Don't forget to factor in the windchill. Waterproof suits are expensive, ranging from around $100 to $400. Why such a wide range? The least expensive garments are waterproofed with a coating of light polymer. Yes, they are better than a rubber rain suit from the Army-Navy store, but the coating on less expensive suits loses its waterproofing capability over time, especially with frequent washings. The top-of-the-line waterproof jackets retain their waterproofing capability much longer and are far more breathable. A lightweight porous membrane is laminated to the shell, allowing heat to escape but keeping out moderate to heavy rain. Make sure the garment is lined so it won't stick to you when you sweat.

Cold-Weather Accessories

Because up to 50 percent of body heat is lost through the head, some head covering is crucial on cold days. You'll want to keep your hands and feet warm as well. Again, select moisture-wicking, breathable fabrics such as Polypropylene, Capilene, DryLete, or DryLite for socks, gloves, and caps. If you tend to suffer from cold hands, keep in mind that mittens offer greater warmth than gloves. Both are available in varying thicknesses and with a range of wind-resisting and waterproofing properties. You can protect your groin area with wind-resistant, moisture-wicking briefs. Ear and face coverings made of a base-layer, moisture-wicking fabric are other valuable additions on frigid days (see list on page 27).

Training Cool in the Heat

The technology used for fabrics designed to keep you cool and dry in hot and humid conditions is actually similar to that used for cold-weather garments. The main difference is that you wear less in hot weather. The fabrics are lighter and usually of a mesh design to enhance breathability and allow sweat to evaporate quickly from the skin, thus keeping you cooler. As with cold, heat is a relative term for runners; some are more tolerant of it than others. Sunny versus overcast conditions can make a difference as well. In general, we can define warm conditions to mean 60 degrees (16 degrees Celsius) and up.

In hot weather, choose fabrics that are lightweight and that have a mesh design that enhances breathability to keep you cool.

The main fabric used for technical summer garments is polyester, with a brushed, cottonlike nylon a distant second. Polyester is lightweight, breathable, soft to the skin, and supple (thereby reducing chafing). It's designed for maximum moisture-wicking capability. The list on page 27 identifies base-layer fabrics that are most appropriate for warm weather, such as CoolMax, Supplex, and Intera.

In this section, we'll guide you through the options available in warm-weather tops, shorts, sports bras, socks, and accessories.

Tops

Technical running tops are made of either a closed-weave or open-weave (mesh) polyester. You have three basic top options for training in the heat: a short-sleeve technical T, a sleeveless T, and a singlet. The short-sleeve technical T is most useful in moderate temperatures. It also provides a little more protection from the sun. The sleeveless T resembles a technical T with the sleeves cut off. The singlet is the most commonly used top in hot weather because it provides the greatest freedom of movement and the least cover. A singlet differs from a tank top in that it is usually made of a mesh fabric; the tank is of closed-weave construction.

You can also find specialty tops such as cropped singlets, stretch tops, and garments with rear cargo pockets. Remember to apply sunscreen liberally to all exposed areas, even on overcast days (the rays of the sun can still cause sunburn and skin damage).

Sun Protection

Protection from the sun is crucial for runners, who spend so much time outdoors, and it applies to both cold-weather and warm-weather running. Sunburn can be painful and annoying in the short term, and studies show that repeated sun exposure (especially intense exposure early in life) over a lifetime can greatly increase the risk of skin cancer, a disease that can be fatal. Here are ways to protect yourself from sunlight while running:

Sunscreen. Cover all exposed skin with a liberal, even coating of sunscreen with an SPF of at least 15 (30 or 40 is better) before going outdoors. Don't forget your ears, eyelids, bald spots, and the back of your neck and hands. Use a waterproof product that won't wash away when you sweat. It's easy today to find products without alcohol, which can sting. Reapply after your run if you plan to remain outside. Use sunscreen on overcast as well as sunny days, especially when running in the middle of the day.

Hats and sunglasses. Protect your head, face, and eyes by wearing a hat with a brim and a pair of UV-protective sunglasses. You'll see better, reduce fatigue of the facial muscles caused by squinting, and reduce your risk of skin cancer and cataracts.

UV-protective clothing. The rays of the sun can penetrate many of today's lightweight fabrics, especially meshes. You can solve the problem either by applying sunscreen underneath these fabrics or by wearing garments made from fabrics that offer protection against the sun. These fabrics should be marked on the label.

Many women have a love-hate relationship with running bras. The secret is to purchase a bra that provides support without discomfort. Running bras fall into two categories:

1. Those made solely as undergarment support
2. External fashion-oriented bras

Undergarment bras come in many supportive variations. The majority of external running bras provide low to moderate support, although a few offer a high level of support by using the type of adjustable straps, hooks, and snaps found in undergarment bras. These garments, however, incorporate cotton in the outer shell, making them heavier (especially when wet).

The bottom band that hugs the rib cage can cause chafing and blistering. You can avoid or minimize chafing by wearing a looser-fitting bra or one with a smaller band; both options, however, can compromise support.

Always try on a bra and move around in it as much as you can before buying. In addition, try replacing your bras every six months to a year (depending on how often you run) to avoid any abrasion caused by fabric breakdown.

Shorts

As with tops, the differences among shorts come down to coverage and freedom of movement. The current trend in shorts is microfiber fabric, with its soft, silky feel; however, the cottonlike feel of brushed nylon is also popular. The majority of shorts are closed weave, although a few are available in mesh, which offers more breathability (without providing a peep show).

Running shorts come in two cuts. Notched shorts are fuller and longer, usually with a two- to four-inch inseam. Split-leg shorts are cut higher with the leg split at the sides for ease of movement. Look for technical running shorts that come equipped with a moisture wicking brief; most also have a key pocket, and some have a drawstring. Some companies have added functional features such as external mesh storage pockets.

Tight-fitting spandex shorts, worn alone or under your running shorts, can be helpful in preventing inner-thigh chafing. Spandex comes in lycra blends, cool max blends, and cotton blends. Choose a blend that suits your personal preference.

Socks

Few clothing items generate as many opinions as running socks. Some socks purport to provide cushioning, and others promise permanent freedom from blisters. The main thing to keep in mind when selecting socks is that they must have moisture-wicking properties. Thick or thin, crew top or roll top, double layer or single layer, if a sock doesn't pull moisture away from your foot it does you no good. Keep in mind that a sock's thickness can have a dramatic effect on the fit of the shoes, so always try on new running shoes with the socks you wear for running.

Accessories

Some accessories marketed for runners are simply gimmicks to avoid. Others meet runners' needs. Headwear and sunglasses help protect the head, face, and eyes from exposure to the sun. Although useful year-round, they tend to get the most use in warmer weather. Caps must be breathable, should wick moisture, and ought to offer water repellency. A mesh cap or visor is best in hot weather because of its breathability; a microfiber cap is more suitable on cold and wet days because it offers more insulation.

A water carrier is useful on long runs with limited water sources. You'll find a plethora on the market—pouches that strap on your back, bottles that fit in a waist belt, contoured hand-held varieties, and more. These are recommended for anyone working out for more than an hour without access to water in some other way (such as a water fountain or garden hose).

Apparel Recommendations

Temperature (°Farenheit)	Lower body	Upper body	Outerwear	Accessories
Below 20°	Double-layer tights	Medium-weight long-sleeve top	Jacket	Head and handwear
20 to 30°	Light- to medium-weight tights	Medium-weight long-sleeve top	Vest or jacket	Head and handwear
30 to 40°	Lightweight tights	Lightweight long-sleeve top	Vest or lightweight jacket	Head and handwear
40 to 50°	Lightweight tights or shorts	Lightweight long-sleeve top		
50 to 60°	Shorts	Long-sleeve or short-sleeve top		
60°±	Shorts	Short-sleeve top		Cap or visor
80°±	Shorts	Singlet		Cap or visor

*Wind and precipitation may affect the above recommendations.

The chart above provides basic recommendations for dressing for running in all kinds of weather.

4

Choosing Your Training Shoes

KIRK ROSENBACH
Member of the Atlanta Track Club's masters competitive team
and a frequent lecturer on running-shoe topics

GREGORY SHEATS
Running shoe analyst and consultant on numerous
running shoe advisory panels

Your everyday training shoe is your most important piece of equipment; quality shoes are essential to achieving any sort of breakthrough.

Selecting the proper training shoe is one of the first and most crucial steps you can take in your quest for breakthrough running. Your everyday training shoe is your most important piece of equipment. Quality training shoes, or "trainers," are essential to achieving any sort of breakthrough in your running, whether it's completing your first two-mile run or setting a world record.

In this chapter we will help you better understand the components of a quality training shoe. We'll guide you in determining your foot function as a basis for selecting the right shoes for you. We'll address myths and misconceptions about the foot, running shoes, and shoe selection and offer some tips on choosing and caring for your running shoes. This chapter focuses primarily on training shoes for road running, with a short section on trail-running shoes. See chapter 18 for information on racing shoes, which are designed for use in races and, if one desires, interval training or speed workouts.

Anatomy of a Running Shoe

The basic components and construction of a running shoe are not complex. Although shoe companies may like you to believe otherwise, all running shoes have the same basic anatomy and use similar construction materials.

Last

The shoe is built around a *last*, a hard, molded form that roughly mimics the shape of the foot. The last defines the shape of the shoe—either straight or curved. The last also refers to the shoe's internal construction; in the finished product, the board is either left in the shoe (board lasted), partially left in (combination lasted), or removed (slip lasted).

A shoe's last was once considered much more important to the function of the shoe than it is today. Now most shoe experts (exercise scientists as well as shoe manufacturers and salespeople) consider the midsole (see the next paragraph) far more important in differentiating training shoes and serving the needs of the runner.

Midsole

Although the last sets the shoe's basic shape, the heart and sole of every running shoe is the midsole, which defines everything else about it. The composition, density, and shape of the midsole largely determine the shoe's cushioning, support (or stability), and flexibility features as well as its weight and overall function. The midsole is made of polyurethane (PU), ethylene vinyl acetate (EVA), or other firm, shock-absorbing material.

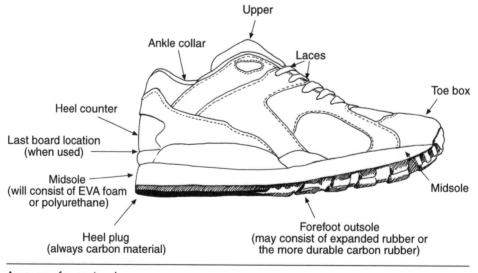

Anatomy of a running shoe.

Embedded in the midsole are the cushioning enhancers, often some type of encapsulated air, gel, or other shock-absorbing material.

The midsole is one of the features that distinguishes the running shoe from other types of athletic footwear, none of which (including cross-trainers) we recommend for anyone who runs regularly. The cushioning properties of the running-shoe midsole, combined with the running shoe's relatively light weight (compared with other athletic shoes), flexibility, and some degree of heel lift, are designed to handle the repetitive impact and stress of running. These characteristics differentiate running shoes from most other athletic shoes, which are designed for activities that stress lateral (side-to-side) movement.

Upper

The upper comprises all materials above the midsole. It is crucial for comfort and proper fit of the shoe, although ultimately its job is to hold the midsole on the foot. The upper can be divided into three sections—the heel counter, the throat or lacing area, and the toe box. The upper is made of light-weight materials, often nylon mesh for breathability and synthetic suede for strength and durability. These materials also resist stretching and maintain shape. The heel counter (including the ankle collar) holds the heel in place with minimal slipping. The lacing area allows you to adjust the snugness of the shoe. The toe box holds the front of the foot, allowing for some flexibility and wiggle room in the toe area.

Outsole

The bottom of the shoe, or outsole, is usually a durable, abrasive-resistant material such as expanded rubber or carbon rubber. Its job is to act as a buffer between the midsole and the running surface.

Determining Foot Function

Before you can select a training shoe that is right for you, you must have a clear understanding of the biomechanics and function of your foot. Between the time the foot strikes the ground and the toes push off again, a biomechanical action called the foot function occurs. We distinguish between foot function (how the foot operates during running) and foot type (high arch, moderate arch, flat foot).

You are probably familiar with the terms pronation and overpronation. These are among the most recognizable, and most misunderstood, terms relating to feet and running shoes. Pronation is the natural tendency of the foot to roll inward as it progresses from landing impact to toe-off, in an attempt to dissipate shock. Pronation becomes a problem (overpronation) when the natural inward roll is excessive, potentially causing stress to various parts of the body from the lower back on down and compromising the integrity of the shoe.

The following are the three foot functions that determine the features and properties of the running shoe that will work best for you.

Stable foot function. The stable foot shows no tendency to roll inward beyond the center to the ball of the foot. Therefore, it does not absorb shock as efficiently as other feet and requires shoes that maximize cushioning and flexibility. Almost all shoes for the stable foot will have midsoles using some version of EVA, a relatively soft, flexible material, rather than harder, firmer PU.

Severe overpronator foot function. At the other end of the spectrum is the foot that exhibits extreme overpronation. Observe someone running from behind and watch his or her feet during the transition from landing to takeoff. If one or both ankles are dramatically collapsing inward so that the anklebone points at a downward angle, we refer to this foot function as a severe overpronator. In most cases this foot function requires shoes with a firm, dense midsole—one that withstands aggressive thumb pressure—along the inner side. Shoes of this type also include a clearly visible stability device—a solid thermal-plastic material incorporated into the midsole along the inner rear side. The midsole composition in these shoes will be either PU or very firm EVA. A wider heel base can further enhance the stability of the shoe.

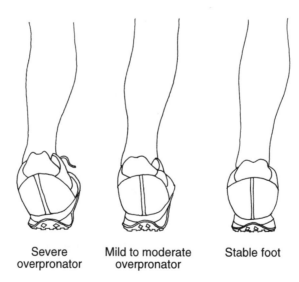

| Severe overpronator | Mild to moderate overpronator | Stable foot |

The three foot functions.

Mild to moderate overpronator foot function. Between these two functions is the foot that has some degree of overpronation, exhibiting some inward roll but nowhere near the ankle-grazing-the-road scenario of the severe overpronator. A shoe with PU in the heel area of the midsole usually has inherent stability that works well here. This is true even if the shoe is not built up or firmer on the inner side because PU is more resilient than EVA. These shoes are designed with a greater degree of cushioning and flexibility than those needed by the severe overpronator, but they still have either denser midsoles or a plastic stability device on the inner side.

Before you buy a running shoe, you'll need to determine your foot function. What's the best way to do this?

Your best resource is a running specialty store, where the salespeople are usually runners and are trained to identify foot function and to recommend shoes accordingly. Most running specialty stores allow you to try on as many shoes as necessary and have a knowledgeable, experienced person to watch you run in them (which is much different than watching you stand or walk in the shoes). An alternative is to find salespeople knowledgeable about running shoes at a general sporting-goods store.

> Have a clear understanding of your biomechanics and foot function.

If neither of these options is available, your best bet is to have one or two other runners accompany you on your shoe-buying expedition and watch you from behind as you run on a level surface. (Having more than one observer helps because you can reach a consensus.) Your observers should specifically look for signs of your foot function. First, try running in a new pair of shoes with no stability features; most shoes of this type (neutral shoes) have a completely white midsole and no plastic stability device along the inner side of the shoe. To be on the safe side, have your observers watch you run in more than one pair of this type of shoe to verify foot function.

If you show no sign of rolling or collapsing in as you make the transition from landing to toe-off, then you'll probably do fine in a shoe designed for the stable foot function (neutral shoe). If you tend to roll inward, have your observers watch you in one or two shoes for the mild to moderate overpronator foot function (stability shoe). If these shoes correct the collapsing tendency, then this is your category. If you're still rolling in, move on to a shoe for the severe overpronator foot function (motion-control shoe).

Shoes vary within a foot-function category, so have your observers watch you in several models. Pick one that is comfortable, fits your foot well, and holds it in a neutral or stable position. Remember that shoes for severe overpronators are likely to be heavier than other shoes because they provide extra support. The extra weight, however, is worth it because the support will increase your efficiency and will likely help reduce the chance of injury or premature midsole breakdown.

Myths and Misconceptions

Let's address some common myths and misconceptions about feet and running shoes. We're amazed at how often we hear these myths perpetuated, even by experienced runners.

Myth #1: *A runner with flat feet (no pronounced arch when standing barefoot) will always overpronate and thus will need a stability shoe.*

Some runners with flat feet overpronate, of course, but plenty of folks with flat feet exhibit a very stable foot function while running. What the foot does when standing or walking does not necessarily indicate what it does during running. Regardless of the shape of your foot, if you have stable foot function you do not need "stability shoes."

Myth #2: *Large or heavy runners are more likely than small or light runners to overpronate and have a heavy footstrike.*

Shoe manufacturers and shoe-buying guides often categorize runners by weight and recommend shoes accordingly. In truth, many big runners (those over 175 pounds) have a stable foot function. Some also float along as if they are auditioning for the ballet. Conversely, small, light runners are assumed to have stable feet and to spring lightly from step to step. Again, this is not always true. Some lightweight runners have moderate or even severe overpronation. Whether a runner strikes heavily or lightly does not correlate to the degree of pronation. The issue here is foot function, not body size and weight or footstrike.

Myth #3: *The way the outer heel strikes as the foot hits the ground determines what type of shoe the runner needs.*

Runners often associate their outer-heel strike with a particular foot function and try to buy shoes accordingly. It is what the foot does after the heel strike that determines foot function and, consequently, the appropriate shoe type.

Myth #4: *A board-lasted shoe is inherently more stable because of the rigidity of the board itself.*

Instead of making the shoe more stable, the board can, in fact, contribute to a platform effect that interferes with the foot's ability to center in the shoe, which in itself can be destabilizing. Some runners also believe that the shape of the shoe (straight or curved) determines its function. That is, they assume that a straight-lasted shoe will be stable because it is straight. This is not necessarily true. Remember that the composition of the midsole is the crucial factor in determining what a shoe does for the foot and for your running mechanics.

It's a good idea to keep a record of shoe models that have and have not worked well for you. You may be able to discern a pattern that can point you toward the right category. Manufacturers often change their shoe models and may discontinue a model that works well for you. If this occurs, ask a knowledgeable shoe salesperson for advice on the best update for you.

Selecting a Running Shoe

Wherever and however you end up shopping for running shoes, here are some tips on choosing them.

Take Your Time

Be prepared to spend some time buying shoes. Don't shop when you're in a rush. Find a salesperson who knows about running and who seems interested in helping you. Avoid a salesperson who is interested only in making a sale.

Don't follow friends' advice when it comes to picking a shoe. What might be great for their needs could be the opposite of what your feet require.

Be Prepared

Take your current running shoes and a pair of socks that you prefer to run in. Looking at the wear patterns on your shoes, particularly areas of stress or compression of the midsole, may help a salesperson pick appropriate models for you. This procedure, however, is not a substitute for having an observer watch you run in new shoes, as described previously. The thickness of your socks can affect the feel and fit of a shoe and thus the size of shoe you buy.

Fit Comes First

Make sure shoe fit is comfortable. There is little consistency in running-shoe sizing, so go by the old adage "If the shoe fits, wear it" rather than relying on the same numerical size. Always try on the shoes before buying them (even if you have bought the same model before). Doing so will prevent you from buying shoes that have been sized incorrectly or that have a manufacturing defect. Shoes should be snug but not tight. The forefoot should have some wiggle room. When standing, allow about the width of your thumb between the end of your longest toe and the end of the shoe. Your running shoes may be a half to a full size larger (or even more) than your dress shoes. In most people, one foot is bigger than the other, so try on both shoes to make sure you have ample room in each.

Depending on your needs, it's fine for men to wear women's shoes and women to wear men's shoes if the fit is comfortable. As a rule, women would buy one and a half sizes smaller than their women's size in a men's shoe, and men would buy one and a half sizes larger than their men's size in a women's shoe. Of course, try shoes on for fit.

> What matters is finding a shoe that is structurally right for you, fits your foot well, and feels good when you run in it.

Try on several different models for comparison's sake. But if a model has worked well for you and is still available, you are probably better off staying with it than switching. You may have several different shoe models to train in, which is fine as long as all the models fit your foot function.

In most cases, more than one shoe model within a foot-function category will meet your needs. This is important because manufacturers are constantly updating, replacing, or phasing out shoe models. Your feet and body are often more adaptable to change than your mind. As change is inevitable, embrace it and run with it.

Don't Fall for Gimmicks

Do not let aesthetics be a significant factor in your decision. What matters is finding a shoe that is structurally right for you, fits your foot well, and feels good when you run in it.

Also do not buy a shoe simply because it has a particular cushioning enhancer. Although these materials can make a good shoe better, they will do nothing to overcome a poorly designed shoe or one that is structurally incorrect for you. Replacement insoles (the material or sockliner that your foot sits on inside the shoe) can help with fit but should not be needed for cushioning in a new shoe. That's the job of the midsole.

Keep in mind also that you do not need specific trail-running shoes if you are doing only occasional trail running or are running on fairly smooth, well-maintained trails. Trail shoes tend to be somewhat more rigid in construction than road-running shoes and may have a firmer platform to give the runner more ankle support and protection from rocks, sticks, and tree roots. Other features of trail shoes include toe guards, water-resistant materials, and tongues designed to keep debris from getting into the shoes. Although these features can be helpful, remember that they tend to add weight to the shoe. In sum, most runners will do fine in their everyday training shoes on most trails. But if your running is almost exclusively on trails or is on rough, backcountry trails, then consider using a trail-shoe model.

Do not write off a shoe company because one of its models did not work for you. You may have tried a model that was not structurally right for you, or perhaps you simply did not like a particular shoe. Ask a knowledgeable salesperson for advice about other models (both within and outside that company) that may work for you.

Remember that the most expensive shoe purchase you make is for the pair that does not fit properly or that is not structurally suited to your needs. Generally, if you shop at a reputable running specialty store or sporting-goods store, you will find no linear correlation between shoe price and quality. We often have to explain this to customers who come into the store and ask for our most expensive shoe, assuming it will be the best. Higher shoe prices generally mean more materials or components, which make the shoes different but not necessarily better. If a shoe is structurally right for you and you like it, then buy it; if you prefer something else, buy that.

Alternating Shoes

There is nothing wrong with alternating two pairs of shoes, either two of the same model or two different models, as long as both are right for your foot function. Alternating shoes allows each pair to dry out between wearings. In addition, you will strike the ground and run slightly differently in different models, even within the same foot-function category. In so doing, you will be shifting the stresses on your body from model to model, which may help reduce your chance of injury.

Replacing Your Running Shoes

In general, running shoes have about 400 to 600 miles of effective cushioning in them before the midsole becomes too compressed. You will be able to feel when this has occurred, when the shoe is no longer providing the cushioning and support you need. Midsoles break down progressively over time (beyond a couple of years), even if you are not using them. Don't run in shoes that are too worn out to support and cushion your feet. Save them for gardening.

Caring for Your Running Shoes

1. If you absolutely, positively must wash your running shoes (we don't recommend it), *do not* immerse them in water. Instead, use a damp cloth or an old toothbrush and mild soap to clean them. If they become wet during a run, take the insoles out and let the shoes air dry. You can stuff the shoes with dry paper towels to absorb some of the moisture.

(continued)

(continued)

2. *Keep shoes away from heat sources!* Heat dries out the cushioning materials and can harden the glues that hold the shoe together. Do not put shoes in the clothes dryer or near heat vents. Do not nuke them in the microwave or bake them in the oven. Do not place them in direct sunlight or leave them in your car in hot weather.

3. If you notice the outsole is starting to wear down, use a urethane shoe-repair product (available at running specialty stores and sporting-goods stores) to slow or halt this process before it even gets close to wearing through to the midsole. Or, if your shoes are over the 400- to 600-mile limit, replace them.

5

Periodizing Training for Peak Performance

TUDOR O. BOMPA, PhD
Founder of the Tudor Bompa Training System and
full professor at York University, Toronto

MICHAEL CARRERA
Executive Director of the Tudor Bompa Training System

By varying stress intensity, you can achieve better peaking and improve the consistency of your performance.

Organized people tend to be more effective than those who are not organized. In the same way, the efficiency of endurance training for running relates directly to how well one plans his or her program. Effective planning, which normally translates into better performance, strongly depends on using periodization in your training.

The term *periodization* comes from *period* (i.e., period of time), which in training time is often referred to as a phase. Periodization breaks up training in both time and type of training, including, for example,

- periodization of the annual plan, or how to divide the annual plan into smaller and easier-to-manage training phases in order to peak for a given set of events; and

- periodization of the motor abilities (strength, speed, and endurance), or how to manipulate training methods and concepts, and in what sequence, to produce a sport-specific quality such as power, power endurance, or muscular endurance.

Organizing your training based on periodization offers two important benefits.

1. It is a better, more effective way of planning a year of training when training loads and stress vary from phase to phase.
2. It emphasizes volume (quantity) and intensity (quality, speed, and power) of training at specific phases of the overall training plan. By varying stress intensity and changing the emphasis of training elements—physical, technical, tactical, and psychological—during preparatory and competitive phases, you can achieve better peaking and improve the consistency of your performance.

Many athletes have benefited from periodization. Canadian sprinters and track cyclists, for instance, never broke a world record and were not even visible on the world sports scene before applying periodization to their training in the 1980s and 1990s. After exposure to periodized training, especially the periodization of strength, these athletes have been among the best in the world, breaking world and Olympic records. The same is true for runners, rowers, and other athletes of many countries. By applying periodization to training, several U.S. college football teams climbed from the bottom of their league standings to the top. Many tennis players, swimmers, and triathletes have also noticed dramatic improvements from using this effective method of planning. Middle-distance runner Gabriela Szabo of Romania is one of the many European and African runners who have followed the concept of periodization for the past six years. Her improvement in the 800 meters through 5,000 meters culminated in 1999 as she won the International Amateur Athletic Federation (IAAF) Grand Prix and was named by the IAAF the 1999 Athlete of the Year.

Periodization of the Annual Plan

You'll want to start your periodization plan by deciding when you want to peak during the year and whether you want to peak for one or two series of races. The chart at the top of page 51 illustrates the structure of a basic annual plan with only one peak, a single periodization, in which you plan to achieve peak performance at the time of the national championships (NC).

Most distance runners use only one peak at the end of the summer, whereas middle-distance runners often use a two-peak annual plan. Often called a bicycle or double periodization, a two-peak annual plan involves two separate cycles, one for each peak (the indoor and outdoor competitions). The

Periodization of a One-Peak Annual Plan

Training phases	Preparatory		Competitive			Transition
Training subphases	General preparatory	Specific preparatory	Pre-comp	Competitive	N C	Transition

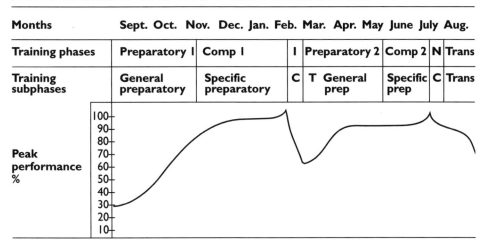

chart below illustrates such a plan. Note the difference in the peaking curves between a mono-cycle and a bi-cycle.

A bi-cycle annual plan has two main peaks—the first in late February or early March for the indoor championships (IC), and the second in late July for the national championships (NC). The dates of the two major competitions dictate the length of training phases and subphases. Therefore, preparatory 1 is longer than preparatory 2, whereas the two competitive phases (comp 1 and 2) are of almost equal length. For the same reason, the general preparatory phase and specific preparatory phase are longer for the first cycle than the second cycle. Between the first and second cycles is a two-week transition (T) phase, whereas after the national championships in July a four- to five-week transition occurs.

Periodization of a Two-Peak Annual Plan

Months	Sept. Oct. Nov. Dec. Jan. Feb. Mar. Apr. May June July Aug.							
Training phases	Preparatory I	Comp I		I	Preparatory 2	Comp 2	N	Trans
Training subphases	General preparatory	Specific preparatory		C	T General prep	Specific prep	C	Trans

Selective Periodization

Training programs for junior athletes often duplicate those of elite athletes. In most cases, however, those using the programs of successful athletes fail to analyze whether junior athletes are ready for a multipeak plan or whether juniors can tolerate the high-intensity training that accompanies the programs of elite athletes.

As you are planning your competitive season and trying to figure out if you should plan around one or two peaks, you'll want to consider the following.

- A mono-cycle is strongly recommended for beginners and junior athletes. The advantage is that it includes long preparatory phases free from the stress of many races, allowing the coach and athlete to concentrate on progressive development and build a strong foundation of physical training.
- A bi-cycle plan is appropriate for experienced or national-class runners—individuals who can qualify for national championships. Even in this situation, the preparatory phase should be as long as possible to allow time to establish the fundamentals of aerobic training without the need to race. The advantage of a bi-cycle is that an athlete can plan to undertake two aerobic phases of training coupled with two phases of event-specific speed and endurance training.

Although the duration of training phases depends on the schedule of competitions, the following chart provides a good guideline for the distribution of weeks per training phase.

Annual Plan Training Phases

Regardless of the number of peaks or cycles in your annual plan, they it will include three basic phases—preparatory, competitive, and transition.

The *preparatory phase* is of enormous importance to the entire year of training. Throughout this period the athlete prepares physically, technically, and psychologically for the competitive phase and becomes familiar with racing strategies. Inadequate training during this period cannot be over-

Suggested Distribution of Weeks for an Annual Plan

Annual plan		Preparatory	Competitive	Transition
Mono-cycle:	52 weeks	32 or more	10 to 15	5
Bi-cycle:	26 weeks	13 or more	5 to 10	3 to 4
Tri-cycle:	17 to 18 weeks	8 or more	3 to 5	2 to 3

Use periodization to maximize training effects and achieve better performances.

come by any other type of training and has visible repercussions during the competitive phase. A significant amount of training based especially on increased volume (quantity of work) would result, in the end, in a relatively low level of fatigue after training and could enhance recovery. Throughout the phase, and especially during the initial part, a high volume of training is essential in creating the basis of adequate body adaptation to the specifics of training.

In general terms, the specific objectives of training in the preparatory phase are as follows:

1. To acquire and improve general physical training (for example, to increase working capacity and ability to cope with fatigue)

2. To increase the aerobic base to the highest level

3. To develop specific psychological qualities that enable the athlete to visualize his or her race and block out unnecessary stress that may negatively affect performance outcome

4. To develop, improve, and perfect technique

5. To become familiar with racing strategies

The preparatory phase can last between three and six months depending on whether climate conditions are conducive to training, whether the runner has attained adequate development, and whether the annual plan is a mono-cycle or a bi-cycle. For instance, beginners should undergo a longer preparatory phase than advanced runners do. The basic rule is that the duration is one to two times as long as the length of the planned competitive phase.

For methodical purposes, it is best to divide the preparatory phase into two subphases—general and specific. The objectives of the *general prepara-tory* subphase are to develop the aerobic base, increase working capacity, and improve technical fundamentals. The foremost objective, however, should be to develop a level of physical conditioning that will facilitate future training and performance. During this phase, perform flexibility training, strength training (anatomical adaptation), long runs, base training, and a small volume of anaerobic-threshold training. Avoid racing during this phase of training. Concentrate on fitness and sport-specific testing.

The *specific preparatory* subphase represents a transition toward your competitive season. Though the objectives of training are quite similar to those of the general preparatory subphase, the character of training becomes more specific to the event. You should participate in events that are longer than your specialty event. Although the volume of training is still high, you should dedicate about 30 percent of total training to event-specific racing endurance. During the specific preparatory phase, emphasize flexibility training, long runs, and base training. Plan anaerobic-threshold training twice per week and focus strength training on medium or long muscular endurance depending on your event. You may choose to participate in competitions during this phase but only as practice runs or as a way of monitoring your pace and learning how to deal effectively with physical and psychological stress caused by competition.

The main goal of the *competitive phase* is to perfect all training factors so that you can improve your ability and thus compete successfully in the main competition or championship meet. Although you are also racing during the preparatory phase, the competitive phase includes the meets or races for which you are peaking your performance. Among the general objectives of the competitive phase are the following:

1. Continuous improvement of aerobic and event-specific endurance (started in the specific preparatory subphase)

2. Perfection of technique

3. Perfection of racing strategy and gaining competitive experience

This phase of training should continue to include flexibility training and base training. Plan to do anaerobic-threshold training twice per week and speedwork once per week. Focus strength training on the development of medium or long muscular endurance depending on your event.

Before the championship competition, there is a short *taper*, or *unloading phase*, the scope of which is to facilitate peak performance, the best performance of the year (see also chapter 20). Figure 5.1 illustrates a tapering strategy for distance-running events.

Of the two training elements, volume (quantity) and intensity (quality), the latter is the more fatiguing and taxing. Throughout the two weeks of tapering, therefore, you need to decrease intensity progressively while also decreasing the volume of training (though to a lesser degree than you decrease intensity). Reduce both volume and intensity below 40 percent of your normal total training per week. In this way, you will preserve your aerobic endurance level while removing the fatigue of high-intensity training.

The *transition phase* is a welcome change for athletes and coaches after several months of stressful training and many competitions. The purpose of the transition phase is to remove fatigue from both body and mind, to relax psychologically, and to regenerate biologically before a new annual plan or the second cycle of a bi-cycle begins. An acceptable level of physical training throughout the transition phase, especially for aerobic endurance, involves the maintenance of 40 to 50 percent of the volume used during the preparatory phase. If you neglect to maintain the acquired aerobic endurance level during the transition period, you will experience a detraining effect, a decrease in physiological functioning. Endurance capacity will decrease about 7 percent in the first two weeks (a 30 percent decrease in the level of

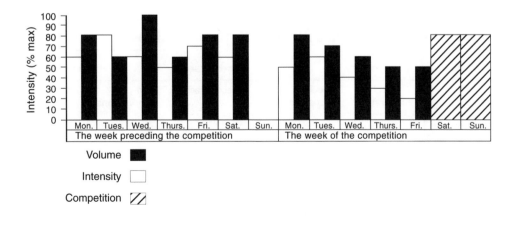

Figure 5.1 Tapering for two weeks before a competition.

hemoglobin and as much as a 50 percent decrease in volume of mitochondria). To avoid too much biological degeneration during this recovery transition period, maintain two to four workouts per week of informal and relaxed training. During the transition phase of training, you should concentrate on maintaining flexibility while centering most of the workouts on long runs and cross-training.

Periodization of Motor Abilities

One of the essential elements in the success of periodization refers to how and when you train the main motor abilities, such as strength, speed, and endurance, during the annual plan.

In several sports, the periodization of motor abilities is not yet known and therefore not applied. For instance, I have seen many 800- to 3,000-meter runners doing speedwork as early as February or March without building a foundation, such as tempo running, to develop an anaerobic-aerobic base. Speedwork performed this early in the year takes away from the necessary training time you need to build a strong and efficient aerobic base.

Periodization of Endurance

During an annual training plan for running, you'll focus on developing your muscular and cardiovascular endurance in several phases. Taking as a reference an annual plan with one peak, you accomplish endurance training in four main phases:

1. Aerobic endurance (general preparatory and transition)
2. Aerobic and event-specific endurance (specific preparatory)
3. Event-specific endurance (specific preparatory and competitive)
4. Maintenance of aerobic endurance (competitive)

The Periodization of Main Motor Abilities

	Preparatory		Competitive		Transition
	General preparatory	Specific preparatory	Precompetitive	Main competitions	Transisition
Endurance	Aerobic endurance	Aerobic endurance Event-specific endurance	Event-specific endurance Maintain aerobic endurance		Aerobic endurance
Specific speed (racing)		Anaerobic endurance	Event-specific speed Anaerobic endurance	Event-specific speed Agility Reaction time Speed endurance	

Each of the suggested phases includes specific training objectives. *Aerobic endurance* is developed throughout the transition phase and early preparatory phases (three to five months). Although each running event may require slight alteration, you can achieve your goals of aerobic endurance through uniform and steady-state running, at medium intensity (heart rate range between 130 to 160 beats per minute). As a general result of such a program, the efficiency of your cardiorespiratory system progressively improves, consequently heightening your working capacity. Parallel with your adjustment to training, you must elevate your aerobic endurance workload, especially the volume (quantity) of training. Aerobic endurance goals can be achieved by participating in long runs, base training, cross-training, minimal anaerobic-threshold training, and strength training in the form of anatomical adaptation training.

Aerobic endurance and event-specific endurance play extremely important roles in achieving the objectives set for endurance training by increasing oxygen delivery and utilization and lactic-acid tolerance. Throughout this phase, which represents a transition from aerobic endurance to endurance specific to your event, you still emphasize aerobic endurance. Elements of anaerobic activity are introduced, depending on the specifics of the event. For example, for a one-mile event, perform repetitions of a quarter mile and a half mile; for a three-mile event, perform repetitions of a quarter mile, a half mile, and a mile; for a 10K event, perform repetitions of a half mile to two miles. An intensive training regimen abused by some runners (short interval training of mostly 200 to 400 meters) may fail unless the foundations of endurance are solidly developed during the second phase. The prevailing methods are uniform, alternative, and long and medium interval training of 3 to 20 minutes (see earlier examples). Perform the longer distance repetitions in the early part of this phase and the shorter distances toward the end of this phase. The volume of training reaches the highest levels during the aerobic phase of the specific preparatory phase of the annual plan. You can achieve aerobic and specific endurance through long runs and base training. Use shorter distance events (a quarter mile to a mile) for anaerobic-threshold training to improve aerobic and specific endurance.

Event-specific endurance coincides with the competitive phase. Selecting the appropriate methods depends strictly on the proportions between aerobic and anaerobic endurance for each event. Event-specific endurance as a proportion of aerobic endurance can be 40 percent for a half mile and a mile, 30 percent for two miles, and 20 percent for 10K. Varying the intensity level should facilitate a good recovery between training sessions, leading to a good peak for the final competition. You need to maintain aerobic endurance throughout the competitive phase. Aerobic endurance training is often used as aerobic compensation or as compensation for days of high training demand or following races.

Periodization of Specific Speed

The periodization of speed training depends on the physiological characteristics of the event, your level of performance, and your competition schedule. Whether for shorter or longer distance-running events, the periodization
of speed may follow variations of these training subphases:

Anaerobic endurance. As the competitive phase approaches, training becomes more demanding, event-specific, refined, and specialized. You incorporate anaerobic training in the program to ensure that you can cope with
the accumulation of lactic acid, especially during the early part of most
races. The suggested proportion of anaerobic training per week is 40 to 50
percent for a half mile, 40 percent for a mile, 20 to 30 percent for two miles,
and 10 percent for 10K.

Event-specific speed and anaerobic endurance training could incorporate
some or all of the speed components, including alactic (sprints of 50 meters
to 100 meters, or 6 to 12 seconds), lactic (sprints or repetitions of 30 to 60
seconds), and speed endurance (repetitions of 1 to 3 minutes), depending on
the specifics of the event. Take the above suggestions regarding the percentage of anaerobic training into consideration. Allowing for full recovery, you
can run repetitions of 100 to 800 meters or longer once or twice a week. You
can combine this form of training in the same day with aerobic endurance
to facilitate supercompensation, that is, glycogen restoration and removal
from the system of metabolites such as lactic acid and other waste products.

Event specific speed. During the competitive phase, you must plan the
intensity of training in accordance with your schedule of races and the
importance of speed in the particular event. For example, a 5K runner
should devote 20 to 30 percent of total training volume to speed training,
whereas a marathon runner should focus only 10 to 15 percent of training
volume on speed training. The shorter the event, the greater the importance
of intensity. Use a combination of high-intensity (alactic and lactic) repetitions and longer repetitions at anaerobic-threshold pace.

Dynamics of Volume and Intensity

The volume and intensity of training play important roles in the loading
strategy of training during the annual plan, besides being crucial elements
in peaking. The *volume* of training is the quantitative element of training that
incorporates integral parts of any training program. These include the
duration of activity, the distance covered in a training session, and the
number of repetitions of a given distance. The volume also refers to the sum
of work performed in a given training phase. Thus, an athlete may perform
24 training sessions in August and 16 in October. The same athlete may run
80 kilometers (48 miles) per week in April and only 72 kilometers (44 miles)

per week in July. In both examples, the volume of training is higher in the first case than in the second.

The quantity of work, or the volume of training, is an important element to train in running events in which endurance is the essential physical quality. In this sport, no one can be successful without performing a high volume of work in training. High volume, therefore, is an important training ingredient, especially during the preparatory phase when you build the foundation of strong cardiovascular conditioning. The high volume necessarily means a lower intensity, such as you will use during long-run workouts (chapter 7) and other base-training workouts (chapter 6). As the competitive phase approaches, decrease the volume of training slightly to allow for some high-intensity training. Remember, however, that you must consistently emphasize aerobic endurance throughout your competitive phase if you expect to achieve a good performance. Consider these guidelines for the percentage of training that should be aerobic: 50 percent for a half mile, 60 percent for a mile, 70 percent for two miles, 90 percent for a 10K, and 95 percent for a marathon.

> The right mix of intensity and volume is crucial for achieving your breakthrough.

The *intensity* of training represents the qualitative component of the work performed in a given period. It usually refers to how fast a repetition is performed (speed) and the psychological stress that accompanies it. The intensity of training is also determined by the amount of rest between repetitions. A partial recovery between repetitions is characteristic of high-intensity training as it inflicts a greater degree of collective fatigue on both the physiological and psychological systems.

Both the volume and intensity of training have a specific interaction during the main phases, such as the specific preparatory phase and the competitive phase, of the annual plan. Figure 5.2 illustrates the dynamics of volume (i.e., aerobic endurance) and intensity (i.e., lactic-acid training) for a two- to three-mile (3,000-meter to 5,000-meter) event. Peak performance is planned for the winter and summer nationals.

On the left of the chart is the kilometrage per week. The dynamics of the aerobic endurance training (volume) and lactic-acid tolerance (intensity) training change according to the training phase. In the early preparatory phases, the volume of training increases in steps, every three to four weeks, alternating with a lower volume, with the purpose of removing fatigue, regenerating the body, and relaxing the mind. Toward the end of the preparatory and early part of the competitive phases (C1 and C2), the volume stabilizes around 100 to105 kilometers per week. As the main competitions approach, and as you taper for the nationals, the volume of training decreases progressively to 50 percent of peak volume (50 kilometers per week). These less fatiguing conditions help you achieve peak performance by promoting psychological regeneration and the removal of lactic

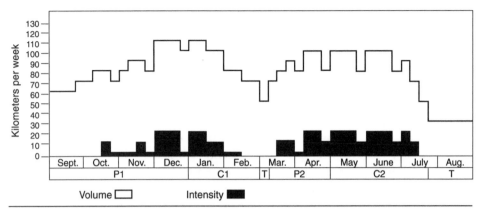

Figure 5.2 Volume and intensity for a 3,000-meter to 5,000-meter event.

acid and other waste products that have accumulated in your muscles because of intense training.

Because the two- to three-mile (3,000-meter to 5,000-meter) event is one in which the proportions of aerobic and anaerobic training are about 80 percent and 20 percent, the kilometrage of lactic-acid training is quite low. Even in months slated for the hardest training—December, January, May, and June in this example—the volume of lactic-acid training is not above 20 kilo-meters per week. Perform training designed to tolerate lactic-acid buildup during most months of the year (see chapter 8).

Conclusion

The fundamental concept for good annual planning is periodization, especially organizing the phases of aerobic and specific endurance training to maximize training effects. The periodization of event-specific speed and endurance represents the manipulation of different training phases with specific goals, organized in a specific sequence, with the ultimate goal of creating event-specific adaptation. When this adaptation is complete, you are physiologically equipped to produce better performances.

Having a good understanding of periodization will also assist you in producing better annual plans and training programs. In doing so, remember first to schedule your competitions to guide your training phases. Also, keep in mind that you must integrate into your program the periodization of nutrition (see chapter 13) and psychological training.

The Tudor Bompa Training System currently offers certification programs for both fitness and sport conditioning. If you would like information, e-mail the Tudor Bompa Training System at tudorbompasystem@home.com or check out their Web site at www.tudorbompa.com. Send mail inquiries to the Tudor Bompa Training System, P.O. Box 95, Sharon, Ontario L0G 1V0.

Building Your Base

MARK CONOVER
Member of the 1988 U.S. Olympic Marathon team
and head track and cross country coach at
California State Polytechnic University in San Luis Obispo, California

Base building creates a platform on which you erect all the other components of a successful training program.

As a runner, you are probably familiar with the concept of building a base for your training. In a nutshell, the purpose of base building is to create a platform on which all the other running components of a successful training program—anaerobic-threshold training, speed training, tapering—are erected. Your running breakthroughs must begin from a solid foundation of mileage run at "training" pace—a pace that, although it taxes your aerobic system, you can comfortably sustain over long periods and use to recover physically and mentally between hard efforts. In terms of heart rate, base-training pace is about 60 to 70 percent of your maximum.

This chapter defines base training and explains why it is a crucial foundation of your training program for making your breakthrough, no matter what your level and running goals.

What Is Base Training?

Distance running is primarily an aerobic activity. Aerobic means "with oxygen." During aerobic activities, your muscles use oxygen from the air you breathe as their primary energy source. The purpose of base training—running at a significantly lower intensity than race pace—is to advance and maintain your cardiovascular endurance and aerobic fitness level so that you can train comfortably and consistently. Proper base training trains your body to do this by conditioning your body to consume submaximal amounts of oxygen as you run. This means that during base-training runs you are not struggling for breath; you should be able to talk comfortably during these training runs. Yes, you are breathing at a higher level than you would be if you were sitting in your living room watching television, but you are not overstressing your cardiovascular system (heart and lungs). You are fully meeting your muscles' need for oxygen without forcing your body to rely on other energy-delivery systems. Unlike these other energy-delivery systems, the system used to supply energy for aerobic activity employs oxygen, which exists in unlimited supply—as long as you keep breathing!

Base training not only helps your body adapt to using oxygen more efficiently as an energy source but also strengthens the muscles, tendons, bones, and ligaments that form the "levers" used for running (your legs and feet, primarily). By consistently training at a pace that does not overtax your cardiovascular and musculoskeletal systems, the body also strengthens itself at the cellular level by creating more mitochondria (the energy-processing units of the cells), which play a crucial role in the muscles' ability to use oxygen. In addition, base training increases the number of capillaries, the smallest blood vessels, which deliver oxygen-rich blood to the working muscles.

Base running at a moderate intensity can serve as active recovery between harder efforts.

The function of base training is to strengthen physiological systems before adding faster-paced workouts. This is essential if you want to build an optimal training routine that leads eventually to a breakthrough performance. Look at your base mileage as money in the bank. Without it, you have nothing to draw upon later when you must cash checks in the form of fast workouts and races.

How do you determine the optimal pace for inducing these changes? As a broad gauge, you should be able to take in the scenery on your base-training runs and not dread the workouts. Rather, you should look forward to them as a form of therapy—a respite from the daily grind, if you will. Running at this moderate intensity also can serve as active recovery between harder efforts (see chapter 27 on building recovery into your training). Your base-training effort, however, should be more than a shuffle. You should feel pleasantly "up" afterward (though not winded).

Base Training Heart Rate at Various Ages

Age	Heart rate range
20	120–140
30	114–133
40	108–126
50	102–119
60	96–112

Many runners monitor their pace more objectively by wearing a heart rate monitor or taking their pulse. Your heart rate when base training should be about 60 to 70 percent of its maximum. A simple way to determine your base-training heart rate is to subtract your age from 220 and multiply that number by 0.6 and 0.7. The chart above gives base-training heart rate ranges for runners of various ages.

Keep in mind, however, that the 220-minus-age prediction formula is just a general guideline and may not be accurate, especially for older and very fit runners (both of whose actual training heart rate ranges will tend to be higher). For this reason, judging base-training pace by perception of effort makes more sense for many runners. You should be able to talk comfortably, though not sing or whistle, without feeling breathless.

When Should You Do Base Training?

Base training—that is, pure aerobic training—should compose the bulk of any distance runner's training, at any level of experience and ability and during all phases of the training cycle. You may be surprised to learn that even the best runners in the world do at least 80 percent of their running volume at conversation pace.

If you are a beginning runner (or coming back to the sport after taking a break from it) you should do *all* of your running at a base-training level. This will allow you to adjust gradually to the physical rigors of running, thus reducing the risk of injury, and will encourage you to enjoy running as a relaxing and nonstressful activity. Remember that the idea behind working toward your breakthrough is to build strength and endurance consistently, adapt slowly, and, above all, avoid injury and overtraining.

Besides putting in base-training miles as the foundation of your running program, you want to run almost exclusively at base-training level for at least two to three months if you are embarking on a training cycle that targets a certain race or racing season. Think of your base training as a foundation of both cardiovascular and muscle-connective tissue strength on which you will build your breakthrough performance by adding all the other components—discussed in upcoming chapters—of a great effort.

At other phases of your training cycle (anaerobic-threshold training, speed training, tapering, and racing), base-training-paced runs allow your body to recover between hard workouts and races, while maintaining aerobic fitness and reminding you why you love running in the first place. Thus, base training serves not only as a foundation for training but as the core of an ongoing training program that allows you to maintain aerobic fitness and recover from high-intensity efforts.

Base-Training Guidelines

Many runners don't know how to respond to a nonrunner's remark that running is boring. Some of us find it difficult to answer the nonrunner's question, "What do you think about out there?" Runners love running for a variety of reasons, including its simplicity, the social aspects, and the opportunity to be in nature. Boredom is rarely a factor. Still, it's possible to get into a rut or have an occasional flat, dull run, especially during training periods in which most of your training is base training. You can avoid this staleness by looking for ways to add variety to base-training runs:

- Vary the location of your runs. Choices include roads, trails, track, and fields. Ask other runners for suggestions.
- Vary the distance from day to day.
- Run with friends. Memorable conversations often arise during these base-training runs. The easy pace allows for conversational give-and-take that readily banishes boredom. No doubt you've had many conversations while running that might not have happened in other circumstances.
- Take your dog with you.

Beginning distance runners should work their total mileage up to 25 miles a week, advanced runners should aim for a high of 50 miles weekly, and elite runners should strive to run between 80 and 130 miles a week. These guidelines apply to runners preparing for distances from 5K to the marathon, with those specializing in shorter distances gravitating toward lower mileage and those focusing on longer distances aiming for higher weekly mileage. In working toward these upper limits, increase the distance of your weekly mileage by no more than approximately 10 percent every three weeks. (Note that these mileage guidelines represent total miles, including both base-training miles and others added at later stages of training.)

To achieve those goals, beginners should first work themselves up to running 15 miles per week and stay at that level for three weeks. They should then up their total weekly distance to 17 miles for three weeks, then 20, finally working up to 25 miles per week after three months. These numbers apply to all beginners, who should not yet be concerned with specializing in a particular distance. This may seem like a long time to spend building up, but a gradual approach will help ensure that novice runners keep the risk of injury low and continue to enjoy regular runs while consistently strengthening their running base.

More advanced runners—those who have been training consistently for at least six months and have a base of at least 25 miles per week—must decide on which race distance or distances they wish to focus. Runners who want to race at distances of 10K and up should build up to running 35 miles per week for three weeks, then 39 miles, then 43, and finally 50 miles per week after three months. Runners who wish to specialize in the 5K to 10K range can moderate their weekly mileage totals by 10 to 20 percent. Younger runners (high school and college age) should keep mileage totals moderate because they are still developing physically and as runners. Aging runners also usually need to back away from high mileage to avoid injury and allow more time for rest and recovery. Elite runners—those speedsters who finish in the top 10 of prominent regional races—would step up their base training from 70 to 77, 85, 94, and 100 miles, and so forth in three-week increments, depending on their training background, their response to mileage increases in the past, and the race distance or distances at which they want to specialize. Those racing only in the 5K to 10K range probably don't need to take their mileage above 80; those focusing on 10K and above will probably need to venture into triple digits to maximize their potential.

A Cautionary Note on Mileage

When determining mileage totals for your training and racing, remember that more is not necessarily better. Your personal mileage totals depend to a great extent on your goals and your running and racing background. For example, if your goal is simply to finish a race, and you're running 35 miles per week with four weekly runs, moving up to six efforts of similar intensity per week and 50 weekly miles probably won't boost your race performance. It may even do more harm than good because such a jump in mileage increases risk of injury or excessive fatigue due to overtraining (asking more of the body than it is prepared to handle). If you are a beginner or coming back to running after a significant break (three months or longer), you should be especially conservative with mileage. Don't start back at an advanced level you may have been at in the past.

Mileage guidelines are a safeguard to protect you from overtraining (which results from increasing the quantity or quality of your runs too quickly), not an absolute prescription to be followed to the letter. You know your body better than does the creator of any set of guidelines, which are prescribed to the general population of runners, not tailored to individuals. You need to monitor your body's response and back off when you feel signs of injury or excessive fatigue, rather than stick blindly to a rigid formula.

Thus, some runners may benefit more than others by running greater mileage. The guidelines offered here are not set in stone; rather, they are intended as helpful parameters that have worked for many runners over the years. Keep in mind that the main purposes of base training are to advance your aerobic capacity and increase muscle strength and endurance. These gains are the result of consistent base-training mileage, built up slowly over at least two to three months.

The chart below offers a broad outline for how runners wishing to improve their race performances should build up their total weekly mileage during the time leading up to their goal race. You should build up to the starting level using the guidelines on pages 66 and 67 for increasing overall mileage from week to week (i.e., no more than a 10 percent increase every three weeks). As noted in the previous section, you should set maximum goal mileage by considering your race distance, your overall fitness level, and your past experience in handling high mileage, physically and mentally.

Begin to taper (reduce mileage and intensity) two weeks before your goal race. For example, Sally, an advanced runner, plans to peak at 50 miles per week in training for a 10K. This is a reasonable weekly mileage goal that would allow her to include a long run of about 12 miles, two speed workout days of 8 or 9 miles (total) each, two easy recovery days of about 6 miles each, a tempo run day of 7 miles, and a day off. Five months before her goal race, she should aim to run 35 miles per week (70 percent of 50). Starting four months before her goal race, she should increase her weekly mileage to 40 (80 percent of 50). Beginning two months from her goal race, up until two weeks before the race, her mileage should average around 50. Remember that mileage goals are ballpark figures. You should shift gradually from one level to the next, not all at once.

Volume of Base Training

Months before goal race	Mileage
5	70% of maximum goal mileage
4	80% of maximum goal mileage
2	Maximum goal mileage

In general, the higher your mileage, the more likely it is that you'll obtain your performance goals if (and this is a big if) you don't overtrain. The problem with overtraining, unfortunately, is that you usually don't discover you've reached that point until it's too late. The secret to successful training is to push yourself to a peak performance level without tripping over the edge into a wasteland of burnout, staleness, and possible injury and illness. See chapter 26 for specific guidelines on avoiding overtraining.

All the mileage recommendations in this chapter are provided as guidelines to prevent overtraining in the base phase of training. Avoiding overtraining depends on keeping an accurate log that records not only what you do but also how your body responds to it. The mileage (which represents total weekly miles run unless otherwise stated) should be comfortable to handle at all stages, so that you can mix in anaerobic-threshold and $\dot{V}O_2$max training at the appropriate stages. If the mileage is not easy to handle,

Mileage guidelines are meant to protect you from overtraining; they are not absolute prescriptions.

© David Madison/Bruce Coleman Inc.

then you need to continue to work on advancing your aerobic capacity before doing training that is more arduous. Keep training at your current level (or back off slightly) before increasing your mileage or intensity.

Building on Your Base

Once you've established a solid base of running, you will need to incorporate faster-paced running into your training mix to maximize your chances of achieving specific performance goals you may have set. After you have built your aerobic base, you can introduce other paces into your training such as lactate-threshold training (see chapter 8) and speed training (see chapter 9).

Remember that you must first prepare your body for these rigorous forms of training by establishing a solid base. Without your base, you will never achieve the breakthrough you seek to achieve through higher intensity training.

> The secret to successful training is to push yourself to a peak performance without overtraining.

Even after you start adding other running intensities into your training, you'll still want to include base training in your program. Use the following guidelines to devise an optimal mix of weekly mileage paces to prepare for breakthrough racing (see also the chart below):

• Run 80 percent of your weekly miles at base-training pace, which equates to 60 to 70 percent of your maximum heart rate. This will work out to roughly one to two minutes slower per mile than your 15K or 10-mile race pace. The most important point is to run at a pace that feels easy, relaxing, and restorative for you, regardless of the numbers on the watch or heart rate monitor.

• Run 15 percent of your weekly miles at anaerobic-threshold pace, which should be about your 15K to 10-mile race pace. The 15 percent figure is approximate and optimal, but you shouldn't worry if you don't achieve it. Even if you run only 5 percent of your weekly miles at anaerobic-threshold pace, you will still be building up your body to prepare for race pace.

• If you can handle close to the 15 percent total, then run 5 percent of your weekly miles at $\dot{V}O_2$max pace. Begin $\dot{V}O_2$max workouts only during the final six to eight weeks of your race preparation. This type of workout will train your body to use oxygen better by consuming it at very fast speeds.

You should follow this training regimen beginning about four months before the target race or racing season, after a two- to three-month period of base training. You can fit in two such training periods per year, each culminating in breakthrough performances, followed by a two-week break before beginning the next period of base training.

Mileage Guidelines for a 40-Mile-Per-Week 10K Runner

A 40-mile-a-week runner who completes a 10K in 43:30 (approximately 7:00-per-mile pace) should train in the following manner:

Type of training	Mileage	Pace per mile
Base	32	8:20
Threshold	6	7:20
$\dot{V}O_2$ max	2	6:55

Endurance Training

RICHARD BENYO
Editor of *Marathon & Beyond* and winner of the
1998 RRCA Professional Journalist of the Year award

Simply put, a long run is roughly two to two and a half times your longest weekday run.

The human body is one of the most adaptive machines on earth. Unlike machines of steel and plastic and rubber that gradually wear out from use, the human body, when used regularly, adapts to that use and begs for more.

It is this "more" that fulfills the desire of the human spirit for greater challenges, providing the springboard to training for and participating in longer and longer endurance events—at the far end of the spectrum, in ultradistance events.

The capacity of the human body for work is phenomenal. Properly trained, a human being can run down virtually any other animal on earth—not through sheer speed but through raw endurance. Ancient man regularly ran prey to the ground by outlasting it. The human advantage comes from a combination of factors: muscle and cardiovascular adaptation, sensible pacing dictated by a larger and better brain, and a complex ability to expel heat built up in the process of physical exertion. A dog can cool itself only from its tongue and the pads of its paws. In contrast, a human being uses virtually every square inch of skin to cool himself or herself.

The ability to build a tremendous capacity for endurance and to refuel along the way has elevated the human being beyond what would seem the natural limits of an organism to endure. The subject of learned and applied increased endurance capacity of the human organism is multilayered, but it is simultaneously the relatively simple science of stress and rest.

Eighty years ago track coaches advised their milers never to run more than three-quarters of a mile in practice because the effort would overtax them and thus ruin them for their ultimate mile effort in competition. Distance running pioneers such as Paavo Nurmi and Emil Zatopek defied that conventional wisdom. They shocked the track world by increasing their long endurance runs and even their track repetitions in practice to volumes that traditionalists thought would guarantee their failure. Instead, however, the success of these athletes is imprinted in the Olympic record books.

In the late 1950s, a New Zealand shoemaker and part-time coach named Arthur Lydiard took a group of neighborhood runners under his wing and, to the dismay of established coaches, markedly increased the distances of their long, slow runs. Lydiard and his charges were rewarded with a shelf of medals at the 1960 Rome Olympic Games.

The Long Run Defined

What constitutes a long run? For every formula, there are a dozen variations waiting in the wings. On a simple level, a long run (often run on a weekend) is roughly two to two and a half times the longest run a person is doing during weekday training. If a long weekday run is 7 miles, the weekend long run would be 14 to 17 miles. Elite runners accustomed to running 10 miles on a weekday afternoon after running a 5-mile wake-up run in the morning would be in the 20- to 25-mile range for a long weekend run.

This chapter is oriented to marathon and ultradistance runners. For the marathoner, the exact distance of the long weekend run depends on where the runner is in the timetable of building for the marathon. Others do the long run to hold their long-endurance fitness level over an extended period.

Some marathon and ultramarathon runners train or race a 20-miler every weekend of their competitive seasons. Many of these racers also regularly flirt with injury because they maintain that level without periodically inserting easier days or rest days. As these athletes age, their bodies demand more recovery time and injuries multiply.

The theory of the long run's success in promoting endurance is based on a simple premise: stress the organism, rest it so it can adapt to that new level of stress, stress it again a little more, then allow it more recuperative rest while the organism adapts still further. This *hard-easy* approach to distance running is based on theories codified during the 1950s and 60s by Arthur Lydiard; all current endurance theory is merely a variation on Lydiard's essential principles. (See chapter 5 on periodization, which details the basic tenets of training.)

A long endurance run once every two weeks is ideal for building toward racing marathons or for maintaining a high level of running and endurance fitness because it allows for a secondary, shorter (or "easy") long run on alternating weekends.

As for intensity, the long run is not a jog. You should run it at roughly 90 to 100 seconds per mile slower than your marathon race pace. The idea of the long run is to build endurance to run, not merely to survive. The consistent stress of running the long run (instead of interspersing walking breaks) effectively elevates endurance capacity all the way to the molecular level, where the mitochondria learn to fire more consistently.

A long run is not a jog.

The secondary long run on alternating weekends would be roughly two to five miles shorter than the long run. Thus, a typical 20-week primary and secondary long-run training program might look something like this:

Week 16—16 miles (primary)

Week 17—13 miles (secondary)

Week 18—18 miles (primary)

Week 19—15 miles (secondary)

Week 20—20 miles (primary)

The shorter long run every other week maintains fitness while allowing the body to rest from the longer long run. It permits some recovery and enhances the ability to go into the next long run more rested and energized, ready to do a better, higher level job, each time extending the outer limit.

Both the long run and the secondary long run are significantly enhanced if the runner also inserts one medium-long run during the week. For example, if a runner is doing 18-mile long runs and 14- to 15-mile secondary long runs on alternating weekends, a good, hard 7- to 8-miler once each week in the middle of the week would contribute to the quality level (i.e., strength or speed) of the long run and the secondary long run.

As for intensity, the midweek medium-long run should be done just below lactate-threshold pace (see chapter 8 for a description of lactate-threshold training)—that is, a good, solid effort after the warm-up, rather than at the 60 to 70 percent of heart-rate maximum effort of training pace. Naturally, this hard midweek run should be scheduled at least two days away from a weekly track workout to allow the body to recover properly between hard or long workouts.

The Long Run Considered

The endurance-training program can be compared to a medical-school skeleton. The long run is the backbone. Without it, all other elements of the training program—from speed workouts to cross-training—rattle to a pile on the floor like so many random, unconnected bones.

Without a regularly executed long run, the runner establishes no outer limit of endurance. The human body cannot perform during a race for which it has not been trained in practice. We have all seen and heard of tremendous endurance accomplishments seemingly beyond the ability of the athlete. On closer examination, though, we find that those startling performances are grounded in similar or related performances in mundane training sessions.

An as yet unexplained phenomenon of the human body is that long and hard training is seemingly imprinted at the molecular level to the point that heroic performances are occasionally achieved on what seems to be insufficient training. Many body cells and body systems have "memories" just as brain cells do. If you perform an action enough times, a muscle, especially the mitochondria in the muscle, begins to know what reaction you expect of it. The action becomes imprinted. This process works in body systems too. Take, for instance, the body's ability and inclination to perspire; the body of a highly trained marathoner will begin to perspire much sooner than the body of an untrained individual. Again, the action is imprinted through repetition. The body can also learn to use free fatty acids instead of electrolytes. In those instances, the long runs of the previous 4, 5, or 10 years may produce accumulated effects that can augment current training to produce a performance not seemingly justified by current training levels.

Such extraordinary performances based on previous years of regular and consistent training are not well understood. They seem to be an extension of the phenomenon of the abrupt success that former athletes enjoy upon suddenly embarking on a training program after years of doing nothing. Compare that with the uphill battle of nonathletes who take up endurance-training programs at a later age.

Those who have trained regularly for decades should not count on this phenomenon. The anomalous performances usually surprise the athlete more than they do the startled spectator. Witness several veteran endurance runners (Max Jones and Jeff Hagen come to mind) who are currently experimenting with how little weekly mileage they can accumulate and still turn in credible—and even noteworthy—performances. Those performances are based in large part on years of consistent high-level training anchored by weekly long runs.

On minimal weekly mileage during 1998, Jeff Hagen won outright the six ultramarathons he ran, despite being 51 years of age. At the 1999 Sutter Home Napa Valley Marathon, Max Jones, aged 71, ran 3:42:04 (faster than 8:30-per-mile pace) on 15 miles per week of training. He sees himself as an

Build up to high mileage gradually, increasing total mileage no more than 5 to 10 percent per week.

© D. Graham/H. Armstrong Roberts

ultrarunner and holds numerous international age-group records in ultra events. Both of these pioneers admit to needing a long run to anchor their experiments. Although they benefit from the cumulative effects of high mileage, most of their current minimum weekly mileage is made up of one long run.

What about those of us who want the secret to handling high overall mileage? The solution is two-pronged:

1. Build to high mileage gradually, increasing total mileage no more than 5 to 10 percent per week.

2. Once at high mileage, don't hang out too long (more than six months) in that rarified atmosphere. Many talented racers reach a high level of endurance and speed and become so infatuated with their performances at that level that they overstay their welcome. This invariably leads to injury. Even the talented, well-adapted body needs rest to rehabilitate itself from high-level performances. Major marathon seasons are spring and fall. For most marathoners and ultrarunners, one serious race in each season with a major cutback over the winter and a similar but less extreme cutback over the summer is appropriate.

Importance of Rest

Rest is a crucial but frequently overlooked element of training, not just for longevity but for improved performance. Both of Derek Clayton's world-best marathon performances in the 1960s came in the wake of forced rest due to surgical repair of overuse injuries. Joan Benoit's gold-medal performance at the Los Angeles Olympics occurred in the same circumstance. If a runner incorporates rest into an endurance-training program, he or she is master of that lull. If a runner does not schedule rest, the body will demand it at some point, often at an inopportune time.

Marathon Training Essentials

The essentials of marathon training are simple:

1. Run a regular long run that builds in length (by no more than two miles every two weeks) toward race weekend.

2. Follow a carefully planned and executed program that builds strength and speed, in addition to endurance, toward race weekend. Running "as you feel" is not the way to train toward a good marathon. Plan a training schedule of 14, 16, or 18 weeks and stick to it. Launch your marathon-training program from a solid foundation of running fitness. A marathon-training program longer than 18 weeks launched from a solid foundation of fitness tends to be too long for most runners, causing performance to drop off.

3. Plan well-placed and periodic rests, especially in the wake of hard or long workouts.

4. Practice good hydration. Drink enough water that you urinate prodigiously six to eight times per day. Water is best because it is universally available, cheap, easily absorbed by the body, has no calories, and does not tire the body by requiring the production of insulin as do sugared drinks. Count on a well-balanced diet to provide other essential nutrients.

5. Perform some high-repetition but low-weight upper-body workouts, especially involving the arms and shoulders. In the latter stages of a marathon, a well-conditioned upper body can keep a runner going faster and farther more comfortably. A runner who begins to sag at 18 miles closes down his or her lung capacity. Additionally, the rhythm of the legs comes from arm swing; tired and ineffective arms in the final miles of a marathon rob the runner of stride length and strength. Consider that losing a half inch per stride in the latter stages of a marathon loses you 87 feet per mile. You'll need to run an extra 87 feet to complete each mile because of your shortened stride.

6. Treat yourself to regular sports massage. Bill Rodgers gets them. So does Joan Benoit Samuelson. An hour-long, twice-monthly sports massage that digs down into those stressed and sore muscles to break up adhesions and restore muscle health is a therapeutic way to head off injury and ensure better runs. Always schedule an easy training day the day after a massage because your body will need time to recover from the wonderful assault on the muscles. Good, hard sports massage deposits a fair volume of toxins in the bloodstream for eventual excretion. The toxins tend to compromise the ability of the bloodstream to carry oxygen and nutrients efficiently to an exercising body. In addition, deep sports massage tends to cause temporary muscle soreness that can make a hard workout more difficult.

7. Don't stretch unless you really know what you're doing. Many "experts" encourage stretching to prevent running injuries. An equal number preach against stretching, period. The experts I trust almost universally advise against most stretching exercises. One of them, podiatrist John Pagliano, an authority on long-running training and racing and a talented racer in his time, has compiled a database of his patients over the past 20 years. His findings indicate that the third leading cause of running injuries is stretching!

If you want to stretch, never do it while your muscles are cool or cold. Joe Oakes, who has been running more than 50 years at every imaginable distance, suggests doing gentle stretches first thing in the morning while you are still in bed and warm from sleeping under the covers. Alternatively, jog a mile or two to warm up your muscles before doing any stretching. Never bounce while stretching; it's a sure way to tear muscle tissue. And always back off a stretch if you feel pain.

8. Never try in a marathon anything you have not field-tested in practice—drinking sports fluids, using running shoes that haven't been gradually broken in at shorter distances, wearing new running outfits, or changing your dietary regimen leading into race day. Try everything you plan to use on race day during and leading into your long runs. Race day is not the time to learn that your new shoes cause blisters in the arch area, that the fettuccine that strikes your fancy the night before the race causes diarrhea, that the racing shorts you just bought chafe your inner thighs. You get the idea.

9. Complete the mundane tasks up front. Pick your marathon and send in your entry early. Secure your plane ticket and hotel room early. Well ahead of time, schedule the time off from work you need for the marathon. Put practical matters behind you early, so they won't clutter the path to your marathon success.

10. Visualize your race performance. On your long runs and on your hard midweek medium-long runs, note your performance. Then, in quiet moments, translate those performances to the course profile of your upcoming marathon. Run through the marathon in an honest, objective examination of what your training indicates is possible. Run through your potential marathon performance repeatedly. If you manage to do this honestly and objectively, on race day it will merely be a matter of painting by numbers the portrait of your best performance based on your training at that point.

Running Into the Great Beyond

What is beyond the 26.2 miles of the marathon? Each year, a segment of veteran marathon runners decides to try an ultramarathon. Technically, an ultramarathon is anything longer than 26.2 miles, but it's usually an event of 50K (31 miles) or longer. Ultramarathons come in an endless array of distances, surfaces, and challenges—from the 50K to a four-month adventure run through most of the states in the United States.

Ultrarunning provides a viable arena for marathoners who feel they have become too old and too slow to do well at the marathon distance but still want to have credible performances; a good marathoner can often do exceptionally well at his or her age group in ultras. Most of the ultrarunners against whom they will compete have not been to a track to do speedwork in years. For most ultrarunners, a track is anathema to their training, yet they eagerly embrace the track as the crucible of 24-hour, 48-hour, 72-hour, and six-day races. Ultradistance running is filled with such deep paradoxes.

A well-trained marathoner is capable of racing a good 50K. A good marathoner, by backing his or her pace down about one minute per mile and lightly snacking on solid foods along the way (after practicing eating on the run during long runs), can usually do a credible 50-miler.

Most ultramarathons in the United States are trail runs. A good road marathoner will not automatically make a good trail ultrarunner. Trail running is a separate art form; runners should practice it during long runs well before competing in a trail ultra. An efficient, low-to-the-ground marathon style doesn't account for exposed roots or rocks. On the positive side, because most ultras in the United States are on trails rather than roads, the ultrarunner will usually benefit from running on a forgiving dirt surface. In addition, thanks to the softer surfaces of trails, runners can often increase mileage without the expected increase in running injuries.

Ultramarathons offer an array of distances, surfaces, and challenges; choose what suits you.

© David Madison/Bruce Coleman Inc.

A marathoner moving up to ultras should also learn to eat while running, choosing snack foods (pretzels, chips, cookies) that quickly restore sugars and salts rapidly burned up in an extended run or race. An ultramarathoner must also be good at drinking a great volume of fluid, especially water. Without proper hydration, an ultra can quickly become a session in hell.

Ultramarathoning, done properly, consumes a great deal of a runner's life. Simply because training and racing distances are much longer and are at a significantly slower pace, long runs become, well, longer runs. Some ultramarathoners race every weekend, using that distance as their weekly mileage and training minimally or even not at all during the week.

Fueling on the Long Run

Some of us are a little cynical about how incredibly complex the simple act of running has become, especially on the matter of nutrition. When Clarence DeMar, Emil Zatopek, and Abebe Bikila were setting course and world records, they trained themselves to do so fueled by plain water and sometimes sugared tea. Some marathoners ran the entire 26.2 miles without any fluid replacement, which may well have undermined the possibility of even greater performance.

Today, endurance athletes are confronted with a cornucopia of sports drinks, bars, and gels, all of which can be beneficial for replenishing muscles with a readily available supply of carbohydrate for energy. As for caloric replenishment, exercising beyond 90 minutes warrants ingesting at least a sports drink, but the simpler the better because simpler foods and drinks are typically cheaper, easier to digest, and more universally available. The more exotic you go, the more likely you are to begin depending on something that is frequently not available. The brain, which operates on sugar, loves to be fed pure sugar after 90 minutes; otherwise, it begins to become sluggish and keeps hinting that it would like the body to stop what it is doing because the rest of the body is burning up the supply of simple sugar it usually has all to itself.

Sports drinks that provide some replacement of electrolytes are also valuable because the body processes electrolytes much more easily than it does free fatty acids, of which it has a nearly limitless supply. It takes careful practice to teach the body to use free fatty acids efficiently, but once the body learns how, its performance greatly improves.

Long runs teach the body to use free fatty acids, available in incredible volume, as opposed to glycogen, which isn't. By beginning long runs without feeding your body a lot of sugar, you teach it to begin changing over to free fatty acids.

Don't become too dependent on specific sports drinks. They may not be readily available at every race. The option of having your own specially marked bottles at aid tables generally is available only to the field of elite, invited athletes. The solution is simple: learn to drink whatever the race is serving and don't begin taking it until at least an hour into the race. Stick to water the first hour. Don't go into a race having snacked on anything containing sugar and don't use anything containing sugar for at least the first 60 to 90 minutes. Why? First, ingestion of sugar sets off an insulin reaction, which consumes a lot of energy, energy you could more profitably use to move the legs along efficiently. Second, ingestion of sugar inhibits the body from changing over to using free fatty acids. Why should it bother to change to free fatty acids if it's getting all the sugar it needs?

As for sports bars, they are a convenient, but expensive, invention. Ellen Coleman, a noted sports nutritionist, advises endurance athletes to buy fig bars instead of sports bars because they provide similar benefits at a substantially lower price. Of course, if you're doing an eight-hour workout, a sports bar may hold up in your fanny pack much better than a fig bar.

Gels have their advantages, but once you begin to use them on a long run or race, you must continue to use them or risk suffering a severe energy drop. Don't begin using gels until 90 minutes or more into a long workout or race. Otherwise, unless you continue to use them, you'll flirt with turning your sugar level into a yo-yo.

The best plan is to train yourself to function on a simple and plain refueling program because those fuels are more likely to be available. Running is a simple sport. You'll perform best by keeping it that way.

For the ultrarunner, the best advice is to learn to eat on the run, everything from pretzels to baked potatoes, all of it in small portions every half hour or so, or at each aid station. Keep your nutrition simple, and problems you encounter along the way will turn out to be simple and easily surmountable. Again, the formulated carbohydrate-replacement drinks are expensive, are not always available, and can cause various problems along the way—especially when consumed in the volume that ultrarunners require. As an example, ultralegend Ann Trason drinks V8 Juice on her 100-milers. She packs containers in dry ice inside her drop packets. Before expensive sports drinks were introduced, we used Nutriment and fruit drinks.

Of course, such a regimen almost guarantees that they will not run ultras well, even if they participate in them regularly.

As you would for the marathon, you should schedule ultras carefully. A runner should go into an ultra well trained and well rested if he or she hopes to do well. (Of course, many people who do ultras, like many marathoners, do them not to perform well but merely to take part.)

The danger of hurting yourself by falling down should be mentioned, if not stressed. Several years ago, I participated in a panel at the Vancouver International Marathon with Jeff Galloway and Joe Henderson. Having done some rather strange adventure runs in my time, I was designated as the token ultrarunner. After the talk, one neophyte ultrarunner castigated me for not stressing the potential danger of falling down while doing trail ultras. What can I say? Some people fall down and hurt themselves, some people fall down and don't hurt themselves badly, and some people never or seldom fall down. So now you've been warned that gravity can be a negative factor.

To do well in longer ultras (100-milers, adventure runs, 48-hour races, six-day races, etc.), the runner should try to teach his or her body to recover on the run. This seems like a concept truly alien to everything we've been saying about hard-easy workouts, yet it is a variation on the hard-easy concept that successful ultrarunners have been using for years. Alberto Salazar also used this concept successfully in his heyday. During one of his New York City Marathon wins, he was so firmly in command at 17 miles that he threw in a sub-4:30 mile and then coasted for the next mile at close to five minutes. At his level of fitness, he was able to recover partially during that "easy" mile before increasing the pace again the next mile.

Ultrarunners can execute this process in the following manner. At least every other weekend, train by running a long run on Saturday (32 to 40 miles at a pace 90 seconds slower than your 50-mile race pace), then come back on Sunday and do another long run (18 to 25 miles at the same leisurely pace). For a well-grounded and well-trained ultrarunner, everything is relative; the 18- to 25-mile Sunday is an "easy" day that allows partial recovery from the 32- to 40-mile Saturday. Together, the two workouts prepare the runner for competing in multiday events.

For longer adventure runs that may be your goal breakthrough performance, such as running across the country, it is better to go into the event relatively undertrained. The day-in, day-out sort of running you will need for long adventure runs will bring you up to top-level fitness during the actual event. If you go into this sort of long ultra at your peak, there is a chance you will crash before the month-long event is over; you may use up your peak in the early going.

By combining basic marathon-training principles (but increasing volume and slowing the pace) and by using an occasional marathon as a long training run, a good marathoner can graduate with honors to the ultraworld. Once inside this world, it quickly becomes clear that the only borders are those imposed by the runner's imagination.

Nowhere is the long run more important than in training for the marathon and ultramarathon. The long run pushes the athlete's body into new distance territory during practice so that he or she can combine that advantage with strength and speed training to race faster for longer distances. The long run is the backbone of any distance-running program—the backbone to which all other elements are attached to create the complete runner. The long run is also the primary element for runners who wish to break through to the next level in their long-distance running. A well-executed long run is one of the greatest confidence builders for the distance runner. And on the completely esoteric level, the runner who performs a long run well comes as close as any runner can to producing a work of art.

8

Lactate-Threshold Training

PETE PFITZINGER, MSc, MBA
Exercise physiologist, coach, 1984 and 1988 member of the
U.S. Olympic Marathon team, and senior writer for *Running Times*

Among all measurable physiological variables, lactate threshold is the best predictor of distance-running performance.

This chapter focuses on how to make a breakthrough in your running performance by training to improve your lactate threshold. Lactate and lactate threshold (sometimes referred to as anaerobic threshold) are defined, and the relationship between lactate threshold and distance running success is explained. This is followed by a look at the physiology behind the buildup of lactate in the muscles and information on how to determine your lactate-threshold pace. Most important, a discussion of how to train effectively to improve your lactate threshold is presented.

Lactate used to be thought of as simply a waste product of muscles in the breakdown of carbohydrates for anaerobic energy production. When glycogen or glycose is metabolized, a substance called pyruvate is formed. When pyruvate is produced more quickly than it can be used to produce energy aerobically, the excess is reduced to produce lactate. It is now understood, however, that lactate is both produced and used as a fuel by the muscles and heart even when you are resting. When you increase your effort from walking to jogging to slow running, both the amount of lactate you produce and the amount you use increase. Up to a certain exercise intensity, the amount your muscles produce and the amount your body uses stay roughly in balance. As you begin to run faster, however, you eventually reach a speed at which the rate of lactate production by your body exceeds the amount of lactate utilization. The highest exercise intensity you can achieve before your lactate production exceeds its utilization is your lactate threshold (LT).

Your lactate threshold is related to the inability of your muscles to use oxygen quickly enough to produce energy. When your muscles cannot use enough oxygen to produce all the energy they need, the lactic-acid system of your muscles, also known as the anaerobic energy system, produces additional energy. Recently, complex theories have been developed to explain lactate threshold. Regardless of the exact reason for its existence, however, your LT occurs when your body produces lactate more rapidly than it can use it.

Most experienced distance runners can run at their LT pace for 40 to 60 minutes. At speeds slower than LT pace, you should be able to maintain a given pace for well over an hour. At speeds faster than LT pace, however, the buildup of lactate (lactic acid) in your muscles soon restrains you. This is because the buildup of lactate inactivates the enzymes that are necessary for producing energy. For beginning runners, lactate threshold is typically 70 to 80 percent of their $\dot{V}O_2$max. For well-trained distance runners, lactate threshold typically occurs at 80 to 90 percent of $\dot{V}O_2$max.

If you are well prepared for the distance, your marathon pace is typically 3 to 5 percent slower than your LT pace. Runners who have trained consistently for several years can run races of 15K or 10 miles at almost exactly LT pace and can run races of 5K to 10K slightly faster than LT pace. Less experienced runners are likely to be able to maintain LT pace for about 8K to 10K. For races shorter than 5K, LT is a less useful predictor of performance. Runners usually run those races considerably faster than LT pace, so other factors contribute more to performance.

Lactate Threshold and Distance-Running Success

Among all the physiological variables that can be measured, lactate threshold has been found to be the best predictor of distance-running performance. Why? In running terms, your LT pace is the fastest running speed you can maintain without a rapid rise in the lactate levels in your muscles and blood. Without realizing it, you set your pace in a distance race according to your LT—if you exceed that pace your muscles will rapidly accumulate lactate, which as previously stated, inactivates the enzymes that are used to produce energy. Thus, in a long race, going out at faster than LT pace means that you will later be forced to slow dramatically when your lactate level rises.

Besides lactate threshold, several other factors contribute to running performance, including mental toughness, smart pacing, running economy (that is, how much oxygen you require to run at a given pace), and your maximal oxygen consumption ($\dot{V}O_2$max, the maximal capacity for oxygen consumption by the body during exertion). For many years, exercise physiologists believed that $\dot{V}O_2$max was the best predictor of endurance performance. In the late 1970s, however, Jack Daniels, PhD, and colleagues investigated changes in $\dot{V}O_2$max and running performance with training and noticed that running performance continued to improve after $\dot{V}O_2$max leveled off. Over the past 20 years, it has become clear that the amount of oxygen a runner can use at his or her lactate threshold is more accurate than the amount of oxygen a runner can consume at maximal effort ($\dot{V}O_2$max) in predicting the runner's performance.

The pace you can maintain while running at your lactate threshold, which also is determined by differences in running economy among individuals, is an even more accurate predictor of distance-running performance. In a classic study, Peter Farrell, PhD, and colleagues investigated the relationship between running ability and several physiological variables—including $\dot{V}O_2$max, lactate threshold, percentage of slow-twitch muscle fibers, and running economy. Of all the variables measured, LT pace was most closely related to racing performance. It appears that race pace for distances above 10K is primarily determined by LT pace, which can be increased either by training the muscles to increase their oxygen consumption at LT or by improving running economy. You can improve oxygen consumption of your muscles at your lactate threshold by performing a certain percentage of your training at your LT pace.

As an example of how your lactate-threshold pace determines your racing performance, consider three hypothetical runners, Alison, Joyce, and Claudia, with $\dot{V}O_2$max values of 60, 55, and 56 milliliters per kilogram per minute (ml · kg^{-1} · min^{-1}), respectively. Holding all other factors constant, Alison, with the highest $\dot{V}O_2$max value, would win a race against the other two runners. Suppose, however, that oxygen consumption at LT for Alison, Joyce, and Claudia represents 70 percent, 80 percent, and 75 percent of each of their $\dot{V}O_2$max values, respectively. Joyce would then be predicted to outperform Alison and Claudia because Joyce is able to consume more oxygen at her lactate threshold [44 ml · kg^{-1} · min^{-1} (55 × .80 = 44)] than Alison or Claudia [42 ml · kg^{-1} · min^{-1} (60 × .70 = 42 and 56 × .75 = 42)].

So far, we have looked at oxygen consumption and lactate threshold but not running economy. Remember that both oxygen consumption at lactate threshold and running economy determine your LT pace. Let's say our three runners want to race at a pace of 6:00 per mile. Alison and Joyce each require 46 ml · kg^{-1} · min^{-1} of oxygen to hold that pace, but Claudia requires only 40 ml · kg^{-1} · min^{-1} because she is more economical (i.e., she can run at that pace using less oxygen than the other two runners due to several factors). Claudia could maintain a 6:00 pace longer than the others could because she would be the only one running below her LT pace.

If you want to improve your running performance while minimizing your risk of breaking down because of injury or overtraining, you should focus your training on improving your lactate threshold.

Adaptations That Improve Your LT

Your lactate threshold improves with the appropriate training because of several adaptations that take place in your muscles. These adaptations occur in a chain that increases the supply of oxygen to individual muscle fibers and improves the ability of your muscle fibers to produce energy aerobically.

More Blood Flow to Your Muscles

Oxygen is transported in the blood. LT training increases the proportion of your blood sent to your working muscles, which enables your muscles to receive and use more oxygen and, therefore, allows you to run faster before reaching your lactate threshold.

More Capillaries

Capillaries are the smallest blood vessels. Several capillaries typically border a muscle fiber. They bring oxygen and fuels to the muscle cells and take away waste products. LT training sessions help increase the number of capillaries bordering each muscle fiber, which improves the efficiency of oxygen delivery.

More Myoglobin

Myoglobin carries oxygen from the outer surface of your muscle fibers to the mitochondria (the part of your muscle fibers where energy is produced aerobically), just as hemoglobin in your red blood cells carries oxygen from your lungs. LT training stresses the ability of myoglobin to transport oxygen to the mitochondria, which stimulates your muscles to increase the amount of myoglobin in your muscle fibers.

More and Bigger Mitochondria

By stressing the ability of your muscles to produce energy aerobically, LT training causes an increase in both the number and size of the mitochondria in your muscle fibers. With more mitochondria, you can use more oxygen before reaching your lactate threshold.

More Aerobic Enzyme Activity

Aerobic enzymes in your mitochondria speed up the rate of aerobic energy production in your muscle fibers. LT training stimulates an increase in aerobic enzyme activity, which increases your lactate threshold by allowing your muscles to produce more energy aerobically.

The pace you can maintain while running at your lactate threshold is an accurate predictor of your distance-running performance.

How Your LT Improves With the Right Training

If you have been training hard for several years, you have probably just about reached your genetic potential in improving your $\dot{V}O_2max$. Your LT, however, will continue to increase with the right training even after you have been running for many years. That is because improvements in $\dot{V}O_2max$ are primarily due to an increase in the ability of your heart to pump blood to your muscles, whereas increases in your lactate threshold also reflect several adaptations in your muscles that improve their ability to produce energy aerobically. Improvements in LT are the most likely area for a breakthrough for veteran runners. Unfortunately, your LT also decreases relatively quickly when you cut back your training. In the lab, we see decreases in LT in runners after six to eight weeks of reduced training.

Let's take a look at a few studies that have investigated how much and how quickly LT can improve with the right type of training. In 1982, Bertil Sjodin, PhD, and colleagues investigated how much LT pace would improve in male distance runners by adding one weekly 20-minute run at LT pace to their regular training for 14 weeks (their previous LT training was not clearly specified). LT pace increased by 12 meters per minute after the alteration in training. This is a 12- to 15-second-per-mile improvement, which would represent more than a minute in a 10K race and more than 5 minutes in a marathon.

> Improvements in LT are the most likely area for a breakthrough for veteran runners.

In another study, a team of Japanese researchers (Tanaka et al. 1986) looked at the relationship between improvements in lactate threshold and race performance. Runners were instructed to continue with their regular training and add two runs per week of approximately one hour at LT pace. At the end of four months, LT pace improved by eight meters per minute (8 to 10 seconds per mile), oxygen consumption at LT increased by 5.6 percent, and 10K performance improved by 95 seconds. Interestingly, the performance of these athletes in a 1,500-meter race—which is run at a pace faster than LT pace—did not improve with LT training.

The results of these studies and others indicate that regular training sessions at LT pace provide a stimulus to improve LT pace and performance in races of 5K or longer. How much and how quickly you improve in response to LT training depends on the amount of specific LT training you do and your genetic capacity to adapt to training. Some runners are "adapters" who improve relatively quickly in response to a training stimulus. Other runners take longer to adapt. Regardless of your genetic endowment, however, you will improve your LT pace—and, therefore, your racing performances—by regularly running sessions specifically designed to stimulate improvements in LT. Before I provide specific guidelines and workouts for LT training, let's first determine your LT by completing the following steps.

How to Determine Your LT Pace

Exercise physiologists conduct LT tests on runners, cyclists, rowers, swimmers, triathletes, and other athletes. An LT test in a lab will tell you your LT pace and heart rate at LT. The physiologist can then prescribe the correct training zones for you. Most universities have an exercise science laboratory that can conduct LT tests. These labs may need subjects for studies, or they may conduct LT tests for a fee.

Alternatively, a coach, trainer, or exercise physiologist can conduct an LT test at the track or on a measured road course using a portable lactate analyzer. (It is important that it not be too hot or too windy or the results of this test will not be as reliable.)

If you do not have access to a lab or a portable lactate analyzer, do not despair. You can estimate your LT pace reasonably accurately using your race pace. If you have been running consistently for several years, you can also estimate your LT pace by using your race pace for 15K or 10 miles. For example, if you race 15K in 65 minutes (approximately a 7:00-per-mile pace), your LT pace will be very close to 7:00 per mile. You can then use this pace to calculate your lactate-threshold heart rate zone. After warming up, run at that pace around a track (on a relatively calm day) and record your heart rate. Check your heart rate after you have been running at least one-half mile at your LT pace. Now add three beats per minute to find the high end of your LT heart rate zone and subtract three beats per minute to find the low end of your zone. You can use your heart rate to pace yourself appropriately when you run an LT session on the roads.

For example, Paul—who has a 7:00-per-mile lactate-threshold pace— does a three-mile tempo run on the track in 21:00, and his heart rate stays in the range of 156 to 160 beats per minute. He would want to maintain his heart rate in that range during his LT training sessions on the roads. Heart rate is actually more useful than pace in maintaining the correct intensity on a windy day or on a hilly course. On a hot day, however, you should adjust your LT heart rate range upward three to five beats per minute because your heart rate will be elevated as more blood is sent to your skin to aid in cooling.

How to Maximize Your LT Through Training

By now you should appreciate that improving your LT pace is a high priority for improving your LT and, therefore, for training successfully for a break-through performance. What is the most effective way to improve your LT pace? What types of LT workouts can you do, how frequently should you do them, and what percentage of your total training miles should you run at your lactate threshold?

Improve Your LT Pace

Studies have shown that the most effective way to improve your LT is to train at your current LT pace, which makes logical sense. By training at the intensity at which your lactate concentration starts to increase rapidly, you provide the greatest stimulus for the physiological adaptations that improve LT (see page 84).

The longer you run at your LT pace, the greater the stimulus to improve. Training faster than LT pace provides less stimulus to improving your LT because during faster running the lactic-acid system supplies more energy and you want to train your body to run faster without relying heavily on this system. Training slower than LT pace provides less stress on your aerobic system and, therefore, provides less stimulus to improving your LT.

A heart rate monitor can help you run at your desired LT pace.

It is easy to regulate LT pace at the track or on a measured course, but you also want to be able to do so on the roads, where you may not know precise distances, and on windy days or hilly courses. Again, the best way to determine if you are running at your LT pace is by wearing a heart rate monitor and keeping your heart rate in the correct range.

Structure Your LT Workout

The best LT workouts are those in which you spend the most time at LT pace. The longer you maintain your LT pace, the more stress you put on the ability of your muscles to produce energy aerobically. By fully utilizing the current capacity of this system, you stimulate adaptations to improve your LT and your running performance. Several LT training options are available.

Tempo Runs

You can accumulate time at your LT pace by doing either one continuous run at LT pace (commonly known as a tempo run) or a series of shorter runs at that pace. Both methods have been popularized in the United States by coach and exercise physiologist Jack Daniels, PhD. Daniels is one of a handful of exercise physiologists with extensive experience working directly with runners from the collegiate to elite levels. For a tempo run, first warm up for 10 to 20 minutes at a pace slower than LT pace and then run for 20 to 40 minutes at your LT pace.

Tempo runs provide a targeted workout yet will not leave you excessively tired or sore the next day. Because tempo runs require you to maintain a hard pace for at least 20 minutes, they are quite difficult mentally (more so than interval workouts because of the extended concentration required), and some runners avoid them. The ability to maintain concentration, however, is crucial in preparing for any race. Keep in mind that a low-key race effort can also serve as a tempo run if you have the discipline not to exceed your LT pace. Be careful, however, because it is easy in that situation to be sucked into racing all out.

LT Intervals

Fortunately, there is another excellent option for LT training called cruise intervals, or LT intervals. In an LT interval workout, you run repetitions of at least five minutes at your LT pace with a short rest between intervals. The work-to-rest ratio should be 3:1 or 4:1—that is, three or four times as much

LT running as recovery. These workouts may consist of two long reps or as many as eight shorter reps. Between each LT interval you should jog or slowly run the rest interval. Relatively brief recovery periods are given between LT intervals because at LT pace you do not build up much lactate in your muscles so you do not need much recovery. I've provided a variety of workouts to improve your LT.

Ten Great Workouts to Improve Your Lactate Threshold

20 to 40 minutes at LT pace

12 minutes at LT pace, 3 minutes easy, 8 minutes at LT pace

3 to 4 × 7 minutes at LT pace, 2-minute recovery jog between intervals

4 to 7 × 1,600 meters (1 mile) at LT pace, $1^1/_2$-minute recovery jog between intervals

3 to 4 × 2,400 meters ($1^1/_2$ miles) at LT pace, 2-minute recovery jog between intervals

2 to 3 × 3,200 meters (2 miles) at LT pace, 3-minute recovery jog between intervals

2 × 4,800 meters (3 miles) at LT pace, 4-minute recovery jog between intervals

10 miles steady including 3 to 4 miles uphill at LT effort

Marathoners' special #1—10 miles steady followed by 4 to 6 reps of 5 minutes at LT pace, 2 minutes at steady pace between reps

Marathoners' special #2—12 miles steady followed by 4 to 6 miles at LT pace

Note: Warm up for 10 to 20 minutes before doing the interval workouts.

How Often Should You Do LT Workouts?

How often you do LT training depends on what distance you will be racing and where you are in your training cycle (i.e., the number of weeks before your goal race). If you are racing a half marathon or marathon, the longer LT intervals are most appropriate. If you race 5K to 10K, select some of the shorter options.

Depending on how much training you are doing and what distances you will race, you should do 3 to 12 miles per week of LT training, representing 6 to 15 percent of your weekly mileage. The chart on the next page provides guidelines for how many LT training sessions to do during your preparation for a major race. The *buildup* column refers to your training when you have more than eight weeks before your goal race. The *race preparation* column refers to the eight weeks leading up to your goal race. Try to allow at least 72 hours between LT workouts.

Frequency of LT Training

Race	Buildup	Race preparation
Marathon	1 per week	2 every 3 weeks
15K to 25K	Alternate 2 per week, 1 per week	1 per week
8K to 10K	1 per week	1 every 2 weeks
5K	2 every 3 weeks	1 every 3 weeks

Marathon. For marathon preparation, LT training is approximately equal in importance to long runs. Marathoners should include a weekly LT training session during the buildup phase of their training. As the race approaches and some faster long-interval training is included to improve $\dot{V}O_2$max (and long runs are continued), LT training sessions should be done two out of every three weeks.

15K to 25K. When you are preparing for races of 15K through 25K, LT training is the most specific and important race preparation you can do. You should include LT training sessions throughout your training program. During the buildup phase, I recommend alternating weeks in which you do two LT training sessions and weeks in which you do one LT session. Then, during the race-preparation phase, do one LT session per week.

8K to 10K. In preparing for 8K or 10K races, LT training is of roughly equal importance to higher intensity $\dot{V}O_2$max training (see chapter 9). Emphasize LT training during the buildup phase; it will become secondary during the race preparation phase. Do one LT session per week during your buildup and then do one session every second week during the race preparation phase (final eight weeks).

5K. LT training is not as important for 5K races as it is for longer races; nonetheless, it is a critical part of training. As I recommended for races of 8K to 10K, emphasize LT training more during the buildup phase than during the last eight weeks before the goal race. Include one LT session in two of every three weeks during your buildup, then cut back to a single LT session every third week during the last eight weeks before the race.

9

Maximizing Your Speed

BROOKS JOHNSON
Coach of runners of all distances since 1957,
of Olympians since the 1960s, and of college teams at
Stanford and California State Polytechnic University

Speed training conditions the body to move faster by working the energy and biomechanical systems of the body, and it toughens the mind to withstand the stresses that are involved in efforts at this level.

Success in our sport is based on moving your body from point A to point B in the shortest possible time. That means that speed is your most critical asset. If that's the case, why do so many runners wait until late in a racing season to insert speed into their workouts? Most runners accept the fact that, from the first day of training, we need to establish an aerobic base by doing plenty of running at so-called training pace (see chapter 6 on base training). Why then should we not also go about establishing a *speed* base, also from day one? After all, if you want the body to adapt to running fast, then the sooner you get it adapted, the better. Anything less invites unnecessary stress—and very likely injury—later.

I always tell runners that it is possible to develop endurance by doing speedwork, but it is impossible to develop speed by doing endurance work. Runners talk about giving 110 percent to a race, but this isn't really possible. It is highly unlikely that anyone runs at even 100 percent for more than one stride. The second stride at 100 percent probably marks the onset of an injury. The point is that the rate of speed at which a race is contested has to be something slower than top end, no matter what the distance. Thus, runners who wish to maximize their potential in races must train to compete at a race pace that is well within their comfort zone. By this, I mean a pace that the body can handle with a minimum amount of stress. As you read in chapter 8 on lactate-threshold training, the more the athlete can train, and therefore race, within what I call a comfort zone—a pace he or she can sustain for relatively long periods without slowing down, often called anaerobic-threshold pace—the greater the athlete's potential for a breakthrough in running performance.

Although anaerobic-threshold training will get you started in improving your sustainable race pace, to see substantial increases you *must* do speed training. As you will see in the following pages, speed training conditions the body to move faster by working the energy and biomechanical systems. Speed training also toughens the mind to withstand the stresses that are involved in efforts at this level.

What Is Speed?

Unlike a sprinter, a distance runner should not do speed training only for the sake of developing raw speed. Rather, the distance runner must develop endurance speed—the ability to sustain a quick pace comfortably for relatively long periods (more than about two minutes)—to have any reasonable expectation of success in distance running.

Some people erroneously believe that an athlete is either born with speed or isn't. Although genetics do play a role, much can be done to develop and improve speed through proper training of the body and mind. Let's look at two marathon runners whose current levels of success differ greatly. The differentiating factor is what I call their maximal functional speed—that is, the fastest pace they are capable of generating for short distances (30 to 60 meters) at a given time.

Both of these runners have trained well at an aerobic level; they have done the long runs that allow them to complete the formidable marathon distance (see chapter 7 for more on training for the marathon distance and longer). Unless struck by sudden illness or injury, they will not drop out of a race. Both are conditioned to run the distance at about 80 percent of their maximal functional speed. This level of effort keeps them within their comfort zones—that is, at or slightly below their anaerobic threshold. The first, however, finishes in 2:30, while the second—also working at 80 percent of his maximal functional speed—finishes in 5:00.

How is the first runner able to complete the marathon in half the time taken by the second? The answer is that the first runner, besides training

The sooner you get your body adapted to running fast, the better.

© Frank Siteman/THE PICTURE CUBE

aerobically, has also trained to develop maximal functional speed. Because he has enhanced his potential to run faster through speed training, he has pushed his comfort zone to a much higher level. As you have seen in chapter 8, you can accomplish this in part through lactate-threshold training, but you must also add speed training to the mix. Had the second runner attempted to run at 2:30 marathon pace, he would have had to compete at well over 80 percent of his maximal functional speed. Eventually he would have had to slow down, despite the fact that he has the aerobic capacity to endure running for five hours.

What Determines Speed?

It is important to note that maximal functional speed varies with each individual. It is determined in part by our functional speed capacity, which is our genetic potential to run fast.

In distance running, the most successful competitors aren't necessarily those with the greatest functional speed capacity. Rather, they are those who have trained to develop their speed to a level closest to their functional speed capacity. In the above example of the two marathoners, most of us would judge the first as more successful than the second. In many cases, however, a slower runner is actually performing at a level closer to his or her functional speed capacity than a potentially faster runner, and in that sense is more successful.

How do you know if you are reaching your speed potential? Actually, you never know for sure; there is no standardized test. And isn't that part of what makes our sport so fascinating, that we never know for sure that we are running as fast as we are capable of running? Did Michael Johnson reach his maximal functional speed when he ran 19.32 for 200 meters in winning the gold medal at the 1996 Atlanta Olympics? The time shattered Johnson's own world record, yet he was running his seventh race of the Games, and so was undoubtedly tired, and he admitted that he made errors in his form during the race that may have cost him hundredths of a second. Though some exercise scientists may argue otherwise, I believe that our speed potential is unknowable. That mystery is a big part of why we keep striving to become faster.

We all raise our level of performance significantly by training to develop our maximal functional speed. When our efforts bring us to (or close to) our functional speed capacity, then we achieve the running breakthroughs for which we strive.

How Speed Training Leads to Breakthroughs

Speed training for the middle-distance or distance runner should affect three critical areas to maximize performance potential: physiological, psychological, and biomechanical speed.

Physiological Benefits

The runner who develops his or her speed potential to the fullest has numerous physiological advantages. One of the most obvious is that by doing a portion of training at a high rate of turnover—faster than race pace— the body learns how to manage the demands of sustained effort at high intensity. The heart, lungs, tendons, ligaments, muscles, bones, and body chemistry all adapt to the stress that sustained high-intensity effort requires. The faster than race pace these efforts are, the easier and less taxing race pace becomes and the longer the body can manage the physiological stress generated at race pace. In contrast to anaerobic-threshold training, which is done at or close to race pace, speed training conditions the energy and biomechanical systems of the body to exceed race pace significantly. The physiological adaptations include an increase in the recruitment of anaerobic energy sources, an increase in the recruitment of fast-twitch fibers, and an improvement in neuromuscular coordination.

For runners who never do speed training, the comfort zone remains mostly within the aerobic range. These runners have not begun to push their anaerobic threshold to a high level. If they continue to train in this way, they may never raise their maximal functional speed capacity above about 65 to 75 percent of their $\dot{V}O_2$max level. At this level, they are not able to be truly competitive.

With the proper training—as outlined later—the runner gains the ability to tap into a comfort zone that includes a measure of anaerobic running. This involves training the body to deal with the buildup of lactic acid (also called lactate), a byproduct of the metabolism of carbohydrate. As you learned in chapter 8, lactic acid is produced at increasing rates as running intensity (pace) increases. Eventually the body reaches a point, known as the anaerobic threshold or the lactate threshold, where it can no longer convert lactic acid back to a usable energy source as fast as it's being produced. You can increase your anaerobic threshold by training at lactate-threshold pace.

Lactic acid does not accumulate in significant amounts during aerobic training, so the aerobic-trained runner doesn't learn to deal with lactate buildup. If race pace exceeds the trained capacity, the runner breaks down. Speed training can be thought of as a step up from anaerobic-threshold training. It gives runners the final boost they need to go into the anaerobic zone for brief periods (such as when going out hard at the beginning of a race to assert a lead, surging at midrace, or, perhaps most important, kicking it in to the finish). Without this arrow in his or her quiver on race day, a runner may always be destined to fill the also-ran spot.

Another important, but often overlooked, physiological advantage conferred by speed training takes place within the muscles and connective tissues. When muscles and tissues are called into action, chemical signals called stretch inhibitors are sent to the brain to cause a reacting contraction. These stretch inhibitors in effect shut down the action of the muscles as a protective mechanism to prevent muscle damage as the muscles fatigue. You can see the stretch inhibitors in effect yourself by punching your arm out in front of you once, then doing so several times in succession. Can you feel your muscles punching with less force with each subsequent punch—although you are far from fully fatigued?

In an athlete who does little or no speed training, these stretch inhibitors activate themselves prematurely at a stress level well below what the body is actually capable of sustaining. These stretch inhibitors, however, can be trained to postpone and then override the signals to shut down the muscles. The more they are stressed, the more stress is required to stimulate them into action. And, you guessed it, one of the best methods of stressing these stretch inhibitors to delay them from causing the muscles to contract is speed training. The faster the muscles and connective tissues move, the more stretch is generated and the higher the tolerance levels of the stretch inhibitors. Thus, speed training conditions the body to work at faster speeds without the risk of injury that can result when the stretch inhibitors prevent the muscles and tissues from elongating as needed during high-intensity efforts.

This is one reason that speed training must be incorporated relatively early in the training cycle. Remember, the longer the muscles and connective tissues go without being stressed, the less tolerant they are to such stress. By delaying the introduction of speed training to late in the cycle, we have prepared the mind and body for one thing (slow-paced running) and are now doing something radical and opposite. The body is reluctant to change, and the result is often injury.

Psychological Benefits

Speed training also plays an important role in training the mind to accept the rigors of the high-intensity work necessary to excel at distance running. If a runner trains regularly and consistently at speeds faster than race pace, then race pace becomes more within the runner's psychological comfort zone. The result is a relaxed and loose mindset before and during racing rather than an energy-wasting feeling of tension.

Conversely, the closer race pace is to the runner's top-end speed, the more mental tension the effort will generate. This is likely to cause a runner to give up prematurely, possibly well before the body is physically tapped out. You may have experienced this at the beginning of a race season when your race efforts feel like more than you can handle although the pace is no greater than what you were able to sustain the previous season. After a few races, you remember that this is what racing is all about. Gradually you become accustomed to the mental stress and even become ready to push to a higher level.

As the runner does increasingly more speed training, the mind adapts to the movement and rate of turnover and senses it as being natural and normal. This reduces the mental stress and fatigue associated with going fast and has a positive psychological impact on endurance potential.

Biomechanical Benefits

When runners do speed training they effect significant changes in their running mechanics and form. These changes allow the body to move with the efficiency necessary to sustain high speeds for a relatively long duration. (For more on running biomechanics, see chapter 2.)

The most important changes include stronger feet and Achilles tendons. During slow-paced running, the action of lifting the heel off the ground is voluntary. Speed training conditions the strong, tough Achilles tendon to perform this action reflexively, which is much quicker and more efficient. I might add that it's important to perform speed training in shoes without too much of a built-up heel because it inhibits the reflex action of the Achilles. In my opinion, most "training" shoes are not designed for speed training. If worn for speed training and racing, such shoes can prevent the Achilles from performing this important function. (See chapter 4 for more on training shoes and chapter 18 for more on racing flats.)

How to Train for Speed

The distance runner cannot and should not do speed training every day. Such a training program will quickly cause breakdown and injury. The quality of speed training is far more important than the quantity, and a little goes a long way. An effective blueprint for a typical week of training includes the following:

- Two days of aerobic-threshold training
- Two days of training in the aerobic range.
- One day of pure speed training
- Two days of rest or active recovery

Anaerobic-Threshold Training

Anaerobic-threshold training is training at a relatively high intensity for medium to long duration. It includes long intervals of 800 to 2,000 meters, as well as anaerobic-threshold running, often called tempo training. The idea is to stress the aerobic system by running at a higher intensity than aerobic pace without allowing the body to recover fully between efforts.

Anaerobic-threshold workouts should be separated by at least 48 hours, and I don't recommend doing them more than twice a week. Doing more risks overloading the body with unprocessed lactic acid. Over time this leads to staleness and a flattening of race performances at best; at worst it can cause chronic burnout and sloppy form and technique that can lead to injuries. Distance runners race at or close to lactate-threshold pace. That means that during race weeks you should do only one other lactic-acid training session. (For examples of lactate-threshold workouts, see chapter 8.)

Aerobic Training

Aerobic training is what most distance runners refer to as "training pace" running, done entirely within a range that can be sustained by the aerobic (oxygen-burning) system. At this pace, very little lactic acid accumulates. Training the aerobic system to function effectively and efficiently is, of course, important; the problem is that many runners do too much of their training in the aerobic range. Two aerobic workouts per week are plenty. The length of aerobic-training workouts depends on your aerobic capacity (roughly how long you can run and talk at the same time), your goal-race distance, and your place in the race-season calendar (see chapters 5, 6 and 7).

Pure Speed Training

Pure speed training (in contrast to the two types of training above) is designed to stress the adenosine triphosphate (ATP) system, which is what the body runs on for distances up to about 100 meters, the distance it can cover without relying on oxygen to fuel the muscles. Most 100-meter runners literally don't breathe during their races. Many distance runners and coaches mistakenly believe that nonsprinters don't need to develop this system at all.

I point to Olympic gold medals that have been won with all-out sprinting in the final 100 to 400 meters: Fermin Cacho, who ran 50.49 for the last 400 meters of the 1992 Olympic 1,500-meter final; and Steve Cram, who covered the last 400 meters of the 1983 World Championships 1,500-meter final in 51.5 (to Steve Scott's 51.7). My favorite example is Miruts Yifter's 23.6 for the final 200 meters of the 10,000 meters in a 1973 track meet in Dakar, Senegal (incredibly, the day after winning a 5,000-meter race). Keep in mind that there are hundreds, if not thousands, of men who can run 1,200 meters in three minutes. But the number who can follow a 1,200 at that pace with 400 meters in 52 seconds or less is very small indeed.

What I have always called pure speed workouts consist of efforts up to 100 meters run all out, with recoveries of five to seven minutes between efforts. The rest intervals allow for full recovery. If the runner does the workout properly, the final effort should be at least as fast as the first.

How do you know how hard to run these efforts? Quite simply, you should "run your heart out," moving your legs as quickly as possible (after a thorough warm-up, of course, and followed by a complete cool-down). Heart rate is a poor measure of exertion during these pure speed workouts because the efforts are not fueled by oxygen. If you do them properly you should not need to breathe while running 100 meters.

I believe that runners training for all race distances from the 5K to the marathon should do these workouts so they will have the ability to run fast when they need it during a race—at the beginning, in the middle, and at the end. These workouts should not be the only speed training you do, of course, but you should not omit them. Most runners, once they try pure speed workouts, find them fun and challenging. Their value is unquestionable when you consider the speeds attained by distance runners in the final 100 to 200 meters of championship races. How can those runners achieve such efforts when they are exhausted if their speed before the final kick represents 100 percent of their maximal effort?

Rest and Recovery

Rest and recovery are whatever you need to do to allow your body to absorb the training done on the other days and thereby progress to a higher fitness level. For many runners, rest and recovery are the hardest parts of training because they fear they will lose fitness and speed. They worry that their rivals are training harder. Actually, it's when the body rests that fitness gains occur.

The best runners know how to make the most of their extremely hard efforts through judicious rest.

Think of it this way: you decide to start training for a marathon 12 weeks down the road. You and your coach determine that you need 150 units of fitness to reach your performance goal. Right now you have 70 units. You go out and do your first workout. At the end, you actually are *less* fit than before you started—you have perhaps only 60 fitness units immediately after the workout. The gains occur the next day when your body, stimulated by the dose of work you've given it, essentially says, "I don't want to feel that again." It therefore goes through a number of changes at the cellular and enzymatic levels to increase fitness units to prepare itself for another similar effort.

I tell athletes that *rest* is not a four-letter word. Sure, the best runners train extremely hard. But they know how to make the most of that effort through judicious rest.

In general, I recommend doing nothing on your rest days other than getting a massage or doing some light jogging. Cross-training is another option, but only in moderation. I've known many athletes who pour so much energy into cross-training that they end up not fully recovered for the important work they must do on the other days. Chapter 12 provides good guidelines for mixing in cross-training in the right doses.

Over time the speed-trained runner learns to run fast while recruiting fewer muscle fibers and still getting the job done. This results in greater speed and, more important, endurance. The necessary biomechanical adaptations occur only through the repetition of fast-paced running.

Less flat-foot running. These adaptations stem from the greater strength of the foot. To increase your speed, your foot must transmit more energy to the ground during each stride. This energy transfer does not happen effectively when the foot lands hard and flat on the ground. Instead, foot contact should be quick and dynamic, with the foot rolling and pushing forcefully against the ground surface at toe-off.

Stronger hamstrings. Again, this adaptation follows naturally from proper speed training. It helps the legs draw the heels to the buttocks so the foot moves in a tighter, more efficient arc through each stride. Besides speed training, I have runners perform drills in which they work on lifting the heels to the buttocks in rapid succession for 30 to 40 seconds.

Stronger hip flexors. The hip flexors at the top of the legs are not adequately strengthened by a steady diet of aerobic training. These muscles need to be strong to catch and accelerate the momentum provided at push-off. Regular speed training helps achieve maximum force application with each push-off.

Lower arms. The legs will run at the tempo set by the arms—not the other way around. The part of the arm between the elbow and wrist is the end of the axis of the arm (starting at the shoulder), so this section should be moving as swiftly as possible to set a quick tempo for the entire body. Strong forearms also help with balance. Although most distance runners tend to focus on strengthening the upper arms and shoulders, it's more important to do strength work for the lower arms.

Exercises for Strengthening the Body for Speed

Although speed training will naturally strengthen all the muscles and connective tissues of the foot, a couple of exercises can help. One is to sit in a chair and pull a towel laid flat on the floor toward you with your bare toes. Another is to pick up marbles with your toes and put them in a hat. I bet you'll initially have trouble moving 20 marbles before your foot cramps. With practice, you should be able to move 40 to 50 marbles.

Too Much of a Good Thing?

In 1971 I wrote one of the first articles critical of the long slow distance (LSD) craze that I saw taking over American running in the late 1960s. Over the years, I have written much more about this phenomenon and the damage it can do to the potential of a middle-distance or distance runner. My articles criticizing LSD training have been readily accepted and printed—usually not because of their training value but because they were considered novel and shocking.

The fledgling running boom of the late 1960s (which really took off in the 1970s) was based on getting many people into running who had not run much before then. The idea was to take as much risk out of the activity as possible. The problem was that many people took the LSD concept to extremes, which created unacceptable overuse risks that led to a high rate of injury. Without speed training and with the overuse injuries that resulted from too much LSD, running stagnated.

These days, though, the pendulum has swung far in the other direction. In some quarters, speed is overemphasized. Because of this, we face an even greater danger than before. Speed is a high-risk training activity, which is one of the reasons runners discarded it back in the 1960s. The problem now is that many runners and coaches who advocate speed training do not understand its basic rationale and the physiological adaptations associated with it.

To build the next running boom, one that will lead to the revitalization of U.S. distance running, runners and coaches must understand the science behind speed and apply it in ways that will help today's runners reach their maximum potential. Speed must be properly combined with all the other elements of training—aerobic work, strengthening exercises, and rest and recovery—to produce fit, race-ready runners. Too much speed or speed incorrectly incorporated into training means unnecessary injuries. The predictable results are frustration and continued stagnation of the sport. When properly applied, however, speed training is a crucial ingredient to any runner's breakthrough performance.

10

Building Strength With Resistance Training

STEPHEN ANDERSON, MS
Wellness consultant and personal fitness trainer

Developing strength with resistance training helps reduce the risk of injury, assures balance, and enhances overall performance.

It would be interesting to survey members of the 1972 United States Olympic track and field team and determine how many of them used resistance training as part of their overall training regimen. It is likely that few track athletes in the 1970s considered strength or resistance training part of their preparation for running. Today, most elite athletes in all sports use resistance training as part of a comprehensive workout program.

For runners of all abilities, building strength could prove to be the missing link to achieving a breakthrough performance. Combined with cardiovascular conditioning and flexibility work, resistance training completes a workout routine that assures balance and enhances overall performance, both athletic and in everyday life.

Reasons for Strength Training

Developing strength with resistance training can benefit both men and women, regardless of age, when attention is paid to technique and form and the amount of resistance used. The exercises shown in this chapter are appropriate and safe for runners at any level. Let's begin by examining some of the reasons why developing strength with resistance training is an essential component to faster running.

First, resistance training can aid in the prevention of injuries. Few runners will enjoy an injury-free career. The physical demands of running warrant a total conditioning program that helps prevent such injuries, minimizes the severity of injuries, and speeds the healing process if an injury occurs. Proper resistance training that builds strength is a runner's best insurance policy for meeting the demands of miles on the road, track, or trails.

Second, resistance training can balance the muscles. The major muscles in our bodies work in pairs. As one muscle shortens or contracts, its opposing muscle lengthens, allowing the body to move in a controlled and efficient manner. A runner's stride provides a good example of muscular balance between the front of the thigh (quadriceps) and the rear of the thigh (hamstrings). As a runner extends a leg, the quadriceps will contract, or shorten, as the hamstrings lengthen. On the return kick, the roles reverse as the hamstrings contract and pull the leg up while the quadriceps elongate. This constant action of shortening and lengthening results in a fluid movement as long as muscular strength is balanced.

Strong muscles, tendons, and ligaments add power to your stride.

© R. Walker/H. Armstrong Roberts

When there is a strength imbalance between a pair of muscles, the mechanics of movement may suffer, leading to the possibility of pain and predisposition to injury. This imbalance, which can occur throughout other muscle pairs in the body, may be preventing you from achieving a breakthrough in your running. By itself, running may not balance the strength you need for optimum performance. Differences in running speeds and changing terrain could overdevelop certain muscles and fail to develop others. By supplementing with resistance training, you can work at balancing strength throughout your body. Think of your musculature as links in a chain; you're only as strong as your weakest link. The following resistance-training routine provides complementary exercises that work each muscle pair, allowing you to maximize the power in your body as you run.

A third benefit of resistance training is increased muscle mass. When you repeatedly overload a muscle or a group of muscles with resistance, your body responds by recruiting more motor units or increasing the size of individual muscle fibers to help move the load, which in turn leads to increased muscle mass and strength. Besides developing stronger muscles, resistance training will increase the strength of connective tissues, tendons, and ligaments. With strong muscles, tendons, and ligaments, you build a line of defense against injury, which allows you to focus on expanding your running goals. A runner has no reason to shy away from strength training. Using resistance to build muscle will only help your running proficiency by adding power to your stride, increasing your muscular endurance, and heightening your ability to hold and compose your body in the most productive position for premium running.

Learning to Move Psychophysically

Psychophysical movement refers to the integration of the body and mind working as one in maximizing an activity. In the world of sports, we pay great attention to the physical components necessary for improved performance. To optimize potential, however, athletes need to address the emotional and mental aspects of training as well. A runner may have all the physical attributes required for success, yet find his or her performance lacking. Psychophysical movement bridges the gap between physical potential and actual performance by linking physical training with psychological training. Thus, the body and mind combine for ultimate movement. In the workout setting this is often described as creating awareness with an exercise. Positioning your body properly for each exercise is crucial to the effectiveness of the movement. A series of steps listed in the exercises that follow place your body in the strongest and safest position before you begin the exercise. By using proper mechanics and paying attention to body landmarks, you can create this awareness. You can then move with intention and concentrate on the muscles for that specific exercise.

Eventually, as you become more comfortable and familiar with each correct movement, your body will become accustomed to the ease with which you move and will naturally follow these mechanics in every activity you do. When you execute movements with full body and mind awareness, you will learn to ignore distractions that can lead to poor habits. This philosophy of exercise will strengthen both body and mind, which will improve your running technique and the power of your body for endurance and strength. The result will be continued breakthroughs in your running.

Strength-Training Program for Breakthrough Running

The exercises provided in this program are essential for developing a strong and balanced body that will help you move toward your goals of a breakthrough running performance. When you perform the exercises properly, your increased strength will enhance your overall running power and improve your endurance. The routine is efficient, effective, and fits into a variety of demanding schedules.

Perform this strength-training program at least twice per week. As your strength improves, you can add a third day but never work the same muscle groups on consecutive days. Remember, you must learn to rest as hard as you work. Muscles need to recover from exertion for repair and growth. My preference is that you perform your resistance training following a run because your body will be warm and fully charged with energy. Experiment with your workouts by combining your resistance program with both hard running days and recovery running days. By listening carefully to your body, you will learn what works best for you. This training program works well throughout the year, regardless of competitive running cycles. Your goal is to master the movements. Before starting the routine, it is important to cover the various principles of this method of training.

Technique and Form

How precisely you perform an exercise movement is the key to maximizing your true potential. It is not only the quantity of the resistance that produces results but also the quality with which you move the weight. Through proper technique and form you isolate the target muscles, optimally increase your muscular strength and endurance, and reduce the potential for injury.

Breathing

Your breath becomes a powerful tool in your strength-training workout routine. It acts as an invisible third hand that assists your body in completing the movement. The breathing pattern during your resistance-training program is a full exhalation during the exertion phase of the movement and a full inhalation when you move the resistance in the opposing direction. Try to envision your lungs and diaphragm filling with air and releasing in coordination with the exercises. Doing this will regulate the pace at which you work. You will inhale and exhale with each individual movement. This deep abdominal breathing will itself energize you.

Repetitions and Sets

In this strength-building program, repetitions represent an individual movement within an exercise. Therefore, the lifting and lowering phase of a movement equals one repetition. The number of repetitions ranges from 8 to 12. This range allows you to blend power, endurance, strength, and definition. The goal is to find resistance in each exercise that you can move for 8 to 12 repetitions without compromising technique and form. When your form breaks, end the movement at that point and move on to the next exercise. Remember that you make breakthroughs from strength training when you move precisely and deliberately, and master the movement.

The number of repetitions for an exercise equals a set. This strength-training program uses one set for each exercise to provide maximum effectiveness in an efficient manner. A change in hand position, angle, or bar attachment will emphasize a different region of a muscle.

Types of Resistance

There are many types of resistance that you can use to strength train effectively. Free hand weights, weight machines, rubber bands, body-weight resistance, and barbells are all excellent tools for building strength. I recommend free hand weights for the majority of your workout. Free hand weights have several advantages:

You'll know it's time to increase the weight when you can easily complete 12 repetitions with correct technique.

- Each side of the body must produce equal effort, thereby balancing strength.
- Free hand weights allow you to follow closely the intended range of motion for the joint action involved with the movement.
- Although free hand weights provide one of the more difficult versions of weight training, once you learn the correct mechanics you can apply them to any resistance-training program.

Sequence

The philosophy of sequence in this strength-building program works a particular set of muscles and then follows with the opposing set of muscles. This ensures muscular balance, symmetry, improved postural alignment, and minimal rest periods. Each movement creates a building block for the next. The cumulative effects of the exercises provide maximum results in a minimum amount of time; this sequence strengthens the entire body in 30 minutes.

Choosing the Weight

To choose the weight for each exercise, select a resistance that you can move with correct technique and form for 8 to 12 repetitions. In the early stages of this program, select lighter weights (much lighter than what you can lift) until you have the sense of how your body responds to the entire program. Once the resistance becomes easy for you at 12 repetitions, increase the weight in small (one- to five-pound) increments. You should be able to perform at least 8 repetitions with the increased weight using good technique.

PUSH-UP

This chest strengthener uses your body weight for resistance. You can perform it at several intensities, ranging from a standing push-up off a wall (using partial body weight), to a kneeling push-up (for half or three-quarter body-weight resistance), to a full horizontal position on the floor. Regardless of body position or amount of resistance, the technique, mechanics, and landmarks remain the same.

- Place your hands slightly wider than shoulder-width apart and turn them inward approximately 45 degrees.
- Align your body with your chest positioned directly between your hands.
- Lower your body until your upper arms become parallel to the floor. This position should form right angles in both elbows and armpits. It is important to stop at the point where your upper arms are parallel to avoid excessive stress on the shoulders.
- Keep your body in the same position throughout the movement. Once this position or form breaks, stop and move on to the next exercise. Do not reinforce poor postural habits.
- Breathe using a full inhalation as you lower your body and a full exhalation as you push up to the starting position.
- Exert equal pressure in both phases of the movement. Let your breath dictate your pace with full, smooth movements. Never hold your breath. Do one set of as many perfect repetitions as you can, stopping when your form breaks or when you reach 20.

PULL-UP

The pull-up also uses body weight for resistance. One of the best exercises for strengthening the back, it is a perfect partner for the push-up. The pull-up is a difficult and challenging movement when performed in a free hanging position. Many facilities have an assisted pull-up machine that will allow you to do the pull-up with good form. You simply add weight as counterbalance at whatever level of difficulty you choose. You can also use a partner to assist you in the lifting technique.

You can use a variety of hand positions in doing the pull-up—overhand, underhand, and palms facing each other. Form remains the same for whatever hand placement you choose.

- Grasp an overhead bar and pinch your shoulder blades together. This will extend your chest toward the bar.
- Tighten your abdomen and maintain this contraction throughout the movement.
- Exhale while lifting your chest toward the bar; inhale as you lower your body back to the starting position.
- Do one set, working toward 12 repetitions.

FLAT BENCH PRESS

When working with hand weights, the movement begins when you first pick up the weights. It is important to transport the weights efficiently.

- Hold the weights in the center of your body as you sit at the end of the bench.
- Roll back onto the bench, holding the weights against your abdomen. Your knees should flow with your body as if they were connected to your

upper body with a string, coming to rest with your feet on top of the bench. This will retain a natural curve in your lower back.

- Bring the weights directly over your chest and push them up toward the ceiling. Turn the weights to face thumb to thumb, with the ends of the weights opposing each other.
- Press your shoulders down into the bench with your arms in a straight position. Now you are ready to begin the exercise.
- Lower the weight with an inhalation until the upper arms are parallel to the floor. You should create right angles at the armpits and elbows, keeping the weight aligned with the chest.
- Push the weights back to the starting position with an exhalation. Keep the shoulders pressed into the bench throughout the set and make sure to stop the weights at the top of the movement before they hit each other.
- When you finish the set, return the weights to your center and extend the weights forward at the same time you extend your legs. This will allow you to rise from the bench in the most efficient manner, keeping your back in a neutral position.
- Do one set of 12 repetitions.

LAT PULL-DOWN

The lat pull-down works the large muscles on each side of the back. You perform this exercise on a cable machine with a weight stack. By changing the bar or the width of your hand grip, you can emphasize a certain region of the back. Regardless of the hand position you use, the mechanics remain the same.

- Set the appropriate resistance on the weight stack.
- Select your bar and hand position and lower your body to a seated position.
- Place your knees under the support pads and extend your feet to create a symmetrical stance.
- Pinch your shoulder blades together and extend your chest up toward the bar. This is the beginning and ending position.
- Pull the weight down in front of your chest by moving your elbows toward the floor.
- Exhale as you pull the bar down and inhale as the bar returns to the starting position.
- Do one set of 12 repetitions.

INCLINE BENCH PRESS

The incline bench press follows the same procedure as the flat bench press. The only difference is the angle of the movement. This exercise emphasizes the upper chest.

PULLOVER

The pullover incorporates many muscles of the upper torso. The body is active in this movement. The exercise provides a great opportunity to focus on your breathing.

- Get into position as you would for a flat bench press but use only one weight.
- Lie on a flat bench with the weight on your abdomen, knees bent, and feet on the end of the bench.
- Hold the weight with a flat grip by opening your palms and wrapping your thumbs around the handle of the weight.
- Lift the weight up directly over your chest by extending your arms upward. In this position, the weight should feel flexible yet secure.
- Lower the weight back behind your head in a slow, controlled manner. When you start feeling tension you can soften your elbows slightly.
- Return the weight to the starting position, directly over the chest with your arms extended straight upward.
- Breathe with a deep inhalation as you lower the weight back over your head, and exhale fully as you pull the weight back to the starting position.
- To exit this movement, use the technique you performed for the flat bench press.
- Do one set of 12 repetitions.

ONE-ARM ROW

The one-arm row is a back exercise that helps balance the strength of your right and left sides. As you equalize your strength and improve postural alignment, your running technique will benefit because your body will be positioned to move more efficiently.

- Kneel on the side of a bench with your entire lower leg making contact. The ankle should be at the end of the bench with your toes pointing toward the floor.
- Hold the support arm in a vertical position, acting as a column to hold the body firmly.
- Raise the weight from the floor, and with a straight arm, elevate and pinch your shoulder to create a squared upper back. Remain in this position while performing the exercise.
- Lift the weight up, with an exhalation, at an angle toward your hip. The motion mimics sawing a board. Using control, lower the weight to the starting position with an inhalation.
- Do one set of 12 repetitions for each side.

SHRUG

The shrug is the first exercise done from a standing position. Besides strengthening the upper back, the shrug also provides a sense of relaxation as you exhale tension. You need to create a strong and balanced body position before beginning the exercise.

- Stand tall with your feet pointing straight ahead, hip-width apart.
- Bend your knees slightly to create a soft-knee position.
- Extend your chest forward to create a natural curve in your back.
- Think of your body as a tree with roots and stay firmly planted in this position.
- For the shrug, hold the weights in a firm but relaxed grip, resting on the front of your thighs. Your legs become the tracks along which the weights will move. The landmarks for the shrug are the tops of the shoulders and the base of the neck.

- Raise your shoulders toward the base of the neck while keeping the arms straight.
- Inhale as you lift up and exhale as you lower the weight slowly to the starting position.
- Do one set of 12 repetitions.

SHOULDER PRESS

The overhead shoulder press works the entire shoulder region. I recommend that you perform this movement from a seated position on a slanted bench, which allows you to lean forward slightly and avoid the tendency to hyperextend your back.

- On a slanted or inclined bench, sit with your feet in a 45-degree stance slightly wider than shoulder-width.
- With the weight held in the center of your body, lift the weights up as they stay close to your body and turn them out to align with your ears. You will be drawing a triangle with the weights. The base of the triangle aligns with the ears, and the apex is directly overhead but still within your field of vision.
- Stop the weights in the overhead position before they touch.
- Exhale as you press the weights upward and inhale as you lower them to ear level.
- Do one set of 12 repetitions.

BICEPS CURL

The biceps curl is an exercise to strengthen the upper arm. Stand with your feet pointing forward at hip-width, keeping a slight bend in the knees.

- Start with the weights hanging straight down at the sides of your body.
- Turn your palms outward.
- The biceps curl raises the palms and lower arms toward the shoulders but stops at the peak of contraction. The elbows should not move and should remain pointing toward the floor.
- Exhale as you raise the weights and inhale as you lower them.
- Do one set of 12 repetitions.

TRICEPS KICKBACK

The triceps kickback, which strengthens the back of the upper arm, is a partner to the biceps curl. The body position for the triceps kickback is similar to the one-arm row position except that for the triceps kickback, the

upper arm is parallel to the back with the elbow pointing directly behind. Keep the arm in this position throughout the set.

- Extend the weight behind you by straightening your arm. Return as far as you can without changing the position of your upper arm.
- Exhale as you straighten and inhale as you return.
- Do one set of 12 repetitions.

45-DEGREE SQUAT

The 45-degree squat is one of the best exercises you can do for your legs. This movement works all the large muscle groups of the lower half of your body. It is also a safe squatting exercise because you use less weight than you use with machines or barbells. You maintain posture and alignment and reduce excessive stress on your back.

Technique and form are especially important when performing this exercise. You can begin the movement using no weight with an exercise stability ball, holding a balance bar, or sitting on a bench. When you are comfortable with the exercise, you can do the 45-degree squat standing and holding a free weight.

- Place your feet slightly wider than your shoulders and turn your feet out to form a 45-degree angle. Align your knees with your toes and retain the normal curvature of your back throughout the movement.

- Pay attention to the knee-to-toe relationship and the angle of the thigh. Do not let your knees extend in front of your toes and do not squat any lower than thigh parallel to the ground.

- If you use resistance, hold the weight in the center of your body with arms fully extended downward. The weight acts as an anchor lowering you toward the floor.

- Squeeze the muscles of your legs as you return to the top of the movement.

- Inhale as you lower your body and exhale as you rise back to the starting position. Remember to stay in the same stance throughout the movement.

- Do one set of 12 repetitions.

CALF RAISE

The calf raise serves two purposes: to strengthen the back of the lower leg and to increase flexibility. You can perform the calf raise on a step or a platform that allows you to raise your heels off the floor.

- Standing tall with the balls of your feet on the platform and holding a balance bar or the back of a chair for support, lift your body straight up, rising on your toes. The sensation is as if someone were pulling you up from a string attached to the top of your head.
- Pause briefly at the top of the movement with a squeeze of the toes, then lower yourself back to the starting position.
- Intensify the exercise by holding a free weight in one hand or pressing up with one leg at a time.
- Exhale as you rise and inhale as you lower.
- Do one set of 12 repetitions.

TOE RAISE

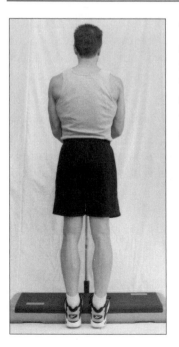

The toe raise is an often neglected movement in an exercise program. Of particular benefit to runners, the toe raise will strengthen the front of the lower leg, thereby reducing the risk of shin splints and related injuries. When paired with the calf raise, the toe raise creates excellent strength and balance in the lower leg.

- Stand tall with your heels over the end of a platform to allow for a greater range of motion as you lift your toes toward your knees.
- Use the alignment and breathing patterns that you used for the calf raise.
- Do one set of 12 repetitions.

LUNGE

The lunge requires strength, balance, and coordination, making it a perfect enhancer of good running technique. The mechanics of the lunge are similar to the 45-degree squat. The thigh goes no lower than parallel to the ground and the knee does not extend over the toes.

- Standing with toes pointing forward and feet hip-width apart, step forward, bending the front knee and lowering the body to create right angles in both legs. The back retains its natural curvature and sinks straight down like an elevator descending.
- Return to the starting position and switch legs.
- Inhale as you lower to the lunge position and exhale as you return to the starting position.
- Keep your hands on your hips to maintain balance. When you need more resistance, you can hold weights in your hands with arms extended by your sides toward the floor.
- Do one set of 12 repetitions.

LEG EXTENSION

The leg extension works the front of your thigh. When done correctly it will strengthen the thigh muscles and create strong and healthy knees. As a runner, you need balanced strength and flexibility in your legs to keep your joints safe.

Perform this exercise on a leg-extension weight machine. Set the chair position so that your knees align with the axis point of the machine and the resistance bar rests just above the ankles.

- Select your weight and create tension by bringing the legs to a 90-degree position. Your feet should be relaxed and your toes pointing toward each other to align your knees properly. This is your starting and ending position; it maintains constant tension.
- Lift your legs while you exhale.
- Inhale while lowering to the starting point.
- Do one set of 12 repetitions.

LEG CURL

As the partner to the leg extension, the leg curl works the opposing muscle groups. The setup for the leg curl is the same as the setup for the leg extension.

- Curl the weight up to a 90-degree angle as you exhale and lower it as you inhale, stopping with a slight flex of your knees.
- Do one set of 12 repetitions.

ABDOMINAL CURL

Strong abdominal and trunk muscles stabilize your body and create improved posture and alignment, which results in more efficient running. A variety of body positions will strengthen the abdomen and trunk. You can perform these movements by using weight machines designed specifically for the abdominals and lower back. You can perform floor exercises on a mat, or you can use a stability ball. All these methods will accomplish your goals.

- Keep your head and neck in the same position throughout and perform the motion by curling your rib cage toward your hips. You can also reverse the movement by curling your hips to your rib cage and bringing your knees to your chest.
- Exhale as you rise and inhale as you lower.
- Do 12 repetitions for each set.

Remember these few simple rules when following this basic strength-training program:

- Work opposing muscles equally.
- Do one set of each exercise.
- Do from 8 to 12 repetitions.
- Let your breathing control your pace.
- Do not work the same muscles on consecutive days.
- Create a strong starting position for each exercise.

A comprehensive resistance-training program provides significant benefits to a runner. Besides injury prevention, this kind of program can result in improved strength in hill running and increased endurance and power for long runs. This strength-training program, when added to a comprehensive running schedule, will create overall improvements in your balance, strength, and flexibility. You will be better able to withstand an increase in mileage and gain the conditioning essential for a breakthrough running performance.

11

Developing Your Flexibility

HEATHER C. LISTON
Freelance writer and contributor to *Running Times*
and *New York Runner*

Maximizing
your flexibility
will help lead
you to a
breakthrough
in your
running.

Flexibility is one of the most common words in a runner's vocabulary. You have to be flexible just to make time to run. You ask for flexibility from your boss, your family, and others to whom you have obligations. You resolve to be flexible about the weather. You strive to be flexible enough to bounce back after a disappointing race or a rough training session.

What, then, does flexibility mean on a physical level? Flexibility, technically, is a measure of the strength and resilience of your tendons, which connect muscles to bones, and your ligaments, which connect bones to bones. If those connectors are strong, elastic, and resilient, they'll help you feel good, run well, and recover from training and races quickly. If they're short, tight, weak, or unhealthy, that will have an adverse effect on your running. Your level of flexibility affects the length of your stride and helps determine whether you'll get injured and how quickly you will heal after an injury.

"Flexible people have a wider range of body motion and thus are able to perform movements that less flexible people find difficult or impossible," says Kenneth Cooper, MD, founder of The Cooper Institute for Aerobic Research in Dallas, in his book *Faith-Based Fitness.* "I've become convinced, after working with thousands of patients and athletes, that a regular stretching routine does help reduce the tendency to pull muscles, ligaments, or tendons, or to injure the back or joints."

On the other hand, a controversial study conducted by David A. Lally, PhD, and reported by Owen Anderson (1994) challenges this premise. The Lally study, performed on athletes who ran the Honolulu Marathon, suggested that white male marathon runners who stretch before running get injured more often than those who don't. This suggestion runs counter to common belief, however, and has not been proven definitively.

If it seems convenient to buy into the theory that stretching is bad for you, keep in mind that stretching improperly can indeed be dangerous, just as using poor form in any sport puts inappropriate stresses on your body. The Lally study did not control the way in which the subjects stretched, so for all we know, they may have been stretching ballistically (see below) and overextending their muscles. If you take the time to learn safe stretches and do them sensibly, you should expect to extend and improve your running life. Incidentally, the Lally study also confirmed what most people already suspected—that stretching *after* running does lower injury rates. It also showed no negative results related to stretching for women or for Asians of either gender. Therefore, despite all the press this interesting study received, we are left with the not-surprising conclusion that stretching carefully and regularly is a good idea (*Running Research News,* May–June 1994).

Your genes determine a significant part of your flexibility. If you were born with short, tight tendons, it's extremely unlikely that you'll have the sort of flexibility breakthrough that suddenly (or even gradually) makes you double-jointed. You can, however, take the best possible care of the body you were born with and maximize your flexibility to help lead you to a breakthrough in your running.

Stretching for Flexibility

The most common and probably most effective way to maintain and improve your flexibility is to stretch. It's not the only way—we'll discuss other, complementary flexibility enhancers later in this chapter—but nearly all runners, coaches, and health care professionals agree that a regular, sensible program of stretching is vital to a runner's ongoing health and development.

Ironically, many more people agree with that idea than practice it. Even world cross country champion Lynn Jennings confesses that she rarely stretches because she thinks it's too boring. Instead, she compensates with a lot of massage. If a professional runner who can presumably devote a lot of time to getting her training right doesn't bother with stretching, it's easy to imagine ordinary runners with full-time jobs and other commitments skimping on it.

Some people skip stretching because they think it's tedious or they don't have time. Others neglect it because they think they're getting away with it. They feel young and healthy and don't notice the negative effects that not stretching may have on their running. Coach Roy Benson warns against that: "When you're young and good-looking and strong, you think you're invincible. But if you keep that up for too long—running without taking care of yourself—you'll eventually find your stride reduced to a shuffle as you kiss your flexibility goodbye."

"As you age," agrees Dr. Kenneth Cooper, "your tendons . . . and ligaments . . . begin to tighten up. The result is a loss of flexibility. But . . . a regular program of flexibility exercise can help keep this tendency toward stiffness with aging at bay."

Runners who take care of themselves and stretch regularly have the potential to break through some of the old myths about the deterioration that accompanies age. "As time moves on, what most runners lose is stride length," says stretching expert Bob Anderson. "Stretching is more for maintenance than for improvement. The most important thing is to maintain what you have; maintain your range of motion and don't let yourself stiffen up."

Stretching Guidelines

How should you stretch? When? For how long? Some of those answers will depend on your personal preference. Opinions vary, and even the experts qualify their recommendations by reminding you to do what works best for you. Still, we have learned a few general principles for stretching.

Ballistic stretching was the first generation of stretching. Remember bending over, reaching for your toes, and then bouncing up and down, hoping to get a little closer each time? Anderson thinks that method was good for camaraderie and bonding. It didn't take much concentration or even regular breathing. When a team bounced through a stretching routine together, they could chat. "Physical education in the 1950s and 1960s all came from the army," remembers Anderson. "My physical education teachers were former drill instructors. They only thought in teams and groups. Your body's need for stretching is too individual to respond to that approach."

Today, it is generally agreed that the ballistic method does more harm than good. Bouncing sets off a stretch reflex that actually tightens you up. Moreover, it's easy to bounce yourself past your body's comfortable range of motion and damage something by straining it too far. Because of the movement involved, some people believed that ballistic stretching also served as a warm-up. But as Anderson says, "You can't warm up by stretching. They're two different things." In fact, most experts agree that it is important to warm up the muscles by jogging or walking briskly for 10 or 15 minutes *before* doing any stretching.

Static stretching came next. When Bob Anderson published *Stretching* in 1975, he led a revolution. Although others realized that bodies needed regular, sustained, gentle stretching, Anderson, more than anyone else, helped people learn how to do it. With simple descriptions of step-by-step stretching exercises for every part of the body and clear, helpful illustrations by his wife, Jean, Anderson made it possible for athletes at all levels to have break-throughs in their performances even if they didn't have coaches or teammates.

"A long, sustained stretch releases muscle tension," explains Anderson. "And another benefit that you can add is mental relaxation." Anderson doesn't ask everyone to follow all the exercises in his book; his recommen-dation is to "learn four to six stretches that you like doing."

For over 20 years, Anderson was the biggest, and almost only, name in stretching and flexibility. Millions of runners and other athletes integrated his methods into their training. Nothing stands still, though, and some athletes, trainers, and medical doctors continued to do research on how the human body responds to stretching.

Active-isolated stretching (AIS) is one result of that research. Aaron Mattes, PhD, was practicing an unusual form of kinesiology in Sarasota, Florida, in the 1980s when Jim Wharton went looking for help for his son, Phil, an outstanding young athlete who was suffering from scoliosis. The Whartons found that Mattes's method of stretching and training the muscles had a dramatic effect on Phil and his performance as a runner. Jim was so impressed that he trained under Mattes and further developed Mattes's method, which, together, they named active-isolated stretching. Wharton soon opened his own clinic and trained athletes in the method. In 1992, Wharton went to the Olympics in Barcelona to work with 33 Olympic competitors.

AIS is based on these four principles:

1. You get a more effective, safer stretch when you isolate and stretch one muscle at a time.
2. All muscles work in pairs, so in every movement there is an agonist, which is primarily responsible for the movement, and an antagonist, which counters the agonist to ensure that it doesn't contract too much. The most effective way to stretch is to actively contract the agonist, the muscle *opposite* the one you want to stretch. The target muscle, or antagonist, will then relax in preparation for the stretch. For example, if you want to stretch the hamstrings (the large muscles in the back of your thigh), you must contract the quadriceps (the set of muscles located in the front of the thigh).

Runners, coaches, and health care professionals agree that stretching is vital to a runner's health and development.

3. If you elongate a muscle too quickly or too far, it will recoil to protect itself from ripping. This reaction, called a *myotatic reflex*, kicks in after stretching for three seconds. Therefore, in AIS you hold each stretch for no more than two seconds. You release the stretch before the myotatic reflex begins, and then you do it again. You work quickly and gently, doing each stretch 8 to 10 times for one and a half to two seconds each time.

4. Breathing is an important component. As in strength training, you exhale during the work phase (the stretch) and inhale as you release the stretch.

Stretching When Injured

After an injury to any muscle or connective tissue, stop stretching that area until you've consulted a doctor—if possible, a sports medicine specialist. Stretching something that's torn or otherwise hurt could easily exacerbate the injury and delay the recovery process. Stretching may end up being a part of your rehabilitation. "If certain kinds of injury happen, then you have to go to therapeutic levels of stretching," says Benson. "Running careers have been reclaimed by people who were finally forced to slow down and learn to stretch properly. They got the tap on the shoulder from the flexibility fairy, and boom—they got faster again."

Stretching: The Practice

So now you have decided you want to fight the effects of aging. You want to keep your body strong and supple to prevent injuries and to help lead you to a running breakthrough. What do you do?

Only you can determine how much stretching is good for you.

If you can make the time, it's good to do a full-body stretching routine every day. "Before a run," says Anderson, "stretch your pelvis, calves, ankles, hamstrings, and upper body. You should also do an extended warm-up of 8 to 10 minutes before you stretch, especially as you get older. After you run, cool down by jogging about two minutes and then walking." Anderson himself finds that it works well to stretch while he watches television.

Only you can determine how much stretching is good for you and how much you're willing to do in pursuit of a breakthrough. If you want to push yourself to new heights, consider buying one of Anderson's books on stretching or *The Whartons' Stretch Book* and trying their comprehensive routines. But if you just want to do enough to keep yourself running well, try the following stretches, which focus on essential areas for runners.

Ankles

Your ankles are the complex joints on which much of your body weight rests; they also absorb much of the shock of running. It is vital that you keep them strong, loose, and ready for action.

ANKLE ROTATION

Stand up straight, holding on to a bar or table to help keep your balance. Lift one foot a few inches off the floor and slowly circle it from the ankle, first one way and then the other (about eight times in each direction), feeling the full range of movement in the front, back, and sides where the foot connects to the leg. Now switch legs and rotate the other foot clockwise and counterclockwise.

ACHILLES TENDON STRETCH

Stand facing a chair with one foot flat on the floor. Put the heel of the other foot on the seat in front of you. Place both hands under the ball of the raised foot and gently pull the front of the foot toward your body. Let go with your hands and point your toes toward the floor, stretching downward as far as you can. Repeat 8 to 10 times, and then do the same with the other foot.

Calves

With every step you take, you're pushing off with the gastrocnemius, your calf muscle, so it's important to keep this muscle strong and flexible.

CALF STRETCH

Sit on the floor with your back straight and your legs straight in front of you. Flex your feet and slowly bend forward, reaching for your toes. Hold for a count of five, then release. Repeat 8 to 10 times.

Hamstrings

The three long muscles in the back of each thigh are the hamstrings. The hamstrings cross two joints (the knee and the hip) and help support those crucial areas. Pulling or straining a hamstring is one sure way to put your running career on hold.

HAMSTRING STRETCH

Lie on your back with your right knee bent, right foot flat on the floor, and your left leg straight out on the floor. Slowly lift your left leg as high as you can, keeping the foot flexed. When you've lifted as high as you can without assistance, put your hands on the back of your left thigh and gently pull the leg a little farther, aiming your toes forward and downward. Alternate legs, lifting each four times.

Quadriceps

The quadriceps, or "quads," the four big muscles in the front of each thigh, do much of the work of running. According to Andy Perlmutter, certified strength and conditioning specialist, another main function of the quads is to control your motion and decelerate you. If your quads are tight, you'll feel pain the day after a long, hard run when you walk downstairs because your quads are working to keep you from tumbling forward.

QUADRICEPS STRETCH

Stand up straight, bracing yourself against a wall or tree for balance if necessary. Bend your left knee and grasp the foot behind you with your left hand. Keeping your body aligned and your left knee aiming straight toward the floor, gently pull the left heel in toward the buttock, feeling the stretch in the front of the thigh. Repeat three to four times with each leg.

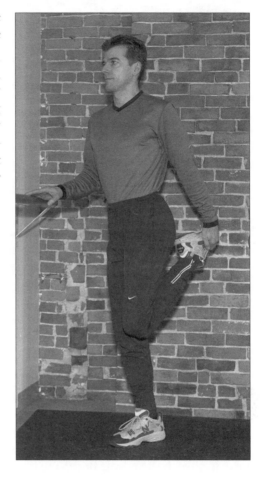

Hip Flexors and Back

With every step you take, you flex your hips as you bring your legs up or down. If the hip muscles are tight, you'll feel some definite discomfort when running. You also use your back muscles when running to keep yourself straight and upright. You'll feel better if your back muscles are comfortably malleable as well.

HIP AND BACK STRETCH

Sit on the floor with your back straight and your right leg stretched out in front of you. Bend the left knee and place your left foot flat on the floor, outside the right leg just above the knee. Put your right elbow on your left knee and pull it gently to the right as you twist your upper body toward the

left. Feel the stretch through your hip flexors, gluteus maximus (buttocks), and obliques (the sides of your abdominal muscles). Repeat on opposite side.

It is also a good idea to stretch your shoulders, arms, back, and neck; additional stretches for your lower body can help as well. Here too, see Anderson's or the Whartons' books (listed in the bibliography, p. 347) on how to stretch the whole body. (To order any of Anderson's books, call (800) 333-1307 or visit **www.stretching.com**.)

Pregnancy and Flexibility

If you work out while pregnant, you may notice that you feel a little more flexible than usual. That's natural, according to midwife Lynn Chapman-Stern. "Relaxin is a hormone in your body whose purpose is to help relax your ligaments. It's more active while you're pregnant in order to help prepare your body for the delivery." If you do a rigorous stretching routine while your body has this extra hormone dose, it is possible to overdo it, says Chapman-Stern. "So be careful: while you're pregnant, you should work at maintaining, but not improving, your flexibility." More information can be found in the videos "Healthy Mother, Healthy Child" and "Yoga Zone Postures for Pregnancy," both available at **www.collagevideo.com** or at (800) 433-6769.

Other Flexibility Enhancers

There are many other methods beyond stretching that can loosen you up and improve your flexibility. Try yoga, massage, or chiropractic care to not only enhance your overall fitness but to help you release tension and stress. Diet and rest can also play role in keeping your muscles and connective tissue healthy and flexible.

> "The best method [is] whatever you continue to do."
> —*Bob Anderson*

Yoga

Yoga for Dummies by Georg Feuerstein and Larry Payne promises that the study and practice of yoga can lead you on the way to being "more flexible, fitter, less stressed out, or more peaceful and joyful." Yoga, as a general term, encompasses a number of different disciplines, or paths. Rooted in the religions of India, all hold enlightenment as the ultimate goal. Along the way, though, several of these disciplines offer physical exercises that can strengthen your body and increase your flexibility even as they calm your mind and integrate your being.

Hatha yoga, often called the yoga of physical discipline, is one of the most common types practiced by athletes of all sports. As you work through the postures of Hatha yoga, your body should feel natural and comfortable while gently extending itself to new levels of fitness and flexibility.

Beryl Bender Birch, the wellness director of the New York Road Runners Club, is a teacher of astanga yoga, also known as "power yoga." The classes she teaches with her husband, Thom Birch, are designed particularly for runners. Birch says of her discovery of this particular yoga practice, "It looked like what I always felt yoga was supposed to be: a balance between strength and flexibility. Hard and soft." Astanga yoga includes many postures borrowed from other forms of yoga. What distinguish it, she says, and make it especially appropriate for runners in training are "the vinyasa, or connecting movement between the postures and . . . the sequential linking of the postures." Astanga yoga offers athletes both the fluidity of motion they need as efficient runners and some serious, focused engagement of the muscles they use in running. (For more information, visit **www.power-yoga.com**.)

Birch's advice to people studying astanga yoga is similar to Anderson's recommendations about stretching in general: "Start slowly, do what you can, go one day at a time, and appreciate the moment."

Massage

"Massage can help loosen contracted, shortened muscles and can stimulate weak, flaccid muscles," according to Elliot Greene, MA, NCTMB, who practices massage therapy in Silver Spring, Maryland. Massage costs money, so most of us can't afford to use it as a regular substitute for stretching ourselves. Still, as Greene points out, "Regarding flexibility, stiff and tight tissues reduce range of movement of the joints. In turn, joints have a way of settling and stiffening when their ability to move fully is reduced. A massage therapist counteracts this by using massage strokes and passive movements to improve circulation, release muscle tension, and free connective tissue that may be binding the joints." In other words, an occasional massage can probably benefit most runners. If you're trying massage for the first time, look for a licensed massage therapist. If possible, find one accustomed to working on athletes, who will be more likely to understand the needs of your hard-worked muscles.

Chiropractic

"A lot of runners have cervical trauma because of the pounding on their bodies," says Harold Steinberg, DC, a chiropractor in Santa Fe, New Mexico. "That means they get pains in their necks. [Chiropractic] can help relieve that pain and tension with an adjustment to the spine." One of Steinberg's patients is a runner who has one leg shorter than the other, a not-uncommon condition that throws the back out of alignment. A chiropractic adjustment can help.

Steinberg, a former runner, says that even with regular adjustments, "You still have to stretch. I can't be with my patients all the time; they have to take care of themselves."

Diet

Proper hydration, perhaps the most important aspect of good overall nutrition, is often neglected by runners. "You must drink a lot of liquids, especially water," says Steinberg. Good hydration promotes adequate blood flow to your muscles.

Healthy ligaments and tendons, like the rest of your body, depend on proper nutrition. If you want to focus specifically on nutrients that may aid your flexibility, you might try an over-the-counter supplement, like glucosamine sulfate, which claims to build cartilage and provide "joint support" by keeping synovial fluid in your joints. Another option is to take an anti-inflammatory like quercetin or shark cartilage. See your doctor or nutritionist for specific recommendations.

Rest

If you want to run, you must rest. It's the same for staying flexible—rest is essential. Overusing your body without letting it recuperate will strain muscles, ligaments, tendons, and bones and may cause you to tighten up, thus interfering with your flexibility. Make sure to build rest days into your training, and rest periods between seasons of hard training and racing. (See chapter 5 on periodization and the chapters in part III on rest and recovery.)

Hot Tubs, Saunas, and Steam

Go ahead and enjoy these invigorating forms of rest, which can help relax taut muscles and make you feel ready to run again. Just be sure to read the posted warnings about not staying in too long. And remember to increase your hydration if you're going to indulge because these treats can dehydrate you.

Finding Your Breakthrough

The breakthrough in Bob Anderson's life, as an athlete and a person, was all about flexibility. "A sense of self is why most people exercise," says Anderson. "It's all about developing your own potential. To do that, you have to know yourself and get to know your own body through a sense of feel." Anderson grew up with the nickname Puggy, and although he played football, baseball, and basketball in high school, he was still out of shape, he says.

In 1968, as a college student, Anderson says, "I was stiff as a board. I took some flexibility tests and realized I had a problem." He never really liked exercise. Today he remembers, "When I got into stretching, I changed who I was." He did a lot of research on the topic, then started helping other athletes stretch and assisting the trainers. "I'm one of those all-or-nothing people. In the case of stretching, it was all." Anderson started running at age 23. By 1999, at age 54, he had run the Pike's Peak Marathon and the Catalina Marathon 10 times each.

What does he recommend for others? "I advise people to try stretching for three or four weeks. If you don't like it, don't ever do it again."

Similarly, Jim Wharton says of active-isolated stretching, "Try it for 20 minutes a day for three weeks. If it works for you, keep doing it. If it doesn't, don't."

It's up to you.

Professional Flexibility Specialists

Athletes, trainers, and others concerned about maintaining their health and reducing the negative effects of aging are increasingly recognizing the value of flexibility. One marker of this is a new credential, Certified Flexibility Technician, developed by Jim Wharton and recognized by the American

Council on Exercise and the American College of Sports Medicine. If you're the sort of person who benefits from the structure that comes with personal attention and coaching, it may be worthwhile to hire a professional to help you develop the flexibility training program that will lead to your personal breakthrough.

"People ask me what's the best method of stretching," says Bob Anderson. "The answer is, the method that you'll do. Some methods are hard to understand, so I don't use them. But whatever works, works—whatever you continue to do."

12

Cross-Training

GORDON BAKOULIS
Editor-in-chief of *Running Times*, coach, and
four-time U.S. Olympic Marathon Trials qualifier

Cross-training
activities supple-
ment running to
enhance aerobic
fitness, while
relieving strain
produced by the
pounding of
running.

Many runners, when they hear the term *cross-training,* think of something they do only when they're injured. "I hate cross-training with a passion," 1996 Olympic marathoner Keith Brantly has said. "My idea of cross-training is pulling weeds in my garden."

Fortunately, at least a few runners, coaches, and exercise scientists have a broader and more positive association with cross-training. Done correctly, as part of a comprehensive conditioning and fitness system, cross-training activities can be of enormous benefit to runners—whether injured or not. In this chapter I tell you what cross-training for runners is all about, itemize the activities best suited to runners, offer guidelines for various ways to incorporate cross-training into your training (how often, how much, and at what points during your season), and show how a cross-training program can help lead to a breakthrough in your running.

Cross-Training Defined

I've never seen a formal definition of cross-training by any official sports or exercise organization or governing body. Although I want to emphasize that cross-training is not an anything-goes concept, it is a somewhat broad-based and loosely defined activity. You shouldn't let someone with several letters after his or her name tell you that what you're doing is or isn't cross-training.

Cross-training can be defined as a segment of an overall training or fitness program in which you participate in a variety of activities in a systematic way to promote balanced fitness. I would modify the definition for runners by noting that for them, running remains the primary fitness activity and continues to engage their interest in performance and competition. Cross-training activities are those that supplement running to enhance aerobic fitness while relieving strain on parts of the body that might otherwise be overstressed by the pounding of running. I do not include in this definition complementary activities such as strength training, stretching, or yoga, which primarily develop fitness other than cardiorespiratory fitness. The goal of a cross-training program for runners is to maintain or enhance cardiorespiratory fitness in the body beyond what the runner can attain solely by running. Consequently, cross-training achieves

- greater strength of muscle groups not used in running (the arms and shoulders through swimming, for example);
- reduction of the injury risk associated with a running-only program, thanks to enhanced nonrunning muscle strength;
- reduction in workout boredom because of increased variety of activities; and
- prevention of the overtraining and burnout that is common among runners, especially at the competitive level.

Cross-training is more than just a break from running. Done systematically, it can improve your running. You can incorporate cross-training activities into all phases of your training. Although it's best used as part of your base training and recovery training (for reasons outlined later), you can cross-train as part of endurance, lactate-threshold, and speed training as well.

Examples of popular cross-training activities for runners include deep-water running, swimming, cycling, rowing, fitness walking, stair climbing, using an elliptical trainer, cross-country (Nordic) skiing, in-line skating, rollerskiing, and snowshoeing. Before talking about these activities in detail, let's take a closer look at why you should include cross-training in your training for running.

Cross-training complements your running and allows you to combine training and socializing.

© Kristen Olenick

Why Cross-Train?

As already mentioned briefly, cross-training offers many benefits. Let's look at these specifically and in detail here.

Reduce Injury Risk

Most running injuries are caused by the pounding, repetitive nature of the sport. We can reduce our injury risk in many ways—by replacing our training shoes regularly (see chapter 4), by sticking to soft running surfaces whenever possible, and by not increasing our mileage or intensity too quickly. Still, despite observing these precautions, the fact remains that with each footstrike a runner lands with a force equivalent to three times his or her body weight. When you figure that we land on our feet around 1,700 times per mile when we run, that's a lot of pounding. For many of us, that pounding is bound to cause injury somewhere along the way.

Cross-training activities for runners can reduce that risk simply by taking the pounding out of aerobic activity. When you push your heart rate up to aerobic conditioning levels and beyond, the heart doesn't know whether you are running, biking, swimming, or Nordic skiing. All these activities can maintain your aerobic (cardiovascular) fitness while sparing your body the pounding associated with running. If you use them to replace a portion (up to 35 percent if you are not injured and thus prevented from running) of your running miles each week, you'll remain as aerobically fit as if you were running all those miles. The payoff is that you'll be much less likely to break down due to injury.

Of course, the *specificity of training principle* says that your greatest improvement in an activity will occur as a result of doing that activity. "Runners run," skeptics scoff when I preach the value of cross-training. They ask rhetorically, "Did you ever see a Kenyan on a Stairmaster?"—the point being that the world's best runners seem to do just fine without cross-training. Both points are valid. It's true that to become a better runner, the bulk of your training must be devoted to running. (No studies have been done on just how much is optimal, but I recommend a minimum of about 65 percent based on my own experience and that of other runners I have known and worked with, unless injury prohibits it.) But isn't it also true that you see the greatest progress during periods when you are able to remain injury free? If you're injured, you can't run—at least not as much or as hard as you'd like. As for the Kenyans, although it's difficult to generalize about such a large, diverse group of athletes, those who train in Kenya tend to compensate for the risk of following a high-mileage, running-only program by running mostly on dirt and grass at altitude and up hills, where speeds need not be as great to produce the same aerobic effect. And guess what? Kenyan runners become injured too, perhaps more than they would if they cross-trained.

Curb Boredom

Some would see this reason as debatable. Certainly those like Keith Brantly would tell me there's nothing more stultifying than spending an hour paddling around in a water-running vest or sitting on an exercycle. If that's how they feel, I'm not going to argue. I would only say that cross-training offers options. When you just can't face one more plod around your regular 4-mile loop, it's refreshing to know you can take a 12-mile spin on your mountain bike instead. How about those days when ice or snow makes an outdoor run out of the question and you'd no sooner hit the treadmill than stick needles under your fingernails? On those days, you can swim laps for 40 minutes instead of sticking a goose egg in your training log.

Let's face it. We all have occasional days when we're just going through the motions on our runs. Too many days like that, and many of us start finding excuses to postpone, shorten, or even skip running. A cross-training plan increases the chance that some activity will inspire us to have a workout that exceeds what we do because we "should." In addition, cross-training may offer more options to combine training with social activities. Are all your friends runners, or do you have some that would prefer to get together with you for mountain biking, in-line skating, or another activity?

Prevent Overtraining and Physiological Burnout

If you're reading this book, chances are you're the type of runner who doesn't have to be told to work harder. If your coach tells you to run six to eight miles, you'll do eight (or more). If your program says to keep your heart rate at 150 to 155 beats per minute (BPM) on your easy days, you'll flirt with 160. Chances are that the extra mileage and intensity you slip in here and there have on occasion led to injury or at least to periods when you felt stale and flat and didn't know why.

You should know by now the importance of periodizing your training—that is, building rest and recovery into your program after periods of hard effort, such as a major race or racing season (see chapter 5 for more on periodization). Still, runners who tend to train on the edge are at risk of overdoing it and burning out at any time. Cross-training, by reducing your total running volume and helping to keep your program varied and interesting, can reduce the risk of physiological (and psychological) burnout and overtraining. Because you are pursuing activities in which you are probably not as proficient as you are in running, you may be less likely to push yourself too hard. I don't overdo the intensity when I swim simply because I can't. My swimming skills and experience are such that I am physically unable to push myself to the levels I'm able to achieve in running. (See When to Cross-Train on page 142 for more on how to incorporate cross-training into your overall training program.)

A word of warning, however. If you're not careful, you can overdo the volume with cross-training activities just as you can with a running-only program. You need to keep careful track of how much cross-training you are doing (both overall and as a percentage of your total training volume) and what that equates to in running terms (more on this on page 145).

Once, early in my competitive running career, I was cross-training through an injury and feeling inordinately tired. After calculating my training load, I realized that I was doing the equivalent of 125 running miles a week in the form of swimming and biking! I'd never run more than 100 miles a week—no wonder I was exhausted. I started spending less time in the pool and on the bike and felt much better.

Promote Balanced Fitness

You probably don't need to be convinced that running is a wonderful activity for promoting fitness and health. Whether you compete or not, running regularly makes you healthier, fitter, and less likely to suffer from hypertension, heart disease, and possibly some forms of cancer. But you may not realize that running is not a total-body exercise. For instance, it does little to strengthen the arms, shoulders, back, and abdominal muscles.

Cross-training can improve your running by improving your overall fitness and strength.

Strengthening these areas can help make daily tasks easier, such as lifting, pulling, and pushing, and can reduce the risk of common back problems. Of course, such strength gains can also improve your running and thereby facilitate the breakthroughs you are striving for in your overall training program (see chapter 10 on strength training for more on the gains you can make from strengthening your muscles). For example, stronger abdominals can allow you to run more upright, which may improve your running economy; stronger arms and shoulders can help you keep moving powerfully in the late stages of a race when you are tired. By choosing cross-training activities that complement running by working the muscle groups that running doesn't target, you will become a fitter specimen overall.

When to Cross-Train

Many uninjured runners who cross-train incorporate their cross-training activity or activities only on their easy training days. They continue to use running as their activity for their long-endurance training, anaerobic-threshold training, and speed training and use their cross-training for some or all of the other workouts, whose primary purpose is aerobic conditioning. The idea behind this practice is that the tougher workouts are designed specifically to improve various aspects of running (endurance, speed, etc.). The remaining workouts are designed primarily for aerobic conditioning, recovery from harder efforts, and active rest (see part III for more on rest and recovery).

This routine makes sense because it saves wear and tear on the body caused by excessive running and allows the cross-training runner to benefit from cross-training activities in which he or she may not have a high level of fitness. But not all of us can comply with this rule, especially injured (or injury-prone) runners, who may suffer from trying to do their longest, hardest workouts as runs. All the cross-training activities covered in this chapter can be used at any point in a training program and as any component of training. If you have a serious knee injury and can't run on the roads

Should You Cross-Train?

A cross-training program makes sense for you as a runner if

- you are injured and can't run (at least not as much or as intensely as you'd like);

- you frequently develop overuse injuries such as plantar fasciitis, tendinitis, and stress fractures;

- you tend to overtrain by doing too many miles, pushing the pace too hard, or both;

- you suffer from selective lack of fitness, that is, weak abdominal, back, or upper-body muscles;

- you feel bored with your current routine of just running;

- you need more training options for convenience or safety; or

- you are starting to exercise for the first time or after a significant layoff.

at all, it's fine in most cases to do your speed workouts as water running (or cycling or some other type of cross-training if your injury will tolerate it). You will just need to keep in mind the specificity of training principle and realize that to get the most out of your training, you will ultimately have to perform the activity (running) in which you wish to excel. If injury or lifestyle constraints make that impossible, however, cross-training is definitely your next-best option.

Choosing Cross-Training Activities

"What's the best cross-training activity to complement my running?" runners ask. That question is as difficult to answer as the ubiquitous query, "What's the best running shoe?" so often directed to running-shoe salespeople. The best cross-training activity, like the best shoe, is the one that works for you— one that you enjoy, find convenient and accessible, and can master without too much difficulty. There's not much sense in my telling you that swimming is best if you live miles from the nearest pool or sink like a stone.

That said, for runners some cross-training activities are, in general, better than others. Likewise, cross-training is better incorporated at some points in a training program than at other points. For example, the latest research suggests that deep-water running (see pages 147-148) while wearing a flotation vest or belt closely simulates land running—thereby allowing you to adhere to the specificity of training principle—yet it completely eliminates the pounding that can cause and aggravate so many running injuries. This doesn't mean, of course, that there's anything wrong with other cross-training activities, as long as they're accessible to you, provide enjoyment, and don't cause or aggravate injuries. All aerobic activities, by their nature, will maintain cardiovascular fitness, muscle endurance, and (to some degree) strength.

Of course, you don't have to limit yourself to one cross-training activity. Let's look at some popular cross-training options one by one to help you determine those that might be suitable for you. We'll also look at how to incorporate these activities into your overall training program.

Cycling

Before the advent of deep-water running, cycling was often touted as the best cross-training activity for runners. Cycling strengthens the quadriceps muscles in runners, which often are weak relative to the hamstrings. This common imbalance in strength between the quads and hamstrings often contributes to knee problems in runners. Thanks in part to the popularity of triathlons, many runners already cycle, so for them there's no learning curve or investment in equipment. For other runners, however, cycling can involve a significant equipment investment. A decent bike costs at least several

Cycling strengthens the quadriceps and involves no pounding, but it can aggravate some knee injuries.

Equating Cross-Training and Running

A running equivalent to a cross-training workout is often hard to gauge. Outdoor activities such as cycling, in-line skating, and rollerskiing are subject to variability caused by hilly terrain, traffic, weather, and other factors. You can't use heart rate equivalents for water workouts because the pressure and the cooling effect of the water on your body decrease heart rate, meaning that you will be working harder than your heart rate would seem to indicate compared with a land-based workout.

Over time, most regular cross-trainers develop a sense of what their various cross-training workouts are worth in running terms. If this is a concern for you, your best bet is to use a heart rate monitor and cross-train with an easily monitored land-based activity such as stationary cycling or elliptical training. Keep in mind that if you are new to these activities, it will take a while (usually four to eight weeks depending on your fitness level and adaptability) before you become fit enough in the new activity that your heart rate accurately reflects how hard you are working compared with a running workout. Don't forget to ease into any new activity (in both time and intensity) to avoid injury, excessive soreness, or discouragement.

hundred dollars, so you're better off borrowing or renting one until you're sure that cycling is right for you.

Although cycling involves no pounding, it can aggravate some knee injuries. Thus, even though cycling can help strengthen the quadriceps muscles, thereby helping to achieve balance with a runner's strong hamstring muscles, cycling may not be the optimal activity if you're suffering from, or are prone to, such problems. Talk to a sports medicine professional about other activities that might be better for you, such as deep-water running.

Outdoor cycling involves a bigger time commitment than running for the same fitness benefit because you get to rest on the downhills. For those with limited time, indoor cycling, either on a stationary cycling machine or using a wind trainer to which you hook up your bike, is a better option. Safety is another concern for cyclists in some areas. On the plus side, you may be able to combine your workout with transportation on a bike. Once you have adjusted to stationary cycling, your running-equivalent workout will probably be roughly the same duration as a running workout, provided heart rates are similar. You can do recovery workouts, anaerobic-threshold (AT) workouts, long-endurance workouts, and speed workouts on the bike.

Most cyclists find it easier to get their heart rate up on a road bike than on a mountain bike, but choose the model that works best for you in terms of convenience and comfort.

Cross-Country (Nordic) Skiing

Like deep-water running, cross-country skiing is an excellent total-body activity that involves virtually no pounding to the joints. A cross-country skiing workout burns more calories than running at the same heart rate level, and it works more muscles, including the shoulders, arms, upper back, and abdominals. Outdoor skiing is a great way to commune with nature in the winter; the indoor version is accessible at most health clubs if you don't want to fork over several hundred dollars for a machine. There's a bit of a learning curve for both activities. Take a lesson if you are a beginning outdoor cross-country skier (even if you're a whiz at downhill). Ask health-club personnel for instruction rather than trying to wing it on a machine. As with any activity, you'll achieve better fitness gains if you learn correct technique.

Because of the intense cardiovascular workout that cross-country skiing offers, as well its total-body nature, ease into the activity if you're new to it by gradually increasing the duration and intensity of workouts. Because the activity uses the entire body, you will likely be able to get your heart rate to higher levels than you can with running. Therefore, your running-equivalent workout on skis should be slightly shorter than your running workout. I would aim for a 35-minute workout on skis to equal a 45-minute running workout. Rollerskiing outdoors is also an option during warmer months.

Snowshoeing

This activity has taken off in popularity over the past few years. An estimated one million North Americans strapped on snowshoes in 1998, up from four hundred thousand in 1996. Part of this dramatic growth has been driven by the development of lighter and smaller snowshoes—unlike those of the past that resembled tennis racquets for the feet. These new shoes, with their smaller and asymmetric frames, make it possible for runners to maintain close to their normal running gait and running form on the snow. Although you may want to start by walking in them to get a feel for the activity, once you get the hang of snowshoeing you can measure the time and exertion level of your workouts to determine the running equivalent. In general, expect your snowshoeing workouts to correspond roughly to your running workouts in duration and intensity. (Don't try to equate miles because the varied terrain and snow conditions inherent to snowshoeing can cause workouts of the same distance to vary significantly.) You can do speed workouts and long "runs" on snowshoes, and races are popular in northern areas during the winter months. Because running on snowshoes is so similar to regular running, most running injuries probably won't stand up well to a snowshoeing workout, although you may be able to walk on snowshoes through some injuries.

Finding the Right Cross-Training Activity for You

Ask yourself these questions when evaluating cross-training options:

- Is it convenient?
- Do I enjoy it?
- Is it accessible most of the time?
- Do I have the necessary skills (or can I learn them without too much difficulty)?
- Will it aggravate or cause an injury?
- Can I handle any financial investment involved (equipment, fees, club membership, etc.)?

Swimming

I've found there's no middle ground among runners when it comes to swimming. Some love it, cheerfully using it to cross-train through injuries or employing it as part of their regular training program. Others categorically refuse to stick a toe in a lap lane. (Many in the former group are either triathletes or former competitive swimmers.) Swimming is an excellent cross-training activity for runners who know how to swim, enjoy it, and have access to a pool. It uses about 80 percent upper-body muscles and 20 percent lower-body muscles, which means that you can swim through most running injuries (be careful with some knee and ankle problems). Swimming doesn't burn as many calories per minute as running at the same intensity, nor does it raise the heart rate as high because of the pressure of water on the body, which causes more blood to return to the heart and more blood to be pumped with each contraction. Your heart will tend to beat slower in cooler water, faster in warmer water. Technique can make a huge difference in swimming efficiency, so take lessons or ask someone knowledgeable to look at your stroke and offer pointers.

Swimming and running are hard to equate in duration and intensity because of the effects of water on heart rate (see page 145). In general, runners will be able to attain only 85 to 90 percent of their running heart rates while swimming. That's OK; the body is still working hard, but the effort is not reflected in heart rate because of water pressure and the cooling effect of water. You can use swimming as a recovery workout, AT workout, speed workout, or endurance workout.

Deep-Water Running

As mentioned earlier, deep-water running is a popular cross-training option for runners, many of whom first try it when injured and then become converts when they see how beneficial and even enjoyable it can be. Deep-water running requires you to run in water deep enough that you can't touch bottom. It's best that you wear a flotation vest or belt so you can put your energy into running smoothly and rhythmically rather than trying to stay afloat. As with swimming, you'll have a lower heart rate and rate of perceived exertion (the sense of how hard you're working) when water running compared with running on land. A rule of thumb is that heart rate during water running is about 10 percent lower than during land running. Getting your heart rate up to 140 BPM when running in the water is roughly equal to working at 154 BPM when running on the land.

Deep-water running will not aggravate most running injuries, including plantar fascia problems, most tendinitis and bursitis, and most stress fractures. Deep-water running is a total-body exercise that works your legs, trunk, and arms and conditions your cardiovascular system.

If possible, find a deep-water running class or at least someone who can advise you about proper technique. Classes can be sociable because people of all levels can work out side by side. Form is important; here are some basic pointers. Stay vertical in the water with your head up, pump your arms at your sides rather than across your chest, reach forward with your feet and follow through behind you, and keep your feet in neutral position (neither pointed nor flexed). Because water lowers heart rate and provides resistance to quick limb movement, you can do interval (speed) training and AT training in water more often than you can on land. By thus varying your workout, you can relieve the boredom of water running. A water-running workout gives about the same aerobic benefit as a land-running workout of the same duration.

Deep-water running is currently considered the best cross-training activity for runners in the sense of maintaining the specific fitness you need to run well. Another positive point is that it has a very low injury rate.

Elliptical Training

This relatively new cross-training option is all the rage at health clubs. The elliptical trainer, introduced in 1995, is made by Reebok, Precor, and other companies. It gets its name from the pattern in which the feet move, through an elongated oval shape rather than in a circle, from side to side, or up and down. The elliptical trainer provides a nonimpact workout that's also weight bearing, so it can help keep bones strong. You can vary your stride—forward or backward—and the incline and intensity of the workout. The machine works all the main muscles of the lower body as well as the arms and shoulders because your hands grip levers that move the arms back and forth. Once you are accustomed to elliptical training (after about four to eight weeks) your workouts should be roughly equivalent to your running workouts in duration and intensity.

The elliptical trainer is a great cross-training option if you have a heel or foot injury such as plantar fasciitis (or are prone to such problems). Be careful with knee injuries. Although the impact is less than with running, you're still bending the knees and asking them to support the body through a full range of motion. It is not difficult to get the hang of the machine, and the full-body workout is a boon to runners. The hamstrings aren't worked as intensely as in running, but you can compensate by doing hamstring curls (see chapter 10 on strength training).

Stair Climbing

Climbing stairs reduces impact on the knees compared with running and provides a great cardiovascular workout. Walking briskly up stairs will get your heart rate up to the level of running at training pace; you can pick up the pace for an interval workout. If you don't have access to a stair-climbing machine, try walking up stairs in a tall building and taking the elevator back down. You'll want to wear running shoes or supportive cross-trainers. Once you are accustomed to the activity, a stair-climbing workout is roughly equivalent to a running workout in duration and intensity.

Fitness Walking and Hiking

Brisk walking with a vigorous arm swing can provide a cardiovascular workout approximating that offered by running, with far less impact. I've known injured runners who were able to maintain close to their running fitness level by walking on a treadmill set to an uphill grade of 3 to 5 percent. Everyone knows how to walk (although race walking takes special skills best learned from an instructor). The activity is accessible to all and requires only a pair of good, supportive shoes. Most running shoes (trainers) are fine for fitness walking. Fitness walking or hiking burns approximately the same number of calories per mile as running; the difference, of course, is that it takes longer to walk or hike a mile than to run it. The intensity is similar only if you adhere to strict race-walking form, with its exaggerated arm swing and hip motion. Otherwise, fitness walking will be somewhat less intense than running, and hiking will approach running intensity only if done up a significant hill.

You can choose more than one cross-training activity to supplement your running.

Cross-Training Schedules

How much should you cross-train? That depends on your goals, the activities you choose, and your injury status. For uninjured runners who

Cross-Training: Who Does What?

A number of elite runners are enthusiastic cross-trainers. Here is what some of the best runners in the business do to supplement their running:

Joan Benoit Samuelson, Bob Kempainen, and Janis Klecker—cross-country skiing

Jane Welzel—swimming

Lynn DeNinno—swimming, cycling

Linda Somers and Bob Kennedy—deep-water running

Anne Marie Lauck—fitness walking

Lynn Jennings—cross-country skiing, hiking

Ed Eyestone—hiking

want to supplement their training to reduce injury risk and increase variety, I recommend a 15 to 35 percent cross-training program. Some runners do more cross-training during certain times of the year, such as runners in northern climes who do the bulk of their winter training as cross-country skiing or snowshoeing. If you are injured you may have to do all your conditioning as cross-training, with a gradual return to running as you heal.

Here are three suggested cross-training schedules for marathon runners that include 15 percent, 25 percent, and 35 percent cross-training. (These schedules are also appropriate for most runners training for 5K to half marathon. Your mileage and time spent working out may differ from those in the schedules presented here. If so, adjust the cross-training times and distances accordingly, maintaining the ratio of cross-training to overall workout time.) Although I have suggested specific cross-training options, you should choose the activities that work best for you with respect to interest, skill, accessibility, convenience, and support of your running goals.

15 Percent Cross-Training Program

Monday—Swim 35 minutes, including 20 minutes of intervals

Tuesday—Run 60 minutes, including 30 minutes of intervals

Wednesday—Run 45 minutes easy

Thursday—Run 65 minutes, including 35 minutes of tempo running

Friday—Cycle 30 minutes steady

Saturday—Run 60 minutes or race

Sunday—Run 120 minutes steady

25 Percent Cross-Training Program

Monday—Nordic ski 40 minutes steady

Tuesday—Run 60 minutes, including 30 minutes of intervals

Wednesday—Deep-water run 40 minutes, including 20 minutes of intervals

Thursday—Run 65 minutes, including 35 minutes of tempo running

Friday—Climb stairs 25 minutes steady

Saturday—Run 60 minutes or race

Sunday—Run 120 minutes steady

35 Percent Cross-Training Program

Monday—Fitness walk 60 minutes steady

Tuesday—Run 60 minutes, including 30 minutes of intervals

Wednesday—Elliptical training 45 minutes, including 20 minutes of intervals

Thursday—Run 60 minutes, including 30 minutes of tempo running

Friday—Snowshoe 60 minutes steady

Saturday—Run 60 minutes or race

Sunday—Run 120 minutes steady

13

Eating to Train

SUZANNE GIRARD EBERLE, MS, RD
Sports nutrition specialist, author, and
a *Running Times* contributing editor

Making smart food choices allows you to get the most from your training efforts.

If you're like most runners, you eat at least three times a day, most days of the year. That translates into more than a thousand decisions a year about what to eat! Healthy eating habits can help you withstand the stress of daily workouts and long runs, and can reduce your chance of catching a cold or succumbing to an injury. You'll feel better and have more energy—just what you need when you're trying to achieve a breakthrough performance.

Unfortunately, many runners squander these daily opportunities to improve their running. Choosing the proper running shoes, heart monitor, or workout seems to take precedence (in training) over cultivating healthy eating habits. You may not realize how much speed you can lose by skipping meals or becoming mildly dehydrated. You may also underestimate the dangers of constant dieting and the negative effects of seeking to be thin in order to run well. Such practices can seriously diminish your running performance.

Choosing foods that taste good and are good for you need not be time consuming and overwhelming. The Food Guide Pyramid can guide you in obtaining the nutrients you need—the major players (carbohydrate, protein, and fat) as well as the supporting cast (antioxidants, B vitamins, calcium, iron, and zinc). Making smart food choices allows you to get the most from your training efforts.

Essentials of a Runner's Diet

If you think the Food Guide Pyramid has gone the way of knee-high running socks, think again. Designed by the U.S. Department of Agriculture (USDA) as a general guideline for choosing a healthy diet, the pyramid provides simple rules relevant to the entire population, even runners. The main adjustment that runners need to make is to consume more than the average sedentary American does—more calories, more carbohydrates, more protein. Runners must also be sure to ingest a steady stream of certain critical nutrients, such as antioxidants, B vitamins, calcium, iron, and zinc.

Refamiliarize yourself with the Food Guide Pyramid (figure 13.1) and the serving sizes it's based on. Using the pyramid, some common sense, and a bit of planning, you can easily obtain the nutrients and other substances you need for good health and quality performances.

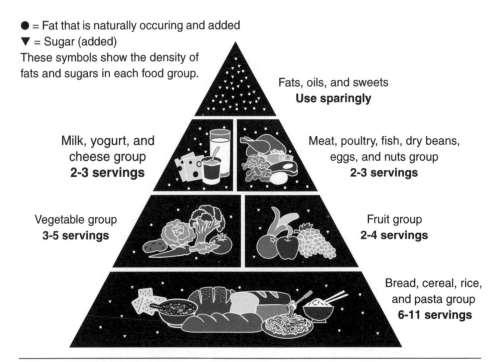

● = Fat that is naturally occuring and added
▼ = Sugar (added)
These symbols show the density of fats and sugars in each food group.

Fats, oils, and sweets
Use sparingly

Milk, yogurt, and cheese group
2-3 servings

Meat, poultry, fish, dry beans, eggs, and nuts group
2-3 servings

Vegetable group
3-5 servings

Fruit group
2-4 servings

Bread, cereal, rice, and pasta group
6-11 servings

Figure 13.1   Food Guide Pyramid.

Food Guide Pyramid Serving Sizes

What counts as a serving? Here are guidelines adapted from those included with the USDA's Food Guide Pyramid.

Milk, Yogurt, and Cheese

1 cup of milk or yogurt

$1^1/_2$ ounces of natural cheese

2 ounces of processed cheese

1 cup of cottage cheese

1 cup of fat-free or low-fat frozen yogurt or ice cream

Meat, Poultry, Fish, Dried Beans, Eggs, and Nuts

2 to 3 ounces of cooked lean meat, poultry, or fish

(1 ounce of meat $= ^1/_2$ cup of cooked dry beans or peas)

$= 1$ ounce of tofu

$= 1$ egg or 2 egg whites

$= 2$ tablespoons of peanut butter

$= ^1/_3$ cup of nuts

Vegetables

1 cup of raw leafy vegetables

$^1/_2$ cup of other vegetables, cooked or chopped raw

$^3/_4$ cup of vegetable juice

$^1/_2$ cup of spaghetti sauce

$^1/_2$ cup of scalloped potatoes or potato salad

1 medium potato, boiled or baked

Fruit

1 medium piece of fruit (apple, banana, orange)

$^1/_2$ cup of chopped, cooked, or canned fruit

$^1/_4$ melon

$^1/_2$ grapefruit

$^3/_4$ cup of fruit juice

$^1/_2$ cup of dried fruit

(continued)

(continued)

Bread, Cereal, Rice, and Pasta

> 1 slice of bread
> 1 small roll, biscuit, or muffin
> 1 tortilla
> $1/2$ small bagel
> $1/2$ hamburger roll
> $1/2$ large pita
> $1/2$ English muffin
> $1/2$ croissant (large)
> 1 ounce of ready-to-eat dry cereal
> $1/2$ cup of cooked cereal, pasta, or rice
> 1 ounce of crackers
> 1 four-inch pancake
> 1 ounce of pretzels
> 2 rice cakes
> 3 cups of air-popped popcorn

Fats, Oils, and Sweets

> No specific serving size recommended; use sparingly.

Major Players

Carbohydrate, protein, and fat are the essential nutrients that supply the energy or calories you need to fuel training and competitive efforts. Most runners need 20 to 25 calories per pound of body weight to support their daily running habit. Figure on 16 to 20 calories if you're moderately active and 25 to 30 calories if you're training for ultra events.

You've probably heard carbohydrates called a runner's best friend. Stored in the liver and muscles as glycogen, carbohydrates are the fuel your body increasingly relies on as you increase the intensity of your run. Your body, however, can store only a limited amount of carbohydrate, which becomes a limiting factor in longer races such as marathons and ultras.

Your body can store only a limited amount of carbohydrate.

Your brain and nervous system rely almost exclusively on carbohydrate for fuel. Moreover, you won't burn fat efficiently or recover from workouts quickly if you don't eat a carbohydrate-rich diet. Most runners do well eating a diet that obtains about 60 percent of its total calories from carbohydrate-rich foods. If you're running an hour or less a day, aim to eat three grams of carbohydrate per pound of

What Is the 40-30-30 Diet and Can It Work for Runners?

Carbohydrates have been shoved to the side lately by the new kid on the block—protein. Featured in best-selling books and touted by famous athletes, 40-30-30, a diet composed of 40 percent of calories from carbohydrate, 30 percent from protein, and 30 percent from fat, promises to make you slim, healthy, and fast. Runners accustomed to loading up with carbohydrates may be especially confused by this trend.

Carbohydrate-rich foods provide the main fuel used by the body in workouts and races, especially as you run at faster speeds. Carbohydrates are also essential for replacing the body's glycogen stores following exercise, thereby allowing you to train every day. A daily diet that obtains only 40 percent of its calories from carbs, compared with the traditionally recommended 55 to 65 percent, isn't likely to support peak performances long term. Followed to the letter, 40-30-30 diets also tend to provide too few calories, which can leave you feeling too weak and tired to train.

If you've taken the runners-need-carbohydrates mantra too far, however, paying more attention to your protein and fat needs can improve your health and running performances. Counting blocks of protein or carbohydrates or computing the 40-30-30 ratio at every meal and snack isn't the answer. A simple solution is to eat mixed meals— to mix carbohydrates, protein, and fats during your meals and snacks. For example, loading up on plain pasta, salad, and bread at dinner delivers primarily carbohydrates. For a better balance, add chicken or shrimp (protein) to your pasta sauce and drizzle low-fat salad dressing (fat) on the salad. Eating a variety of foods makes eating more fun and is more likely to give you all the nutrients you need, in the correct balance.

body weight per day. If you are a runner who trains strenuously for one to two hours daily, strive for four grams. If you exercise more than two hours each day on average, take in five grams of carbohydrate per pound of body weight per day.

This leaves plenty of room for the other two major players in a well-balanced diet—protein and fat. You need protein to build and repair muscle tissue, generate red blood cells, synthesize enzymes and hormones, and keep the immune system in good working order. An adequate protein intake for runners, 12 to 15 percent of total calories, equates to 0.5 to 0.75 grams of protein per pound of body weight per day. Vegetarian runners can meet their protein requirements by consuming a variety of plant proteins (soy products, legumes, nuts, and seeds) throughout the day. Eggs and dairy foods also provide ample amounts of protein.

Fat, besides providing essential fatty acids and a concentrated source of energy, helps transport and store fat-soluble vitamins in the body. Fat also makes foods tastier. Obtaining 20 to 30 percent of calories from fat, or 0.5 grams per pound of body weight per day, is reasonable for most runners. This allows you to make nutritious choices and still enjoy your favorite foods.

How can the Food Guide Pyramid help you keep all these numbers and percentages straight? Building your diet around plant-based foods, as the pyramid recommends, essentially guarantees you'll be eating a carbohydrate-rich diet. Grains such as rice, bulgur, quinoa, breads, cereals, and pasta, as well as fruits and vegetables, boost your carbohydrate intake without adding much fat to your diet. These foods (except for fruit) also supply small amounts of protein, which augment your daily protein intake as you eat the recommended number of servings.

Rounding out your diet with the recommended amounts of protein-rich foods, such as dairy products, meat, poultry, fish, eggs, dried beans, or soy foods, ensures that you'll meet your daily protein needs. Dried beans (such as kidney, garbanzo, or black beans) and dairy foods (such as milk and yogurt) also supply ample doses of carbohydrate. Of course, you can rack up too much fat by routinely indulging in foods such as fast-food hamburgers, fried chicken, and cheese. These foods, although they may supply protein, can easily put you over your daily fat requirement. On the other hand, entirely eliminating the milk and meat food groups isn't necessarily a healthy choice. Choosing lean meats and low-fat dairy foods or soy foods and eating dried beans several times a week is a healthy compromise.

A sprinkling of high-fat foods, such as margarine, salad dressing, and an occasional bowl of ice cream, adds necessary fat to your diet and makes eating an enjoyable experience. High-sugar foods, such as candy, fat-free cookies, and soda, although they provide carbohydrates in the form of sugar, offer little else of nutritional value.

Bottom Line

Concentrate on eating a balanced diet. Include foods in the recommended amounts from all five food groups. Enjoy your favorite high-fat and high-sugar foods in moderation without letting those choices crowd out food-group foods.

Supporting Cast

In your quest to improve your running performances, an optimal intake of vitamin C, vitamin E, beta-carotene, calcium, iron, and zinc will speed you on your way. These nutrients do not contain or provide energy, but they help your body function at peak efficiency in other ways. By making smart food choices, you can easily obtain the U.S. recommended daily allowance (RDA) of these vitamins and minerals.

Antioxidants

Beta-carotene (converted to vitamin A in the body) and vitamins C and E protect cells and tissues from the damaging effects of free radicals—the by-products of strenuous aerobic exercise, pollution, cigarette smoke, and other environmental toxins. Saturating your tissues with these nutrients, preferably from food rather than from supplements, may translate into less muscle-tissue damage, a speedier recovery, and a stronger immune system.

Beta-carotene and vitamin C are easy to get by eating a variety of fruits and vegetables. Develop a taste for richly colored varieties such as mangoes, apricots, sweet potatoes, broccoli, strawberries, and dark leafy greens (spinach, collards, and kale). Vitamin E is found in vegetable oils, margarine, nuts, green leafy vegetables, wheat germ, and whole-grain products.

RDA of Antioxidants

Vitamin C—60 milligrams per day for adult males and females

Vitamin E—10 milligrams per day or 15 international units (IU) for adult males and 8 milligrams per day or 12 IU for adult females

Beta-carotene—No current RDA; experts recommend 6 milligrams per day

B Vitamins

Thiamin, riboflavin, niacin, and other B vitamins are used by the body to help convert carbohydrate, fat, and protein into energy. You need more of these B vitamins as the number of calories you consume increases. Of course, the easiest way for runners to meet their high calorie needs and subsequent higher vitamin B needs is simply to eat more nutrient-dense foods they enjoy. Vitamins B_6, B_{12}, and folic acid are necessary to form healthy red blood cells. Whole and enriched grains (cereal, bread, etc.), legumes, nuts, seeds, fruits, and vegetables, as well as lean meats, poultry, eggs, and dairy foods, will supply all the necessary B vitamins.

RDA of B Vitamins

Thiamin—1.2 milligrams per day (adult males), 1.1 milligrams per day (adult females)

Riboflavin—1.3 milligrams per day (adult males), 1.1 milligrams per day (adult females)

Niacin—16 milligrams per day (adult males), 14 milligrams per day (adult females)

Biotin—30 micrograms per day (adult males and females)

Pantothenic acid—5 milligrams per day (adult males and females)

Vitamin B_6—1.3 milligrams per day for adult males (1.7 milligrams for males over 51 years), 1.3 milligrams per day for adult females (1.5 milligrams for females over 51)

Vitamin B_{12}—2.4 micrograms per day (males and females)

Folic acid (folate)—400 micrograms per day (males and females)

The information provided on thiamin, riboflavin, niacin, biotin, and pantothenic acid is no longer listed on food labels because deficiencies are rare. It's easy to get enough by making wise food choices. Athletes eat more calories and more food, so they should easily be able to get the B vitamins they need, especially because grain products are fortified. All multivitamin supplements provide the water-soluble B vitamins also (often in very large doses). Why put in amounts needed? No one actually tracks them and adds them up! That's the beauty of focusing on eating a variety of foods from all five food groups in the recommended amounts rather than trying to track the 40 or more individual nutrients needed on a daily basis.

Calcium

Crucial for building strong bones and teeth, calcium also helps muscles contract and helps nerves send messages. Consuming too little calcium can contribute to the development of stress fractures. It also sets you up to develop osteoporosis (a condition characterized by weak bones that break easily). Eating dairy foods is the easiest way to accumulate the 1,000 milligrams of calcium you need per day (1,300 milligrams for runners age 9 to 18 and 1,200 milligrams for those over 50). One cup of milk or yogurt or a serving of cheese ($1^1/_2$ to 2 ounces) provides 300 milligrams of calcium.

Calcium can be found in foods from all five food groups, so include alternative sources if you don't consume dairy foods. Try calcium-fortified orange juice, soy or rice milk, tofu made with calcium sulfate, dark green leafy vegetables, baked beans, canned salmon or sardines (with bones), and fortified breakfast cereals.

Iron and Zinc

Your body needs iron to form hemoglobin and myoglobin, the oxygen-carrying portion of molecules in the blood and muscles. Consuming too little iron can result in iron-deficiency anemia. You'll feel tired, run down, and unable to maintain your usual running pace. An adequate zinc intake bolsters the immune system, allowing wounds and injuries to heal properly (including the cellular microdamage from daily mileage), and boosts your resistance to infections and illnesses.

If you routinely or regularly eat red meat, poultry, and fish or shellfish, you're most likely meeting your need for iron and zinc. Milk, yogurt, and cheese are also good sources of zinc. Plant sources contain less absorbable forms of iron and zinc, but most runners can still satisfy their needs by eating a variety of foods such as dark green leafy vegetables, dried beans and lentils, dried fruit, tofu, textured vegetable protein, soy milk, oatmeal, nuts, seeds, and enriched breakfast cereals.

Bottom Line

Make the effort to eat the nutrients you need. Include a variety of foods from all five food groups. It's quick and easy to pop supplements, but the nutrients found in foods are generally absorbed better. Food provides packages of nutrients that work together, as well as yet-to-be-identified health and performance boosters that don't appear in any supplement.

If you routinely eliminate whole food groups or skip meals, however, take a multivitamin or mineral supplement. Consider a calcium supplement to round out your dietary intake (check food labels to determine what you routinely consume and limit your supplemental dose to 500 milligrams at a time). Take extra iron if a routine blood test determines you have an iron deficiency. Add vitamin E (100 to 400 international units) if you exercise in heavily polluted areas, train at altitude, or follow a very low-fat diet.

Preventing Common Dietary Mistakes

Making smart food choices ensures you'll have the fuel on board to train harder, a stronger immune system, and more energy in general. Many of the training lulls and poor performances that runners suffer from can be attributed to poor eating. Some of the most common mistakes include skipping meals, not eating enough during the day, eating too few or too many carbohydrates, ignoring fluid needs, and running to eat instead of eating to run.

Avoid Skipping Meals

Most runners cram an amazing amount of activity into a day—school or work or both, family responsibilities, errands, personal interests, and running or other forms of training. Many go through the day without properly refueling. Then, starting in the late afternoon or evening, they pile in the calories that would have served them better earlier in the day.

Sound familiar? Break this cycle by eating regular meals and snacks. It's normal to be hungry every three to four hours when you're awake. It's not normal, or healthy, to go long periods without eating, nor can you expect to perform at your best. Eating within an hour or two of rising helps replenish the liver glycogen your body used overnight as fuel. Your blood-sugar level won't plummet midmorning, and you'll be able to concentrate and be more productive. Breakfast eaters also fare better at losing weight and keeping it off.

If you're not hungry when you get up, it's probably because you eat too much or too late the night before. Stop eating one hour earlier and keep moving the time back until you wake up hungry enough to eat breakfast. If lack of time is your excuse, rearrange your schedule and carve out five minutes for a bowl of cold cereal or oatmeal heated in the microwave. Instant breakfast drinks come in handy, or try the ultimate quick breakfast—a glass of milk and a glass of juice or a piece of fresh fruit. Eating breakfast following a morning workout is particularly important.

Breakfast eaters tend to do better losing weight and keeping it off.

The next step is making lunch a priority. Eating lunch can reduce stress, enhance productivity, and recharge you for the afternoon, especially if you train late in the day. Remember that the goal is to eat your calories during the day when you need them. If time is tight or you're squeezing a run in at lunchtime, be prepared by brown bagging it or leave a few minutes to swing by the cafeteria. As with all meals, aim to include foods from at least three food groups.

Even if you eat lunch, making it all the way until dinner can be unrealistic. Keep healthy snacks on hand, especially if you run at the end of the day. Think of snacks as minimeals. Try to include one or more food-group foods in your snacks. Cookies dunked in milk, for example, make a healthier snack than soda and chips.

Eating dinner gives you an opportunity to unwind, reconnect with family and friends, and refuel for the next day. You don't have to prepare a gourmet meal. Keep some staples on hand to throw together quick, nutritious meals—scrambled eggs and toast, pasta and sauce, canned chili and crackers, and so forth. Round out your meal with juice, fruit, or vegetables served raw or cooked (keep frozen or canned varieties on hand). You can always buy part of your meal, such as a rotisserie chicken, and add healthy side dishes. Other timesaving prepared foods that are good options include canned beans, grated cheese, skinless and boneless chicken breasts, instant-cooking grains, salad-bar produce, and prewashed salad greens. Stock your kitchen with timesaving devices such as a sharp knife, small electric or handheld food chopper, vegetable steamer, microwave and microwave-friendly cookware, and a Crock-Pot or slow cooker. If you find yourself ravenous or eating right up until bedtime, then you haven't eaten enough calories during the day.

Balance Your Carbohydrate Intake

The recent fanfare about high-protein diets may have you confused about the role of carbohydrates in a runner's diet. On the other hand, perhaps you've fallen into the carbohydrate-overload trap. Either circumstance, eating too few or too many carbohydrates, can keep you from meeting your running goals.

Best Way to Avoid Carbohydrate Overload

Don't eat your grains plain. Instead of eating two bagels, have one with peanut butter. Toss shrimp, chicken, or lean ground beef into your pasta sauce. Instead of demolishing a box of crackers, have a handful with low-fat cheese. You'll eat a balanced diet—enough carbohydrates and adequate protein and fat, too.

High-protein diets, on the other hand, may leave you eating too few carbohydrates. Valued for their ability to promote quick weight loss, they tend to provide too few calories for active people.

Protein can serve as an energy source during exercise, providing up to 15 percent of your energy needs in the late stages of a long race. Our muscles are designed, however, to burn primarily carbohydrate and fat for fuel. A sound training program helps spare the use of protein and glycogen for energy by enhancing the ability of the body to burn fat during exercise. Eating more protein won't give you more fuel for exercise and by itself won't promote the growth of muscles. You need a strength-training program as well as adequate calories to build muscle. (See chapter 10 for information on strength training.)

Including high-quality protein sources at meals and snacks makes sense. Protein helps keep blood-sugar levels in the normal range, and you'll be less likely to overeat on carbohydrates. But don't skimp on complex carbohydrates such as whole grains, pasta, bread, rice, cereal, beans, and fruit. Eaten in reasonable amounts, these foods provide a steady supply of energy to fuel peak performances.

Carbohydrates should make up the majority of the calories you consume. Some runners may do well on a diet of 50 to 55 percent carbohydrate. Some marathoners and ultrarunners may need closer to 70 percent. No matter what the exact percentage you eat to perform at your best, all runners will benefit from consuming adequate carbohydrates at two key times—following daily runs and before long races.

Many runners fail to eat enough carbohydrates to replenish their glycogen stores. Unexplained fatigue, sore muscles, and an inability to maintain a normal running pace are common symptoms. Capitalize on the power of carbohydrates by consuming carbohydrate-rich foods or drinks within 15 to 30 minutes after exercise, as well as every two hours for the next several hours. It makes sense to load up on carbohydrates (approximately 0.5 grams per pound of body weight) during this window of time because your muscles are most receptive to replacing glycogen. You'll recover more quickly and feel better during your next run.

If you don't feel like eating immediately following a run, drink your carbohydrates in the form of sports drinks, juice, milk, or a fruit smoothie (fruit mixed with yogurt or blended with milk). Ease in carbohydrate-rich foods such as yogurt, bagels, fruit, and energy bars, as tolerated. The sooner you can eat a balanced meal including both carbohydrate and protein, the better. Protein has also been shown to speed recovery by further enhancing the resynthesis of glycogen in muscle cells.

Runners preparing for races lasting longer than 90 to 120 minutes can also benefit from boosting their carbohydrate intake. Pack in the carbohydrates (up to 70 percent of calories) for three days before a long race. Besides topping off glycogen reserves, muscles hold on to three grams of water for every gram of carbohydrate stored, so by glycogen loading you enter the race better hydrated too.

Overloading on carbohydrates is a pitfall common in active people. Living on fruit, salad, bagels, pasta, and sweets can leave you dangerously low in essential nutrients, such as protein, calcium, iron, and zinc. If you eliminate entire food groups, such as milk or meat and beans, it's easy to end up eating too many carbohydrates. Instead, work on finding alternative sources for the food groups you don't eat much of; for example, if you don't like or can't tolerate cow's milk, substitute calcium-fortified soy or rice milk.

Stay Hydrated

Many runners fail to monitor the most important nutrient of all—water. One of the quickest and simplest ways to boost your performance is to make sure you're well hydrated. Without proper hydration, you'll feel light-headed, tired, irritable, and headachy. And that's before you start running.

Head out for a run in a dehydrated state, or ignore your fluid needs as you exercise, and you can quickly run into trouble. You will find it more difficult to tolerate the heat, and you risk suffering from heat cramps or, worse, heat exhaustion or heat stroke. Your performance will suffer too. Even mild dehydration—a 2 percent drop in body weight due to the loss of fluid (3 pounds for a 150-pound runner)—can decrease by 20 percent your ability to perform mental and physical tasks.

Fill up before you head out the door by drinking at least two cups (16 ounces) of fluid an hour or two before exercise. Drink another cup (8

Is dehydration slowing you down?

© Index Stock Photography

ounces) 15 minutes before you plan to run. Water, juice, milk, and sports drinks will all do the trick. Alcoholic and caffeinated drinks cause you to urinate and lose fluid, so be sure to match each glass of these beverages with an equal glass of water.

Don't wait until you feel thirsty to drink—that means you're already dehydrated. Keeping tabs on your urine is an easy way to monitor your hydration. You should be able to produce ample amounts of pale yellow or straw-colored urine. Producing scanty amounts of darkly colored urine indicates that you are dehydrated.

> Ignoring fluid needs can decrease performance and, in the worst case, be dangerous. When in doubt, drink more than you think you need.

During exercise, plan to drink another 4 to 8 ounces every 15 to 20 minutes depending on what the weather is like and how well you hydrated beforehand. If you run for an hour or less, know where to locate water along your route or carry it with you. For runs lasting over an hour or during intense efforts, such as interval workouts, choose a sports drink, which replaces the water and electrolytes lost through sweating more efficiently than plain water. You'll also get a boost from the carbohydrates these beverages provide.

If you think dehydration may be slowing you down, weigh yourself before and after you run. Replace every pound lost by drinking at least two cups of fluid. Next time you run, try to drink that amount in the few hours before you exercise. Eating salty foods will also help you hold on to the fluids you drink. Pay particular attention to your fluid needs on hot and humid days and on low-humidity or windy days when you may not be as conscious of sweating.

Eat to Run, Don't Run to Eat

A serious trap many runners, especially women, fall into is running to eat. That is, running becomes a means for losing weight or a way to burn calories to earn the right to eat certain foods. If you're trying to run well by eating as little as possible, or if what you eat depends solely on how much you've run, you need to rethink your eating habits.

Food is the fuel that allows you to run in the first place. You won't enjoy running or perform well if you feel tired all the time. Constant dieting usually backfires in the end. Eat too few carbohydrates or calories, and your body will use protein from your muscles to help meet energy needs. Much of the weight loss associated with diets is actually a loss of muscle tissue. Muscle tissue burns calories even at rest. Lose muscle and you reduce your metabolism and end up needing fewer calories. Depriving yourself doesn't work either. It often leads to poor food choices and overeating when you finally address your hunger.

Disordered eating patterns, such as very low-fat diets, set female runners up for a more serious condition called the female athlete triad (disordered eating, amenorrhea, and osteoporosis). Eating too few calories is thought to lead to amenorrhea (the loss of menstrual periods). The hormonal changes associated with amenorrhea put women at increased risk for osteoporosis. Amenorrhea and frequent stress fractures are warning signs that your current eating habits and training program are out of balance.

Eating Disorders

When the desire to be thin or have the perfect runner's body gets out of control, an eating disorder can be the tragic result. Eating disorders, such as anorexia nervosa and bulimia nervosa, are serious emotional problems that can have life-threatening consequences. Anorexia nervosa, a condition characterized by self-starvation and excessive weight loss, affects as many as 1 percent of all women and an even higher percentage of young women ages 15 to 24. Bulimia nervosa, a secretive cycle of binge eating and purging, is even more common. It's been estimated that one of every five college-age women suffers from bulimia. Although complex in nature, low self-esteem appears to be the common factor among individuals with eating disorders.

Being involved in a sport such as distance running, where low body weight is deemed advantageous, increases the risk for developing anorexia or bulimia. By nature, runners tend to be self-disciplined, competitive, and compulsive. The same traits typify the personality type vulnerable to an eating disorder. Running usually doesn't cause the eating disorder. Rather, people who are at risk tend to gravitate toward running; being involved in the sport triggers or precipitates an eating disorder in someone predisposed to developing one.

Some of the warning signs associated with eating disorders include

- intense preoccupation with weight and body image,
- marked decrease in weight not related to a medical condition,
- compulsive and excessive training beyond purposeful training,
- abnormal eating habits (e.g., refusing to eat with others, bizarre food rituals, etc.),
- self-induced vomiting (bathroom visits following meals),
- abuse of diet pills or laxatives, and
- amenorrhea.

Adhering strictly to a vegetarian eating style has also been linked to the development of eating disorders, particularly among young athletic women.

Runners preoccupied with their weight tend to be highly self-critical and appear anxious or depressed. They may deny obvious fatigue and complain of dizziness, feeling cold, and abdominal discomfort upon eating. Bulimia may be harder to detect because weight loss is usually not as significant. Swollen glands, bloodshot eyes, knuckle scars, and worn tooth enamel are signs.

Prevention is the real key when it comes to runners and eating disorders. Start by accepting your body type and shape. Focus on establishing healthy eating habits that allow you to accomplish your training and racing goals without endangering your health. If amenorrhea occurs, recognize it as a sign that your body is not healthy and that you need to seek medical treatment. Often, reducing your training slightly and gaining as little as five pounds can make a difference. If you coach or advise runners, don't weigh athletes and don't support or promote the fallacy that losing weight will make an athlete run faster.

The best chance for recovery from an eating disorder lies with early intervention. If you struggle with weight and body-image problems, or someone you train with or coach does, seek help immediately from someone you trust. Your goal or responsibility when dealing with a friend or teammate is not to change the person's behavior but to get them into treatment. Working with a team of professionals who specialize in treating eating disorders, such as a physician, a registered dietitian, and a therapist, gives the best results.

If you weigh yourself, don't fixate on a single number. Most runners perform their best by maintaining their weight within a range of a few pounds. If you're trying to lose weight while training, don't reduce calories by more than 20 percent and don't try to lose more than a pound a week. Keep the Food Guide Pyramid handy. If you have trouble balancing your running and eating habits or accepting your inherited body type, seek help from a registered dietitian or a mental-health expert who specializes in disordered-eating issues. Dieting can often be the trigger for developing a full-blown eating disorder, such as anorexia or bulimia nervosa.

Performance-Boosting Snacks

Think of snacks as minimeals. Include at least one food from one of the five food groups in each snack. Add a glass of water, juice, milk, or some other noncaffeinated beverage to help you stay hydrated.

- Instant oatmeal with dried apricots
- Cereal and low-fat milk
- Peanut butter and jelly sandwich (half or whole)
- Pita bread with melted low-fat cheese
- Rice cakes or crackers with humus or low-fat cheese
- Slice of pizza
- Microwave-baked potato topped with cottage cheese, salsa, or low-fat cheese
- Cup of soup and crackers
- Raw vegetables dipped in low-fat salad dressing
- Fruit smoothie or low-fat milk shake
- Fresh fruit dipped in yogurt or chocolate-flavored syrup
- Banana bread and milk
- Angel food cake with fresh berries or dipped in yogurt
- Cookies and milk
- Trail mix (nuts, raisins, dried fruit, etc.)

Training at Altitude

PETE PFITZINGER, MSc, MBA
Exercise physiologist, coach, 1984 and 1988 member of the
U.S. Olympic Marathon team, and senior writer for *Running Times*

Does a training system exist that can provide the hemoglobin-boosting benefits of breathing thin air without the potential fitness-lowering effects of training at altitude?

In their search for that elusive edge, many distance runners have looked to training at high elevations to enhance their natural abilities and the hard work they do at sea level. Can training at altitude, generally defined as elevations above 5,000 feet (1,600 meters), improve distance-running performance? If so, what exactly brings about these improvements? What are the best ways for runners to approach altitude training for maximal benefit and minimal risk of over-training and other possible complications?

The benefits to distance runners of living and training at high elevations were perhaps most notably on display at the 1968 Summer Olympic Games in Mexico City, which is located approximately 7,500 feet (2,300 meters) above sea level. There, athletes racing distances of 1,500 meters or longer who had lived or done at least some of their preparation at high elevations, such as the Kenyans, Ethiopians, Mexicans, and some

Europeans, had a distinct advantage over those who had done little or no high-altitude preparation (including most of the American team). Consequently, those who trained or lived at altitude before the Games dominated their events.

The results of those Games showed definitively that to compete well at high altitude, it is necessary to live and train at high altitude. What is much less clear, however, and what has been the subject of extensive research over more than 30 years, is whether living and training at altitude provides an advantage for competitions held at sea level.

Anecdotal reports abound of the advantages of being an altitude-trained runner in sea-level competitions. Some have argued that runners from the highlands of Kenya and Ethiopia have dominated the world distance-running scene because they have lived and trained all their lives in comparatively thin air and therefore have developed the heart and lungs to perform well in such conditions. The belief that the high-altitude living and training provide a performance advantage is seen in the popularity of running enclaves such as Boulder, Colorado, and Albuquerque, New Mexico. Both locations are filled with world-class athletes and hopefuls who are convinced that by training there they will achieve a long-sought breakthrough in their running.

But researchers who have performed well-controlled studies on the supposed altitude advantage have found mixed results. When athletes train at high elevations to prepare for sea-level races, they do not consistently perform better than when they train at sea level. By taking a look at the physiological effects of high-altitude living and training, and the latest ideas on how it can improve performance, runners can better answer questions about whether altitude training in any amount makes sense for them as a way to optimize their running performance.

What Does Altitude Training Do?

The primary benefit of training at high elevations is an increase in the natural production of the hormone erythropoietin (EPO). EPO in turn boosts the hemoglobin content of the blood. Oxygen attaches to hemoglobin for transport in the blood, so therefore a rise in EPO levels leads to an increase in the oxygen-carrying capacity of the blood. More oxygen reaches the working muscles without harder pumping by the heart. The result is that the runner can produce more energy aerobically and therefore maintain a faster pace. Furthermore, if your body isn't expending as much energy, you are able to maintain this faster pace longer. Additional benefits of altitude training include increases in the size and number of mitochondria (the part of the muscle fiber where energy is produced aerobically) and in the quantity of aerobic enzymes in the working muscles.

Can altitude training help you achieve a breakthrough?

© David Madison/Bruce Coleman Inc.

Training at high altitude, however, has one definite downside. Because of the reduced oxygen content of the air you breathe during training, you are not able to train as intensely as you can at sea level. Less-intense training produces a less-fit athlete. This probably explains why studies of athletes training at altitude to compete at sea level have had inconsistent results.

Altitude training practices vary among world-class athletes. Some live and train at altitude year round, some go to altitude for two to four weeks at a time, and others train at altitude for several months at a time.

Living High, Training Low: A New Variation on Altitude Training

More recently, the research findings about altitude training for distance runners have led exercise physiologists, coaches, and athletes to search for a training system that could can somehow provide the best of both worlds—that is, the hemoglobin-boosting benefits of breathing thin air without the potential fitness-lowering effects of training at altitude. The thought is that the ideal combination involves living at high altitude and coming down the mountain to do high-intensity training at a lower altitude. When athletes live and do all their training at altitude, the lowest beneficial altitude is thought to be approximately 5,000 feet (1,500 meters). When athletes live at altitude but do their high-intensity training at a lower elevation or at sea level, the lowest beneficial altitude for living and doing low-intensity training is open to debate but is generally thought to be 6,000 feet (1,800 meters) or greater. A low altitude for doing high-intensity training is considered anything below 3,000 feet (900 meters). By living and training in this way, the body increases its production of red blood cells, but the runner is able to maintain high-intensity training.

Several uncontrolled studies have been conduced on the benefits of living high and training low, and have found improvements in performance at sea level of up to four percent. For example, Chapman and colleagues conducted a study (Chapman, Stray-Gundersen, and Levine 1998) in which 22 elite runners lived and performed easy running at 8,000 feet (2,400 meters) but did their high intensity training at 4,000 feet (1,200 meters) for four weeks. The investigators found average improvements in 3K run time of 1.2 percent (approximately 6 seconds) after this live high and train low regimen. In addition, a great deal of anecdotal evidence exists in which athletes have lived at high altitude and trained at lower altitude and have run great races several weeks later.

A scientific study from Australia (Telford et al. 1996) found that a group of runners improved their two-mile run times by 7 percent after altitude training. Their control group, who trained together at sea level, also improved by 7 percent, which suggests that the improvements came from the training-camp environment (being away from day-to-day stresses, being able to train with other athletes, etc.) rather than the altitude.

Fortunately, Levine and colleagues have now conducted three well-controlled studies with distance runners on the benefits of living high and training low (Stray-Gundersen, Chapman, and Levine 1998; Levine and Stray-Gundersen 1997; and Levine, Stray-Gundersen, and Duhaime 1991). In these studies, one group of runners lived at 8,000 feet (2,400 meters) and trained at 4,000 feet (1,200 meters) while another group lived and trained at sea level, so that the benefits of living high and training low could be separated from the training camp effect. Those studies lasted four weeks and found additional improvements by the test group in 5K run time of 2.3 to 4.3 percent (approximately 14 to 26 seconds) and in $\dot{V}O_2$max of 3.1 to 5.4 percent. These studies clearly show that living high and training low leads to a benefit in running performance at sea level.

The optimal altitude for "living high" is 7,000 to 8,000 feet (2,100 to 2,400 meters).

At the February, 2000 International Altitude Training Symposium in Flagstaff, Arizona, Levine presented new data indicating that the optimal altitude for "living high" is 7,000 to 8,000 feet (2,100 to 2,400 meters).Living at altitudes of 9,000 feet (2,700 meters) or higher actually led to smaller improvements in performance than living at 7,000 to 8,000 feet. The problem with high-low training, of course, is logistics. Only a few places in the world allow you to live at a high altitude and quickly and conveniently travel to a low-altitude workout venue.

Altitude Living and Training Options

How can you bring the mountain to you? All right, suppose you're convinced of the potential benefits of living high and training low. If you're like most people, this is not a practicable option, given your current lifestyle and responsibilities. After all, how many of us can just pack up and move?

As a result of the growing interest in living high and training low, a few entrepreneurs have developed a variety of ingenious altitude simulators that artificially create high-altitude environments. Currently on the market are at least five different altitude simulators, which fall into three categories.

Houses or tents

This category includes two options. The first is the nitrogen house (also called an altitude house), which is a complete living area sealed off and brought to a low-oxygen concentration (as you would find at high altitude). The idea is to live in the house full time (except when training) and to breathe the thin air, thus developing high-altitude adaptations.

Altitude houses are permanent facilities available in only a few locations around the world. Of the methods discussed here, the altitude house simulates high altitude most closely and is the most generally accepted method. A study conducted with 22 world-class cross-country skiers and triathletes living in an altitude house in Finland (Rusko et al. 1999) found increases in red blood cell hemoglobin levels and $\dot{V}O_2max$ after 25 days of living at simulated altitude and training at sea level. Twelve athletes lived in the altitude house for 12 to 16 hours per day at a simulated altitude of 2,500 meters (8,200 feet), while the other 10 served as a control group. $\dot{V}O_2max$ increased by 3 percent, and red blood cell mass increased by 5 percent in the altitude-house group, while no increases occurred in the control group. This study clearly shows a benefit from living in an altitude house and training at sea level.

The other option is the altitude tent, a smaller sealed unit that you set up over a standard bed and sleep in at night. The cost is about $5,000 (U.S.). Over the past three years a number of elite runners, cyclists and triathletes have used altitude tents to obtain the benefits of high altitude living without having to travel to the mountains. Preliminary results of studies currently in progress indicate that sleeping in an altitude tent leads to performance improvements of 1 to 2 percent.

Hypoxic (low-oxygen) training chambers

These chambers, found in some health clubs, permit you to work out at simulated high altitude while you live at your normal residence. Using this method, however, contradicts the live-high, train-low model, and thus would seem to offer little benefit. It's possible, though, that training in the chambers could increase red blood cell count slightly in the endurance athlete. The theory seems to be that exposing red blood cells to high altitude during training might stimulate a training effect. As of now, good studies on the effectiveness of hypoxic training have not been completed, and little to no evidence is available to support use of the live-low, train-high method.

Intermittent hypoxic training

This method of taking advantage of the effects of high altitude, also known as high-altitude intervals, uses a device called a hypoxicator that allows the athlete to breathe air that simulates an altitude of up to 22,000 feet (6,700 meters) in five-minute intervals. At the UniSports Centre for Sport Performance in New Zealand, researchers use different settings for different athletes, depending primarily on the amount of arterial oxygen desaturation they experience, and intersperse such low-oxygen intervals with five-minute intervals of breathing sea-level air. In studies conducted in 1999 and 1998, the researchers at the Centre used the hypoxicator in their lab for three weeks with a 27:44 10K runner and several world-class triathletes. They found increases in hemoglobin of 0 to 5 percent. Another study, conducted in 1998 by Dr. John Hellemans in Christchurch, New Zealand, found similar increases in hemoglobin in a group of 10 runners, cyclists, swimmers, and triathletes after using the hypoxicator for 20 days. Dr. Hellemans found increases in hemoglobin of 4.3 percent, hematocrit of 5.0 percent, and improvements in time trials of 2.9 percent. Unfortunately, neither of these studies included control groups.

It's interesting to note that athletes exhibited much variation in both in how they felt using the hypoxicator and in how they responded physiologically. This reinforces what other studies have shown about altitude training—that athletes do not all respond to it in the same way.

The 1998 Chapman, Stray-Gundersen, and Levine study, published in the *Journal of Applied Physiology,* found large differences among subjects' responses to altitude training. Why the large differences? The current theory is that athletes who do not improve performance with altitude training are thought to have an EPO response that is insufficient to increase production of red blood cells. The message to the distance runner is that altitude training is not a sure bet for achieving breakthrough running.

My advice to the runner interested in altitude training, by whatever method available, is this. Before making plans to live high and train low, either by driving up and down mountains or investing in an altitude simulator, make sure you have a good coach and have put in several years of well-planned training. At that point, the slight benefit you may gain could be the difference between making an Olympic team and staying home to watch the Games on television.

Questions and Answers About Altitude Training

Q. If I plan to race at an altitude above 5,000 feet (1,500 meters), should I consider altitude training?

A. Yes, if you are racing at 5,000 feet or above, then you will definitely benefit from altitude training.

Q. What if I'm just doing one race per season at altitude, and it's not the Olympics or world championships?

A. If the race is not that important, then your decision should be based on the cost to you of training at altitude and the availability of a suitable training site.

Q. What type of training should I do at altitude and what type should I do at lower levels?

A. Low-intensity training (base training, easy aerobic running) can be done at altitude. If possible, you should avoid doing high-intensity running (intervals, repetitions) at altitude because you will not be able to train as intensely and will therefore induce less of a stimulus to improve.

Q. Should I change my diet at all in preparation for altitude training and while training at altitude?

A. It is important to have adequate iron levels before going to altitude. Have a blood test two months before going to altitude so you will have time to raise your hemoglobin levels or iron stores (ferritin) if they are low. Also, make sure iron intake is adequate while at altitude, either through diet alone or through diet and supplementation.

Q. What about hydration when training at altitude?

A. Low humidity levels at high altitude can lead to dehydration. Take care to remain well hydrated during sojourns to altitude.

Q. What other precautions about altitude training should I be aware of?

A. The sun's ultraviolet (UV) rays are stronger at high altitude because they have not been absorbed as much by the earth's atmosphere, so use sunblock and avoid prolonged exposure to direct sun.

PART II

Breakthrough Racing

In part I we focused on training—that is, conditioning the body and mind to rise to a higher level of performance by following a progressive, systematic program of running and other activities and lifestyle enhancements. Part II turns to the testing ground for that breakthrough performance, which for many distance runners is the competitive arena, racing. The 10 chapters in this section outline for distance runners at all levels the philosophy behind racing, the many and varied choices in the competitive realm, and how to prepare and execute optimally in a race situation.

Part II is in many ways inseparable from part I of the book, and it builds on the lessons learned in the first 14 chapters, which you have most likely already read. As we noted at the beginning of part I, everything you do to improve your running is connected to everything else. Again, you will find as you read the words of the experts who contributed to this section that each has his or her perspective on how you can be the best runner you can be, and what being the best means. You will again find that our group of experts all agree that a comprehensive, holistic approach to running and all that supports it is the best way to enjoy and benefit from the sport. Here is a closer look ahead to what you will find in part II.

Why we race is the topic of chapter 15, on racing philosophy, by *Running Times* editor-in-chief Gordon Bakoulis. Indeed, many long-time runners rarely or never race; others pin on a number only for certain special events, such as a run to benefit their favorite charity. They race for fun rather than for the competition. But for the majority of runners interested in achieving a breakthrough, the racing scene—roads, track, cross country, or trails—is where they test their mettle. In this chapter, Bakoulis draws on the stories of more than a dozen runners who at some point made the transition from runner to racer. These individuals describe in their own words just what prompted that shift, what it felt like, and where wearing the racer label has led them in their running and in the rest of their lives. The chapter also includes a section on race goal setting and a checklist of responses to the runner's question, "Should I race?" It provides a setup for the rest of the section, as well as motivation for both the novice racer and the veteran runner who, at some point, may have grown stale on racing.

Chapter 16 is a trip through both history and the contemporary racing scene, guiding runners through the varied competitive options available to them. Running writer and 34-minute 10K runner Jonathan Beverly leads the tour, which explores the origins of track, cross country, road, trail, and ultradistance racing, including explanations of how runners can become involved in all these genres. Beverly, whose own racing experience ranges from fell (mountain) running in rural Ireland to European marathons to extensive track and cross country, brings his enthusiasm and wide-ranging research to this delightful guide. Runners of all levels and backgrounds will learn and gain motivation by realizing the many options out there.

In chapter 17, veteran apparel industry manager Teresa Gibreal of Phidippides running store in Atlanta discusses the all-important topic of what to wear to the races. As Gibreal makes eminently clear, the choice of race-day apparel is much more about function than simply looking good (although that counts too, and it isn't precluded, given today's array of functional running gear that also looks fabulous). The chapter features discussions of dressing for both heat and cold on race day, including mention of the latest performance fabrics designed for sleekness and speed as well as protection from the elements. You will benefit from carefully absorbing this information, whether you're a veteran of the days of sweats and itchy nylon track suits or a newcomer to the competitive scene.

Chapter 18 concerns the footwear that some runners wear for their competitive outings, commonly known as racing flats. Veteran members of the retail running industry Kirk Rosenbach and Gregory Sheats, both of Atlanta, explain the need for these speed-promoting shoes among some (but not all) runners attempting to achieve a breakthrough in their running. The material builds upon information and advice presented in chapter 4 on training footwear, also authored by Rosenbach and Sheats. The writers draw comparisons between training shoes and racing flats, and detail the occasions when runners might want to consider using the latter option in their racing and possibly their fast training. Also included is a section on selecting racing flats, using the same foot-function criteria that the authors explained in chapter 4.

Chapters 19 through 22 are really the meat of this section of the book, as they spell out exactly how the performance-oriented runner can best prepare the mind and the body for race situations. In chapter 19, prominent coach and former world-class runner (2:12 marathoner) Tom Fleming tells runners how to peak for their competitive endeavors. The chapter, divided into physical peaking and mental peaking, covers such topics as how long a runner can hold a peak, the value of a coach, and a step-by-step, week-by-week guide to peaking at various distances. Fleming draws on his experience as a fiercely competitive athlete all over the world, as well as his coaching of such athletes as Anne Marie Lauck, Joe LeMay, and Elaine Van Blunk. It's a vital chapter to read in the context of this overall section of the book.

Chapter 20 builds on the information presented by Fleming. Here we have harnessed the writing talents and drawn upon the experience of running writer and 2:15 marathon runner Jim Hage, winner of two Marine Corps Marathons. Hage writes here about the whole process of preparing to race, which can include peaking but also encompasses buildup races, which many runners train through as part of their preparation for a more important competition. The information gathered and presented here by Hage ranges from down to earth (don't forget to pack your timing chip in your race bag the night before the race) to esoteric (how to ready your mind for competition).

Every runner who has sought to improve in the sport knows what a powerful tool the mind can be. In chapter 21, sport psychologist, running coach, and former elite runner Andy Palmer, PhD, presents compelling evidence about just how essential the mental component is to breakthrough racing. Palmer structures the process of developing a racing mindset into a six-step process: making the decision, consulting knowledgeable resources, deciding what's negotiable, determining goals, planning for success, and learning to balance your life. Palmer's chapter leads readers through that process and, most important, shows how runners of all levels and backgrounds can apply it. He draws upon three areas—his knowledge of psychology, his coaching background, and his experience as an elite runner.

All the preparation and mental techniques that a performance runner brings to racing, important as they are, count for little without a properly developed set of tactics or strategies to get through the race itself. Chapter 22 is a nuts-and-bolts look at the various methods runners can use once the gun goes off to ensure a successful race performance. Team coach and former U.S. Olympic Marathon Trials qualifier Randy Accetta brings all his experience and insight to the topic. The chapter builds on information presented elsewhere in the section (particularly the introductory chapter on racing philosophy) by including a discussion of what distinguishes runners from racers. Also included are a list of dos and don'ts for racing and a set of specific instructions for track racing that detail tactics to employ in various positions within a pack.

We've already provided information and guidelines in chapter 13 on how to fuel yourself for healthy and performance-oriented training. Chapter 23 expands on that material with a discussion of how runners can best fuel themselves for their competitive endeavors. In this chapter, sports nutritionist Jackie Berning, MS, RD, answers such important questions as what to eat and drink the night before and morning of a race, and how to eat and drink to promote recovery from racing various distances. Berning presents her material in the context of a discussion about fueling runners for optimal performance with a diet that includes a balance of carbohydrate, fat, and protein intake and adequate fluids, vitamins, and minerals. She affirms that no magic pill is available that runners can take to perform their best on race day. Rather, a runner will race his or her best consistently by adhering to a sensible, adequate, and balanced diet during all phases of training as well as near the time of an important race.

A refutation of the concept of a magic bullet to produce breakthrough race results is carried into chapter 24, which concerns one of the darker aspects of competitive running, the use of illegal performance-enhancing drugs and techniques. In this chapter, running journalist Jim Ferstle, who has extensively covered the drug issue in competitive sports, outlines runners' search for the competitive edge through drug taking as it has gone on from the 1950s, starting with the use of amphetamines, into the 21st century. It's a sorry tale in which some athletes in endurance sports, including runners, literally risk their lives through their use of banned drugs and techniques with potentially serious health consequences. Clearly, although drug-taking may have provided short-term benefits for some runners over the years, this is not the way to attempt a breakthrough. Ferstle casts a glimpse into the future, expressing hope that athletes, including runners, will care enough to join the leaders of their sports to level the playing field and restore a sense of fair play to competition.

Part II as a whole demonstrates to the performance-oriented runner that many routes are open to making a breakthrough in the competitive arena of the sport. These routes are interconnected and overlapping, and in truth, the runner must follow all in some way to maintain a breakthrough approach to running over time. After completing this part of *The Running Times Guide to Breakthrough Running*, the runner will be equipped to combine the training methods explored in part I with various approaches to maximizing success on race day. These approaches carry over the philosophy of consistent and dedicated effort presented in part I, reminding the runner that any running breakthrough takes time and commitment if it is to be lasting and real.

The Racer in You

GORDON BAKOULIS
Editor-in-chief of *Running Times*, coach, and
four-time U. S. Olympic Marathon Trials qualifier

> In what other sport do world-class athletes toe the same starting line and cover the same ground as those just getting started in the sport?

Running is a unique athletic activity because virtually anyone can do it. Moreover, anyone who chooses to do so can become involved in the competitive aspect of the sport. You don't have to pass a test, learn a complex set of skills, join or form a team, invest in expensive equipment, or (in most areas) travel great distances to find an event. Any individual can enter a race and participate—even if it's the first time he or she ever slipped on running shoes.

Some people who enter road races do no running at all apart from the actual races. Of course, it makes more sense to prepare for races with training, even if the runner has no interest in winning or beating others. The point is that running is just about the most accessible and egalitarian sport there is. In what other sport do world-class athletes toe the same starting line and cover the same ground as those just getting started in the sport?

Part II of *The Running Times Guide to Breakthrough Running* is for those whose goals in running include performing to their competitive potential. Reading and absorbing the information and ideas in this section, although it won't guarantee you PRs, will help you see what steps you need to take to put it all together on the starting line. Your adjustments may be physical, such as learning to control your early pace so you don't run out of gas miles before the finish. They may be mental, such as developing a more competitive mindset. They may be logistical, such as remembering to pack your bag for a race the night before instead of the morning of, when you're nervous and scatterbrained. These adjustments and others are discussed throughout part II of this book.

Of course, many people run for years—even a lifetime—and never once race. These folks run for the fitness and lifestyle benefits—including weight control, socializing, mental health, and being part of a popular and admired activity. The idea of putting their fitness to the test against other runners does not interest them. Moreover, many participants enter road races not to compete or test their performance limits but to enjoy the social and recreational aspects or, increasingly, to support a charitable cause. If asked, these people would not consider themselves racers.

For many runners, making the step from running for fitness and recreation to racing represents a significant breakthrough. We asked a number of runners who run and compete at different levels to describe their transition from runner to racer. The responses we received describe experiences that fall into several general categories.

Making the transition from runner to racer involes physical, mental, and logistical adjustments.

Runner to Racer: Making the Transition

Every racer's story of how he or she became competitive in the sport is different. I asked a handful of runners to share their experiences and got the responses presented here. These anecdotes speak powerfully about both the attractions and challenges of being a competitive runner.

Doing It for Myself

I have been running since I was 12 years old. Middle school and high school track and cross country tried to suck me into the spirit of competition, but it was never enough. Often I found myself running because my coach was pacing me on a bicycle yelling, "Pick it up! Run!" rather than running because I wanted to better my condition, my time, or my finishing place.

After my 16th birthday, a group of boys enticed me to run the Houston Marathon with them. "What's a marathon?" I naively asked. I gave a firm, unwavering, "No!" when I learned it was 26.2 miles.

Something, however, grabbed me about this idea, especially since the young men egging me on were well-known couch potatoes. "If they can do it, then surely I can do it," I thought. I committed myself to showing them up. Five months later I completed my first marathon in 4:02, beating those boys by 45 minutes. I was the victor just for crossing the finish line. I never returned to track. Instead, I found my heart swept away by road races, especially marathons. Soon, just pushing for the finish line was not enough. I wanted more. At the 1998 Dallas White Rock Marathon, I decided to compete against the clock to qualify for the 1999 Boston Marathon by running under 3:40. As I finished, taking first in my age group with a 3:29:55, I puked four times. But I had qualified.

The urge to compete is now in my blood. I want to be faster, better, and more focused. I want those digits on that clock to drop, yielding to my determination every time I run. I will race the clock and I will hope each time to win.

  Andrea Schettler, 22, Austin, Texas

If anyone had told me I would become a competitive runner, I would have laughed. As a kid, I was fat and not very coordinated. At age 33, however, frustrated with a very busy spouse, three kids, and graduate-school demands, I decided to try what my husband did every night—head out the door for a run.

My first efforts were feeble. After several weeks I found I could make it around a long block. I also discovered that I really liked the freedom and solitude. By the time I returned from my 20-minute jaunt, my husband, Hap, usually had all three kids in bed. For more than a year, running around the block was all I did. The first time I ran home from my parents' house, less than two miles away, I suggested Hap leave later in the car so he could pick me up at the mile mark if I was exhausted. When he passed me, I waved him on.

Hap sometimes ran in races, and after I had been running about two years, he encouraged me to start thinking about running a St. Patrick's Day race that started near our house. The distance was five miles, which seemed formidable even though I had increased my mileage and was running to graduate school and back, three miles each way. The week before the race I ran five miles all at once and felt OK.

Conditions on race day were windy and cold and there was some snow and ice on the route. About 100 men, 3 women, and 5 St. Patrick's Day Queen contestants lined up at the start. I looked at the queen hopefuls in their jeans and loafers and vowed to beat all of them.

I passed most of them by the second mile; I don't think any finished. I was, however, one of the last in the pack, and by the third mile I was told I had to run on the sidewalk because they were opening the streets to traffic. Still, I was wearing a big smile as I rounded the last corner and ran downhill to the finish line. I was the last woman but I beat six or seven men. I was hooked.

Judy Lutter, 60, founder and president of the Melpomene Institute, St. Paul, Minnesota

Finding a Hidden Talent Within

I was never athletic. My high school had no girls' teams or even physical education. Until age 29 I had managed to rarely break a sweat. In the summer of 1978 I was finishing my master's degree and had lots of spare time. I noticed many joggers on campus and since I had coached my middle school girls to three straight district titles, I figured I could be a jogger.

I went to the track, where I humiliated myself by not being able to go around the oval. My type A personality would not admit defeat, and I kept at it until I was able to complete the cross country parcourse. A month later I heard there was a five-mile race on campus. I figured I could do that and stood on the front line. I passed the mile mark at seven minutes and then died a painful death. At two and a half miles I passed the dorm and was tempted to bag it. Nevertheless, I finished and won an age-group ribbon. A racer was born.

One August one of my daughters joined me on my daily runs. We entered a 5K on Labor Day and finished dead last. This time, however, we earned a T-shirt (which is still a favorite). You would have thought we were champions as we lorded those shirts over the other half of the family. In time both my husband and our other daughter joined us.

I joined a local running club and met other runners. I began to do track work with a wonderful volunteer coach. I was not the most talented, but I worked hard. He took us to a race and entered about 10 of us. As I approached the finish line, I heard my coach asking where all of my teammates were. They were all behind me.

Our family returned to the Labor Day 5K the following year, and I won in 18:32. Since then I have won hundreds of trophies and met some of my most wonderful friends. Running got me through my doctorate, a divorce, and many of life's ups and downs. On a good day I can still break 40 minutes for 10K, and I still love competition. I never set out to be a racer, but I have never wished it any other way. At age 50 I continue to race and beat most of the women in the field. It only gets better.

  Carolyn Mather, Morganton, Georgia

I was a basketball player who ran to stay in shape for basketball. One Labor Day weekend, a girlfriend asked me to join her in a half marathon in St. Francis, New Brunswick, Canada. I was just going to run with her when my dad told me that he was going to come watch. Since it was my dad, I figured I had to push, but I had no idea how to run a race of that distance.

It was a small race, about 50 people, and I started conservatively. At about the one-and-a-half-mile mark we had to cross a railroad track. A train was coming. I was in about the middle of the field and was the last one to get across the track before the train came. I was quite a ways behind the leaders, but it was a long train and I figured that no one was going to catch me so I could take some chances. I just began to focus on the people in front and reel them in one by one. I ended up finishing fourth in 1:17:36. I was pretty happy. The next day there was a four-mile race in Caribou, Maine, in which I finished in fourth again in about 22 minutes. At that point I decided I could be a competitive runner.

  Andy Palmer, PhD, sport psychologist, coach, and former Olympic
  Marathon Trials qualifier, Atlanta, Georgia

Discovering Self-Confidence

I was very happy doing my 3-mile run as many days as I could get out there. I'd rush home from work, toss off the heels and stockings, and pull on the tights and running shoes. Heading out the door, I would enter another world, calm and serene. This went on for some years until a friend convinced me to run a marathon. The leap from 3 to 26 miles seemed insurmountable, but I was determined. The training programs said I should try a shorter race first. I had never been to a road race, nor cared to participate in one. I didn't view myself as competitive, although I had played college lacrosse and could still recall the rush of scoring a goal.

My town was holding a 10K race, so I decided to bite the bullet and enter. It wasn't difficult to increase the miles, as I did it in a planned manner so as not to injure myself. I wasn't interested in time, only endurance—seeing if I could finish without stopping. The day of the race I was very nervous. The entire town comes out for this event, and the streets were lined. All of a sudden, I could sense the enormous difference between my daily runs and this major event. I was shaking when the gun went off. I ran as fast as I could in an uncontrolled manner, never stopping for water or changing my pace. Adrenaline pumped through me, urging me on faster and faster. I had no idea where I was in the pack. When I turned the corner and saw the finish line, there was one woman ahead of me. I knew I could take her if I ran harder, but I didn't want to seem aggressive, so I slowed down and politely followed her into the chute. Later on, I learned that my politeness cost me second place in my division. I was furious. If I ever doubted that I had a competitive streak, here was proof that I definitely possessed one! Never again would I allow myself to hold back for anyone. In that once instance, I discovered the racer hidden beneath the runner.

Gail Waesche Kislevitz, freelance writer, Ridgewood, New Jersey

I hated what I saw in the mirror. I was 11 years old, 10 pounds overweight, and miserable. I was insanely jealous of the "popular" kids at school. I knew it wasn't considered cool to talk to your parents, but in desperation, I confided in my mom.

Mom had an idea. I was skeptical, but I listened. Her idea was for me to run around the block—about one mile—before dinner each night. I had been involved in sports when I was younger and swam on a swim team in the summer, but during the school year I wasn't involved in anything athletic. I decided to give it a try.

The next afternoon, Mom and I started our first run. Within a quarter mile I was walking, doubled over with agonizing cramps. Discouraged, I started to turn back, but with some incentive from Mom, I kept going and walked the rest of the mile.

Weeks went by. Every day, Mom and I would go for our run. I worked up to running the entire mile and then two miles. With my new self-confidence, I decided to try out for the cheerleading squad. I was cut, so I tried out for the soccer team and went on to play field hockey, swim, and run track in high school. Although I was recruited to play hockey at Lehigh University, the allure of running was too much. I had run a few races and found myself longingly watching the cross country runners disappear into the cornfields while I attended hockey preseason camp. Within a week, I handed in my hockey stick and became the cross country team's only walk-on. By senior year, I was a captain and in love with running and racing.

One day, when I was home for Thanksgiving break my sophomore year, I asked Mom if she'd like to go for a run. She said that she hadn't really thought about running lately. I insisted, she changed, and off we went to do our old one-mile loop. After a quarter mile, Mom had to stop, doubled over with cramps. She said she thought she'd turn back and I said, "How about walking the rest of the way?" She did.

It's been 20 years since my first run around the block. Since then, Mom has run four marathons, and I just completed my sixth. I'll be running in the 2000 Olympic Marathon Trials, and Mom will be there cheering.

Laurie Corbin, writer and nutritionist, Morristown, New Jersey

I began by running just a few times on a short, flat course before my coach encouraged me to extend my distance. As I got into better shape, my personal competitiveness and the feeling of being stronger got the better of me, and I enrolled in my first race, a 10K. I suffered through it, sustained a foot injury, recovered, and went on to four more years of injury-ridden competitive running, which included two badly run marathons and dozens of races at various distances, including my favorite, the half marathon. I left running, four years after I had started, after my third triathlon to move and get married.

After taking several years off I began running again recently, and now find myself in the same place I was 11 years ago—running for exercise and mental health and, unlike the first go-round, actively trying not to get caught up in an overly competitive mindset. I will have a second chance now that I'm returning to see if I can keep my competitiveness under control as I have a tendency toward stress fractures and tendinitis.

Tony Candela, 45, Bronx, New York, the first blind runner to participate in the Central Park Triathlon

Competing for a Larger Purpose

This transition was very vivid to me. Several things happened. First, when I was a marathon runner from 1967 to 1972, the whole issue was first just completing a marathon, and then campaigning for women's official inclusion in the sport. We were officially included for the first time in a major marathon in the United States in Boston in 1972. It was a landmark, officially acknowledging us as real athletes. Up to that point I felt I had to keep showing that I could always look feminine and tidy, have a smile, never show hurt or exhaustion. I was always afraid that, as happened in 1928 when women lost for 32 years the right to compete in Olympic events involving more than one lap of the 400-meter track, it could be taken away from us.

So in 1972, official at last, I decided to really push. Also, I didn't want to get to 40 years old and realize that I'd never given it all I had to be all the athlete I could be. I knew I didn't have a lot of basic talent, but I wanted to go to the absolute limits of myself. I didn't want any regrets or wondering.

When I ran 2:51 in Boston in 1975, on a perfect day with a tailwind, after three years of doing 110-plus miles a week, I felt elated, like I'd "arrived" at last. When I looked at the time at the finish, the order of women's marathon rankings clicked over like the timetable in Penn Station. I was number three in the United States and number six in the world! I felt also like I'd run myself right to the limit. It was the first time I couldn't wait to run the marathon, with no sense of dread, only that I wanted to attack the course. I felt utterly fearless at the start, and throughout the race the road seemed to come to me rather than me slogging over it.

At the time there were not always enough women around to know you'd have a race. But there were a few of us, and for the first time in races around that time, I actually raced other women, neck-and-neck stuff. It was just a whole different feeling.

While I'm happy being back to being a jogger, nothing is quite so dizzying as that feeling of being in the best shape of your life, and then of laying your hand across your own thigh and really, physically feeling it to the touch!

Kathrine Switzer, director of Avon Running, New York City

Finding My Competitive Niche

In the world of ultrarunning, especially in ultras that take place on mountain trails, every racer who completes the event is a winner, and anyone who survives is competitive. Although I always enjoyed running as a soccer player in high school and college, it was not until I started competitively running marathons after college that I would say I broke through from runner to racer.

The marathons lead to triathlons and, in turn, to ultradistance running. My real breakthrough as a racer came at age 30, when I started to win or place in most of the ultras in which I competed. I was drawn to the idea that I could enter a trail ultra and just enjoy being out there with so many people, taking in the scenery and wildlife and adventure of the event without any competitive BS getting in the way. The sense of spiritual assistance that you receive from the field is amplified in ultras in ways I cannot begin to explain. It was that spirit and the incredible momentum that I received both from being in front of the field and pushing to do so from race to race that made my transition from runner to racer happen.

Now, having entered the most challenging race of my life, parenthood, I wonder if I will be able to weather the transition back from racer to runner *without suffering too much. I am optimistic that the change back (or forward) will be a temporary one.*

   Adam Chase, attorney and ultrarunner, Boulder, Colorado

Keeping My Running Fun

My childhood friend Holly Chase unwittingly helped me become a competitive runner. I was seven years old when I succumbed to "strategic abandon," for a sort of planned-out free-for-all that typified (and still typifies) my running. Strategic abandon made me change from "runner" to "racer."

   Holly and I competed in everything. She was the tallest kid in our class, I was the shortest, and we made quite a pair gutting it out for those kickballs. What always tickled me was the idea of outrunning others—or at least matching them stride for stride, since I had a weirdly long stride for my height. During the coed track season in middle school, I was urged to "give the boys a run for their money."

   It was when I ran in an all-girls cross country race, however, that I became serious about racing. Competition now allowed me, a goofy little nonthreatening redhead, to make a competitive statement: I'm starting as fast as I can, and I'm finishing as fast as I can. I didn't say it out loud, but I acted it out loud.

   In high school cross country, I was always in the racing mode. I had a wonderful coach who introduced me to team strategy, but I still ran hard from the start. Real-life troubles hounded me during those years, but none mattered whenever I ran. So I ran a lot. My training took on the edge of insanity during summer vacations. Every day I'd run morning, midday, and evening, amassing at least 15 miles. Back at school, I became just rested enough to race undefeated and win the interscholastic cross country championships.

   These days, my strategy is to shift between risky fun (competition's strategic abandon) and my old-time childhood type of frisky running (noncompetitive wild abandon). My major transition to racer had happened long ago, when I first realized that running became a lot more fun when I had a secret little plan to carry out along the way.

   Fiona Bayly, freelance writer, New York City

Clearly, being a competitive runner involves making some sort of commitment to getting faster or holding to a certain standard. The anecdotes included here—and they are just a sampling of many more stories that have been told to me by runners of all backgrounds and competitive levels—show that runners embrace competition because it is fun, offers a challenge, and helps them uncover aspects of their nature that they often did not even know were there. Women especially, often socialized to be meek and deferring, learn by competing as runners that it's OK—it's great!—to be winners in sport, and therefore in life.

The competitive standard that a runner strives for and achieves varies widely, of course. It depends entirely on the individual and can change over the course of one's involvement in running. A young runner, for example, might strive to make her high school or college team. Once there, she may endeavor to score for the team, place highly in team races, and perhaps qualify for state, regional, or national championships. After college, the runner might try to make it as an open track, cross country, or road runner. Or she might choose instead to join a road-running club, compete on the local road-racing scene, or simply run for fitness and camaraderie. Some runners get into the sport later in life and become drawn to age-group competition in their 40s, 50s, and beyond. Some move toward marathons and ultras as their experience deepens in the sport. These days, a number of runners gravitate toward duathlons, triathlons, adventure racing, and other competitive outlets that include running and are becoming increasingly common. Runners are fortunate that their sport can accommodate all these levels and types of involvement. Happily, runners can participate in their sport in a variety of venues—roads, track, cross country, trail, and mountain running—and can easily carry over their skills to sports such as cross-country skiing and snowshoeing.

> Runners embrace competition for the fun, the challenge, and to uncover aspects of their nature that they did not even know were there.

Setting Racing Goals

It's said that you must have goals in order to succeed. I'm not entirely sure that's true, because some of my best races were ones in which I stood on the starting line, looked around at the competition, and said to myself, "Omigod, I'm gonna croak!" In other words, my only goal as the gun went off was to survive the race experience! Seriously, though, I believe it is essential for a competitive athlete in any sport to develop an overall plan, to have a sense of how you are going to achieve it, and—most important—to hold on to that goal and plan when competing.

If you ask a group of competitive runners about their goals, most of them would say that they'd like to get faster. (A group of 40-and-over runners might say they'd like to slow down as little as possible.) For the first year or so of my competitive running career, improving my times was my only wish. Quickly, though, my goals took on more concrete form. I started breaking down my races into various sections and focusing on specific aspects, such as getting a clean start, not falling asleep and losing the pace in the middle miles, and striving to have a kick at the end. I also aimed to improve my times mile by mile (say, 10 seconds per mile), which added up to significant overall improvements in my times.

Runners can participate in their sport in a variety of venues that accomodate different levels and types of involvement.

© Irene Owsley Spector

Racing offers two basic types of goals—time goals and place goals. Different goals might be appropriate for different situations. For example, you might run a race on a flat course under perfect conditions and decide that today is the day to go for a PR because you may not have another such opportunity. Runners who competed in the 1994 Boston Marathon, with its memorable tailwind, say they felt that way on the starting line. It was a day for great times, a day that produced both men's and women's course records; positions mattered far less. At other times, place is everything. Who remembers the winning times in Olympic final events? (OK, we remember Michael Johnson's 19.32 in the 200 meters in Atlanta in 1996.) What matters is who winds up with the gold, silver, and bronze. Months or even years in advance, athletes set their race-day goals accordingly for these particular events.

Some athletes are generally more motivated by goals of beating others or placing well than by time-related goals. I tend to fall into that category. Although I improved early in my career by setting ever-faster time goals for myself, what really propelled me once the gun went off was winning the race or placing as highly as I could. I'm very competitive with other people, and I wanted to beat the women I saw as my rivals. I wanted to outduel them in head-to-head battles; I wanted to break the tape. I still do. I'm proud of my PRs, and no one can ever take those times away from me. But in the heat of the moment, I'd rather have a win than a fast time. Of course, by setting my sights on winning and seeking out races that offered excellent competition, the times took care of themselves.

I find it hard to imagine that a runner can improve competitively without setting goals. In fact, as noted in chapter 1, it's important to have goals as a motivational force in your running even if you don't race. Setting goals such as improving health and fitness will get you out the door to run when it's dark, cold, and rainy, when you "don't have time," when you just plain don't feel like it. Having a competitive goal simply adds fuel to your motivational fire.

The authors of the chapters in part II will have a lot to say about how setting goals relates to making breakthroughs in racing. Let me just add my thoughts about how to set useful goals:

- Set a racing goal that makes you gulp or curl your toes. If it's too easy, it won't motivate you to give your all.
- On the other hand, don't set a ridiculous goal. A marathoner who's only run 3:30 after 10 years in the sport is unlikely to win an Olympic gold medal. Use pace charts and prediction formulas to help you set pace goals for distances you haven't yet attempted.
- Write down your goal. Look at it frequently and say it aloud. This will make it more real, more a part of you.
- Set intermediate goals along the way to your ultimate goal. For instance, if your ultimate goal is to qualify for the Olympic Marathon Trials, have one of your intermediate goals be running a half marathon that predicts a marathon in the range you'll need to achieve.

Why Race?

It's useful to ask yourself why you race, especially if you are new to racing, coming back to it after a break, or looking for motivation to continue racing. In the stories of runners becoming racers included earlier, some runners said they sometimes wished they could go back to being just runners, without all the pressure and physical pain of racing. Yes, racing is hard. It requires discipline, sacrifice, and risk taking, and it dramatically increases the risk of injury. Many runners just don't want that from an activity that's supposed to be relaxing and good for them.

Here are some reasons you may want to consider if you're wondering whether you should race.

- Racing is rewarding. You've heard it said that nothing important in life comes easy. That's certainly true of racing. The harder you work, the greater the feeling of satisfaction you receive from a well-executed effort.

- Racing is progressive. Running is a sport in which, perhaps more than any other, effort equals achievement. If you work hard, train smart, and avoid injury, you will get faster, plain and simple. Of course, at a certain point you will plateau and then eventually see a decline. The trick then is to set alternative goals, such as placing well in your age group.

- Racing is fun. You'll enjoy tremendous camaraderie in being part of the racing scene, whether it's your high school or college team, a series of all-comers track meets, the local road-race circuit, the trail-running or ultra network, or a group of triathletes. Regular racers develop great respect for their competition. In many communities, battles among running teams or clubs are fierce—but all in fun. One New York City runner said that running a race in Central Park feels like playing those big games of kick-the-can at the playground when you were a kid.

- Racing is a mystery. When you step to the line, you never know exactly what's going to happen between the time the gun goes off and the moment you cross the finish line. When I'm one of the top entrants in a race and a reporter asks me, "So, how do you think you're going to do out there?" I feel like saying, "I don't know, that's why I'm going to run the race!"

Although your training should give you a fairly good idea of what to aim for in a race, you don't know what kind of a day you're going to have or how your competitors will fare. That's what makes you tingle to the tips of your fingers as you stand there waiting for the gun to fire. Pin on your number and take your chances!

16

Preparing for Your Race Distance

JONATHAN H. BEVERLY
Running writer for *Running Times, Runner's World, New York Runner,* and other publications; 34-minute 10K runner

Racing gives our running focus, encourages planning and goal setting, and adds an extra shot of motivation.

A student once made an insightful comment to me. "When you don't have a final exam," he said, "it takes all the energy out of the class." Many runners find the same relationship between running and racing. Races are the finals that put energy into our running. Although we run for reasons other than preparing to race, just as we study for objectives beyond passing an exam, racing gives our running focus, encourages planning and goal setting, and adds an extra shot of motivation to each run. Racing provides punctuation for our running lives.

Races, however, are much more than an external prod to encourage our running—they are themselves an absorbing and addictive pleasure. The late philosopher-runner George Sheehan called racing "the lovemaking of the runner." Racing is the consummation of our running passion—part performance, part dance, part parade, part test, part bloody battle. Few experiences hold the range and intensity of a race well run.

Different reasons draw different runners, and different runners are drawn to different races. Fortunately, the running world lays out a smorgasbord of choices with events catering to every personality, body type, and competitive style.

Road Racing 5K to Marathon

The road race is the staple of the American runner. On prime weekends of the year, you can find a road race in nearly every county in the country. Sponsored by local clubs, businesses, and community organizations and often offering musical entertainment, postrace refreshments, gifts, prize drawings, and, of course, souvenir T-shirts, road races combine elements of a county fair with athletic competition.

The defining characteristic of the road race is its venue—on the streets and highways of our cities, parks, and countryside. Most road races grow out of grassroots efforts: local associations or individuals conceive, organize, and direct them. Their relationship to national or international governing bodies often extends only to the official measurement of the course, if that.

Road races are also open—they welcome all who pay the entry fee and have the courage to pin on a number declaring themselves official participants. All competitors (female and male, fast and slow) start together and run the same course, which is wide enough to accommodate large packs of competitors.

The tradition of open races can be traced back to community games that have surrounded fairs and markets of Scotland and Ireland for centuries. These races often commemorate historic stories of races held by kings and lords to select messengers or even brides (the winner of one such race reputedly ran away when she saw her "prize," leading one to question the nobleman's selection method!). Later we hear of races staged by English gentry in the 17th and 18th centuries between their professional "footmen."

The upper and middle classes entered the racing scene as running became popular in schools of the Victorian era as a way to build health and moral fortitude. The Olympic movement in the late 19th century and the amateur athletic associations in the United Kingdom and the United States formalized "amateur" competition among the upper classes, relegating traditional open races to "professional" status.

During the 19th and early 20th centuries in the United States, athletic clubs whose memberships were based on ethnicity or class hosted amateur races of various distances throughout the year. Communities and associations also continued to sponsor professional races that drew large crowds of spectators. Resembling boxing matches more than today's participant races, these staged contests between small groups (sometimes only two, in one-on-one duels) were considered arcane and dangerous by spectators. Public

Road races welcome all who pay the entry fee and have the courage to pin on a number.

© Les and Viola Van/Unicorn Stock Photos

interest in the spectacle of running waxed and waned throughout the first half of the 20th century, and runners remained a small, obscure population.

This all changed with the fitness craze of the 1960s and 1970s. When masses began "jogging" for health, they also started gathering at weekend races. Yet old strictures still stood, insisting that runners be members of clubs to be eligible to race in official "amateur" events, thus excluding women, blacks, and lower-class runners. Led by members of the Harlem-based Pioneers Club, runners formed their own association—the Road Runners Club of America (RRCA)—which was instrumental in opening the sport to all and breaking down the artificial division between amateurs and professionals.

The RRCA also led the way in certifying course measurements, securing liability insurance for races, and recognizing the achievements of all runners with age-group awards, finisher's T-shirts, certificates, and medals. Many of today's races were born in the running boom of the late 1970s, and more are added each year in the open and encouraging climate of today's running world. The 1990s have witnessed what many call the second running boom. The new climate has opened the door not only to all races and classes and both genders but to all speeds as well. The new breed of runner often cares more about having a good time than running a fast time. Although median finish times in road races have plummeted, participation has soared to new heights. New races often raise money for charities, making the events vehicles for specific causes rather than ends in themselves.

Despite their occasional carnival atmosphere, road races are also serious competitions. Most road races award prizes to the top finishers and the top runners in each age group—usually in 5- or 10-year divisions. In the larger races the top runners compete for significant prize money. The first finishers enjoy racing in its purest form—in head-to-head competition where all can see who crosses the line first.

In age-group competitions it is often difficult to identify your competitors (especially because runners never show their age), so an award may come as a surprise when the event is over. A recent trend is to award prizes based on age-graded performances—adjusting finish times based on statistical tables of world bests at each age. This method produces a fairer competition but lessens the element of head-to-head competition. Still, runners compete at all levels of a road race, whether or not their competition earns official recognition. All racers share the adrenaline surge that results from the pursuit, and they compete with those near them. Some of the best competition occurs long after the winners have finished their cool-down, when friends and rivals still on the course test their fitness and resolve against each other.

Road races serve as the social center of the running community.

Regardless of your ability or ambivalence toward competition, once you toe a starting line you are a competitor. Few can resist the motivational power of the event: starting en masse at the sound of the gun, being swept forward by the synergy of the pack, accepting water from volunteers and cheers from spectators, crossing beneath the finish-line banner, reading your name and a precise measure of your effort on the posted results.

Besides providing a competitive venue, road races serve as the social center of the running community. Perhaps the reputed loneliness of the long-distance runner is what drives us to such heights of sociability, for the scene before and after a road race competes with the liveliest of parties. Some converse extensively during the race, while others discover a different kind of camaraderie. "Socializing in running," wrote Dick Goodie in *The Maine*

Quality of Running, "is realized through the sharing of a violent combat—the gutsy Maine road race." This intimacy of shared hardship should not be underrated. I have rarely felt closer to a friend than after a tough half marathon in which we ran shoulder to shoulder at the edge of our ability yet spoke no more than a handful of words for over an hour.

Although we can and do compete with each other, we share the common rival of time, displayed prominently on digital clocks, called out at checkpoints, and printed in results. The pursuit of better times spurs runners to greater excellence, and accurate measurements of both course and time are essential for a well-organized race. Many racers talk about their personal records, or PRs, over popular distances as measures of their success and as motivational goals.

This pursuit can become obsessive, however, exaggerating the importance of accurate split times, smooth open roadways, and a speedy course (*flat* and *fast* are the buzzwords). A slavish attention to time obscures one of the unique aspects of road racing—the variety of terrain and the character of the locale in which the race is run. A pleasant side effect of road racing is the opportunity to tour new places. Some of the best races sacrifice ease and speed to take in a scenic or historic route. Times run in such a race can be compared only with themselves or with others in the same event. Because of this variation in difficulty, runners cannot set official world records in road races. Records for road distances are considered world "bests," and the specific course is mentioned when referenced.

Road races range in size and style from small-town events drawing a dozen local runners, with numbered Popsicle sticks to mark finish order and chamber of commerce gift certificates for prizes, to giant commercial events involving tens of thousands of participants and volunteers, with high-tech timing systems, worldwide media coverage, and thousands of dollars in prize money. At either extreme, and throughout the spectrum, they reflect and celebrate their running communities.

Finding and Choosing a Road Race

You can often find entry forms for local races at your local running specialty shop or at athletic clubs. These forms detail the date, time, location, and course. Larger races also advertise in local or national running publications, and increasingly on the Web; the Road Runners Club of America (**www.rrca.org**) site is a good place to start. Registering in advance can save you a few dollars and usually guarantees a T-shirt. Several popular races now limit the size of their fields, requiring preregistration sometimes months in advance.

Choosing a race depends largely on your goals and preferences. Select the distance based on your training level as well as your plans and goals. If this is your first race, the distance should be well within your reach, and you should run it without any goals or expectations (easier said than done). As you gain race experience, plan a schedule that fits races into a larger pattern (see chapter 5 on periodizing your training for racing). With each race, decide if your primary goal is a fast time or a tough test, a competitive field or a scenic escape. Entry forms usually provide a course description, estimates of the size of the field, and clues to the style of the race. Make sure the course is certified if your primary goal is time related.

Small local races let you stand out—at either the front or the back—and often reflect regional and ethnic character. Larger races provide more amenities, competition, and excitement; running behind the world's best can be both motivating and humbling, and the crowded pack of a large race generates a unique energy. The world of road racing offers a banquet of choices, and you need not restrict your diet.

Racing the Marathon

The marathon serves as the capstone event in the schedule of many runners and running communities. Although marathons are commonly road races, this classic distance deserves special mention. The marathon is a race for romantics—a larger-than-life quest that inspires heroism.

The marathon is any footrace of 26 miles, 385 yards. This unique distance is a legacy of a circumstantial compromise at the 1908 London Olympics. That race was meant to be 40 kilometers (about 25 miles) but was lengthened a little over a mile so that it could be started by the Princess of Wales on the lawn of Windsor castle and still finish in the Olympic stadium. The distance stuck.

The race itself, and its name, date from the first modern Olympics held in Athens in 1896. The event was designed as a special commemoration of a legendary run from a battlefield on the plains of Marathon to the capitol at Athens. The runner, a messenger named Pheidippides, allegedly arrived in Athens after his 25-mile run, announced, "Rejoice! We conquer!" and promptly fell over dead. Although historians reject the accuracy of the story (Pheidippides was an experienced messenger who more likely ran 150 miles to Sparta a few days earlier to request aid in the battle), the modern Olympic race was a great success. More than 100 years later the marathon's legacy and mystique are still growing. A large part of this mystique stems from its unique distance, for although an average trained runner can race up to 20 miles without significant distress, the final 6 require months of training and a disciplined will. Those not fully trained for the distance (and even some who are) hit the infamous wall somewhere during those last 6 miles—the point where the body says in no uncertain terms that it has gone far enough. The appeal of the marathon is linked to this extreme exertion. Those who attempt it are aware that they are going beyond normal limits, that success is not guaranteed.

Yet the fear of the marathon has greatly subsided, due in part to enhanced training information and in part to redefined expectations. Today, finishing a marathon has nearly become a rite of passage for young professionals in American society, alongside graduate school, marriage, and buying a house. Many consider it a once-in-a-lifetime challenge. At the other extreme, it becomes as common as a weekend long run for some, such as the members of the 50 & D.C. Club, who try to run a marathon in each state—often completing them all in two to three years. Many runners choose a moderate middle, running a marathon once or twice a year. This provides time for a thorough training and recovery program and gives the race its due respect for those wishing to maximize their performance.

Like shorter road races, marathons come in a variety of sizes and styles. Some large races have legendary status. Boston has held its marathon every April for more than 100 years and is the only one that requires a qualifying time. New York City's five-borough extravaganza stole the limelight in the 1980s and established the standard for a big-city marathon, which has been copied throughout the world. Smaller marathons lack the crowds (which can be a good thing for those seeking fast times) and provide calmer, more intimate events. Courses range from flat loops designed for speed to challenging tours of scenic countryside.

Finishing a marathon has nearly become a rite of passage.

Because you can run a marathon well only a few times a year, the choice of which marathon to run takes on greater importance than the selection of which shorter race to enter. A would-be marathoner must consider the course profile, size of field, average temperature, ease of getting to the start, refreshment available on the course, race history, and his or her goals for the race. Every type of marathon has a time and season.

Trail and Mountain Racing

Trail races celebrate the wild side of running. These events leave the smooth and level asphalt for rough, narrow, hilly trails. This contrast in venue transforms more than the style of shoes—trail racing has an entirely different culture than road racing. Strength, agility, and toughness reign here, rather than pure speed. Entry forms brag about the difficulties of the course, and finishers proudly emerge from the woods mud splattered, scraped, torn, and bleeding (bleeding is not mandatory but certainly not discouraged). Times and distances mean far less in this world than on the roads, and runners rarely settle into a steady pace or rhythm.

Being closer to nature, trail courses differ throughout the country, reflecting both the terrain and the geology. In the northeastern United States, runners contend with roots, mud, and underbrush; in the Rockies the challenges are altitude and, well, rocks. In any part of the country, the trails present remote and beautiful views accessible only on foot. Trail runners maintain a relaxed camaraderie and a sense of humor about their events— a fraternity of shared strangeness that recognizes and delights in the indifference of the mainstream.

Although nearly all trail runs feature hills, some make them their main selling point. Mountain running traces its roots to the outer reaches of the British Isles, where they have been racing up and down their mountains in fell races since the Middle Ages. Pikes Peak, the most famous mountain race in the United States, was first run in 1956 as a challenge between smokers and nonsmokers (none of the smokers finished, incidentally) and now offers the choice of the full up-and-down marathon or just the ascent. This option reflects the great division among mountain runners as the ascent requires pure strength, whereas those who descend also need fast feet, balance, and a bit of recklessness. The annual World Mountain Running Championship, sanctioned by the International Amateur Athletic Federation, is held at different venues throughout the world. It currently alternates between ascents and full mountains, with pure ascenders abstaining on the odd-numbered years.

Another growing trend is adventure racing, challenges that combine sports such as kayaking and climbing with running. The granddaddy of these events, the French-inspired Raid Gauloises, changes its venue to a new exotic locale each year. More accessible events such as the Eco-Challenge and XTerra series are expanding the participation base of the sport.

Orienteering, long popular in Europe, is another variation of trail running that is gaining popularity in the United States. An orienteering course consists of a specified number of sites, called controls, that competitors must locate with the aid of a detailed map and compass. Competitors can choose their own routes to each control, and even the order in which they visit them. Superior map reading and quick-thinking, strategic decision making help balance the leg speed and log-jumping skills necessary in these races.

Ultramarathons

Beyond the marathon is a world into which few venture—although more travel there each year. The term ultramarathon includes every race longer than 26.2 miles, ranging from a 50K (31-mile) road race in Central Park to a 150-mile jaunt through Death Valley from the lowest point in the continental United States to the highest.

Although many indigenous cultures encourage ultradistance running, the recorded sport originated in Britain with the "pedestrians" of the 18th century competing in go-as-you-please challenges and races. These early athletes set remarkable records such as 100 miles in 19 hours and 500 miles in six days. In the late 19th century, six-day face-offs conducted on small indoor tracks in the United States and Britain drew crowds and press coverage. Interest died soon after the turn of the century, and not until the 1950s did more than a handful of athletes attempt ultradistances.

Ultrarunning continues to be popular in the country of its birth. Ted Corbitt of New York, a leading ultrarunner of the 1960s, once said, "I always considered ultramarathoning a disease and the British had it with fever to spare" (Kislevitz 1999). The 52.5-mile London to Brighton race has been contested since the early 1800s, with the official British Road Runners Club race dating from 1951. On the Web site *Ultramarathon World*, Milroy (1998) reported that "from the 1960s until the 1980s it was the premier ultra-marathon in the world—effectively the Ultra Distance World Championships." Official world championships are now held at a different site each year, but London to Brighton remains a favorite event.

Another classic ultra is the Comrades Marathon, a race much longer than the standard marathon, covering 90 kilometers between the South African cities of Durban and Pietermaritzburg. Each year the direction alternates between uphill and downhill (although there are climbs to spare in both directions) from the coast to the plains or back. Despite the strict 11-hour cutoff time, tens of thousands have completed the event since its birth in 1921. The experience is reportedly addictive, drawing runners back year after year.

Trail ultras officially got their start in 1974 when Gordy Ainsleigh's horse was unable to compete in the annual Western States 100-mile one-day ride in California's Sierra Nevada. Rather than skip the event, Ainsleigh ran it without his horse and finished within the 24-hour cutoff. Others followed his lead, and by 1977 the Western States 100-Mile Endurance Run became official. Now a popular and competitive championship race, Western States inherited and passed on the tradition of awarding a silver belt buckle to those finishing in less than 24 hours. "To buckle" is now a standard goal in 100-mile races throughout the country.

In all ultras, finishing the distance is the primary goal of those who enter. "Go as you please" still describes the ultra pace—although some please to go remarkably fast. Competitors often break for short walks or rests during these efforts. All must master the art of eating during the event (see chapter 23 for tips on what and how to eat during an ultra event). Physical and mental endurance distinguish successful ultrarunners, who tend to keep their own company and eschew mainstream trends in clothing, training, and nutrition. Runners who find they're just warming up after several hours on the road or those seeking a new challenge might find their niche in ultras.

Track Racing

Track is racing distilled—scientific experiments to test speed with all extraneous variables eliminated or minimized. Tracks have no hills, a uniform surface, and, in shorter races, competitors run isolated in individual lanes. Tracks are intentionally standard distances. Although the composition of the surface may differ slightly among tracks, track races held anywhere in the world, for the most part, can be compared and unequivocal world records set.

As with roads or trails, the venue describes the event, but politics also lie behind the distinction. Modern track began with the Olympic Games in 1896. The games set out to re-create athletic contests of ancient Greece, with track events at the core. The games also borrowed heavily from the mores of the time, including the ethos of "amateur" athletics, emphatically enforced by the Amateur Athletics Union (AAU) in the United States.

Although the distinction between amateur and professional athletics has blurred, track racing continues to be primarily organized by official track federations and open only to members of school teams or track clubs. Yet open events can be found. Reportedly started by legendary coach Bill Dellinger in Oregon and known as all-comers meets, they allow less-gifted and aging legs the opportunity to fly around the oval. Unlike road racing, track events are seasonal; indoor track runs from December through mid-March, outdoor from late March into September.

One loop of an outdoor track (on most tracks) covers 400 meters. Indoor track circumferences vary, usually falling between 150 and 300 meters. Track events consist of sprints (100 to 400 meters outdoors, 60 to 400 meters indoors), middle distance (800 to 1,500 meters or the mile), and distance (3,000 and 5,000 meters indoors and outdoors, and 10,000 meters outdoors).

Because the distances of many track events end where road races pick up, they appeal to those with a greater percentage of fast-twitch muscle. Many of us were introduced to competitive running on the tracks of our local grade schools or high schools. Those of us less gifted happily leave the track for longer events as soon as our school days end. Yet training and racing these shorter events can help those specializing in longer events maximize their speed and efficiency. The small circumference and tight corners of the track enhance the feeling of speed as well as provide exciting moments as runners jostle for position in races over 400 meters, making track racing not quite as sterile as it appears at first glance. The track allows spectators to see the full race. The stadium encloses and enhances their cheers, giving track the highest adrenaline rating among running events.

> The small circumference and tight corners of the track enhance the feeling of speed.

The same characteristics make it impossible to hide and all too possible to be lapped (sometimes repeatedly) in distance events. But even those of us who suffer from speed deprivation can occasionally thrill to the feel of rounding the final corner and sprinting down the straightaway—perhaps discovering we possess more speed than we believed. Regional chapters of USA Track & Field (USATF) provide information on local events (visit **www.usatf.org** for contacts). You might also ask at schools or colleges about intramural and all-comers meets.

Cross Country Racing

Cross country running is to track what trail running is to road racing. Cross country races generally range from 4K to 15K on off-road courses. Course roughness varies by region and organization, but courses tend not to be as difficult as those in open trail races. Many are run on golf courses or groomed trails, but mud is a common hazard, and hills are considered almost mandatory.

Cross country is a team sport; racing strategy and pack-running tactics figure prominently in every event.

Unlike other running events, cross country is a team sport. Finish positions for the top five runners are added together, and the lowest score wins. Time takes a back seat to racing strategy, as each course has unique challenges and few allow for smooth running or even pacing. At the start a mass of runners break from the line and try to gain position before the trail narrows. Along the course, hills and turns present both obstacles and opportunities to gain an advantage, such as the strategy of accelerating after a corner to widen a gap while you are out of sight. Teammates pull each other along and discourage opponents with pack-running tactics, sometimes sacrificing personal victory for the greater team good.

High school, collegiate, and world-class runners compete in cross country events in fall and into winter under the supervision of their respective athletic federations. As in track, occasional open meets sponsored by colleges or local running clubs welcome all comers. Joining a pack of brightly clad runners crossing an open field on a crisp, fall day is the perfect antidote for running staleness.

Racing Into the Future

At the beginning of the 21st century, races continue to hold a strong place in the life of a runner. Participation in races across the board grows each year, with marathons, ultras, and adventure events growing most rapidly.

Races give each runner an opportunity to define his or her goals and measure success. Breakthroughs occur when we push back boundaries, however we define them. In this era of relative peace and prosperity, we follow quests that motivate us to transcend the path of least resistance. We seek our stronger, nobler selves; we are willing to work and sacrifice and suffer. Races of all types will continue to provide such quests for those of us who pursue them.

17

Suiting Up to Race

TERESA GIBREAL
Assistant manager of Phidippides Running Store in Atlanta

The right racing apparel lets you focus on your race and forget about what you're wearing.

At any local race you will see an amazing variety of apparel choices—not just in fashion but also in function. Some runners, you will notice, tend to stick to everyday, tried-and-true garments, whereas others are decked out in the latest new and shiny running attire. A few go for a slicker, aerodynamic look.

As a runner, your choice of racing apparel depends on what feels most comfortable and practical for you. Your total racing environment—the weather, the distance, the terrain, and your perception of these aspects—should always determine the garments you wear for your race. Using the following guidelines can help ensure that you are geared up for success. Also refer to chapter 3, "Gearing Up for Training." Much of the advice on training gear also applies to racing gear, especially the discussions of fabric choices and dressing for the weather. A separate chapter on racing gear is included, however, to discuss the choices you make on race day.

Choosing Your Racing Gear

The following tips will help you select the optimum race-day apparel. Then, once the gun goes off, you can focus on your race and forget about what you're wearing (except as motivation along the way as you think about how fabulous your high-performance outfit looks):

- **Be true to yourself.** As mentioned in chapter 3, we all have different built-in thermostats. Because of the climate in which we were raised and our inborn responses to heat and cold, our individual responses to different race conditions will vary. A 10K run in 40-degree weather (4 degrees Celsius) will see some runners in shorts and singlets (and a few wearing even less), others in tights and T-shirts, and some bundled up in fleece tops, jackets, hats, and mittens. All these choices may be fine; the important thing is that *you* are comfortable while running at high intensity. Being comfortable leaves you free to concentrate on your race, not on the sweat dripping into your eyes or the cold nipping at your bare fingers.

- **Follow the "add 20 degrees" rule.** Remember the rule of thumb for dressing for a training run: Add 20 degrees (11 degrees Celsius) to the temperature (including windchill or heat index if applicable), then dress accordingly. Because you will be running hard in a race, you might want to add even a few more degrees to your estimate before making your apparel decisions. You'll have to experiment to find the race-day body-coverage choices that work best for you. Look around at the start of a race and you will see a wide range of choices, no matter what the conditions. Some runners are so enamored of feeling fleet and light that they will race in a singlet and shorts even in temperatures in the 30s (just above 0 degrees Celsius) and colder! Others prefer more coverage. Part of the purpose of your warm-up is to gauge the conditions and make a final apparel decision before the gun.

- **Consider the distance.** Your racing attire also will depend on the distance of the race. You will most likely dress differently for a 5K race on a sunny, 50-degree (10-degree Celsius) day than you would for a marathon under the same conditions. Because you heat up more while running at the high-intensity pace of a 5K, you'll probably want to wear very little; shorts and a singlet should do it for most runners, unless you are just jogging through the event. In the marathon, a bigger concern will be sun exposure, which can hasten dehydration and cause discomfort and possible skin damage. Therefore, you might want to cover your shoulders with a T-shirt and wear a hat with a brim to shield your face. And don't forget to put on sunblock. (See below for more on dressing for the distance.)

- **Be prepared for several options.** If you are traveling to a race, arrive prepared for a variety of conditions. The Boston Marathon, held in mid-

Your total racing environment should determine the garments you wear for your race.

April, has been held on days when the temperature topped 90 degrees (32 degrees Celsius), with sun and high humidity. In other years, the day of the race has had snow and freezing rain with temperatures in the 30s (just above 0 degrees Celsius). If the forecast is iffy on race morning, bring a variety of gear to the start, then make your decision as close to race time as possible.

• **Wear layers to warm up.** It's important to be comfortable for your warm-up. The last thing you want to do is pull or strain a muscle by trying to warm up when you feel cold. On the other hand, you don't want to overheat because you're overdressed.

In half marathon, marathon, and ultramarathon races, it's common for runners to wear a throwaway garment (such as an old cotton long-sleeve T-shirt or sweatshirt) to the start and remove it when the gun sounds. (Volunteers at the New York City Marathon collect literally tons of such castoff items and donate them to charity.) You can also take off and discard items along the course (but please do so responsibly) so you'll remain comfortable as the race progresses. Gloves, hats, and, for your forearms, long socks with the toes cut out, are some helpful options. If you choose your apparel incorrectly in longer races, you will be uncomfortable, and possibly even in danger, for long periods. If you can't bear the thought of tossing out a perfectly good item of clothing, use the old trick of wearing a plastic trash bag before the start. Just be careful that you don't become so overheated that you feel a sudden, dramatic chill when you take it off. When it comes to breathability, plastic makes cotton feel like a high-tech fabric!

- **Be prepared for changes en route.** Weather can change suddenly and dramatically *during* a race, and the longer you're out there, the greater your chance of running through a change. If you become warm, don't hesitate to discard items along the way; losing your favorite technical long-sleeve top isn't as bad as overheating and becoming dehydrated. If you can, ditch a garment with a spectator you know. Or drop it as you pass an aid station; perhaps some kind-hearted volunteer will bring it to the finish line.

  If you're worried about getting cold in a race's late stages—which can happen in a marathon if you hit the wall and have to slow dramatically—arrange for a friend to be at a designated point along the course to hand you something to put on if you need it.

- **Do the layered look.** Dressing in layers is the cardinal rule anytime you're exposed to conditions for a lengthy period. In a race, layering will allow you to make adjustments en route. Make your layers as light as possible; that way if you don't want to ditch them you can tie them around your waist or tuck them into your shorts and keep racing with minimal drag and distraction.

- **Note your apparel in your log.** This can be an invaluable resource for making future race-day clothing decisions. Looking back six months and seeing "10K, 45 degrees, light rain (shorts, thermal T, cap)" will help guide you in picking an outfit for today's half marathon on a windy, 40-degree, overcast morning. Notations on apparel choices for your training runs can be useful too, although you'll probably want to go a bit lighter when racing because of the increased energy expenditure.

- **Bring cool-down clothes.** Always have a warm, dry outfit to change into for your cool-down, especially if it's cold. You will have perspired heavily during the race (even on a cold day), and as you cool off afterward, the moisture can make you feel colder. You can become chilled or develop muscle cramping and tightness even on a warm day. On a hot day it just doesn't feel (or smell) very good to warm down in your sweat-drenched race gear.

Warning! Wear It in Training *First*

Whatever you decide to wear for a race, always make sure you have first worn the complete outfit on a few training runs. This is especially good advice when running a half marathon or longer race. New clothing may cause chafing, blistering, and other discomforts that you don't want to deal with when you're trying to focus on performing your best. You would never wear a brand-new pair of shoes for a race; the same goes for running apparel.

Dressing for Half Marathons and Beyond

When you are racing a half marathon (13.1 miles, or 21.1 kilometers) and longer, the effects of weather changes, fatigue, and general wear and tear on the body can dramatically impact race performance. It's crucial at these longer distances to make smart apparel choices to maximize your chances of a breakthrough performance.

First, as noted above, realize that the weather during the race may vary dramatically. Not only might the temperature rise or fall, but the wind, cloud cover, precipitation, and humidity could all change as well, affecting your comfort level and body temperature. This is especially true in ultradistance races held in extreme conditions. During the Western States 100-Mile Endurance Run, held in the High Sierras of California, competitors typically negotiate snowfields in the early stages, then later run through canyons where temperatures can top 100 degrees (38 degrees Celsius). Typically, in longer races the body temperature starts relatively cool, warms up in the

As your temperature rises, discard layers, tie them around your waist, or tuck them into your waistband to keep racing with minimal drag and distraction.

© iPhotoNews.com

middle, and then starts cooling down during the later miles as fatigue sets in. Moreover, many of these races start very early in the morning when it's cool or cold, with temperatures warming up, often significantly, as the race progresses.

Dress in layers to prepare for dramatic temperature changes you may experience during long races that start early in the morning.

We recommend that you assume that the temperature (or factors affecting it, such as windchill) will vary by at least 10 to 20 degrees (6 to 11 degrees Celsius) during a half marathon or longer race. It's vital to stay warm before the race by wearing appropriate warm-up gear. It's also a good idea in cool conditions to invest in a jacket or vest that can fold into its own waist pack for easy, lightweight carrying. For recommendations on fabric choices, refer to chapter 3, page 29.

During long races it's crucial to wear garments that reduce the risks of chafing and blistering. The characteristics of these garments are explained in detail in chapter 3 (page 27). During long events, men who experience nipple chafing, which can be extremely painful and bloody, can wear bandages over their nipples or purchase a pair of nipple protectors (available at running specialty stores and from catalogs). It's important to dress to prevent chafing in races of all distances, of course, but you won't have to suffer as long in the shorter events.

Garments and accessories that help you easily transport fluids and nutritional aids (gels, sports bars, etc.) can be a big bonus during long races. Such items are a virtual necessity for ultra events, in which to bonk is to forfeit any hope for a comfortable race experience, let along a breakthrough performance. (See chapter 23 for a discussion of the importance of proper hydration and fueling during races.) Another option, of course, is simply to drink and eat at aid stations, but carrying your own replenishment puts you in the driver's seat, so to speak. Pocketed tops and shorts and waist packs allow you to carry fluids and solid items.

Summing It Up: Choosing the Perfect Race Outfit

- Test garments and accessories before wearing them in a race.
- In races, less is more. You want to be light and aerodynamic.
- Be prepared for all types of conditions on race day.
- For half marathons and longer races, anticipate a temperature change of 10 to 20 degrees (6 to 11 degrees Celsius).
- Don't hesitate to discard layers as temperatures rise.
- Dress warmly for your warm-up and cool-down to prevent muscle cramping.
- If needed, have a plan for transporting fluid and fuel during the race.

Selecting the Right Racing Flat

KIRK ROSENBACH
Member of the Atlanta Track Club's masters competitive team, and a frequent lecturer on running-shoe topics

GREGORY SHEATS
Running shoe analyst and consultant on numerous running shoe advisory panels

Racing flats can give both a physical and psychological boost to runners of any speed and experience level.

In this chapter we discuss a type of shoe often associated with breakthrough running—the racing flat, which is how most runners describe the shoes they race in. You may want to refer back to the material in chapter 4 on training shoes. Much of the information in that chapter about the anatomy of a running shoe, foot function, and selecting and buying shoes pertains to racing flats as well.

The racing flat is a shoe designed to be worn during competition and speed or interval workouts. Although racing flats come in several variations, some common features generally distinguish them from everyday training shoes. Compared with training shoes, racing flats

- are lighter in weight;
- have a thinner outsole or an outsole made of a lighter, less durable material (a softer rubber compound);
- have less midsole cushioning material (ethylene vinyl acetate or polyurethane);
- have a lower heel elevation because the midsole is thinner;
- have a cut-away or more contoured arch; and
- have lighter weight materials in the upper, foregoing some strength and durability.

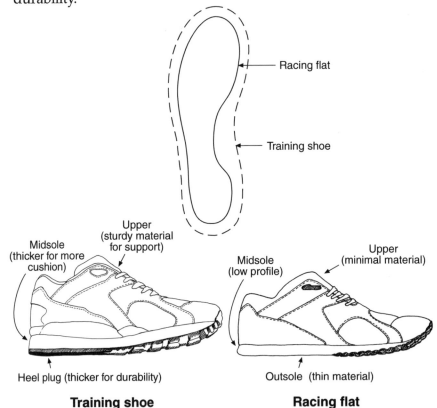

Training shoe   **Racing flat**

The diagram above illustrates some of these differences between training shoes and racing flats.

Racing Flat Dos and Don'ts

Before we take a look at selecting a racing flat for your type of foot function, let's start with some basic information and advice about racing flats. These pointers should clear up some misconceptions you may have heard at running specialty shops, workouts, and races:

1. Don't think that racing flats are only for elite, world-class athletes. Racing flats can give a physical and psychological boost to runners of any speed and experience level who enjoy racing and are trying to better their times.

2. Don't buy into the notion that racing flats are only for small, lightweight runners and not suited for big or heavier competitors (those over 175 pounds). As with training shoes, your foot function (see chapter 4), not your size and weight, is the critical factor in determining whether you could benefit from racing flats and in choosing the type of shoe you need.

3. Don't expect a miraculous improvement in your training and racing just because you wear a pair of racing flats. The benefits are hard to quantify and may be as much psychological as physical. Although this psychological effect should not be discounted, the bottom line is that your natural talent and training are still the key determinants of your racing performance.

4. Do remember that although racing flats may improve your racing performance, less shoe is on your foot than with a training shoe. Thus, depending on your foot function and other factors, such as the distance and terrain of the race or the speed of the workout you are performing, using racing flats can adversely affect your running biomechanics and increase the impact on your muscles and joints. These alterations can more than offset the advantages of the lighter weight. To protect your body and preserve the psychological advantage of wearing your sleeker, lighter, racing flats for racing, we strongly encourage you to do most, if not all, of your speed or interval workouts in your training shoes.

5. Don't think that a shoe you wear to race always has to be a shoe specifically designed as a racing flat. Rather, think of a racing flat as any shoe lighter than the shoe you train in. Any such shoe should help you run faster, or at least feel faster. Your foot function, the length and terrain of the race or speed workout, and the weather are some of the factors that affect your choice of footwear.

6. Do ease into using racing flats if you've never worn them before. Never wear them in a race right out of the box, especially in a long event like a marathon. If you run into trouble you'll jeopardize both your health and your performance. Try them on an easy run before using them in a workout. If possible wear them in a speed workout before using them in a race.

Selecting a Racing Flat

As with training shoes, you should select your racing flats primarily by considering your foot function. (Refer to the discussion in chapter 4 for a more detailed definition of the three basic foot functions summarized here.)

Stable Foot Function

The stable foot function exhibits no tendency to roll inward beyond the center to the ball of the foot. If you have this type of foot function, you are a good candidate for a shoe that is designed as a true racing flat.

If that's the case, remember that not all racing flats are created equal. As with training shoes, some models will be a little more cushioned and protective of the feet than others or will give you a greater sense of support, important even for those with a stable foot.

When you buy any racing flat, take into account the type of races for which you plan to use the shoes. For example, if you are using them for shorter distances (5Ks and some 10Ks) you could consider some of the lightest and sleekest models. These might not feel like enough shoe, however, for races such as half or full marathons. You will have to make this judgment as you try on the shoes and test them on runs.

Running surface also makes a difference. Although racing flats are designed for use on the roads, they may be a poor choice if the surface is wet, icy, or snowy because many racing flats have poor traction compared with training shoes. If you are racing on trails or grass and choose not to wear spikes, wearing lightweight trainers may make sense for maintaining good traction. Although spikes can be worn on most outdoor and some indoor track surfaces, they are not necessary for successful track racing and training.

Take into account the type of races you intend to run and the running surface you will use.

Mild to Moderate Overpronator Foot Function

Those of you with foot functions in this category have two viable options. First, you might try a racing flat built with some degree of inner midsole support and with a slightly wider base of support than is typical of the genre. You can usually recognize these shoes by a darker colored midsole on the rear inner side. This type of racing flat may also be less cut away or contoured in the arch area than other racing flats. Second, you could consider using a lightweight training shoe meant for the stable-footed runner. Although not specifically designed as racing flats, these shoes will likely feel lighter and more flexible than your training shoes. They would not be appropriate for your everyday running, but they would offer more performance than your trainers and more protection and running efficiency than actual racing flats. The point here is that you should keep an open mind about what shoe is best for you.

Severe Overpronator Foot Function

If you are a severe overpronator, be careful if you decide to race in a lighter shoe than your trainer, especially for a distance longer than 10K. Because

Racing flats may be a poor choice if the surface is wet, icy, or snowy.

© Photo Run

you have a foot that rolls inward excessively, you must do your everyday running in a shoe designed to control this inward motion. If you were to switch to a traditional racing flat, or even a lightweight cushioned trainer (such as that used by the stable-footed runner), you would significantly increase your chances of running inefficiently and becoming injured.

Still, you may want something lighter for your racing. We suggest that you use a training shoe that is normally designed for the mild to moderate overpronator foot function. These shoes are typically somewhat lighter and more flexible than your training shoes but will still give you some degree of support. Even so, we strongly recommend against using these shoes for distances longer than 10K or in any off-road race.

Other Considerations

Very few models of racing flats are made for women. As a rule, women buying racing flats should buy one and a half sizes smaller than their women's size in a men's shoe. Thus, a size-eight woman would buy a size six and a half men's shoe. (Of course, try shoes on first for fit.)

If you use orthotics or inserts in your training shoes, you should think carefully about whether you should use them in your racing flats or whether you should even use racing flats. Some reasons *not* to use orthotics in your racing flats are the following:

1. They add weight, which you are trying to eliminate by using racing flats.
2. Racing flats and lightweight trainers often have shallower heel cups and trimmer profiles, so you may find that your orthotic does not fit particularly well or that your foot slips up and down in the heel, which you don't want.

The advantage of using your orthotics or inserts in your racing flats, of course, is that you retain their corrective function. If you do not use them, and at the same time go to a lighter, less stable shoe for racing, you significantly increase your chance of becoming injured or running inefficiently. If that happens, you are more than counteracting the advantage of not wearing your orthotics.

You will have to decide if using racing flats at all is a good idea if you regularly use orthotics for running. If you decide to try it, find a shoe for racing that accommodates your orthotics. We do not recommend running any race longer than a 10K without your orthotics. Pay attention to how you feel afterward compared with how you feel when you use orthotics. If courses are comparable, note whether your times vary significantly using the two options.

Racing Flat Summary

We urge you to review the tips on shoe selection and care in chapter 4 (pages 45-47), which apply to racing flats as well, except for the advice about life or mileage expectancy of shoes. Because the design of a racing flat is inherently lighter and less durable than that of a training shoe, you will not get anywhere near the mileage out of your racers that you will out of your training shoes. You should expect somewhere between 100 and 175 miles of effective cushioning.

If you have a mild to moderate overpronator or severe overpronator foot function and end up using lighter training shoes for racing (rather than actual racing flats), you can expect them to hold up a bit longer. But because you are using a shoe that gives you less support than normal and are doing hard running in the shoes, do not attempt to extract the full 400 to 600 miles that you typically get from training shoes. A reasonable estimate would be 225 to 325 miles.

Unless you are competitive at the highest levels, you will probably be better off using your racing flats (be they true racing flats or trainers-as-racers) only for race distances below the half marathon. When you get beyond that distance, the added benefit of the lighter shoe is likely to be more than offset by the increased likelihood of running inefficiently and having your body absorb the extra pounding and stress, which can cause injury or, at the least, tired, dead legs.

In sum, racing flats selected and used wisely can help you achieve breakthrough running performances. But do not expect miracles. Remember that proper training, not shoe selection, is your best preparation for great races.

19

The Art of Peaking

Coach of adidas Running Room and two-time winner
of the New York City Marathon

A peak race requires meticulous planning and preparation months before you line up at the start.

Which race or championship are you peaking for this competitive season? Every runner dreams of running his or her perfect race, or reaching his or her *peak performance*, if you will. What do I mean by *peak*? To my mind, a peak race is one that goes 100 percent right. Often your running seems effortless, and you just can't believe it's all so easy! On such a day you may achieve a new personal best or triumph over runners you previously thought were unbeatable.

The history of our sport is packed with wonderful examples of peak races. The one that first comes to my mind is Joan Benoit's victory at the inaugural women's Olympic Marathon in Los Angeles in 1984. When Joan started to pull away from the field at the three-mile mark, we all thought she was making a huge and costly mistake. We didn't know (and perhaps she didn't either) just how "on" she was that day. She was primed. In one of the greatest peak performances

Elija Legat sets a race record at the 1998 Prague International Marathon

© Courtesy of Prague International Marathon

in the history of sport, Joan ran 2:24:52 for the gold medal, finishing well over a minute in front of silver medalist Grete Waitz. Although Waitz and the rest of the field tried to catch Benoit once they realized her move was for real, they couldn't narrow the gap. Benoit said the race was so easy she felt she could have run another 26 miles after finishing.

Another great example is Bill Rodgers's winning run at the 1979 Boston Marathon, where he demolished the field and set a course record and American best of 2:09:27. Unlike Benoit, Rodgers did not take the lead until 21 miles into the race. He held off a challenge from Japan's Toshihiko Seko at 22 miles. I was in that race, and although many of us ran well that day (the conditions were excellent—low 40s [about 6 degrees Celsius], overcast, and no wind), we recognized that Rodgers was in another zone. Seko had beaten him the previous December at the Fukuoka Marathon and in a recent 10K, so Rodgers knew he had to use every resource to turn the tables. Bill gradually inched away over the final 4 miles to win by 45 seconds. He was utterly spent at the finish, especially after sprinting the final 600 meters to secure the age 31 world record by one second.

Peak Versus PR

It has been said that our worst races are often our hardest. Conversely, a peak race may feel easy, almost effortless, even as you exceed your highest goals. In my experience and in watching the careers of other runners, peak races and personal records (PRs) don't always coincide. Take Joan Benoit's example. The 1984 Olympic Marathon was probably the best race of her life, the ultimate peak, yet it wasn't a PR at the time and it's three and a half minutes slower than Joan's career PR and American record of 2:21:21, run the following year in Chicago. During that Chicago race, Joan has said she felt flat and worried the entire time about being beaten by world record holder Ingrid Kristiansen; it wasn't an easy or enjoyable experience. Alberto Salazar pushed himself close to the point of no return in his peak races. Bill Rodgers happened to peak and attain a PR on the same day in Boston in 1979; his 2:09:27 remains his personal best time, and he'd probably say it was the best race he ever ran. Olympic and world championship track finals, for which athletes aim to peak, are often tactical races won in slow times. Part of peaking for these races is knowing how to hold back and then go all out in the final stages of the race. Similarly, peaking for a cross country world championship involves racing strategically (often by tucking behind sacrificial teammates who do the hard work of setting the pace) and knowing how to negotiate difficult courses under often treacherous conditions. Five-time world cross country champion Paul Tergat has won in driving rainstorms and fierce heat by being ready for anything—fast pace, slow pace, taking the lead early, and coming from behind—and by using his Kenyan teammates to assist him in securing a victory. His times in these races matter far less than his ability to adapt his talents and training to the course and race conditions.

As for myself, my PR of 2:12:05 was set in Boston in 1975, one of the toughest races I ever ran. I tried with everything that was in me to catch Bill Rodgers, who ended up running 2:09:55 to set American and course records. Once I lost Rodgers the wind went out of my sails, and I finished despondently, letting Steve Hoag pass me in the last mile. On the other hand, in the race I consider my peak (Los Angeles Marathon, 1981), I ran 2:13:15. I felt as if I jogged it and won easily. Looking back, perhaps I should have recognized that I was having one of those perfect days and pushed for a PR. Sometimes we just don't know we're having a peak day until it's over.

A peak race can be one in which you take charge early with a steady, fast pace and win going away. It can be a contest in which you follow your coach's advice by using a sit-and-kick strategy, letting the other runners fight for the lead while you bide your time and then blowing by them in the final 800 meters. And, of course, you don't have to be an elite runner to run a peak race. John Doe's 3:59:59, a 20-minute PR beyond his wildest hope, is just as much of a peak as Rodgers's 2:09. The results of a peak vary from one runner to another based on goals, experience, and performance standards. For all runners, though, a peak is both a physical and mental experience that concentrates many varied resources at your disposal.

Whatever your race-day strategy, a peak race requires meticulous planning and preparation months before you line up at the start. Occasionally, it will seem to you that a peak race just happens, but more often than not you will have orchestrated it. Better yet, when you continue to train correctly you can often hold a peak for several weeks and continue to see more breakthrough performances. (See chapter 5 for information on periodizing your training for peaking.)

How Often Can You Peak?

How often you can expect to reach a peak in running depends on the race distance, your fitness, and your competitive background, but I can offer some guidelines. Most successful distance runners do best on a training cycle that prepares them for two peaks per year. We can find many examples of distance runners who have peaked successfully, even spectacularly, three times in one year, but I believe that over time such a schedule will break down even the strongest runner.

Two yearly peaks conveniently break up the year into two six-month training cycles (each including about four months of training, plus rest and recovery weeks). For many distance runners, that means a spring peak and a fall peak, leaving the periods of rest, recovery, and early-season buildup for high summer and the dead of winter. (Of course, in planning your peaks, where you live makes a huge difference. I'd hesitate to peak in August in Atlanta, for example, or Minnesota in February.) As a runner, you should look at the races you want to peak for and set your training schedule to build toward those dates.

In choosing a peak race, think about when you race best. Factors to consider include weather, your family, work, and community obligations (don't choose a peak fall race, for example, if you're committed to coaching your daughter's soccer team during that season), and, of course, races available at that time of year. If you have no choice (say, you are competing in a national or world championship that is held only once a year), you may have to adapt specific training strategies to maximize your potential during that season. For example, I've trained runners for summer world championship races by working specifically to adapt them to the heat by training at midday rather than in the cool of the morning or evening.

When I was competing at the elite level, I always had my best peaks in the spring. Although I live in the northeastern United States, I never had a problem training hard through the cold, dark, snowy winters and then unleashing the results in April and May. I never did as well coming off a summer of training in the heat and humidity. If you follow a similar pattern, you might want to plan your "ultimate" peak to follow your best training period and to scale back your other peak a bit.

How Long Can You Hold a Peak?

The span of time over which runners can maintain peak performance is a controversial subject among coaches. My rule of thumb is three weeks, and I'll stick with that despite many coaches I respect insisting on shorter or longer peaks. If you can get in two PR races in three weeks, you're going to be ecstatic, right? Attempting a third, in my overall experience, is often asking too much of yourself. Quit after two weeks, however, and you may squander an excellent opportunity.

Interestingly, I've often seen remarkable peak races at short distances a month or so after a runner has run a peak-effort marathon. The runner rests physically and mentally for a couple weeks, resumes light training, then goes out and pops a great 5K or 10K. It doesn't always work, but if you're a marathoner, it's worth a try sometime, preferably under the guidance of a coach.

Physically Preparing to Peak

Rarely does a peak comes out of nowhere; rather, it is the result of months of preparation during which you may sacrifice other things in life as well as short-term success (by "training through" certain races to maintain a high level of fitness) to reach your full potential on peak-race day. Like most coaches, I believe in a carefully planned training schedule that starts with recovery from the previous peak followed by base building, speedwork of gradually increasing intensity (including tune-up racing), and finally tapering as you head into your peak-racing season. Your plan should incorporate your entire training development, including base training, anaerobic-threshold running, speed training, cross-training (if you include that), and strength and flexibility work. Think of each stage as a building block that must be strong and sturdy to support the next block, or stage. After recovering from the previous peak, you work a bit harder in each stage as the next peak period approaches. (See chapter 5 for more on this progressive approach to training.)

Benefits of Having a Coach

A coach can help you considerably in achieving a peak performance. I recommend that all competitive runners have some sort of formal coaching. Sometimes we need an objective voice to tell us what to do. Good places to start looking for a coach include your local running club, local college and university teams, the Road Runners Club of America (RRCA; see Web site address, page 199), and the Internet. Here's how a coach can help:

- **A coach makes the decisions.** As you near your peak race, it's easy to second-guess yourself. Should I do 4 or 5 × 800 today? Do I need a day off? A coach removes the guesswork. A skilled coach (especially one who knows you and your training response well) is better at assessing what you need and don't need. Leaving the decision making to someone who knows how to train you relieves the pressure. All you have to do is execute.

- **A coach can help you plan race strategy.** On race day you likely feel an overwhelming temptation to just run as you feel without a strategy for exactly how you will reach the goals you've trained so hard to reach. With a coach you can plot a detailed race strategy, including when to hold back and when to surge, how to respond to moves by your competitors, and when to unleash your final kick.

- **A coach can remind you that you're awesome.** It's easy to become so caught up in training that it starts to feel mundane. A coach can step back and remind you how incredibly hard you've worked and what tremendous potential you'll have on race day. You should feel that way yourself, but it's helpful to be reminded.

Let's break down each stage in your training schedule, including competitions leading up to your peak race. What follows is an outline of the basic seasonal schedule I use for my athletes (who include runners specializing in distances from 1,500 meters to the marathon), including elements of both physical and mental peaking.

Step by Step to a Peak Race

Early season (four to six weeks)

- Select your desired peak race and write it down in your training log. To peak, you must plan your training backward from there.
- Develop a strong distance base, working on aerobic endurance and strength (for more on base training, see chapter 6).

- Train at higher intensities no more often than once every 7 to 10 days
- Write down your goals for your peak race in your training log. If you need guidance, consult a coach or someone with experience in competitive running. (For more on goal setting, see chapters 1 and 15.)

Midseason (four to six weeks)

- Arrange the schedule of tune-up races that you will do in preparation for your peak race. Race over various distances, usually shorter than the distance you have planned for your peak race. These races will supplement your training, accustom your body to racing, test your fitness, and allow you to see your progress. Ideally, I recommend running two to four races during this phase—enough so that you feel race sharp, but not so many that you feel overraced by the time of your peak race.
- Continue to develop your aerobic strength by keeping the bulk of your training in the aerobic range (60 to 80 percent of maximum heart rate).
- Incorporate workouts that help build your speed and turnover at least once every seven days.
- Start to prepare yourself mentally for your peak race by using positive thinking and visualization about your race efforts.

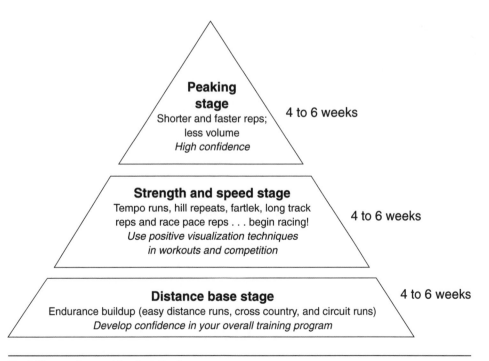

Tom's Training Pyramid for Peak Performance.

Late season (four to six weeks)

- For speedwork, do shorter and faster reps than what you were doing in midseason. Run at the pace of your peak race, with less recovery, to hone the speed you will need on race day.

- Taper by incorporating more easy training days between the more intense speed workouts (for more on tapering, see chapter 20).

- Reduce the duration of your longest workouts (both long runs and speed sessions) as well as your overall mileage.

- With your coach or advisor, discuss and plan your race strategies and tactics (for more on racing tactics, see chapter 22); discuss strategies that your competition might use.

- Visualize yourself achieving complete success in your peak race.

Mentally Preparing to Peak

Achieving peak performance requires more than being physically ready. Particularly as your peak race draws near, you must focus attention on the mental aspects of peaking. Although I believe that the physical part of preparation (your training) counts for more than the mental part, you cannot ignore either. I've seen many runners put all the physical elements of a peak race in place but fail to reach their potential on race day because they were not mentally prepared. Your emotional frame of mind can make all the difference. Let's look at three key ways to prepare your mind to peak along with your body.

The will to win

Everyone wants to be a winner, right? You'd think so, but I find that most runners are afraid of succeeding. I'm not sure why. Maybe it's because they fear the pressure of having to maintain a certain standard. Maybe they retreat from the attention of others or worry about all the work it will take to hold on to their place at the top.

As long as you harbor fear of success, you will fall short of your potential. You must embrace a winning attitude. Positive self-talk—repeating mantras such as "I am a winner" and the like—though valuable, can only take you so far. What I've found more important is to view your peaks—no matter how lofty—not as ultimate achievements but as stepping-stones to the next level. When Bob Kennedy won the NCAA cross country title as a freshman, he and his coach, Sam Bell, talked not about the incredible achievement but where Bob would go from there.

Working with a coach can be helpful in overcoming a fear of success. I sometimes ask an athlete, "Are you afraid to be successful, to be a champion? Are you training to be the absolute best you can be?" Athletes must answer these questions positively, and truthfully, to themselves in order to peak.

The best runners I know have one thing in common: They never stop believing they can be better. This belief keeps them constantly pushing to get to the next level, whether they are just starting out or world class.

The fear of losing, of failure, is not necessarily a bad thing. This is a normal feeling, and it can be motivating. If you're leading a race, a fear of being passed may drive you to keep pressing during a surge or compel you to maintain pace during a long uphill. Just don't let the fear become so overwhelming that it deters you from throwing yourself into competition in the first place.

Sisu

Finland has produced some of the greatest runners of all time. The runners from Finland have a word, *sisu*, that they use to describe a sort of mental toughness. The word has no direct translation into English, but the closest approximation is *guts* or *willpower*. I've known several runners who epitomize sisu, most notably Alberto Salazar. A runner who races so hard that he has to have an IV drip put into his arm and be given last rites at the end of a marathon is gutsy enough by my standards.

Where does sisu come from? It comes from somewhere deep inside an athlete. The attitude is, "I'm going to do my best today, no matter what." Sisu cannot be coached or taught; an athlete either has it or not.

Controlled emotional readiness

How exactly do you want to feel as you stand on the start line of your peak race? Excited and motivated—but not too much so. The key to a peak performance is to be fired up and raring to go but also to have control of those feelings. This is important at any race distance, particularly in the marathon (and beyond) in which going out too hard can spell disaster.

You can be in the best shape of your life, but if you don't control that preparation in the final days before your peak event and early in the race itself, you will not achieve your peak. Overexcitement can lead to training too much in the last days before the race or making judgment errors near race day (like suddenly trying a new sports drink or radically changing your planned race strategy).

> The best runners I know never stop believing they can be better.

To avoid these problems, remind yourself as the race draws near that you have done all you can to prepare yourself physically; squeezing in one more hard workout will do more harm than good. You should do your final speed sessions with control, not as all-out efforts. Tell yourself that you are ready to execute, to reap the rewards of all that hard work—on race day, when it counts, not before. Repeat frequently, "I have worked very hard and I am in great condition. I will now be successful in this race."

Although it's important to set goals for your peak race, as the event approaches you need to remind yourself that the most you can do is try your best. Every race can't be a PR or a win. Certainly, you should set goals that challenge and motivate you, but unrealistic goals will put negative pressure on you. Learn to appreciate slow, steady improvement. (See chapter 20 for more on race preparation and chapter 21 for more on developing a racing mindset.)

Are You Ready?

How do you know you are ready for a peak race? Like many coaches, I try to help my runners recognize they are in peak shape by designing workouts that prove their fitness to them. The runners perform these workouts close to the peak race but not so close that the workouts rob them of the energy and focus they will need on the big day. Here are three examples:

1,500 meters. Track specialist Brooks Johnson told me about this workout. Warm up thoroughly, then run 1,000 meters all out. Rest as long as you need to for full recovery, then run 500 meters all out. Cool down thoroughly. The combined time is what you are capable of for 1,500 meters.

5K to 10K. Jog for at least 10 minutes to warm up, then do some strides to get loose. The workout is simply 800 meters all out. Cool down with a few more strides and at least 10 minutes of light jogging. This workout will remind you that you are not only strong but fast.

Half marathon or marathon. Warm up thoroughly, then run 2 × 1 mile, recovering fully between efforts. Cool down. Again, you will see that you have tremendous speed as well as strength.

You can use these workouts to visualize success in your peak race. Remember, though, to hold something back for the big day!

Remember the components of a peak performance and prepare yourself for amazing results:

1. **High-level fitness.** You should feel, based on your training, that you are as fit as you can be at this time.
2. **Good tune-up race results.** Ideally, a 5,000-meter runner will have run close to a PR for 1,500 meters, and a marathoner will have turned in a good 10K performance. (Don't despair, however, if your tune-up results have been less than spectacular, especially if you trained through those races.)
3. **Envisioning success.** Visualize yourself succeeding and experiencing the desire to embrace victory.
4. **Control.** Keep control of the excitement and anticipation you are feeling.

Preparing to Race

JIM HAGE
Contributing editor of *Running Times* and winner of
two consecutive Marine Corps Marathons

Even if you don't race for your supper, you can adopt and adapt some of the strategies that professional runners use.

Training day to day, while at times monotonous, is more often mesmerizingly delightful. The feelings of fitness and vigor and the predictability of our repeated forays on the road, track, and trails are a large part of what training is about. We don't run solely to race; rather, we race to measure ourselves, mentally and physically, to see the progress we have made through our training. Interim goals provide motivation throughout our training routines and keep our running fresh and challenging.

Of course, elite runners have a necessarily narrower focus than recreational runners, and they train almost exclusively to race to the peak of their abilities at a given time. Those elite athletes are in their physical prime. They may or may not be running, even for fitness and recreation, 20 years from now. Racing—getting the most out of themselves here and now—is their raison d'etre.

At the opposite end of the spectrum are those runners who simply live to train and couldn't care less about racing. I have a friend who works out on the track twice a week but rarely races. "It messes up my training," he says in all earnestness.

If you are reading this book you likely are not as obsessive—or obtuse— as my friend is, and chances are you are not a professional runner. But even if you don't race for your supper (or plane tickets, television sets, and trophies), you can adopt and adapt some of the strategies employed by these professionals so that you too can get the most out of yourself when it comes time to pin on your race number.

If we can use some of the physical, mental, and practical tips elite runners use to gain an edge before racing, we should certainly do it. Let's face it. Compulsive behavior is a big part of just about every runner's psychological profile. Most avocational runners excel at being highly motivated and logging miles in all sorts of weather and despite numerous obstacles.

Where the common runner falls short, however, is in executing the finer points of race preparation, namely tapering before a race and following commonsense procedures on race morning. Taking these important prerace steps can make all the difference between a breakthrough performance and one that falls far short of your true potential.

Physical Taper

You may find tapering to be the most enjoyable aspect of training. Tapering is the easing-off phase of training after months of buildup and strength phases. Tapering comes after all the hard work is done. Consider it the calm before the storm. Physically, a proper taper gives your body a chance to be at its peak on race day. Mentally, a respite from the rigors of training will allow you to focus on the task at hand. After all, starting your taper often means that you have completed the hard work (highest volume and intensity) of training.

For some runners, of course, tapering is far from their favorite part of the sport. Physically, at least, many runners see the runner at rest as a contradiction in terms. Our hero is usually happiest in intense training mode, methodically cranking out miles and tough speed sessions and then blissfully savoring that pleasant, justifiably fatigued feeling. Runners at rest tend to be excitable and cranky because they are without the calming and soporific effects of a long run or track workout.

Properly apportioned, however, the tapering phase of between 10 days and 3 weeks before a marathon, and between 7 days and 2 weeks before a key race of the half-marathon distance or shorter, should sharpen both your racing body and soul in preparation for maximal effort.

Tapering allows your body to be at its peak on race day, and your mind to focus on the task at hand.

You will obtain the best results following the tapering phase when you are content with what you have achieved during the base-training (see chapters 5 and 6) and race-preparation (see chapter 5) phases. Otherwise, the temptation is to get in one last long run or one more speed session. Thus, the starting point for a successful taper begins months before your goal race, when you plan for a tapering phase in your overall training cycle leading up to the goal race. Whenever you chart and follow a solid training program, the tapering phase before the race itself should be a welcome and well-earned respite. Although a taper will not substitute for proper training and preparation, it can prime the runner for his or her best effort.

Carbohydrate Loading: Old and New

Back in the dark ages of marathon training—the early 1980s, to be precise—many runners practiced carbohydrate depletion and loading. In a nutshell, the strategy was to deplete the muscles' stores of glycogen (stored carbohydrate) by doing a long run and then starve the muscles of carbohydrates by limiting food to proteins and fats for several days after the run.

In theory, the carbo-deprived muscles would then have an enhanced capacity to store carbohydrates when you reintroduced potatoes, pasta, breads, and the like during the few days before the goal race. In practice, however, such a radical diet serves to confuse the body's chemistry during the all-important prerace week.

My experience with the deplete and load technique is perhaps typical of many who tried this extreme form of muscle-fuel manipulation. Six days before the 1982 New York City Marathon, I decided to accelerate the depletion-loading cycle I was planning to execute. I completed my last long run of 17 miles along the Charles River in Boston on the Monday night before the Sunday marathon. Then, to implement the next step of the carbo loading practice, I essentially starved myself of everything but proteins and fats for the next three days. For the last three days before the marathon, I commenced carbo loading, which I kept up until race morning.

By this time, my body was so confused I didn't know whether I was hungry or not. My goals for the race were to be in the top 50 and break 2:20:00. I had trained well, and my general fitness carried me to a PR of 2:20:09 and 51st place. But I'm convinced that if I had limited myself to just two major mistakes before the race, rather than knocking back the trifecta—a long run just six days before the race, depletion, and loading—I'm sure I would have easily met my goals.

Today, a proper dietary taper would include carbo loading but would eliminate the old-style depletion phase because of its limited utility and high risk.

Tapering Defined

Basically, tapering includes a reduction in total mileage from peak totals as well as a reduction in the quantity and intensity of interval training. Ideally, a well-executed taper seeks to find the proper balance between training volume, interval and anaerobic-threshold work, and resting. Numerous studies have demonstrated that proper tapering is effective and can enhance performance by about 3 percent. When you consider that one more long run, or one last track workout, will provide approximately a 1 percent improvement in fitness, it is nearly always better to err on the side of resting rather than continuing to train when in the tapering phase.

Keep in mind, too, that tapering is a sometime kind of thing. See chapter 5, on periodization, for more on how tapering fits into an overall training program. Tapering differs significantly from merely reducing mileage a few days before racing. Don't plan on tapering more than once a season, as when peaking for a marathon or some other particularly significant event that is your goal race. It will make more sense to train through most other races—not significantly reducing mileage or the quantity or intensity of workouts.

Tapering obviously doesn't require the effort of the strenuous buildup and high intensity that peak training entails, but in other ways the "work" of tapering is just as difficult. With the big race looming and the runner's fitness nearing a peak, he or she must intentionally run fewer miles and run them at a lesser intensity. For example, a runner who has been training 100 miles per week, with one long run and a track workout, must cut total miles in half, eliminate the long run, and drastically modify a 4-mile track workout into less than a mile of striders. Making errors in the final few weeks of preparation can waste all the hard work of training.

My Marathon Taper

Working off one hard track session, done at midweek, I generally begin my taper 10 days before the race by limiting the total distance of intervals, but not the intensity. For example, during the base-training cycle I would run a speed workout of 5 × 1 mile at 5K race pace (4:45 for me) with a two-minute or one-lap rest. My first taper workout would consist of three or 4 × 1 mile at the same pace and with the same rest. Physically and psychologically, I should finish that workout feeling reasonably rested and ready (if not tanned).

My final track session, done three or four days before the race, would consist of short intervals of 200 or 400 meters, adding up to no more than one mile and perhaps a few 100-meter strides. This session is intended to engender some leg turnover and burn off pent-up physical and nervous energy. I would reduce my total mileage for this period as well.

Remember that the two keys to effective tapering are a reduction in mileage, complemented by a lessening in training intensity. Keep in mind, however, that one runner's hard week is another runner's easy one. So just as the number of taper days will vary among runners, so will the percentage reduction in mileage. In general, however, research and anecdotal evidence have provided guidelines that indicate mileage should be reduced by approximately one-third for the week two weeks before a marathon and by about 50 percent for the final week. Depending on one's training level, fitness level, and goals, a more gradual taper may commence as long as three weeks before a marathon.

For distances from 10K to a half marathon, try tapering by cutting mileage and intensity somewhat less. Again, individual needs and goals will dictate how much less, but a not quite inversely proportional decrease in total mileage for shorter races should work well. In other words, for a half marathon, taper about half of what you would for a full marathon. For a 10K, the taper should be about 25 percent of the marathon taper. Whereas a longer period of rest is necessary to prepare for a marathon, the sharpness needed for shorter races tends to dissipate more quickly than does the strength- and endurance-oriented training critical to a successful marathon. Thus, tapering for a 5K is much less—say, 10 percent or so—than that recommended for a marathon.

No matter what the distance, the trade-off is between maintaining (but likely not improving) the fitness levels you've worked so hard to achieve and harboring strength for maximum effort on race day. The tables below, adapted from one prepared by two-time Olympian and exercise physiologist Pete Pfitzinger for *Running Times*, provide details on marathon and 10K tapers.

Tapering Schedule for a Marathon

Weeks out	Mon	Tues	Wed	Thurs	Fri	Sat	Sun	Total weekly mileage
3	5 to 7 miles easy	5 to 7 miles easy	12 miles with 12 × 100 m strides	5 to 7 miles easy	5 to 7 miles easy	11 miles with 7 of those miles at marathon pace	16 miles steady	59 to 67
2	5 to 7 miles easy	5 to 7 miles easy	3 × 2K at 8K race pace	9 miles steady	5 to 7 miles easy	6 miles with 10 × 100 m strides	10 miles steady	48 to 54
Race week	5 to 7 miles easy	5 to 7 miles easy	8 miles with 3 miles at marathon pace	5 to 7 miles easy	4 to 5 miles	4 to 5 miles easy	Marathon	31 to 39 (prerace)

Tapering Schedule for a 10K

Weeks out	Mon	Tues	Wed	Thurs	Fri	Sat	Sun	Total weekly mileage
2	5 to 7 miles easy	5 to 7 miles easy	6 × 1K at 5K race pace	5 to 7 miles easy	9 miles steady	5 miles easy	7 miles with 10 × 150 m strides	42 to 48
Race week	5 to 7 miles easy	6 miles with 6 × 200 m 1,500 m pace	5 to 7 miles easy	5 miles with 8 × 100 m strides	5 miles easy	4 to 5 miles easy	Goal 10K race	30 to 35 (prerace)

The tapering schedule for a 10K race assumes that your mileage peaks at 55 miles a week and that you ran a 5K tune-up race on Sunday two weeks before your goal 10K race.

1992 Olympic Trials

I executed my most successful marathon taper in the three weeks before the Olympic Trials Marathon. In the month before the race, my training mileage peaked at 127. I raced well during my buildup phase at shorter distances without cutting back my training but didn't race at all in the three weeks before the race, when my mileage dropped from 115 to 90 to 55. My taper was systematic, and I knew I had prepared carefully in every way. Most important, I was confident in my race plan, which was to run evenly and pick off the dozens of runners who I was sure would go out too fast.

In a friend's prerace odds-makers pool, I predicted I would finish 8th. On a warm day, which forced last-minute adjustments of my pace goals, I was 38th at 10 miles but steadily moved up and finished in 2:16:27, good for 8th place.

Mental Preparation

All things be ready if our minds be so.
William Shakespeare, Henry V

The king, as quoted by the Bard, was referencing war, not running races, although the statement is applicable to either. The best physical training and taper can be rendered moot by an inadequate mindset on race day. As long as a training foundation is carefully laid upon a reasonable race plan, executing that strategy race morning should be a matter of simply going through the motions, right?

Of course, that is the challenge of racing, particularly in longer distances such as the marathon. Countless variables, throughout training and tapering, not to mention on race day, can undo the most well-conceived race plans. Here are some strategies for eliminating (or at least reducing) the multiple risks of trouble.

Eliminate Variables

The best way to avoid unforeseen problems is to prepare yourself for race morning well before the alarm goes off. Before big races, most runners—anal-compulsive types that we are—will have already picked up their numbers and pinned them on their singlets. Right there, they've eliminated numerous potential problems, from registration difficulties to a lack of safety pins. Other potential missteps are not so easily prevented, but there are ways to reduce their likelihood.

Countless training, tapering, and race-day variables can undo the most well-con-ceived race plans.

The night before the race, not on race morning when you may be fuzzy headed or rushing around, pack your bag to take to the start. Include your racing shoes (with timing chip if applicable), Vaseline, Band-Aids, toilet paper, spare socks, water, energy foods, extra T-shirts, a few bucks, and whatever else you might need to make yourself comfortable before, during, and after the race. If it's cold, include extra clothes, a hat, and gloves. Pack your sunglasses if it's sunny.

A friend of mine does a variation of the military checklist. Then, as he walks out the door, he double-checks for his watch, bib number, and racing shoes. Anything else, he figures, he can do without. Finally, when traveling to a race by plane, don't trust your essentials to airline baggage goons—use those overhead bins.

Technology Trips Up Veteran Campbell

You might think that with more than 30 years of international racing experience, New Zealand's John Campbell would be beyond rookie mistakes. Well, guess again. At the 1999 Boston Marathon, Campbell, 50, seeking to set a veterans' age-group record, wore new racing flats. Compounding that error, Campbell triple knotted his timing chip in his shoelaces to be sure it wouldn't come off. Well, glorioski, his new flats caused blisters. Campbell wanted to stop and adjust his shoes and socks, but realized that unlacing his shoes was not feasible given his impossibly knotted laces. After a strong first half of the race, the Kiwi was grounded and forced to drop out. It just goes to show you that even experienced runners can be felled by a simple error made in the hours before an important goal race.

Focus on Your Specific Goal

Mental preparation is one area in which the fast really are different. One major reason elite runners excel is that they are nearly always physically prepared and mentally sharp.

Ask a non-elite runner about expectations for an upcoming marathon, and he or she will likely kick the ground and modestly or sheepishly say something about hoping to finish. If you are able to extract an honest answer from an elite runner, on the other hand, you will hear a precise litany of anticipated splits, projected finishing time, and probably more personal

Fatuma Roba and other elite athletes have confidence in their training programs and in themselves.

© Photo Run

strategy than you care to know. The biggest difference between the two answers will probably be the confidence with which the elite runner makes his or her case.

It's not so much the power of positive thinking; it's that the elite athlete possesses belief and conviction based on his or her training. Such poise is not a simple switch that can be turned on and off; it's the product of time and experience. The harder one works, the better the results one achieves and the more confidence one has in a particular training plan. This is another reason having and following a written schedule based on short- and long-term goals is critically important to performance-oriented runners of all levels.

The eye of the tiger stuff can therefore be overstated. If you haven't adequately prepared for the race, there is little point in trying to fool anyone, including yourself, about expectations. For more on goal setting, see chapter 1 on training philosophy and chapter 15 on racing philosophy.

Visualize Your Race

Elite athletes employ mental techniques that are nearly as important as their training methods. Just as you wouldn't walk into an important job interview without having anticipated certain questions or practiced various responses, no runner hoping to peak at a specific race should step to the starting line without a comprehensive race plan. That doesn't mean your notions of realistic splits and relative position in the field are necessarily sacrosanct or that you must maintain goal pace at all cost. But you should have a viable range of expected performance in place, subject to last-minute adjustments for weather, course conditions, and any specific physical ailments you may bring into the race.

Practice for the toughest mental segments of any race just as you train for the physical parts. While training, imagine how you will be feeling at, say, the 20-mile mark, or with a mile to go in a 10K. Try to conjure the physical strength required to work through that segment of the race. Such visualization techniques make the real event seem more familiar and less intimidating. You will have the sense that you have been there before and that your body knows how to respond appropriately to the physical and mental challenges.

Concentration during the event itself is just as critical and might be the greatest difference between performance-oriented racers and strictly recreational runners. Many runners hear early on about the benefits of disassociation, whereby conversation with a friend or music from a headset can make the miles fly by. Some of today's most popular marathons attract runners with their scenic courses or by having a band every mile. Although such niceties can undoubtedly make certain training runs less tedious and less onerous mentally and physically, serious racers have no use for anything but full-on focus during their competitive efforts.

Use the Energy Around You

Drawing energy and inspiration from cheering crowds, particularly during a marathon, is a double-edged sword. Many marathoners love to run New York City, where as many as two million wildly cheering spectators line the course. And although the rush from the roar of tens of thousands on First Avenue in Manhattan, 17 miles into the race, is guaranteed to lift the spirits

Mental Race Preparation: Two Contrasting Styles

In the quiet hour just before the start of the 1998 Boston Marathon, the elite athletes relaxed and stretched in the basement of a church next to the starting line. The contrast in the athletes' prerace styles was stark and revealing.

Ethiopia's Tesfaye Bekele bantered about like a rooster, engaging anyone who would listen in conversation, hyping his country's chances against the Kenyans. All the while, Ethiopia's best hope, Olympic gold medalist Fatuma Roba, lay prone on the floor in a corner, as if severely depressed.

Halfway into the race, Bekele, after running with the leaders and gesticulating wildly for spectators and cameras, began to fade. In contrast, in the women's race Roba moved methodically down the road, winnowing the lead pack until only she remained. While Bekele finished in 2:33:40, more than 20 minutes off his PR, Roba won the second of her three consecutive Bostons in 2:23:21, improving her 1997 time by more than three minutes.

of the most flagging runner, both elites and novices alike have paid the price of running too hard at that point and banging rudely into the wall just a few miles later in the lonely South Bronx.

Particularly in a marathon or an ultradistance race, such unscheduled surging will typically lead to disaster. Again, your race plan, developed unemotionally, objectively, and over months of preparation, is the best guide to expending race-day energies. On the other hand, every runner should maintain at least some swagger. Jason Giambi, a baseball player for the Oakland Athletics, describes his mindset as "feeling sexy" every time he goes to bat.

So what's the best mental approach? Obviously, it is open to debate. But road racing is not like football, in which aggression and high levels of excitement generally enhance performance. Nervousness and anxiety before a big race are natural and may lend an appropriate sense of gravity to the occasion. They may spur the runner to double-check prerace lists and eliminate extraneous variables that might erode performance. At worst, the adrenaline rush at the start, if properly controlled, will lend a legal chemical boost to overall performance.

Sharpening Your Racing Mindset

ANDY PALMER, PhD
Former 2:16 marathoner, sports psychologist, coach, and founder of Maine Running Camps

The ability to monitor your body and accurately read the feedback will enable you to realize your true potential.

Any athlete who wants to make a breakthrough to the next level of performance must first make a positive commitment to do so. This commitment does not yet involve specific racing goals; to make such goals requires a great deal of personal input. Developing a racing mindset requires asking yourself the simple question, "Do I want to get better?" If you can honestly say that you are willing to devote the energy it takes to improve, this chapter will help you clarify that decision and structure the process. Be prepared to take the following steps:

1. Make the decision.
2. Consult knowledgeable resources.
3. Decide what's negotiable.
4. Determine your goals.
5. Plan for success.
6. Learn to balance your life.

Make the Decision

In making the decision to commit to racing, you will not simply be deciding to run a certain time or race. You will be deciding how to realize your potential. Choosing a specific racing goal comes later in the process. Making the decision to be your best, to strive to break through to the next level, is the impetus to begin. Letting go of the outcome will enable you to realize higher levels of performance.

Numbers themselves, such as a specific time in an event or a placing, are limiting. This can be illustrated by the chase in the 1950s to break the four-minute mile. Once Roger Bannister broke the four-minute barrier in 1954, many other runners followed. Society had created the barrier by giving so much power to a specific number.

To develop a racing mindset, don't measure yourself by your watch or your heart monitor. Instead, use them as tools to better understand your body and its response to training. Being able to monitor your body and accurately read its feedback will enable you to realize your true potential and avoid creating a contrived barrier. To develop a positive racing mindset, you must get past the outcome orientation.

For many runners, the most obvious way to begin maximizing potential is to choose a race and set a time goal for it. This procedure is not only frustrating but also limiting. A specific race time is rife with value judgment. It does not, it cannot, account for other factors. Removing this judgment from the process of realizing your potential is essential to achieving and developing your racing mindset.

Now you have made the decision to up the ante. You are on your way to creating an environment of change in your life as a runner. What's the next step?

Consult Knowledgeable Resources

Begin by informing yourself about your specific interest in running. That is, find resources that educate you about track running if you are on a track team, about road running if you plan to race 5Ks or 10Ks, or about marathon running if you plan a breakthrough in your next marathon. Every athletic endeavor possesses a physical window of opportunity. To take advantage of it, an athlete must learn from the mistakes that others in the field have already made. If you can learn from those mistakes, you are much more likely to realize your goals.

Most training successes and failures have been well documented by coaches and runners. Learn from the experts by reading magazines, training guides, and reference materials. Read and study the chapters of this book. Online information is easily accessible, and you can't beat the price. It is also

Having resolved to be your best, let go of the specific outcome. Avoid creating a contrived barrier.

helpful to find an expert you trust—doctor, coach, nutritionist, or trained athlete—to help you wade through all this information. A word of caution: many people and publications share misinformation and offer unreliable advice. You must become an informed consumer.

One quick and relatively easy way to begin is to find a coach with a proven track record, so to speak. Taking this step will require diligent research. Word of mouth may be the best way to start. Choose a coach who will meet you at your point of entry; athletes at different levels have different needs. Make sure you and your coach can agree on basics like long- and short-term goals, training methods, and performance objectives.

Decide What's Negotiable

Unless you are among a handful of elite athletes, you probably fit your training into an alarmingly busy schedule. The demands of family, friends, and career leave little time for the commitment it will take for a break-through performance. Here is where the delicate art of negotiation comes into play. You can think of this as "when push comes to shove."

To reach the next level of achievement, you need to spend more time, energy, and concentration on training. This will likely mean that other areas of your life, for the time being, must take a backseat to your pursuit of this goal. Maybe you'll need to get up a little earlier in the morning for a quality track workout. You might have to skip lunch with your coworkers to fit in a strength-training session at the gym.

Family life and work commitments present some very real, nonnego-tiable obligations. These are different for every athlete. Determine the areas in your life in which you have some flexibility and use them to accommodate your new goals. If you have a coach or mentor, work with that person to create an achievable plan for your breakthrough performance. Start by figuring out how much time you have to spend on training and racing and then figure out your racing goals with that guideline in mind. Doing this will also require figuring out what time is negotiable and what time is not.

Determine Your Goals

Once you have armed yourself with knowledge and a support system, including the support of family and others in your life, and you have deter-mined the amount of time and energy you can devote to the task, it is time to determine your destination. It is important to set positive, realistic goals. Goals that are too easy won't challenge you; goals that are too difficult will lead to frustration. A good coach or knowledgeable training partner can prevent untold heartache by helping you set realistic goals (see also chapter 1).

We are all familiar with the idea of result goals. These can be as lofty as qualifying for the Olympic trials or as straightforward as completing a 10K under 45 minutes. In setting this specific goal, the object is to create an atmosphere of success and develop a positive spiral of achievement. This spiral will build self-confidence and set the stage for your breakthrough performance.

With this in mind, you should set your goals as a series of attainable, sequential steps. You would not want to set an initial goal of winning a 10K if you were a beginning runner. Rather, you would want to train for your first race and finish it strong and motivated. Your next breakthrough might be a specific time goal. Success at each level reinforces your achievements and helps motivate you to go to the next level. You want to establish a sequence of measurable result goals that lead to the ultimate goal. You'll need to reevaluate and readjust these goals from time to time.

Plan for Success

It is important to set up a realistic plan to attain your goals. Some people call these action goals. I like to view these as a mental road map showing you the way to your ultimate goal. If you are a high school runner whose goal is to win the state meet, how do you proceed? First, you need a training plan that prepares you physically and mentally for this event. How do you structure this training? What psychological training is necessary? What are your nutritional needs? How much rest do you build into your training?

Action goals are the minimum daily, weekly, and yearly requirements necessary to achieve results. Plan these carefully with your coach or mentor. Discuss your plans with family or friends who will be affected by your schedule. Don't appropriate someone else's training plan because it worked for him or her. Design and customize your training to meet your specific needs and goals.

Your goal is not to follow a plan, but rather to achieve you best results.

Learn to Balance Your Life

You have a goal, you have a plan, and you're ready for a breakthrough! Now is the time to accept the idea that at some point in the process you may need to make an adjustment. Almost everyone in our culture has embraced the idea that we should "just do it." Sometimes, however, just doing it is impossible. Your goal is not to follow a plan but to achieve your best result. Sometimes other circumstances in life can get in your way. Running a scheduled 20-miler when you have the flu simply doesn't make sense. It is important to have a plan, but you must be flexible enough to account for bumps along the way. You should be able to revise your plan as necessary and still achieve your goal.

Establish and follow a plan but understand that compromise may be necessary. The elite athlete may rightfully state that training and racing allow no compromise. Becoming a world-class athlete is an enterprise that does not welcome concession. For most runners, however, life and training involve constant compromise and concession. When we talk about "no compromise," we talk about what is best for realizing our goals, not what is best for completing a specific training program.

Allow the Breakthrough to Happen

After you've done everything you possibly can, then it's time to
slow down and let yourself be open to the outcome.

Spinoza

Now that you have learned about the preceding six steps, you will want to know how to carry them through to your breakthrough performance. My experience in coaching and counseling athletes of all abilities has shown that negativity and doubt affect almost everyone's training. These emotions frequently hinder performance and will stymie the quest to develop an effective racing mindset. Learning how to let go of these harmful, confusing feelings is difficult but well worth the effort.

Up to now we have talked about what it takes to prepare for a breakthrough performance. It's time to learn the attitude and skills that will allow your breakthrough to happen. To help develop the ultimate racing mindset, four skills will be particularly valuable. They will free you from many dated, irrational ways of approaching a race and allow you to achieve a racing breakthrough. Practice each of the following steps:

1. Open your mind.
2. Become self-aware.
3. Learn detached awareness.
4. Turn on your automatic pilot.

Open Your Mind

You might think that opening your mind would be easy, but in reality it is incredibly difficult. We all have judgments and preconceptions about ourselves, all of which affect our performance. Many of these judgments were conditioned into our psyches long before we had any say in our programming. Much of that programming was either negative or limiting or both. Shad Helmstetter, in his book *What to Say When You Talk to Yourself,* says that by age 18, a person has been told what she or he cannot accomplish 150,000 times, and this is in a "positive, healthy" home. This same person, Helmstetter suggests, may have been told what she or he can accomplish a few hundred times, in the best circumstances.

We must learn to challenge our restrictions and limitations, but before we can challenge them we must recognize what they are. Think about some of your most essential beliefs. Determine how you came to believe them. Do you have proof of them or have others told them to you?

It can be easy, once you begin to recognize your limitations, to blame them on parents, coaches, teachers, and others who have affected your life. *Don't!* First, it's counterproductive. Second, most of it was probably done with the best intentions. Third, look at yourself and recognize how often you do it to others. See how easy it is to be caught in the trap?

Begin the process of becoming open-minded by reframing the word *failure.* Rather than giving it a negative power, let's reward people who are strong enough to continue striving, whether they achieve their goals or not.

The second step toward removing the stigma of failure is to challenge the competence of the people setting the standards and restrictions. If someone is competent, listen carefully to what she or he has to say and learn from it but remove your value judgments. If you suspect that someone giving you advice isn't competent, ignore that person. If you are unsure, challenge the person. When someone runs from a challenge, you have a good idea of her or his competence. Many people around you are in the habit of limiting themselves and are more than ready to pass those limits on to you. Do not accept the baton.

MIND-OPENING DRILLS

1. **Positive affirmations.** Create personal, positive, present statements that begin the reframing process. Much of the negative thought pattern we deal with comes from a constant bombardment of limitations tossed our way as we grow. The same bombardment in a positive direction can challenge the negative. I like to think of this as positive brainwashing. I prefer to use the simplest of affirmations, for example: "I'm relaxed, calm, and cool . . . I can bend like a willow . . . I am a 2:50 marathoner."

2. **Triggers.** Find music, videos, books, quotes, places, and people that make you feel good about yourself and that allow you to learn what is available to you. Surround yourself with these things and people.

Become Self-Aware

If you want to make a breakthrough you must develop your physical and mental self-awareness. Awareness is a tool that you cultivate through self-observation in an objective frame of mind. Observe and make a note (in your training log) of everything from what you eat and how your body reacts to it to what events upset you emotionally. Learn to recognize when your body is leaving a relaxed state and when it is entering a state of stress. The sooner you are able to recognize these changes in your body and mind, the sooner you will be able to control them or know how to use them to achieve your breakthrough.

SELF-AWARENESS DRILLS

1. **Keep a log.** Most of us go through the day with only the vaguest idea of what we are thinking and feeling. We find it difficult to recall the details of a training workout from even a week ago. The log records physical stats as well as mental ones. Keeping a log will help you organize, prioritize, and examine your life and your running. The log should contain your training schedule and meal plans, but it should also be a place for you to examine ideas, thoughts, and feelings—both negative and positive. It's an excellent place to record positive thoughts about your training and your life. You can also use it as a repository for negative thoughts that need an exit route out of your head.

2. **Act "as if."** Many of us have an idea of what we want to present in competition. All of us have role models. Observe the people you admire and determine what it is that you admire about them. From those qualities, assemble a persona and begin to act as if you have already achieved those characteristics. You can also act as if you have achieved your goals (because they are more personally driven).

Learn Detached Awareness

Developing detached awareness overlaps with opening your mind and becoming self-aware. Having detached awareness means that you are able to remove the value judgments that we discussed earlier. In reality, you must train yourself to let go of a lot, to create a split personality of sorts.

In striving to achieve personal greatness, you must learn not to care about the outcome. You must learn to think in contradictions. The race itself must become the most important thing at the moment; you cannot care about the outcome. Any energy you put toward the outcome is energy that you take away from the process of getting there (the race itself). By removing the emotion and value judgment related to the result, a runner is able to use the energy to focus on what is happening right at that moment. The secret to detached awareness is to remove the emotion that inhibits you and to feed off the emotion that enables you.

DETACHED AWARENESS DRILLS

1. **Meditation.** The best drill to achieve detached awareness is meditation. Many people find that doing a progressive relaxation drill beforehand can help considerably. Find a quiet setting free of distractions. Begin with deep abdominal breathing in which you focus on the release of stress and

tension with each exhalation. Follow the relaxation drill with a tense-relax session for the different muscle groups. Starting with the shoulders, hold each muscle group tense for 10 seconds and then release the tension. Pay attention to what the tension feels like and what the release of the tension feels like.

Next choose a mantra. It can be a word, a thought, or even your breathing. The idea is to clear your mind, to bring you to the emotional climate in which you will be able to detach yourself. Most athletes would not want to use this particular exercise right before a competition. (Many books are available to facilitate relaxation and meditation. I like Herbert Benson's *The Relaxation Response*.)

2. **Cognitive reframing.** Examine a belief that you hold. Determine if it is helping your performance or hurting it. If it is hurting you, challenge its validity. Is it a truism or the result of constant programming and subconscious thought? We trust the validity of many suspect thoughts when we really should challenge them.

Turn on Your Automatic Pilot

When athletes talk about great performances, a number of terms come up—sweet spot, the zone, in the groove, automatic. The feeling of automatic movement is described by John Jerome in *The Sweet Spot*: " in the brain-vs.-brawn arguments, it is inescapable that our bodies are often smarter than our minds, if we could only learn to trust them."

Trusting the body is difficult in a society that encourages us to be distant from our bodies. Recapturing faith and trust in the potential of your body is a gradual process. While you are running, let all thoughts and judgments fall away. Deeply feel your body as it moves. Revel in its strength and power. Imagine that you are a metronome with amazing powers of adaptation. Try to find the place where you feel you could run forever and concetrate on committing that feeling to muscle memory.

AUTOMATIC PILOT DRILL

Self-hypnosis. This tool allows you to enter a state of willing suspension of disbelief. This disbelief is similar to what you would experience from a good movie or book when you develop physical symptoms as though you were an actual participant. Self-hypnosis allows you to narrow your attention drastically, to become deeply relaxed, and to experience increased suggestibility.

Use these hints for learning self-hypnosis:

• Find a quiet, comfortable place.

- While sitting quietly, take deep abdominal breaths while concentrating on your breathing.
- Allow your muscles to relax. The feeling is similar to what you feel when you sigh.

The most difficult part of self-hypnosis is believing that it is open to your control. Despite the fact that most of us do it daily, we are unaware of the powers at our command. Slowing down long enough to pay attention is the key to success.

The positive impacts for mental, physical, and emotional training are these:

- Increased ability to control respiration and heart rate.
- Better coping skills. A limited ability to deal with pain or discomfort can limit performance.
- Exceptional concentration skills. When an athlete enters a hypnotic state, the ability to concentrate is greatly enhanced.
- The ability to relax while in a state of intense mental focus. All emotion is removed.

Arriving at a breakthrough performance in your racing is a demanding and exhilarating task. To achieve such a performance, you must change from within. Learn to trust yourself and you will be on your way. Then you must understand that, in the end, a breakthrough performance is defined by hard work.

A runner who wants to realize her or his potential must be prepared to work at it. Not one of the hundreds of training "secrets" will work unless the runner does. Mental, emotional, and physical growth is a lifetime proposition and well worth the effort. Charlie Spedding, bronze medalist in the 1984 Olympic Marathon, passed this advice on to me: "It is not enough to work hard. To realize your best, you must be willing to work hard and smart."

22

Planning Your Racing Tactics

RANDY ACCETTA
Former U.S. Olympic Marathon Trials qualifier, coach of
Team in Training and the Workout Group in Tucson, Arizona

When we race,
we seek to run
fast, we seek to
run far—and we
seek to beat
others.

Training and racing are altogether different animals. The goals of training are varied: to get in shape, lose weight, or perhaps be able to run along a mountain trail just for fun. But the goal of racing is a simple one: to become a killer. When we race, we are like the sleek and deadly leopard—swift, strong, and thirsty for blood. Like the leopard, racers thrive on the chase. They live for the chance to cover ground swiftly, to pounce on their prey. The only difference is that our prey is different from the slower, clumsier baboon that the leopard sometimes stalks. Our prey consists of three creatures—time, distance, and place. When we race, we seek to run fast, we seek to run far—and we seek to beat others.

Racing is perhaps the most satisfying part of running because we can succeed on several levels every time we toe the line. If we run fast but still lose to another, we've still run fast. If we run a slower time but manage to stave off our competitors, then we're still victorious. And in some instances, like the marathon, we rarely compete against others: simply completing the distance is our challenge and our victory.

This chapter provides strategies and tactics to run faster and beat your competitors. A discussion of the various ways you can run your fastest in a given race is followed by a discussion the tactics you can employ to beat your competitors.

Keep in mind that before you can apply these strategies you must prepare your body and mind. That is, you cannot expect to succeed at a strategy if you have not practiced that method of running. As Percy Cerutty, the great Australian distance running coach, wrote in his book *Middle Distance Running* "It is unrealistic for us merely to train, mostly with little realism in the planning, and then go on to a track and believe that we will be able to race as we should."

A word to the wise: you cannot expect to race at 100 percent if you have not trained at 100 percent. Most of the following material will be particularly helpful if you have built a solid base and are capable of doing some form of lactate-threshold or interval training (see chapters 6, 8, and 9).

General Strategies: Three Choices

The three basic approaches to running your fastest time in a race are these: starting fast (or positive splits), starting slowly (negative splits), and even pacing.

Positive Splits

The objective here is to establish a quick early pace, quicker than you will be able to maintain throughout the race. The idea behind starting fast is to get away from your opponents and get a head start on your goal time. Of course, you want to slow down as little as possible as you progress through the race.

Although this approach can work well for advanced runners, starting too fast is often a recipe for trouble in longer races (what you consider a longer race depends on your background and specific strengths as a runner). This strategy will most likely bring you a fair amount of discomfort because you get into oxygen debt early and you have to react to that debt for the rest of the race.

Although the positive-split tactic isn't advisable for beginning runners, if you are well conditioned and can handle the psychological and physical rigors of running above your comfort level from the start, starting fast may set you up for a breakthrough race. Often, inexperienced runners start too swiftly in races, thus putting themselves in oxygen debt and jeopardizing a quality race.

You can practice for a positive-split tactic by starting your speed-training sessions with intervals that induce oxygen debt. A good rule is to do 20 to 30 percent of your workout at a pace that is a few seconds per quarter mile faster than your goal pace. Then return and do the rest of the workout at goal-race pace. For example, if your goal is to run under 16:30 for 5,000 meters, your training will include lots of 400-meter intervals run at 78- to 80-second quarter-mile pace (5:20-per-mile pace). Consequently, if you want to prepare for a hard opening pace in a race, you may start your workout with four intervals of 400 meters at 73 to 75 seconds with a short recovery. After completing one mile of especially quick intervals, return to goal-race pace and do two miles of intervals at 5:20-per-mile pace. (See chapter 9 for more on interval training.)

Likewise, if your goal is to complete a road race at close to 6:00 per mile, then to prepare for a quick start you will want to practice running closer to a 5:30- to 5:40-per-mile pace. If your speed workout consists of four miles, then spend one mile (25 percent of the workout) running at a pace faster than your goal-race pace. For instance, if the standard workout is four one-mile repeats at 6:00 per mile, start the workout by doing the first mile at 5:40 or by doing two half-mile repeats at 2:45. Then go back to the 6:00-per-mile repeats. The goal is to shock the system and get in oxygen debt immediately so that you can train your body and mind to handle this initial discomfort during the rest of the workout. (For more on fast-paced training, see chapters 8 and 9.)

Negative Splits

If you run negative splits, you expect to race the second half of the event at a significantly faster pace than the first half. In other words, you start slowly and speed up throughout the race. To ensure a negative split in longer races such as the marathon, you want to be certain to start slower than your goal pace. We tell our Team in Training novice marathoners that they should check their pace at the one-mile mark of the marathon, then, regardless of their pace, slow down a bit. After all, it is always more enjoyable for the novice to start slowly and gain speed later rather than start too fast and have to slow down. This is especially important in courses that have downhill sections in the later miles, such as the Boston, Big Sur, or St. George Marathons. To succeed in these races, you need to be as fresh as possible late in the race to take advantage of the hills.

Negative splits are often necessary in shorter events when runners are vying more for place than time, like championship races, cross country team competitions, and preliminary heats of the 800, 1,500, 3,000, and 5,000 meters. In these types of races, athletes run conservatively in the early stages, starting to run at maximum effort only as the race draws to a close. This sort of race tends to benefit natural kickers, though we can always improve our kick by training (see chapter 9 on speed training).

Train to run a negative split race by running hard-effort workouts that start slower than goal pace, then move to goal pace, and then finish faster than goal pace. For instance, if your goal is a sub-33:00 10K, you would do three two-mile repeats—the first at 5:25 to 5:30 pace (for a total time of just under 11:00), the second at 5:20 pace (10:40), and the third at 5:00 pace (10:00) if you can. The goal is to practice running faster when you are tired. You can do the same workout during a tempo run. Keep the first 10 minutes moderate, the second 10 minutes at close to race pace, and the last 10 minutes at 90 percent effort.

You can train yourself to handle a long closing finish by practicing sustained sprinting at the end of workouts, such as 150- to 300-meter sprints. You can also train yourself to sprint at the end by incorporating 50- to 80-meter repeats with full recovery at the end of your training sessions.

Even Pacing

The objective of even pacing during a race is to run as close as possible to the same pace throughout the race. This tactic works well in races over one mile long. After you train your body to handle a specific pace, you can sustain that cadence in a race. If you run too fast early in the race, you may go into oxygen debt. If you haven't trained to handle this oxygen debt (see positive splits), you may have a miserable day.

When I ran in college, the qualifying time for Division III nationals in the 5,000 meters was 14:40. I never achieved that time in college (my best was 14:50), but I continued to reach for it after graduating. I joined the Reebok Aggie running club, and my new coach, Tom Craig, believed that the best way to break 14:40 was to practice running the same pace repeatedly, in this case, a 4:40-per-mile pace. He had me run interval after interval at that pace—35-second 200 meters; 70-second quarters; 2:20 half miles. I remember one workout in particular when I was supposed to do 16 quarters in 70 seconds. I felt good during this workout, and at one point cruised to a 66. Tom pulled me aside and said kindly but sternly, "No, the goal of the workout is 70 seconds. Now go run a 70." After I ran the next quarter in 67, Tom called out, "OK, that's it. Off the track. If you can't run 70 seconds, then don't run anymore tonight. You can try again next week." I was embarrassed and not a little ticked off. But he was the coach, so I threw on my sweats, cooled down, and went home.

Tom wasn't being a tyrant. He was merely making a point. The goal of the workout was to practice pace work, and by speeding up I was not achieving that specific goal.

If your goal is to break 14:40 for 5K, suggested workouts include the following: 20 intervals of 400 meters at 70-second pace with a one-minute rest; 6 to 8 intervals of 800 meters in 2:20 with a two-minute rest; 4 intervals

In races longer than a mile, try running an even pace that you can sustain throughout the race.

Courtesy of Examiner Bay to Breakers

of one mile in 4:40 with a four- or five-minute rest. Adjust the times to your goal. If your goal is to break three hours for the marathon, then you will need to average 6:52 per mile. A workout for our advanced Team in Training runners is 8 to 10 intervals of 800 meters in three minutes with three-minute recoveries. Although this pace is faster than marathon goal pace, the workout teaches them to handle the sustained effort required for the marathon.

Track workouts are not the only way to practice pacing. Wearing a heart rate monitor can also help you pace yourself evenly in workouts and through the first portions of a race. You can transfer this pace-effort work from the track to the roads by training your body to know what a particular pace feels like.

Different races call for different methods of running, so you will want to practice all three approaches. Pick low-key races and experiment to see which approach works best for you. Remember, to succeed at a particular race strategy, you need to train your body to execute it.

Specific Tactics

"Hurry, hurry. Catch up to that pack." You've heard this sort of remark yelled out at a road race or track meet. Heck, you might even have yelled it yourself. "Get up there. Pass 'em on the hill!" Of course, it is a lot easier to give advice than it is to follow it. Although no mind game can substitute for accurate and demanding training, some tactics can help you make the most of your abilities. Many of these tactics are especially helpful when racing on the track, whereas others are more suited to the roads or cross country racing.

Know Thyself—and Thy Competition

To race well you need to be smart as well as strong. You need to know your strengths and weaknesses. If possible, you need to know your competitors' strengths and weaknesses. For example, if you train on hills and know that your competitor trains in the flatlands, then you will want to push the pace going up and down the hills. On the track, if you have built an excellent endurance base but do not have a healthy finishing kick, you will most likely want to push the pace at some time during the race to avoid being caught in a kicking duel. If you have excellent sprinting speed compared with the other runners in the field, you will want to stay near the leaders and launch your sprint toward the end.

Remember too that you can always gain new strengths. Just because you haven't developed a kick doesn't mean that you'll never have one. Just because you don't run fast uphill doesn't mean that you never will. You have to practice, drill, and train your body and mind to do what you want to do. Adapt your training to work on your weaknesses. For instance, to develop your hill-running ability, incorporate stadium stairs during your base-training phase. (For more on base training, see chapter 6.)

Know the Course

You need to know the terrain that you will be covering, particularly in cross country and marathon races. If possible, train on the course before race day. For instance, many marathons provide group training runs along the course in the months leading up to race day. If possible, join these group runs and prepare your body and mind for the specific terrain. If you cannot practice on the course, study the race maps and prepare on terrain that is similar to what you will compete on. For example, if you plan on running the Boston Marathon, do your long runs on a course that rolls gently for the first 10 to 12 miles, climbs uphill for the next half hour or so, and then has some downhills and flats for the last portion. By training on a course that mimics the Boston course, you will be better prepared on race day. You can also plan your surges (after you round a corner and are briefly out of sight of your closest competitor), points where you plan to break away, and so forth.

Think on Your Feet

Although you may have planned a specific strategy for the race, you need to be able to adjust your plans according to the way the race unfolds. If you had planned to run a negative-split race but find that the pack is running faster—and you feel relatively strong—quickly change your plan and stick with the pack. Maintaining a training log will help you prepare for races. Write down the details of each race you run and refer to these notes when you are planning a strategy for upcoming races. Once you learn your patterns of strengths and weaknesses, you can better prepare yourself for specific races.

This doesn't mean changing your mind willy-nilly. I was running a marathon once with Greg Wenneborg, a 1996 and 2000 Olympic Marathon Trials qualifier. At the three-mile mark, he suddenly started running faster than his goal pace, trying to catch a pack of runners 100 yards ahead. "I feel good," he said when I cautioned him to slow down. Of course he felt good—it was the three-mile mark! He was supposed to feel good. Fortunately, instead of trying to catch the pack in front of us, he slowed back down to his goal pace. Ten miles later, we were still running strong and had caught all those who went out too fast. We eventually ran 2:19 that day, with Greg finishing one second ahead of me.

Keep Elbows Out at the Start

Don't be bashful about establishing your position. It doesn't matter if the race is an indoor mile or a big-city marathon; protect yourself by angling your elbows outward so you create space between you and other runners. Although I don't advocate shoving the grandmother running next to you, don't hesitate to establish your place. This is especially true at the start of a track race when you need to gain an advantageous position quickly.

Be Patient

Unless the course is so narrow that you will not be able to move up during the race, it is best to start within yourself. Remember, you don't want to get into oxygen debt too early. An easier beginning will allow you to pass others with authority and surge when needed. Find someone you know with comparable ability and work together through the beginning stages.

Be Aggressive on the Hills

Once you've worked your way into the race, attack the course. Surge up short hills. Be patient during long hills, then surge at their crests. Work the downhills. Many runners tend to relax at the top of a hill rather than maintaining a hard effort. You can use gravity to help you run faster downhill while still recovering from the demands of uphill running. If you find yourself discouraged while running uphill, remember that this, too, will pass. You'll be able to recover on the next flat or downhill.

Pass With Authority

Racing is a head game, and you can break your competitors by running fast when they don't expect or want you to. Throw in a burst of speed for 50 to 200 meters as you approach or round corners. Surge at the crest of a hill or on a flat section at the bottom of a hill. If you can dash past tired runners and quickly distance yourself from them, often they'll be too discouraged to catch up. If possible, keep the pressure on for several meters after such a surge.

Relax

You cannot sustain a sprint throughout the race, so be willing to relax at times. Run in a group and let others take the pace. This is especially crucial in long races when you need to run under control for a lengthy period. Train yourself to sit in a pack and let the miles slide by.

Cover the Break

When a group breaks away from you, go with it—you don't need to lead the break, but you must be willing to keep contact. Even if you are fatigued, maintaining contact with the group ahead of you will keep you motivated and focused. When you recover from the surge, you will be well positioned to advance further. Of course, it is easier to run in the middle of a pack than it is to run by yourself, so let the pack carry you along.

Cut the Tangents

Run the shortest distance possible by knowing the course and knowing when to cut angles. You get no brownie points for running farther than anyone else. Geoff Smith learned this the hard way when he lost the 1983 New York City Marathon to Rod Dixon because he followed the blue course markings while Dixon cut the tangents and ran the shortest legal distance. (Of course, do make certain that you complete the required course.)

Follow Those Who Pass You

When someone passes you, don't let him or her create a gap between the two of you. This is especially important in the late stages of the race. Stay on your competitor's shoulder and run with him or her as long as you can. Often, keeping up with someone who passes you will give you a burst of positive psychological energy that allows you to maintain the quicker pace. In addition, your competitor may lose enthusiasm if he or she knows you are determined to keep the pace. This is especially important in a track race. When you are passed, remain on the person's outside shoulder; otherwise, you run the risk of being boxed in.

Think Quick Feet

You can speed up your running cadence by getting your feet down fast and bringing your heels around quickly. Cross country courses in particular force your body to adapt to varied terrain, and quick feet will help you navigate treacherous sections. Instead of trying to run farther with each stride, keep your strides short but move through the running cycle more quickly.

Think Quick Hands

Quick hands lead to quick feet, so use short, quick arm strokes leading with the hands to drive you forward. On uphills, lean into the hill and keep your hips forward. On downhills, lean down the hill and let gravity give you speed. Many runners lean backward in a breaking motion when running downhill, but this only slows them down. Avoid windmilling your arms and keep a normal, fast arm swing. Let gravity carry you and maintain your normal running form.

> Cross country courses and trail races force your body to adapt to varied terrain. Using short, quick, strides will help you navigate treacherous sections.

Be Tough

In almost every race you will reach a point where continuing at your pace seems impossible. Your legs will ache, your breathing will be labored, and your mind will urge you to back off and save yourself. If you wish to race well, however, you won't give in to this seductive voice. Instead, you will change your cadence and run on. Regardless of the discomfort, you will soon recover.

Racing Don'ts

We must avoid doing harmful or inefficient things when we race. The following list is a reminder of the tactical errors that can ruin a runner's opportunity for a successful race.

Don't Start Like a Wild Dog

In the novel *Once a Runner,* John L. Parker Jr. writes that no mile race is ever won in the first lap. This principle applies at every distance. Learn to control yourself in the early stages so you can make the best of your training.

Don't Finish Like a Wild Dog

If you find yourself with a blazing finish, chances are you didn't push yourself enough during the rest of the race. It's important to have enough for a fast close, but be certain that you extend yourself during the latter portion of the race.

Don't Give Up

Don't become discouraged when someone passes you. Eventually everyone gets tired, so keep close and be ready to pounce on your rival when he or she slows down. Use landmarks to help you. Pick a tree to focus on and run fast to it, then run fast to that next mile marker.

Don't Give In to Pity Form

I'm sure you've seen what I call pity form—head back, mouth open, arms carried high, breaths coming in short, high-pitched gasps. We run this way because we want everyone to know how tired we are. In reality, though, we still have a lot of running left in us if we just drop the head, take deeper breaths, and drive the arms. Another benefit is that you will look stronger to your competition.

Don't Slow Down Before the Finish Line

Who has the world record in the 200 meters? Not Carl Lewis. Great as he was, the nine-time Olympic gold medalist slowed and waved to the crowd when he could have set a 200-meter world record. Never, ever slow down before the finish line. Run every step of the way through and past it. Practice this in speed workouts, making sure that you don't slow down before the end of each interval. Instead of finishing your intervals at the finish, run 10 meters farther to practice running through the finish line.

Choose a landmark or mile marker to run to, to break up the race and keep you focused on the task at hand.

A word to the wise: don't drop out! Unless you have a clearly damaging injury or are suffering from extreme heat, cold, or energy depletion, don't step off the course. Once you commit yourself to a race, you owe it to yourself to finish, even if things don't go your way. Quit once and it's easier to quit again.

Track Racing Tactics

I began track racing back in the days of cinder tracks. Our coach at Wesleyan University, Elmer Swanson, was also the old-fashioned kind, a man of few words. We would stand at the starting line readying ourselves for the race and from the sidelines we would hear Elmer call out to us, "Remember, fellas, take your first left."

On the roads, position isn't too important because there is so much room to maneuver, but on the track it's everything. If you are boxed in for even a step or two, you might not be able to cover the break. Let's look at some of the benefits and drawbacks of each of the positions runners assume when racing on the track.

Position 1

This is an emotionally and physically draining place to be. It takes a special runner to handle front running from start to finish. As Percy Cerutty wrote, "As soon as you can be, be a front-runner. Do not be afraid to be the hare in races that may comprise the world's best in the field. On the other hand, it is equally foolish to go into the lead, to run at a pace that you cannot ordinarily maintain." If you thrive on the pressure of leading and you want to control the pace, this is the place to be.

1			
2	3		
4	5	6	
7	8	9	10
11		12	13
14			

Track positions.

Benefits

- You can control the pace from the front of the race.
- You have clear vision of everything in front of you.
- Your arms and feet are relatively clear of the jostling that occurs in the middle of the pack.
- You are on the inside and are therefore running as short a distance as possible.
- If someone tries to pass you, you can cover any break immediately.
- There is something emotionally invigorating about leading.

Drawbacks

- You have no idea what is happening behind you.
- Your heels can be clipped.
- You have to set the pace for everyone else.

Position 2

This is an excellent place for the early stages of the race, but you have to be willing to make a move through others to follow the leaders; otherwise, you run the risk of being boxed in when you need to get out.

Benefits

- You are running on the inside and are therefore running as short a distance as possible.
- You can respond to any move by the leader.
- You have a clear vision of everything in front of you.
- You can push your way out of the box created by #1 and #3 if you need to cover a break by another runner.

Drawbacks
- You are caught in a small box and may have to push your way out.
- You cannot respond immediately to a move on the outside.
- You have to worry about being clipped or pushed from behind or the side. You may also inadvertently step on the heels of runner #1.

Positions 3 and 6

From here you are able to attack when you want to and you can cover a move if necessary. During a 10K you may want to move to the inside for most laps. In the #6 position be aware that you are running in the outside lanes. Many people think that the #3 position is the best during a 3K or 5K.

Benefits
- You have a clear picture of the front of the race.
- You can make a move at any time to follow a runner on the outside, follow the leader, or make a surge of your own.
- You are relatively clear of the jostling that occurs in the middle of the pack.
- You have the psychological advantage of being near the front.

Drawbacks
- You are running a bit outside, though the freedom of movement makes up for the extra distance.

Positions 4, 5, 7, 8, 9, 11, and 12

These are excellent positions during the slower stages of a longer race, but it is hard to compete from here. You have to be alert to the bodies around you. Staying in the pack may help you run a fast time, but it may hinder your chances of winning. Avoid spending too much time on the outside.

Benefits
- You can settle in and let the pace carry you.
- You get the help of the draft.
- You don't have to worry about the pace.
- Those on the inside don't have as far to run as those on the outside.
- You have the psychological comfort of being with the main group.

Drawbacks
- You run the risk of being boxed in and missing the break.
- You have to deal with jostling and pushing.

- You may have to alter your form by keeping your elbows wide and chopping your stride.
- You cannot control the pace.

Positions 10 and 13

Both these positions require you to run too far to the outside during a long-distance track race. Unless you are planning to make a surge to the front, try not to spend much time here.

Benefits

- You are clear of all the pushing and have a clear vision of the field in front of you.
- Most likely you can cover any break made by a front-runner.
- You can surge to the front without fighting through a crowd.

Drawbacks

- You are running farther outside and therefore covering more distance.
- If you drift too far back you cannot cover a move made by the leaders.
- If you are too far outside you lose the advantage of the pack's energy pulling you along.

Position 14

It takes a special runner to compete from the back of the pack. But if you have good sprint speed and can make up ground in a hurry, this may be a safe place for you during the early stages of a race, as long as you are mentally and physically able to make a move through or around the pack.

Benefits

- You have a clear vision of everything in front of you.
- Your arms and feet are relatively clear of the jostling that occurs in the middle of the pack.
- You are on the inside and are therefore running as short a distance as possible.

Drawbacks

- You are far behind the leaders and may not be able to cover a break.
- You are far behind the leaders.
- You must mentally deal with being last.

Hurry Back

Knowledge is power. The more we know about our abilities, the more power we have over our three opponents—time, distance, and other runners. So practice these various tactics in training. Pretend that your training partners are archrivals and that the midday workout is the Olympic Games. Daydream and see yourself winning the gold in world record time. Remember, regardless of our natural speed, all of us can be great racers.

Finally, now that I've presented such a lengthy list of strategies and tactics, I should tell you the most important one. My old college coach, Elmer Swanson, used to give this advice during cross country season. Over the years, he's coached Jeff Galloway, Amby Burfoot, Bill Rodgers, and a slew of Olympic trials qualifiers. When you next stand at the starting line, after you double-tie your laces and tuck in your shirt, remember Elmer's words: "Have fun out there, and hurry back."

23

Fueling Your Body for Racing

JACKIE BERNING, PhD, RD
Assistant professor, University of Colorado, Colorado Springs

Preparing your body for racing begins with good daily nutrition. Most of the energy for exercise comes from foods eaten hours or days before the start of the race.

Achieving your breakthrough performance depends on a number of factors including your goals, genetics, training, and motivation. You had no say about your genetic makeup, of course, and you may find other elements difficult to control. A busy schedule or unforeseen events may cause you to reduce training time. Your motivation may wane. You may find that you have to modify your goals. But one factor you *can* control is selecting foods that will contribute to a breakthrough race. Like all athletes, runners require a nutritionally balanced diet rich in nutrients to sustain normal daily activities as well as the additional demands of training and competition. Making wise food choices and learning when to eat what, before and during competition, provides muscles with the proper fuel and allows runners of all abilities to race to their potential.

As you read in chapter 13, fueling your body consistently for training allows you to prepare your body to withstand the stress of daily workouts and long runs and helps reduce your chance becoming run down or injured. For example, John is preparing for his first half marathon. During his final weeks of intensive training, he notices that after two or three days of hard mileage, he cannot recover properly for the next day's training session. Like many endurance athletes, John finds that his carbohydrate stores are limiting his ability to train intensely.

A nutritional concern for most endurance runners is consuming enough carbohydrate to fuel their muscles. Glycogen (stored carbohydrate) is used as the major fuel during moderate- to high-intensity workouts and races. If John does not consume enough carbohydrates in his diet, he will not be able to replace his muscle glycogen and his performance will diminish.

Carbohydrate is the most important nutrient for working muscles. But because the body has limited capacity to store carbohydrate, it is the least abundant nutrient within muscles. Work conducted by Dr. David Costill (1988, 1986, 1980) showed that runners who do not consume enough carbohydrate in their diets experience chronic glycogen depletion and fatigue.

Focus on Daily Nutrition

As a runner, keeping your daily nutritional needs met will help you train optimally and, therefore, race optimally. Your daily energy needs depend on the duration and intensity of your training program. Many runners train intensely for more than 90 minutes per day and expend from 1,000 to 1,400 calories during the workout. A 150-pound runner exercising at this intensity and duration needs to consume about 3,500 calories per day to stay in energy balance. Good daily nutrition sets the foundation for breakthrough racing. That is, prerace fueling doesn't start a few days before the big race.

As you've learned in chapter 13, a diet composed of 60 percent carbohydrate, 15 percent protein, and 25 percent fat with an adequate amount of calories is necessary to provide the proper fuel mix for optimal performance. To ensure a carbohydrate-rich diet, most runners should eat at least 500 grams of carbohydrate per day, or 4 to 5 grams of carbohydrate per pound of body weight, to restore carbohydrate levels. The table on the following page lists high-carbohydrate foods that can help you meet your muscles' energy demands.

Runners who train twice a day besides working full time and participating in other activities may find it difficult to consume enough carbohydrate. In these situations, I often recommend a high-carbohydrate supplement. These products are not intended to replace carbohydrate-rich foods but to supply extra calories and meet your daily carbohydrate requirements. These carbohydrate-loaded drinks can be consumed in the days leading up to a race or after a race, either with or between meals. They help by

High-Carbohydrate Foods

Food Group		Serving size	Calories	Carbohydrates (grams)
Milk	Milk (low-fat)	I cup (8 oz)	121	12
	Milk (skim)	I cup	86	12
	Milk (chocolate)	I cup	208	26
	Pudding (any flavor)	1/2 cup	161	20
	Yogurt (low-fat, frozen)	I cup	220	34
	Yogurt (low-fat, with fruit)	I cup	220	43
Meat	Meatloaf	3 oz.	230	13
Fruit	Apple	I medium	81	21
	Apple juice	I cup	111	28
	Applesauce	I cup	194	52
	Banana	I medium	105	27
	Cantaloupe	I cup	57	13
	Cherries	10	49	11
	Cranberry juice cocktail	I cup	147	37
	Dates (dried)	10	228	61
	Fruit cocktail (in juice)	1/2 cup	56	15
	Fruit roll-up	I roll	50	12
	Grapes	I cup	58	16
	Grape juice	I cup	96	23
	Orange	I medium	65	16
	Orange juice	I cup	112	26
	Pear	I medium	98	25
	Pineapple	I cup	77	19
	Prunes	10	201	53
	Raisins	2/3 cup	300	79
	Raspberries	I cup	61	14
	Strawberries	I cup	45	11
Vegetables	Black-eyed peas	1/2 cup	99	78
	Carrots	1/2 cup	31	7
	Corn	1/2 cup	88	21
	Garbanzo beans (chickpeas)	I cup	269	45
	Lima beans	I cup	217	39
	Navy beans	I cup	259	48
	Peas (green)	1/2 cup	63	12
	Pinto beans	I cup	235	44
	Potato	I large	139	32
	Refried beans	I cup	270	47
	Sweet potato	I large	118	28
	Three-bean salad	1/2 cup	90	20
	Water chestnuts	1/2 cup	66	15
	White beans	I cup	249	45
Grains	Bagel	I	163	31
	Biscuit	I	103	13
	Bread (white)	I slice	61	12
	Bread (whole wheat)	I slice	61	11
	Breadsticks	2 sticks	77	15
	Cornbread	I square	178	28
	Cereal (ready to eat)	I cup	110	24
	Cream of Wheat	3/4 cup	96	20
	Graham crackers	2 squares	63	11
	Hamburger or hotdog bun	I	119	21
	Malt-O-Meal	3/4 cup	92	19
	Noodles (spaghetti)	I cup	159	34
	Oatmeal (flavored)	I packet	110	25
	Pancake	I	61	9
	Rice (brown)	I cup	232	50
	Rice (white)	I cup	206	50
	Saltines	5 crackers	60	10
	Tortilla (flour)	I	95	17
	Triscuit crackers	3 crackers	60	10
	Waffle	I	130	17

providing carbohydrate to the muscles to replenish reduced glycogen stores. Keep in mind that high-carbohydrate drinks are too concentrated in carbohydrates to be an effective fluid replacement during racing. Their purpose is to help you keep your fuel levels constant throughout the day. Such supplements may also aid your postrace recovery.

Consider Carbohydrate Loading

One of the primary ways runners avoid fatigue associated with low glycogen stores is to consume a diet high in carbohydrate before racing. This practice, known as carbohydrate loading or glycogen supercompensation, serves to increase muscle glycogen reserves for race day.

The practice and principles of carboloading involve two phases:

- Depletion of muscle glycogen stores (with exercise and low carbohydrate intake) to make the muscles more receptive to storing glycogen
- Supercompensation for this glycogen depletion in the last few days before competition by increasing the percentage of carbohydrates consumed and reducing training intensity

During races that exceed 90 to 120 minutes, such as marathons or ultramarathons, muscle glycogen stores become progressively lower and drop to critically low levels if not replenished during the event. This depletion in muscle glycogen results in your not being able to maintain high-intensity exercise beyond 90 to 120 minutes. In practical terms, you become exhausted and must drastically reduce your pace.

By using carbohydrate-loading principles before a marathon, however, you can increase your muscle glycogen stores by 50 percent to 100 percent. The greater your prerace muscle glycogen content, the greater your endurance potential.

Classic Regimen for Carbohydrate Loading

In the 1970s runners used a more classic carbo loading technique. Starting the regimen six days before their event, they would first deplete their muscle glycogen stores through exhaustive running and maintaining a low-carbohydrate diet (virtually 0 percent) for three days. Then for the three days just before the race, these runners would increase their carbohydrate intake to 70 percent while decreasing their exercise. This regimen of low carbohydrate intake followed by high carbohydrate intake allowed the muscles to store more glycogen, resulting in longer performance times before exhaustion, even though glycogen use was greater.

But this regimen has some drawbacks. Maintaining effective training workouts is difficult when your carbohydrate stores are low during the depletion phase. When the quality of your workout suffers, you increase your risk of injury. Moreover, performing three days of exhaustive running four or five days before a competition is difficult.

Practical Carbohydrate Loading

Fortunately, Michael Sherman, PhD, of Ohio State University developed a modified carbohydrate-loading regimen that was without the drawbacks of the classic regimen. His technique showed that runners can obtain glycogen supercompensation in the six days before a competition by consuming a diet of about 50 percent carbohydrate for the first three days and then consuming a diet of 70 percent carbohydrate for the three days before the event. During this six-day period, exercise duration is progressively decreased from 90 minutes on day one, to about 40 minutes on days two and three, to about 20 minutes on days four and five, to a very light day or total rest on day six (see table below). Keep in mind that excessive exercise during this period will use too much of the stored glycogen and defeat the purpose of glycogen loading. This method has been shown to raise glycogen levels comparable to those seen in the classic regimen but with fewer side effects.

It is important to remember that carbohydrate loading is for endurance activities that last longer than 90 minutes. Marathons and other endurance events will benefit most from structured carbohydrate-loading techniques. Greater than normal glycogen stores will not enable a 10K runner to push harder nor will it allow an 800-meter runner to run faster. If your event is 90 minutes or less, you will not gain as much benefit from carbo loading as an athlete preparing for a longer event. Still, carbohydrates are important for your ability to race shorter distances. A 5K or 10K runner should eat a balanced diet (60 percent of which is carbohydrate) and be sure to top off her or his carbohydrate tank before, during, and after racing.

Practical Approach to Carbohydrate Loading

Day	Training time	Carbohydrate intake
1	90 minutes	50% carbohydrate or 5 g per kg body weight
2	40 minutes	50% carbohydrate or 5 g per kg body weight
3	40 minutes	50% carbohydrate or 5 g per kg body weight
4	20 minutes	70% carbohydrate or 10 g per kg body weight
5	20 minutes	70% carbohydrate or 10 g per kg body weight
6	Rest	70% carbohydrate or 10 g per kg body weight
7	Event	Event

To figure your body weight in kilograms, take your weight in pounds and divide by 2.2. The result is your body weight in kilograms. For example 185 lb ÷ 2.2 kg/lb = 84 kg.

Bloating and Carbo Loading

Some runners complain of feeling bloated or having heavy legs after a week of consuming high carbohydrates and doing less training. The heavy feeling likely occurs because every gram of glycogen you put into the muscles causes you to store three to five grams of water. Before competition in the heat, gaining this water weight may be an advantage because it provides the body with more water for sweating.

Plan Your Prerace Meals

Runners often ask me what they should eat before an intense practice or competition. Unfortunately, it is not uncommon to see runners who have upset stomachs or fuel deficits because they haven't picked the best foods to eat before they started their event.

The precompetition meal serves two purposes:

1. It keeps you from feeling hungry before and during the event.
2. It maintains optimal levels of blood glucose for your working muscles throughout the competition.

Many runners don't eat before they race, especially if the event is in the early morning. Many cite nervousness, not having enough time, or feeling more comfortable competing on an empty stomach as the reasons they don't eat before their event. But not eating before an early morning race of any distance (after fasting 6 to 10 hours overnight) lowers your liver glycogen stores, can cause lightheadedness, nausea, and fatigue, and can impair performance. Eating several hours before competition replenishes liver glycogen stores and ensures that adequate energy is available. On the other hand, you don't want your stomach to be full during a race. In general, it can take from one to four hours for the stomach to digest a meal and empty it into the intestines. If a runner is nervous about his or her performance, the digestive process may take even longer. Food that remains in the stomach during the competition may cause indigestion, nausea, and possibly vomiting. Eat your preevent meal one to three hours before the start of your competition. That way, your stomach will be relatively empty during the event.

Choosing Precompetition Foods

The preevent meal should include foods that are high in carbohydrates and that are removed rapidly from the stomach and intestines, such as breads, pasta, rice, cereals, bagels, English muffins, bananas, apples, oranges, potatoes, corn, and peas. Because these foods are digested quickly, you won't be competing with a full stomach and the carbohydrates provided in such foods can help you restore suboptimal liver glycogen stores, which may be called on during a long race such as a marathon. In a shorter, higher intensity race, such as a 5K or 10K, you rely on the stored carbohydrate in the muscle (glycogen) and blood glucose. You won't use glycogen supplied by the liver until your muscle glycogen and blood-glucose levels are diminished.

How much carbohydrate should you consume in your preevent meal? Current research suggests that you should consume one to four grams of carbohydrate per kilogram of body weight one to four hours before exercise. For example, a 150-pound (68-kilogram) runner should aim to eat 68 to 272 grams of carbohydrate. To avoid stomach and gastrointestinal distress, reduce the carbohydrate content of the meal as you come closer to the start of the event. For example, a carbohydrate feeding of one gram per kilogram of body weight is appropriate immediately before the exercise, whereas four grams per kilogram of body weight can safely consumed four hours before the exercise. Use the list below when planning your precompetition meals.

Ideas for Precompetition Meals

- Cereal, bread, pasta, muffins, pancakes, rolls, bagels, tortillas, rice, and other grain products
- Fruits and vegetables, particularly starchy vegetables like peas, corn, and potatoes
- Low-fat milk, yogurt, and frozen yogurt
- Dried beans and peas like refried or baked beans, black-eyed peas

Does Consuming Sugar Before Exercise Improve Performance?

Runners often consume simple carbohydrates such as sugar, honey, candy, or soft drinks just before exercise thinking it will provide them with "quick energy." Unfortunately, eating sugary foods won't provide a boost for muscle glycogen. Remember, most of the energy for exercise comes from foods eaten several hours or even days before the start of the race or competition.

Although new evidence suggests that sugary foods consumed 35 to 40 minutes before exercise may benefit a runner by providing glucose to the exercising muscles, the practice could harm the performance of runners who are sensitive to fluctuations in blood sugar. Evaluate whether you are sensitive to a lowering of blood glucose by trying various amounts of carbohydrate before exercise during training.

Because of their short gastric emptying time, you can consume liquid meals (such as Carnation Instant Breakfast, Exceed, Boost, GatorPro, or your own concocted smoothie) closer to the competition than you can solid foods. Runners who are nervous or tense and have an associated delay in gastric emptying may find that consuming liquid meals helps prevent precompetition nausea.

The hot dogs, donuts, nachos, potato chips, and candy bars found at most concession stands are extremely high in fat and do not digest quickly. These foods eaten as preevent meals will likely stay in your stomach much of the morning or afternoon and thus impair performance. Avoid or limit eating these and other high-fat foods in the preevent meal.

Dehydration of as little as 2 percent of body weight can adversely affect athletic performance.

Eating During Races and All-Day Events

For runners who compete at all-day events such as track meets, making nutritious food choices may be a challenge. The runner should consider the amount of time between eating and performance when choosing foods at all-day events. The following are suggested menus for 5K or 10K events as well as for all-day events.

One hour or less before competition (single races or track events with multiple heats)
- Fruit and vegetable juice such as orange, tomato, or V-8
- Fresh fruit such as apples, watermelon, peaches, grapes, or oranges
- $1^1/_2$ cups of a commercial sports drink

Two to three hours between competition
- Fresh fruit and fruit and vegetable juices
- Bread, bagels, or English muffins with limited amounts of butter, margarine, or cream cheese; low-fat yogurt
- 4 cups of a commercial sports drink

Three to four hours between competition
- Fresh fruit and fruit and vegetable juices
- Bread; bagels; baked potatoes; cereal with low-fat milk; low-fat yogurt; sandwiches with a small amount of peanut butter, lean meat, or low-fat cheese
- $7^1/_2$ cups of a commercial sports drink

Replenishing Fluids

As you may remember from chapter 13, fluid replacement is probably the most important nutritional concern for runners. Approximately 60 percent of your body weight is water. As you compete, you lose fluid through the skin as sweat and through the lungs by respiration. If you don't replace this fluid at regular intervals during exercise, dehydration can occur. A dehydrated runner has a decreased volume of circulating blood. Consequently, the heart pumps less blood with each beat, exercising muscles do not receive enough oxygen, and performance suffers. In addition, body temperature increases, which further reduces performance. Simply put, the muscles shut down. Research has repeatedly shown that dehydration of as little as 2 percent of body weight can adversely affect athletic performance. Thus, a 150-pound runner who loses 3 pounds during a workout or long race has affected his or her ability to run fast.

Preventing Dehydration

The best way to prevent dehydration is to maintain body fluid levels by taking in plenty of fluids *before, during,* and *after* a workout or race. Often runners do not realize how much body fluid they are losing or that they are affecting their performance by being dehydrated. You can monitor hydration using two techniques. One is to weigh yourself before your run and again after the run. For every pound you lose during the workout you need to drink two cups (16 ounces) of fluid to rehydrate the body. A second way is to check the color of your urine. If it is dark gold, then you are dehydrated. If you are well hydrated, your urine will be pale yellow or lighter. Runners often wait to drink until they are thirsty. Thirst, however, is not an accurate indicator of how much fluid you have lost. If you wait until you are thirsty to replenish body fluids, you are already dehydrated. Most of us do not become thirsty until we have lost more than 2 percent of our body weight.

Proper fluid replenishment is the key to preventing dehydration and reducing the risk of heat injury in runners engaged in training and competition.

Similarly, if you drink enough only to quench your thirst, you may still be dehydrated. For best results, keep a fluid bottle available when working out and drink as often as desired, ideally one-half to one cup (four to eight ounces) every 15 to 30 minutes.

Including Nutrients With Fluids

Sports drinks containing 6 to 8 percent glucose or sucrose are absorbed by the body as rapidly as water and can provide energy to the working muscle that water cannot. A growing body of evidence suggests that consumption of a sports drink containing 6 to 8 percent carbohydrate can delay fatigue and possibly improve performance. Runners who consume a sports drink, especially during long endurance events, can maintain blood-glucose levels even when muscle glycogen stores are diminished. This allows the body to continue to use carbohydrate at high rates.

It seems doubtful that drinks containing less than 5 percent carbohydrate can provide enough energy to enhance performance. Therefore, runners who dilute sports drinks are most likely not getting enough carbohydrate in their sports drinks to maintain blood glucose. On the other hand, drinking beverages that exceed 10 percent carbohydrate (most soda pop and most fruit juices) is often associated with abdominal cramps, nausea, and diarrhea, which can be detrimental to performance. Furthermore, carbonated beverages tend to take up more space in the stomach and make a runner feel full.

Many sports drinks also supply the body with electrolytes such as sodium. The ingestion of sodium during exercise may maintain or restore plasma volume—the volume of fluid in the blood. By maintaining good fluid levels in the blood you are able to prevent the body from overheating during exercise and recovery. Consuming sports drinks containing sodium helps retain water in the body and aids in hydration by increasing the absorption of fluid from the intestines into the muscles. Recent research has suggested that a 6 percent carbohydrate sports drink with about 110 milligrams of sodium per eight-ounce serving empties faster from the intestines than plain water.

Some runners worry that sports drinks may contain too much sodium. Most sports drinks, however, are lower in sodium than many other processed and prepared foods that athletes consume.

Ideal Fluid Replacement

The ideal fluid-replacement beverage is one that tastes good to the athlete, does not cause gastrointestinal discomfort or distress when consumed in large volumes, promotes rapid fluid absorption and maintenance of body fluid, and provides energy to working muscles during intense training and competition. The following guidelines will help you maintain your body fluid balance. By maintaining hydration you may even be able to improve your performance in the heat and prevent heat-related illness.

- For intense training and long workouts or races (over 60 minutes), a sports drink containing carbohydrates may provide an important source of energy. A 6 to 8 percent beverage appears to be effective in maintaining fluid balance while supplying the muscles with fuel. If the workout is longer than 60 minutes, replenish your fluids every 15 to 20 minutes and refuel your carbohydrate stores at the rate of about 1 gram of carbohydrate per minute (14 to 15 grams every 15 minutes).
- The fluid should contain a small amount of sodium and electrolytes. The sodium may promote quicker absorption.
- The beverage should be palatable and taste good. Both coldness and sweetness enhance palatability.
- Hyperhydrate with 10 to 16 ounces of cold fluid about 15 to 30 minutes before your competition. If the race is over 60 minutes add carbohydrates to the beverage at a 6 to 8 percent concentration.
- Rehydrate with one-half to one cup (4 to 8 ounces) of cold fluid during exercise at 10- to 15-minute intervals.
- Start rehydration early in the race or workout.
- Avoid carbonated drinks, which can cause gastrointestinal distress and may decrease the volume of fluid consumed.

- Avoid beverages containing caffeine and alcohol because of their diuretic effect.
- If you have never used a sports drink, don't start on race day. Practice consuming fluids while you train. Use a trial and error approach until you find the sports drink or fluid that works for you.

Does Caffeine Improve Performance?

Studies have shown that caffeine may improve endurance performance. Initially, it was thought that caffeine stimulated a greater use of fat for energy so that less glycogen was burned. More recent caffeine studies, however, don't support the glycogen-sparing effect of caffeine. When caffeine improves endurance, it does so by acting as a stimulant.

But caffeine does not help everyone. Some individuals are extremely sensitive to it and have a negative, hypersensitive response. Side effects of caffeine ingestion can include nausea, muscle tremors, diarrhea, and headache. In addition, caffeine is a diuretic. Excessive caffeine intake can stimulate the production of urine and increase water loss, especially in hot weather, which may contribute to dehydration and impaired performance.

Since caffeine is found in everyday foods and beverages such as chocolate, coffee, and tea, the International Olympic Committee has put a limit on the amount of caffeine athletes can consume. Athletes who test above this limit can be banned from competition. At no time should athletes use caffeine-containing tablets before or during competition.

Eat, Drink, and Be Faster

Optimal nutrition is an integral part of peak performance and can enhance your health and athletic potential, whereas an inadequate diet and lack of essential nutrients, like carbohydrates and fluids, can limit your potential for maximum performance. Whether you run at an elite level or in the middle of the pack, making wise foods choices and fueling the body properly will allow you to feel good during exercise and take your running to the next level. A certain amount of fuel is necessary for the body to function properly. But after you satisfy these requirements, proper nutrition and hydration cannot substitute for hard work. They merely promote your hard work and offer a key to the door of success.

24

Drug Use and Racing

JIM FERSTLE
Freelance writer for *Running Times, Runner's World, Road Race Management,* and other publications

Ergogenic aids are a form of fool's gold. A running breakthrough is the product of talent, proper training, and hard work, not the result of performance-enhancing drugs.

A percentage of you who read this a book will almost certainly have entertained the idea of using performance-enhancing drugs to achieve a breakthrough in your running. Perhaps some have thought, "If only there were a pill a runner could take that would allow me to reach that next level." Though most runners are aware of some of the dangers of illegal performance-enhancing drugs, much is yet to be learned. Drug-making technology usually outruns detection technology. As new drugs arrive on the scene, they must be evaluated individually—a laborious and inexact undertaking.

The belief that there are shortcuts to success or magic pills that will somehow transform an otherwise ordinary individual into someone extraordinary is the great lie of modern sports. The belief is present not only in sports but in the nonsporting population as well. In sports this manifests itself in the use of performance-enhancing drugs or techniques. Stimulants, anabolic steroids, blood doping, and recombinant erythropoietin (rEPO) are only some of the methods used by athletes in an attempt to win races, medals, money, and sporting glory. These ergogenic aids, artificial enhancers of performance, are thought by many to be shortcuts to better performances. In many cases, the substances are easy to buy and administer, adding to their allure.

In the final analysis, however, such ergogenic aids are all a form of fool's gold. A breakthrough in running or any sport is the product of a combination of physical and psychological gifts, proper training, and hard work, not the result of performance-enhancing drugs. Although drugs may aid some elements of the athletic success formula, they are no substitute for training, genetically granted talent, and hard work. The use of such drugs would never transform Jack or Jill Jogger into an Olympic gold medalist. But at the rarified Olympic level, where the differences among the top athletes are miniscule and any small advantage has obvious rewards, athletes and their coaches may accept the physiological and legal risks of taking certain ergogenic aids. And because Olympic athletes are role models for their sporting contemporaries, when it is revealed that Olympians have used drugs, some others assume that the same substances will work wonders for them and these individuals may not see the downside of taking such drugs.

Temptations for Runners

At the 1988 Seoul Olympics, Canadian sprinter Ben Johnson was caught using anabolic steroids after winning the 100 meters. The unfortunate response among many athletes was not applause that somebody who cheated was caught, but rather, "Where can I get some of those drugs?" Helen Kelly, MD, a family physician in Minnesota, was outraged when the parent of a high school wrestler came to her attempting to get a prescription for anabolic steroids for her son.

The publicity surrounding home run king Mark McGwire's use of androstenedione, a testosterone precursor, caused a huge jump in sales for this product, which is sold over-the-counter in health food stores in the United States and on the Internet. No one demanded a national examination of why an athlete in one sport is allowed to use a performance-enhancing substance while those in Olympic sports are not. Elite athletes, or those who aspire to be elite, are always looking for an edge, according to Jim Reardon, a psychologist and former collegiate discus thrower.

In some ways, it's a character trait. "It's not cheating if everybody else is doing it," was the rationale Johnson's coach, Charlie Francis, used to explain his athletes' drug use. It is exactly that ethos that has tempted many individuals to begin using drugs. Chuck DeBus, a coach based in Santa

Monica who was banned from the sport by USA Track & Field (USATF) for promoting drug use, would tell his athletes that their competitors were using drugs and they would have to so they could compete on equal terms.

Because the drug-testing systems of most national and international sport organizations do not test for certain substances that can improve performance and are often ineffective at detecting others, the so-called doping gurus tell people that only stupid athletes are caught using drugs. Muscle magazines routinely advertise products that are supposedly undetectable by current drug tests or that will mask the presence of drugs. The cumulative effect of this is that elite athletes are forced to make a choice. Do they believe the hype that one cannot win an Olympic gold medal without using drugs? Or do they remain convinced that drug use is not as rampant or pervasive as they are often told?

For some elite athletes the choice is not that simple. Steve Plasencia, a masters runner who has enjoyed a long and successful career that started when he was Minnesota state mile champion in high school and continued through two Olympic teams and masters competition, talks of a simpler rationale for being a clean athlete. "What satisfaction is there in an athletic performance that was achieved by taking a pill?" Plasencia asks. "Athletics—sport—is supposed to be about personal achievement, challenging your body and your mind, not about better sport through better chemistry. Was it me or was it the pill is the question you have to live with if you choose that route."

Werner Franke, the German cancer researcher who uncovered the secrets of the German Democratic Republic's (GDR) state-run doping program, likes to tell the story of a GDR biathlete who refused to take the drugs the GDR sports authorities wanted her to take. She and her father, who was her coach, adamantly refused to be part of the GDR doping machine. Because of this stance, the GDR sports authorities ostracized them, but history intervened. The Berlin Wall fell, and she was able to train free of the oppression of the GDR government. In 1992, she won the Olympic gold medal in the biathlon at the Winter Olympics. Her story is but one graphic example that disproves the notion that drug use is necessary to win gold medals, says Franke. It is another exposé of the lie that pills lead to medals.

Ironically, Ben Johnson also offers additional support for this viewpoint. Testimony at the Dubin Inquiry into drug use in sport in Canada revealed that Johnson had been put on a drug program in 1981. It wasn't until six years later, however, that Johnson set a world record in winning the International Amateur Athletic Federation (IAAF) World Championships at 100 meters. If drugs were a magic potion, would his route to the top of his specialty have taken so long?

One of the alleged advantages conferred by the use of anabolic steroids is that it allows an athlete to train harder. Studies done on the use of the drugs tend to support the notion that drug use combined with hard work produce the greatest benefit. Thus, it would appear, the drugs are not a magic potion for success but merely an aid in athletes' pursuit of a goal. And, as Reardon notes, highly competitive, elite athletes are always looking for aids, something to give them an edge over their peers who also have extraordinary genetic talent and a strong work ethic. In running, where tiny gradations separate the Olympic medalists and world champions from the also-rans, the search for that edge can become all consuming.

Drug-induced success carries a price tag. Besides the guilt one might feel about a chemically enhanced performance, one must also employ subterfuge and deceit to hide the use of banned substances from everyone. For a complete listing of prohibited substances, visit **www.nodoping.org**.

History of Drug Testing

Drug testing in Olympic sports was first adopted in the 1960s in an attempt to protect athletes from what were perceived to be unscrupulous coaches, trainers, and advisors. Athletes, including those in track and field, were supplied with substances such as amphetamines in an attempt to win races. After several athletes' deaths in the 1960s were connected with the use of amphetamines, Olympic authorities established an International Olympic Committee (IOC) medical commission and began developing methods of sports drug testing. The rationale was not so much to catch cheaters but to deter athletes from using drugs. The theory was that if athletes knew they were going to be caught, they would never attempt to cheat.

At the same time another, more sinister form of competition was taking place. The Cold War between the Soviet Union and the United States was in full bloom, not only in the military and intelligence communities but also on the athletic battleground of the Olympics. American athletes had heard of Soviet use of the male hormone testosterone during the 1950s. During that period, U.S. physician John Ziegler, MD, developed a synthetic form of testosterone—anabolic steroids—for use by American athletes. Compounds with the trade names Deca Durabolin and Dianabol soon became common in the Olympic community as athletes began to experiment with anabolic steroids as a training aid or enhancer.

When 1956 Olympic hammer-throw champion Harold Connolly testified before a congressional hearing in 1973, he openly admitted that many Olympians used anabolic steroids. Testing for stimulants had been instituted beginning with the 1964 Olympics, but testing for steroids did not begin until 1972. As the testing advanced, so did the methods athletes used to avoid detection. The GDR files uncovered by Franke contained several examples of the lengths to which the GDR government went to hide drug use by its athletes. From sabotaging tests to developing substances that were hard to detect in drug testing, GDR scientists and government officials waged a clandestine battle to hide any proof that GDR athletes were guinea pigs in the largest sports-doping experiment ever conducted.

The GDR research indicated that female athletes benefited most from the administration of male hormones. This was most graphically illustrated by the disproportionate success of GDR female athletes in Olympic competition. In effect, the women became "shemales," with their endocrine systems altered to add more muscle through the administration of testosterone. Training methods could be modified, allowing the athletes to do a greater volume of training, which recently prompted Australian swim coach Don Talbot to comment that today's swimmers have to relearn how to train. Before the truth about the GDR drug use became known, coaches would often try to duplicate the high-volume training regimens of the GDR women swimmers. Swimmers were trained on a program that emphasized strength and volume of training, not speed or technique. According to Talbot, now that the sport is being cleaned up coaches have to relearn how to train their athletes.

Besides altering the training methods of athletes, the GDR research produced a new generation of performance-enhancing drugs that were specifically designed to escape detection in drug tests. Androstenedione, a testosterone derivative commonly referred to as "andro," was first identified by GDR researchers as a performance enhancer in the early 1980s when they were searching for a substance to use in case the IOC drug testing became sophisticated enough to detect testosterone use.

In 1987, another substance, recombinant erythropoietin (rEPO), was brought on the market to treat people with severe anemia. American pharmaceutical companies developed the drug for legitimate medical reasons, but the underground athletic drug network, which monitors medical research, soon discovered it. The substance rEPO quickly found a use among athletes, in particular those in endurance sports. EPO is a hormone that the human body naturally produces in small quantities to stimulate the production of red blood cells. Taking rEPO increases the amount of this hormone in the blood, thus increasing the oxygen-carrying capacity of the blood. Endurance athletes had sought similar benefits in the 1970s though a method called blood doping, in which blood would be withdrawn from the athlete and stored. The athlete's body would respond by producing more red blood cells to counter those lost. After this recovery, the blood that had been removed would be reinfused, creating a higher volume of fluid and a greater red blood cell count. This would enable the blood to transport more oxygen to the muscles and thus, theoretically, improve endurance capacity.

This process was believed to increase performance significantly but was fraught with hazards. Whenever blood is removed or reinfused, there is the danger of infection. For blood doping to work, according to research done on the process by scientists led by Mel Williams, PhD, blood must not only be removed in precise quantities but also stored properly. Several things can go wrong with the process due to the number of steps involved, their complexity, and possible problems with needles (unsterile conditions). It was alleged that a biathlete from the former Soviet Union collapsed in the Olympic village and was hospitalized during the 1992 Winter Olympics because a blood-doping procedure had gone wrong.

Use of rEPO eliminated many of the hazards of blood doping by transfusion, but it created health risks of its own. Too much rEPO injected into the body produces an excess number of red blood cells. The blood becomes very thick, and it can be difficult for the heart to pump it. A "sludge for blood" scenario could develop in which heart failure could result from the added strain to the heart. Doctors representing Amgen, one of the producers of rEPO, held a media briefing at the New York City Marathon shortly after the product went on the market to warn of the potential fatal side effects of misuse of rEPO. The risk was acute, they said, because the effects of rEPO are not immediate. It takes the body a while to produce the new red blood cells, so the dose and the timing of rEPO administration require careful medical monitoring to insure that a red blood cell overdose does not result.

The cycling world is full of anecdotal stories of rEPO abuse by elite cyclists. According to these reports, cycling team physicians administer blood thinners or substances known as plasma expanders to keep the blood from becoming too thick. Because cycling and cross-country skiing governing bodies have instituted blood tests that require set hemoglobin values, it is the team physician's responsibility to ensure that riders' or skiers' red blood cell counts stay below the cutoff. Many criticize this as being tacit approval of rEPO use by these athletes, who know they can dope up to a set level. Because of insufficient funding, legal concerns, and the complexity of developing a test for a natural endogenous substance—a substance that naturally occurs at some level in the body—no test is currently in use to detect the use of rEPO. Thus, speculation and accusations abound about who is or isn't using the drug to enhance performance.

German distance runners Damien Kallabais and Stephen Franke were embroiled in controversy in the fall of 1998 when it was revealed that they had asked for and received treatments with a plasma expander before competitions. Researchers noted that use of the plasma expander alone, even though it was not on any banned list, might be a way of enhancing performance in endurance events because one of the limiting factors on performance is the loss of fluid. Starting with a full tank might provide an advantage to athletes who were able to attain that status through the use of the plasma expanders. The athletes were admonished for the practice and warned not to do it again, but little can be done to ensure compliance because the practice is virtually undetectable.

Drug Testing Today

These and other problems with drug testing continue today. Detection of endogenous substances, such as EPO, testosterone, or human growth hormone (hGH), has been a major problem for those attempting to establish a comprehensive drug-testing system. Because human beings are not static organisms, it is difficult to establish universal levels of these hormones, which in megadoses (levels that likely do not occur naturally in the body) can be used to enhance an athlete's training and performance.

In addition, it has been difficult to raise the money necessary to do the required scientific research to establish a medical and legal basis for testing for these substances. The IOC has rhetorically attacked the use of performance-enhancing drugs and declared a war on drugs in sports. As of 1999, however, it has spent only $1 million on research into methods of detection (specifically on detection of the rampant use of hGH). That may change with the commitment of $25 million of IOC funds toward the development of a World Anti-Doping Agency (WADA) as called for in the Lausanne Declaration on Doping in Sport.

The IOC has said it will commit whatever funds are necessary to solve the doping crisis but that it also needs the support of individual sports federations and governments to develop a truly effective sports drug-testing program. Don Catlin, MD, who heads the IOC-accredited drug testing lab in Los Angeles, has likened the political difficulties in setting up and administering a worldwide antidoping effort to the negotiations between the United States and the former Soviet Union over nuclear weapons. Each party in the negotiation mistrusts the other side somewhat, and each is reluctant to give up any edge they may have for fear of putting themselves at a disadvantage.

Striving for a Level Playing Field

The chauvinistic nature of Olympic sports commonly causes countries to hurl accusations at one another regarding who is or isn't tacitly or directly aiding the use of performance-enhancing drugs by their athletes. The most obvious area where this has been rampant is in the out-of-competition testing programs. To monitor use of training aids, such as anabolic steroids, athletes must be tested year-round, not merely at competitions. Year-round testing is costly and difficult to administer. Some of the poorer countries, for example, can barely afford to send their teams to competitions, let alone pay for out-of-competition drug testing.

Because drugs such as hGH and rEPO are expensive, the argument can be made that athletes in Third World nations cannot afford to be on doping regimens and are therefore at less risk of being doped. But in today's global economy, athletes are able to live outside their countries and train and gain access to sophisticated medical care. So, how does one deal with the inequalities? Sports federations, such as the International Amateur Athletic Federation (IAAF), conduct extensive out-of-competition testing programs. The IAAF has also instituted a requirement that athletes who have not been tested twice out-of-competition are not eligible for prize money in IAAF events. Only 10 of the 34 sports federations under the Olympic umbrella perform out-of-competition testing, however, and some would argue that even the IAAF program cannot test everybody.

WADA is supposed to improve this situation by conducting research, creating an out-of-competition testing agency that will test athletes in all sports, and conducting education programs that would help deter athletes from considering the use of drugs. British professor Jim Parry said at the Lausanne conference that punitive drug testing is just an acknowledgment that education programs directed at deterring drug use among athletes have failed. Angela Schneider, PhD, an ethics professor from Canada, emphasized that the doping crisis in sport is an ethical problem, not a scientific or medical one. Engaging in a cat-and-mouse game of drug-use detection through testing solves only part of the problem, she said. The core of the issue is athletes' attitudes toward drug use.

Do Athletes Care?

If the core culture of the athletes is to win at all costs, no amount of drug testing will ever be effective in catching all drug users. But if a culture of ethical values based on principles of fair competition and respect for one's rivals is established, widespread drug use will be less likely to occur. An athlete's attitude toward drug use is learned behavior. All athletes can be influenced by the culture. Unless the trend toward a culture of drug taking is reversed, Schneider says, the war on drugs is not likely to succeed. Initially, Olympic sports administrators attempted to convince athletes that drug use was harmful, even deadly. Because the risks associated with the use of performance-enhancing drugs are not obviously life threatening or severe in the short term, athletes have come to view this attempt to deter drug use as misinformation and scare tactics.

"Ask athletes, 'If nobody else doped, would you?' and the answer is 'No,'" says IOC vice president Dick Pound, himself a former Olympic swimmer. "There are a few who do it to get an edge. All the rest do it because it's the lowest common denominator."

Sports administrators need to create an environment where athletes do not believe that others are doping, where they are not tempted to join the lowest common denominator death spiral, says Schneider. That process starts and ends with the athletes. Schneider and others want to see more athlete involvement in Olympic antidoping efforts. Athletes are not well represented in the halls of Lausanne. It is the athletes, however, who set the norms for the culture of sports. To develop programs that will be true breakthroughs in doping control, sports administrators have to bring the athletes into the process to establish the culture. This is a daunting task, but the future of drug control in sports lies not only in the efficacy of drug tests but in the atmosphere surrounding elite sport.

PART III

Breakthrough Recovery

You've read and absorbed the information on breakthrough training in part I of this book and on breakthrough racing in part II. What is left?

Plenty, and it concerns the most often overlooked aspect of success in running—rest and recovery. Most of us runners who commit ourselves to improving our performance in the sport eventually come to embrace the hard, diligent work required to approach our potential. We do the progressive, multifaceted training, we invest in the proper equipment, we adopt a lifestyle that includes fueling ourselves properly and engaging in other activities that support our running, we work on our runner's mental skills, we hone our racing tactics so that we can take advantage of every opportunity to excel once the gun sounds. The one thing many of us don't get right is the aspect of running that seems to go against the runner's very nature—rest and recovery from all that hard effort.

In truth, recovery is the crucial ingredient without which all the work we put into running means virtually nothing. In addition, proper recovery involves as much effort as any other aspect of training and racing. Physiologically, it is during periods of rest when the fitness improvements we seek from our training actually occur. Rest is also an essential ingredient to running success psychologically, because training and racing without ever taking a break eventually leads to mental indifference that can extinguish one's passion for a once-beloved activity.

Part III of *The Running Times Guide to Breakthrough Running* guides the performance-oriented runner through proper rest and recovery techniques. Mastering the art of successful rest can create a first-time breakthrough for the inexperienced runner and add years of continuing breakthroughs for the runner who has seen success but may find it waning as time passes. In many ways, we believe this is the most important section of this book, because the information and advice is so hard to incorporate fully into a breakthrough running program.

Chapter 25 presents the case for learning to rest, in times of hard training and racing as well as the times interspersed between them, to allow the body and mind to restoke completely for hard work. Few runners have worked harder in the sport than the author of this chapter, six-time New Zealand Olympic qualifier and road-race champion Anne Audain, now director of the Idaho Women's Fitness Celebration 5K. Yet over the years this wise and insightful athlete and leader in the sport has also learned the value of designing her training and racing to allow herself to recover, physically and mentally, from the many stresses of running. Audain talks about her running experiences, beginning as a preadolescent on a low-key, low-mileage training routine with a club team in Auckland, a program that allowed her to develop gradually and maintain a constant enjoyment of running. She outlines the philosophy she tries to communicate to the thousands of women who run and walk the Fitness Celebration: work hard, then take it easy—you've not only earned it, you need it, too.

One of the primary reasons rest is so important to runners is that it reduces risk of injury. As healthy and life affirming as running is, it is also a stressful physical activity and thus carries a high injury risk—one made higher by failing to back off when signs of an impending problem are clear. In chapter 26, sports podiatrist and 27-year running veteran Amol Saxena, DPM, gives runners valuable guidelines and insights on how to keep injury risk low and remain dedicated to pursuing a breakthrough in the sport. The chapter includes information and advice on stretching, using ice and heat effectively, heeding the warning signs of injury, starting back after a layoff for injury, choosing proper running surfaces, and keeping running muscles conditioned to handle the stresses of the activity. Saxena incorporates his experience both as a runner and as a physician who has treated thousands of runners at all levels for injuries and general wellness counseling.

As we learned in chapter 5 on periodization, runners must incorporate rest and recovery into their training cycles, both day-to-day and between seasons of hard effort, to reach their full potential. Chapter 27, by massage therapist and wellness expert Rex Baird, MEd, CSCS, shows runners how to extract maximum gains—and enjoyment—from their running by making sure rest is part of the training plan. Baird compares training for a performance breakthrough to walking a tightrope and reminds us that it is a dynamic, not a static, concept. He explains that to see progress as a runner, you must not only overstress your body but also back off from that hard work to consolidate the gains you are attempting to make. The chapter includes practical tips on recognizing the signs of overtraining and learning to avoid this common pitfall. Some of the information here is an extension of the information on periodization presented in chapter 5. It also shares the philosophies of all the experts included in *The Running Times Guide to Breakthrough Running*, presented in a concise and useful way for the runner who needs just a bit more convincing that *rest* is not a four-letter word.

Some runners are willing to believe in the value of rest and recovery but aren't always exactly sure how to do it. Chapter 28, on restoring and resting the body, outlines the various and sometimes surprising ways a runner can rest as part of training. In this chapter Rex Baird joins Linda Jaros-Osga, sports massage therapist and certified personal trainer, in introducing (or perhaps reintroducing) runners to many different forms of rest, including active rest (easy, nonstressful activities), massage, yoga, meditation, and water activities. Jaros-Osga and Baird present a framework for incorporating rest into a training program that involves the three Ps—planning, physical restoration, and psychological restoration. All are essential ingredients to maximizing running performance and striving for a breakthrough. After reading this chapter, rest will no longer be simply an abstract concept for runners but a clearly spelled out formula that can be easily integrated with any training plan.

When all this information has been read and absorbed, some runners may wonder, "How does this apply to me?" or "How does a real performance-oriented runner apply this?" Chapter 29 answers both questions. In it, Olympic Marathon gold medalist Joan Benoit Samuelson (you can't get much more performance oriented!) explains how she has learned over the years to balance her training and racing with the many other demands in her life—family, work, and community responsibilities—in a program that also allows her to rest, recover, and keep going at a high level. Samuelson, the American record holder in the marathon (2:21:21), relates some advice that her brother, a physician, once gave her: "Rest is the basis of all activity." She then writes candidly about how she hasn't always successfully incorporated that truth into her running lifestyle, although now, as a top masters runner with children and dozens of other responsibilities and commitments, she does. Samuelson explains how she now tapers for races, takes several easy days after races and hard workouts, cross-trains, and manages a balancing act between running and the rest of her busy life. Through her words, runners can come to believe in the value of letting the seasons dictate running patterns, tuning into the rhythms of the body, and focusing on outcomes of performance, health, and improved well-being rather than compulsively adhering to a predetermined schedule (doing workouts when ill or running junk miles to make a training log look good).

Reminding us that we all, no matter what our level of achievement in running, are much more than running machines, Samuelson concludes her chapter, and we conclude here, with words that should guide all runners seeking a breakthrough: "Making running a part of a healthy and diverse lifestyle creates balance in the life you share with family and friends. The secret to a breakthrough running performance may well be achieving this kind of overall balance in our lives."

25

The Need for Rest and Recovery

ANNE AUDAIN
Six-time New Zealand Olympic qualifier
who has been called the "winningest road racer ever"

> It was my ability to maximize the three Rs—rest, recovery, and relaxation—that led to my running success, my longevity, and an injury-free career.

When the editors of *Running Times* contacted me about contributing to their guide to breakthrough running, I was delighted. In running, as in other aspects of life, working toward the next level of success can be frustrating. But with the help of friends and experts, the breakthrough can be a thrilling moment of accomplishment.

Although my 22-year racing career would qualify me to speak to issues of breakthrough performances in the training and racing parts of this book, it was, in the end, my ability to maximize the three Rs—rest, recovery, and relaxation—that led to my running success, my longevity, and an injury-free career.

My achievements in running are a wonder to my family to this day because I was born with foot deformities. I endured surgeries and endless months of rehabilitation simply to be able to walk normally. I had my last and most critical surgery when I was 13. After

I had fully recovered, nearly a year later, I joined a track club in my native New Zealand and took up my life's passion—running.

I'm convinced that growing up in New Zealand set me up for future success. A healthy and balanced lifestyle is the norm for us Kiwis. We believe in eating healthy meals, taking lots of exercise, and participating in a variety of sports. Life down under comes with fewer stresses than the lives that most Americans experience. Kiwis emphasize the process more and the result less. For instance, many children in New Zealand participate in track and field. People of all ages join track clubs and participate at various levels. Of course, these clubs have competitions, but more important, they place great emphasis on teamwork, health and nutrition, and family participation. Parents are actively involved and even participate in meets and events sponsored by the clubs. In the end, these activities emphasize fitness and a positive lifestyle much more than competition and winning. The rewards I reaped from growing up in this system have served me well throughout my running career.

I believe that to gain consistency and therefore improve your running, you need to take an active role in staying healthy and strong. Taking the time off that is necessary to prevent injuries and recover completely helps you continue along the path to your breakthrough with minimal delays. It's amazing to me how often I hear runners talking about their pains and injuries as though they were badges of honor. They are accepting and expecting injuries almost as part of their training programs. That need not be the case. My first coach always told me, "It takes more guts to take a rest day than to train hard." Those are words to live by!

All of that said, here is a list of things I did during my career to maintain good health. I apply many of these principles in my day-to-day life as well as in my running. I believe they can help you achieve a breakthrough in your running too.

Sleep

Sleep is the most wonderful and underrated healer. Most people, especially those who are very active, need *at least* eight hours of sleep each night. Often, as you increase your mileage, you will need more sleep. This can include a restorative half-hour nap during the day if you have the luxury of doing so, though most runners find it more practical to go to bed a half hour earlier at night.

The quality of your sleep is as important as the quantity. Mattresses and box springs do not have an indefinite life. If yours are more than 10 or 12 years old, replace them. Try to go to sleep and wake up about the same time every day. A consistent schedule of sleep allows your body to maximize the healing benefits of rest. It is difficult for your body to make up for lost sleep.

Exercise early and enjoy a metabolic boost throughout the morning

© Eric Stanford/International Stock

Sleeping late on the weekends to try to compensate for lost sleep during the week will not fill up an empty sleep bank; it will only disturb your sleep patterns.

You can also improve your quality of sleep by avoiding caffeine in any form for at least three hours before bedtime. Iced tea, soda containing caffeine, and chocolate can be just as upsetting to sleep patterns as coffee. Also, avoid heavy meals or big snacks for three to four hours before you go to bed. Your body cannot efficiently digest food and relax for sleep at the same time.

Finally, avoid exercising three to four hours before you go to bed. The metabolic boost your body gets from a workout is counterproductive to the process of active rest that sleeping provides. Scheduling workouts in the morning has a double benefit. You will not overlook your workout in the flurry of a busy schedule, and you will have the added benefit of a slightly higher metabolism throughout the morning. If you must work out in the later hours of the day, try to do so as early as possible so you will have sufficient time for your body to relax completely before you go to bed.

Replenish With the Right Foods and Fluids

Watch when someone pulls a high-performance car into a gas station. My bet is that you won't see her put low-grade fuel into it. Similarly, as you are preparing your body and mind for a breakthrough running performance, don't use second-rate fuel. By eating properly, you serve all aspects of your life. When you demand a lot from your system, sound nutrition is even more important to restoring balance.

Fresh fruits and vegetables are always an appropriate food source. Low-fat meats, chicken, and fish are excellent sources of protein, as are soy-based products like tofu. Brown rice and whole grains provide us with much-needed carbohydrates (see recipe below). Water, fruit juices, and low-fat milk are all excellent ways to provide fluids for a demanding runner's system, with water at the top of the list. Chapters 13 and 23 provide more details on fueling your body for optimal training and racing.

Mum's Fruit Loaf

Many cookbooks and magazine articles offer excellent recipes for nutritious food to fuel your body. Here is one of my favorites. I call it a "Kiwi power bar."

I remember my mum making these fruit loaves. We would toast slices for breakfast as well as have slices in our school lunches. Full of goodness!

1 cup of flour
1 cup of bran
1 cup of whole meal or oatmeal
1 cup of dates (chopped)
$1/2$ cup of walnuts (chopped)
$1/2$ teaspoon of salt
1 egg
$1/2$ cup of sugar
1 tablespoon of melted butter
$1/2$ cup of milk
1 teaspoon of baking soda
$1/2$ cup of hot water
$1/2$ cup of golden syrup (This is unique to New Zealand. You can substitute molasses or Karo syrup.)

Preheat oven to 375 degrees (190 degrees Celsius). Sift flour into a bowl and add bran, whole meal, dates, nuts, and salt. Beat egg and sugar together, add warmed syrup and melted butter, and then add milk. Mix into dry ingredients. Add soda dissolved in hot water. Mix well. Bake in two greased loaf tins for 45 to 60 minutes.

Seek Professional Interventions

One way to encourage your muscles to relax and your body to stay in proper alignment is professional intervention by a massage therapist, a doctor of chiropractic, or a doctor of osteopathy. Keep in mind, however, that not all professionals in these fields excel, or are even adept, at working with athletes, so don't choose a massage therapist or doctor without doing some research and getting recommendations from other runners. A professional who specializes in treating athletes, however, can help you avoid a myriad of problems down the road. He or she can also help you recognize subtle signals from your body that might otherwise go unnoticed. Listening to your body and keeping it relaxed and aligned is an important component of the breakthrough in your future.

Choosing and Working With a Health-Care Provider

- Choose someone who runs or is involved in sports and fitness. Find someone who believes as strongly as you do that running is good for you.

- Survey other runners. Ask for recommendations.

- Choose a massage therapist who works specifically with runners. Some therapists will answer your questions while they set up massage areas after a marathon.

- A good sports chiropractor uses muscle kinesiology as well as manipulation.

- Wellness care and preventative medicine can stop an injury before it starts.

Recover for Race Preparation

If your breakthrough goal is participation in a particular race or achieving a goal time in a race, you will find that rest, relaxation, and balance are crucial. Over the years of my racing career, I observed that many elite runners went into races without giving themselves the rest necessary to get their best result. Failing to get enough rest not only affects performance on race day but also gives rise to future injuries. It was my habit to take three easy days before a race, especially if travel was involved. After a race I gave myself two easy days to recover. Again, the key to racing success is consistency. Three months of hard training and three months of recovery from an injury will not lead to a breakthrough performance.

For some of you, your breakthrough goal may be a marathon. Do not minimize the amount of work necessary to reach this goal. The distance deserves both respect and caution from all who undertake to run it. It is a daunting task, especially for those who will complete it in more than three hours. Consider the amount of time it will take to train properly to run 26.2 miles. Many people must make sacrifices in other areas of their lives to run a marathon. Undertake this grand goal only after you have been honest in assessing your reasons for choosing it.

The simple concept of hard work followed by recovery leads to improvement.

The simple concept of hard work followed by recovery leads to improvement. Fatigue is a necessary by-product of this equation. It is important that we push our bodies through physical barriers and then allow them to rest and make adjustments for improvement. At the same time, we must push through some difficult mental barriers to allow for a breakthrough.

Avoid Overtraining

Overtraining without proper rest, relaxation, and recovery leads to chronic fatigue and poor motivation. It also encourages irritability, poor performance, injury, and illness. In extreme cases, it causes a runner to become a cyclist (or swimmer, or tennis player, or worst of all, couch potato). Here are some classic symptoms of overtraining: a higher-than-usual resting heart rate, difficulty sleeping, irritability, loss of appetite, loss of enthusiasm, and consistently sore and tight muscles. Don't be afraid to take a critical look at your training regimen. If you are experiencing more than one or two of these symptoms, honestly evaluate not only your training routine but also your motivations. It may be time to take a few weeks off so that you can return with freshness and enthusiasm to a carefully planned and reasonable schedule.

Set Appropriate Goals

Setting and accomplishing short- and long-term goals trains you to be patient and allows you to maintain good health. Be realistic about setting goals. Remember that they must fit into your lifestyle. Be honest about what you want to achieve and do not let other runners and their goals influence your own. Your aim is to achieve a breakthrough in your running performance, not create additional stress in your life!

Keep in mind that goal setting is something that you do for yourself. Don't allow your goals to be dictated by what other runners are doing. Even elite athletes can fall into the trap of setting goals for themselves based on the workouts of their competition. When I was competing professionally, most elite runners were running at least 100 miles a week. The 100-mile week became the standard for all top runners. I would watch some athletes run back and forth in the parking lot on the last day of the week to get to that magic number. I never once ran that far in a given seven-day period. That is simply too much mileage for me. Had I run that much, I surely would have suffered the consequences.

Here are a few simple goals, but keep in mind that this is only a jumping-off point. Customize your goals to set yourself up for the breakthrough you deserve.

- To run a certain route without stopping
- To build a consistent weekly mileage
- To build to a weekly endurance run
- To train for a specific race or a specific race time
- To improve your body composition

Keep a Diary

Many runners keep a training log, which normally includes mileage, workout descriptions, observations about road and weather conditions, and general level of health and rest. But keeping a diary requires you to do more.

There is no right way to keep a journal or diary, but including more information than you would in a simple training log will help you examine more closely your road to a breakthrough. Committing your goals to paper is one step to making them real. A food diary is an excellent way to keep track of your eating habits—both good and bad. After a while, those French fry entries start to look suspect no matter how much you enjoyed them at the time. Recording your negative feelings of doubt is an excellent way to acknowledge them, accept them, and move on. Recording your positive feelings of confidence felt during a run or race (or in other aspects of your life) will help reinforce that confidence in your mind. Even recording your sleep habits will teach you about the amount and quality of rest that your body requires.

That said, the reason to keep a diary is to help you understand your body and mind and to track your progress. But you'll defeat the purpose of keeping a diary if you become a slave to the process. If you run only to add miles to your diary or you perform a task only so you can make a diary entry, you've missed the point of keeping the diary in the first place. In addition, don't play catch up. Don't try to repeat a great workout every week. Conditions and environment change continually. Allow your diary to be a tool in your breakthrough, not an obstacle.

One of the best things about keeping a diary and committing to goals is that you can plan your workouts. This allows you to focus on what you are doing now. You can also look back at what you've done and see patterns in your training that may have led to tiredness or overtraining, or patterns that may have led to breakthrough races. A breakthrough in your running will be the result of this careful planning. One area of a training schedule often not sufficiently considered is planning for rest. Coaches and athletes alike almost universally characterize rest days by two words—"off" and "easy." With so much explanation devoted to the other components of a schedule, let's give "off" and "easy" a little more thought.

If you are a younger athlete, you are probably able to subscribe to the "one day hard, one day easy" rule. If you do a hard workout on Monday and take it easy on Tuesday, then you can probably go hard again on Wednesday. As we get older, our bodies tend to require more time to recover from a hard workout or race. With some athletes extending their careers well past the age of 70, we need to acknowledge that there is honor (as well as good sense) in resting as long as it takes after a hard workout. For example, if you are experiencing fatigue, you need to evaluate what kind of fatigue you are feeling. We need to be able to train with a certain level of fatigue; that's how our bodies become stronger. But you should not take it to the level where you are stiff, sore, and tired throughout your workout. Pushing beyond this kind of fatigue can frequently result in injury.

As many of you already know, hard days may consist of one or more of the following:

- Long runs
- Hill workouts
- Speed workouts
- Tempo runs
- Races (I always took two easy days after races.)

Easy days, on the other hand, should truly be easy:

- Leave your watch at home.
- Don't run more than about an hour.
- Stop and walk or stretch occasionally.
- Meditate—think positive, wonderful thoughts.
- Choose a relaxed running environment—avoid traffic and noise.
- Meet a friend and talk the whole way.
- Use an easy day to cross-train—swim, bike, in-line skate. (See chapter 12 for recommended cross-training activities but remember that cross-training is not necessarily rest. Take it easy in whatever activity you choose if it is a planned easy day!)

- Walk—it's therapeutic after a particularly hard "hard day" and much underrated. Walking is an excellent way to promote movement in the legs, hips, and arms without the pounding produced by running.

And finally, let's consider a day off. All runners arrive at a day when they just need a break. The need can be for a mental break as much as for a physical one, but we all need a day just to lie back. Take the time you would have used working out to get a massage or make that perfect pot of vegetable soup. See a movie or have a makeover. Sit in the hot tub and think about nothing. Start that book you've had on your nightstand for three months. No one has ever lost fitness by a day of rest, but many have been reenergized by it and have returned to their training with new vigor.

Balance Your Life

Only a few people in the world make a living by running. Everyone else who runs must fit running into the rest of his or her life. Our responsibilities to our families and our jobs create stresses that we should not take into our daily workouts. Whether your training schedule tells you it's a hard day or an easy one, keep in mind that relaxation during both kinds of workouts is important to your success. If you find that you are tense as you begin a run, concentrate on your breathing and form. Consciously relax your shoulders and arms. Sing a song for the first few minutes of your run. It is impossible to obsess about your boss while entertaining yourself, motorists, and pedestrians with your own version of "My Way."

Keep in mind that travel creates unique stress. Whether you are traveling for business or pleasure, know that it will take a toll on your running, especially if you are crossing more than one time zone. Be especially careful about what you eat and drink when traveling, sticking with bottled or boiled water in foreign countries. Travel by air can quickly dehydrate your system. If you are flying to your destination, be sure to drink plenty of water before, during, and after your flight. Avoid caffeinated or alcoholic beverages during the flight as these will exacerbate the dehydration process.

The concept of using rest and recovery to achieve a breakthrough in your running is relatively simple to understand. It is infinitely more difficult to implement because logic tells us that the harder we work, the sooner we will achieve our goals. As runners, many of us are already type A personalities who have a need to tackle any problem with an abundance of energy and drive.

The concept of rest and recovery is anathema to many runners. Yet when we embrace it and incorporate it into a training program, we can achieve extraordinary results in both the short run and the long run.

26

Reducing Your Injury Risk

AMOL SAXENA, DPM
A podiatrist specializing in sports medicine at
the Palo Alto Medical Foundation in Palo Alto, California

> Getting faster
> and more fit is
> like sharpening a
> pencil; the
> sharper the tip,
> the more easily it
> will break.

What does it mean to *break through* in running? It can mean different things to different people, but I think we can all agree that no matter what, it requires being healthy enough to train consistently and well.

Unfortunately, becoming faster and more fit is like sharpening a pencil. The sharper the tip, the more easily it will break. Many runners become injured or sick when they are close to or at their physical peak. Perhaps they are walking the fine line between being in peak fitness and overtraining. In fact, some studies show that 50 percent of marathoners get sick after a marathon.

I have been a runner for 26 years and have experienced my share of injuries. I am also a podiatrist, specializing in sports medicine for 10 years. I have treated and operated on more than three thousand runners, including Olympians and world record holders as well as high school and recreational athletes.

Lay people often do not recognize that elite athletes are not only physically gifted but also extremely motivated to become better faster. Like those sharp pencils, they can also be more vulnerable to illness and injury. On the other hand, elite runners have better resources, such as easier access to training rooms and physical therapy, than most runners do. Moreover, they tend to know their bodies well, recognizing (sometimes) when they are heading for trouble and making changes to avert disaster. But the non-elite runner can also do many things to help reach his or her maximum potential. The most important one, as I mentioned earlier, is staying healthy and free of injury.

I've found several basic tenets to staying healthy. Most of these ideas are easy to adhere to and follow the rules of common sense. But as Mark Twain said, "Common sense isn't all that common." For instance, how many runners do a new and unfamiliar workout or race just because their friends are doing it? What about the runner who says, "I'm hurting today, but I'll do my long run anyway, and then rest for two days"? These circumstances set us up for failure. A big part of why we need coaches and medical staff is because we can't avoid such situations.

As runners, we need to realize that we are not all designed the same. Some runners just aren't meant to be sprinters. Others aren't meant to be marathoners. We vary in flexibility, biomechanics, running gait, and foot type, among other factors. Therefore, we are prone to different injury patterns.

People with flatter feet (excessive pronation) are more likely to develop patella-femoral problems (runner's knee) and pain on the inside of the shin

Shattering Two Big Myths of Injury Prevention

- **Myth #1**: *Let pain be your guide.* The fact is, everyone's tolerance for pain is different. What you may consider a slight twinge could be excruciatingly painful to another runner. Your best bet when in doubt is to err on the side of conservatism—take a day off or at least go easy. If the feeling continues, have the trouble spot evaluated by a medical professional.

- **Myth #2**: *If you can walk on it, you can run.* That is sometimes true but certainly not always. When you walk, you always have one foot in contact with the ground, so the activity produces much less impact than running. Running exerts a pressure equivalent to three to five times your body weight with every step you take, and your feet hit the ground approximately 1,700 times per mile. Ouch!

with regular running. Those with high arches, on the other hand, seem to contract more resistant cases of Achilles tendinitis (heel cord inflammation) and plantar fasciitis (arch-heel ligament strain).

Doctors and coaches can be a great resource in your quest to stay off the injured list. Be aware, though, that much of what doctors and running coaches profess is dogma. For instance, some doctors say, "Let pain be your guide." Unfortunately, this is open to interpretation because the pain tolerance of runners varies. Some runners will tolerate just about anything to get in their daily run, whereas others will put a goose egg in their log at the slightest twinge. A coach may say, "If you can walk on it, you can run." Well, I know that's not always true, and you probably do too.

My experience has allowed me to challenge some of the myths and thereby help runners prevent major injuries. Observing the rules that follow will help you avoid breakdown so you can prepare for your breakthrough.

Stretch Correctly

Runners often obtain information on how to stretch but not necessarily on how long or when to stretch. Research has shown that muscles stretch more easily after they're warmed up, especially if the stretch is held for 15 seconds or longer. Research has also shown that stretching both before and after doing strengthening exercises is helpful. See chapters 10 and 11 for more on strengthening and stretching.

So what do I profess? Stretch any sore body part for 30 seconds before you run. I recommend walking around for a few minutes before you stretch to warm up and loosen the muscles. Then start your run slowly, even if you're just going a few easy miles. I usually average 6:00 to 7:00 per mile during a run, but I do my first mile in about 8:30. That feels almost like a walk, but it helps my muscles warm up gradually and, I believe, helps prevent me from becoming injured.

Take 10 to 15 minutes to stretch all areas, the legs and the upper body, before speed sessions and drills. Then, sometime later in the day, work on your stretching again for five minutes or so. For me, that time often occurs in the office while I'm demonstrating stretching exercises to patients. I realize all of you don't have jobs like mine, but be creative. You can stretch while talking on the telephone, waiting for a bus, watching television, or cooking dinner. Another great time is at your kids' bedtime. I often chat with them about the day's events as I stretch away. Your kids probably think you're weird anyway, so why not?

Following are some excellent stretches for runners. Refer also to the stretches provided in chapter 11. Perform these stretches on a level surface after you have warmed up.

CALVES

To stretch your calves, stand facing a wall or other support, with one foot at least a foot in front of the other and your hands in front of you pressed against the wall. Lean into the wall, making sure you point your toes straight ahead. Keep your heels flat, put your weight on the front leg, and don't bounce. Straighten the back knee and hold the stretch for 30 seconds, then bend the knee and hold for another 30 seconds. Switch legs and repeat.

HAMSTRINGS

Stretching the hamstrings can be tricky, but doing so is extremely helpful for runners. Start in the same position as the calf stretch. Place your weight on the back leg (the one opposite the one you'll be stretching). Keeping the back leg straight, press your back foot into the ground. Bend your front leg slightly and flex your front foot until you feel a stretch in the hamstring. Hold for 30 seconds, then straighten the front knee and hold for another 30 seconds. Switch legs and repeat.

GLUTEALS

One of the best stretches for the gluteal muscles (the large buttocks muscles) is the pretzel. Lie on your back and bend both knees. Place your right foot over your left knee. Move the left knee toward you, feeling the stretch in your right gluteal muscles. Hold for 30 seconds, seeking a deeper stretch if you can. Switch legs and repeat.

Use Ice and Heat Properly

Icing works as an anti-inflammatory method to reduce the swelling of an injured or overworked area by limiting the blood flow to the area. In general, icing is appropriate for both chronic and acute injuries. The cold shrinks (vasoconstricts) the blood vessels, thus reducing the flow of blood to a body part. This decreases the amount of swelling that can occur.

The ideal way to ice is to put ice cubes in water to create a solution with a temperature of 45 to 50 degrees (7 to 10 degrees Celsius). Put the mixture in a sturdy plastic bag to create an ice pack that is malleable for use on various parts of the body. I recommend icing for 10 to 15 minutes, ideally immediately after exercise.

Rolling your foot on a frozen water bottle or a cube of ice formed from a

paper cup for five minutes is great for plantar fasciitis (arch and heel pain).

Chemical (blue ice) packs can be dangerous, judging from my experience and the experience of some of my patients. Use them with caution, as I've had several patients unknowingly get mild frostbite because the packs were much colder than the conventional ice pack that I described above.

Shattering Two Myths About Icing

- **Myth #1**: *You should stop icing after 24 to 72 hours postinjury.* This is not so. The 24- to 72-hour time window refers to the period when you should not use heat on an injury. You can continue to use ice for months after joint injury and surgery with beneficial effects.

- **Myth #2**: *Ice needs to be applied directly to the body part that is injured.* This is not the case. Alternatives are available if the injured area is bandaged, in a cast, or otherwise difficult to ice directly. Ice will cause vasoconstriction (contraction of the blood vessel) above an injured area, cutting off the swelling at the pass. You can effectively ice your ankle, for example, by placing the ice pack on the front of your shin or behind your knee. This is convenient if you have a cast on the ankle. Similarly, you can ice your knee by placing an ice pack on your thigh. If you have a bandage on your knee, try placing an ice pack on your inner thigh, where you feel your pulse. If you can get to the injured area, however, it is more effective to ice the injury directly.

Heat warms and loosens stiff muscles and joints, facilitating easier movement. It also draws blood, which contains oxygen and nutrients, to an injured area, thus aiding the healing process. Use heat before exercise or during rehab. Heating generally can be initiated when bleeding (bruising and throbbing) has subsided, which is normally at least 72 hours postinjury. Moist heat such as that provided by a Jacuzzi or hot tub is ideal. Make sure the temperature is set at 100 to 105 degrees (38 to 41 degrees Celsius). Alternating hot and cold, four minutes at 100 degrees (38 degrees Celsius) and one minute at 50 degrees (10 degrees Celsius), works well for ankle sprains a few days after the injury. The alternating temperatures cause a flushing out, or pumping action, of blood flow. Repeat for three cycles, then leave your ankle in the cold water for four to five minutes after the third cycle to "ice down" the injury.

Don't Fool Yourself

If you suspect an injury, knowing whether to run or continue training can be difficult. Common injuries like Achilles tendinitis and plantar fasciitis typically don't hurt much during your run unless they are severe. Because of this, runners give themselves a false sense of security—they don't think they're hurt as badly as they really are. Thus they don't do the preventive icing that perhaps they should.

Be smart. When in doubt take a day off, or at least replace a planned speed workout with something short and easy, preferably on a soft surface. Losing one training day now makes more sense than facing a forced layoff of several weeks right before your big race. See chapter 12 on cross-training for more about alternative activities to running that can allow healing to occur while you maintain fitness.

When in doubt, take a day off or take it easy.

If you're like most runners, you won't see a doctor until circumstances are dire. I see too many runners limp into my office on seriously damaged legs and feet. Most should have come in weeks earlier so I could guide them in nipping a simple injury in the bud. Don't worry about being too cautious or appearing to be a hypochondriac! Use the following guidelines to evaluate a potential injury and determine whether you need a medical evaluation:

- Pain accompanied by swelling is never normal and should be evaluated. Any swelling, bruising, or lump warrants a medical evaluation.

- If you have pain immediately after running or are limping a few hours later, you probably shouldn't be running, but you may not need medical attention. Take a day or two off, ice, and keep the area elevated as much as possible. Then try running again for just 10 or 15 minutes. Ice four or five times a day for acute injuries. If the pain persists, take another couple days off. If you still feel pain when you try to run again, see a doctor.

- If you have a brief period of stiffness in the morning or at the beginning of your run the day after feeling pain—without any swelling—it's probably OK to continue running as long as you decrease your mileage and intensity and increase the icing and gentle stretching.

- If you cannot bear weight or stand on your toes without pain, you should not attempt to run and should probably see a doctor. Bone and joint injuries (stress fractures, arthritis, and severe sprains) and tendon tears tend to get worse as you run, so you are playing with fire if you attempt any running on them.

Does Running Cause Arthritis?

The latest studies suggest that running does not cause arthritis in the joints. Instead, it provides a protective function. Research comparing long-term swimmers and runners has shown that the swimmers have more arthritis than the runners do in their weight-bearing joints. But if you have arthritis in a weight-bearing joint (such as your knee), you can aggravate it by running. Anecdotally, I've found that such runners can usually manage only 10 miles per week. I encourage them to spread those 10 miles out among several short runs rather than using them all in one long run. I've seen arthritic runners meet for the weekend long run and then limp through the rest of the week.

We've all felt pressure of one sort or another to run when we know we shouldn't, or to run faster or farther than is good for us. Peer pressure, in particular, can have a negative effect. Many runners identify themselves with their running circle. If all their friends are training for a marathon, they jump in and train with them. Not everyone is designed for the rigors of marathon training. If you want to run with your marathoning buddies, start out with them on a run that has a shorter bailout option.

> **People who try to maintain running streaks are more likely to break down than break through.**

Similarly, work and family obligations can limit your training time, causing you to skip icing and stretching when you need to do it. Being aware of these preventive measures and planning them as part of your total training time will help you remain healthy.

Finally, you should never be afraid to take a day off. I strongly believe that six days a week of running is plenty for the nonprofessional runner. Rest is essential. People who try to maintain running streaks are more likely to break down than break through.

Start Back Sensibly

"How soon can I get back into running?" I hear this question often from injured runners, particularly those who have undergone surgery for an injury. Of course, you want to get back into your regular training and racing program as quickly as possible after being laid up with an injury. But the speed of your return to training depends on several factors.

If you have cross-trained while you were recovering from injury, you will retain some cardiovascular fitness. Cross-training, however, may not translate directly into top running fitness because you will have lost strength and endurance in the muscles that are specifically taxed by running, such as the hamstrings. I recommend cycling or walking while injured if your injury will allow it. Cycling or walking intensely for 30 to 40 minutes is approximately equal to 10 to 15 minutes of running. (For more on cross-training, see chapter 12.) As you heal, running in the shallow end of the pool (use aqua socks to protect your feet) is a good way to reacquaint yourself with running biomechanics if your injury permits it. Deep-water running wearing a flotation vest or belt is also appropriate.

As a rule, I recommend that you allow twice the amount of downtime to build back up to your usual routine. For example, if you have to stop running for three weeks, allow six weeks to return to your regular mileage and speedwork. Some injuries, such as stress fractures, don't tolerate daily running initially, whereas soft-tissue injuries, such as tendinitis, heal better with a daily run to keep the tissue flexible. If you don't know whether you are ready to run, have your doctor or physical therapist check whether your injured side is close to the uninjured side in size, range of motion, and strength.

What's the best way to start running again? People often mention the 10 percent rule as a way of increasing running volume (increase by no more than 10 percent a week), but that doesn't help much when you are starting from scratch. Instead, try running easily for 15 minutes the first time out, then take a day off to assess any soreness. If you're OK, then run 15 minutes again. Take another day off and then run 20 minutes. After a few runs, you may feel a bit of soreness from your return to running. This is normal and not a reason to stop running.

You can continue to increase your runs by five minutes every other time you run but maintain the schedule of running only every other day. When you get to 40 minutes, you can alternate 30 minutes of easy running one day with 15 minutes the next day and build up from there.

I get many questions from runners who want to know how much running they should do after a marathon. It's usually a good idea to walk for a few days, even if you feel like running. Walking will flush out toxins and allow your muscles to repair some of the damage done by running 26.2 hard miles. I recommend not running for longer than an hour at a time for the following month. Use all that extra free time to recuperate, rest on your laurels, and turn your attention to other things in your life besides running.

Know Your Surfaces and Gear

"What's the best running surface?" is another question I hear frequently. I can tell you the worst—concrete! Research has shown concrete to be at least six times as dense as asphalt. Stay off sidewalks if you want to avoid injuries. If it's impossible for you to run on a smooth dirt or asphalt path or along the side of a road safely, you're far better off to find a track (stay in the outside lanes unless you are doing speedwork and switch directions periodically) or use a treadmill indoors.

There's much to be said for training on dirt. It's softer than asphalt and thus reduces pounding. That said, I believe you should do a significant portion of your training on a surface similar to the one you will race on. Marathon runners (unless it's a trail race) need to do some of their long runs on the roads because most marathons are run on asphalt.

Many runners seem to think that running on grass is good, especially when they are injured. I don't think it's such a great idea (unless you are training for cross country) because most grassy surfaces, other than golf greens, are unstable. A much better bet is to find an even dirt surface such as a smooth, wide trail, especially if you are recovering from an ankle sprain. Track training is important if you're going to be racing on the track, but you must ease into it gradually if you are a first-timer or if you are just beginning the track season. This is especially true if you wear spikes. Many masters runners come to me because they've developed arch or Achilles strains from being too aggressive during their first track speedwork session of the season in spikes. The left-hand turns of the track and the lower-heeled shoes are two elements that can contribute to injury.

Running in worn-out shoes is also a major cause of injury. Mark in your training log when you started wearing your shoes or, if you're unlikely to check there, write the date in pen directly on your shoe where you can't miss it. As a rule, you should get new shoes every 300 to 500 miles. Shoes are your most important equipment, so take time to buy the correct shoe for your foot type, body weight, and running surface. (For more on training and racing shoes, see chapters 4 and 18.)

Build a Strong Base

I believe that most runners need to do strengthening exercises for their lower legs to avoid common lower-leg injuries. Here are three exercises to help you:

STORK

This is a great way to regain your balance sense (proprioception) after ankle sprains and to help prevent sprains by building up the stabilizing muscles in the legs. Stand relaxed and raise your arms to the sides. Bend one knee, raising the foot behind you. Try to balance for at least 15 seconds. Waving your arms makes it harder and builds the hip and knee stabilizers.

TOWEL SWOOSHES

This exercise works best on a slippery surface such as a kitchen or bathroom floor. Stand barefoot with a small towel in front of you on the floor. Use the toes of one foot to gather the towel and then spread it back out. Swooshes help strengthen your ankle stabilizers. Do the exercise in both directions on a slippery floor for five minutes in each direction, then switch feet.

HEEL RAISES

These are a great way to build up the inner-calf muscles, which are frequently injured in runners who are experiencing shin pain. Stand with one foot in front of the other, knees slightly bent. Point your toes slightly inward, then rise up on your toes. Hold for a second, then slowly lower. Add to the challenge by doing them one leg at a time, starting with three sets of 20.

Don't Get a Pain in the Butt

Many runners are plagued by chronic hamstring, piriformis (the deep buttocks muscle), and low-back pain. They think there's nothing they can do about these problems. It's true that once these injuries become chronic it's hard to eradicate them. The trick is not developing them in the first place, and you do that by strengthening and stretching the muscles in those areas.

Unless they sprint or run a lot of hills, distance runners do not properly develop many of these muscles. Moreover, many of us have desk jobs that keep these muscles in cramped positions for long periods, especially if we are not sitting up straight. In addition, we tend to lose our flexibility as we get older. I find that many distance runners with chronic lower-leg problems have weak hip stabilizers. On the other hand, few sprinters develop these types of problems; to figure out why, just look at how they're built.

The exercises below should help maintain your strength and speed. Remember to stretch after any type of strengthening exercises. (See chapter 10 for more on strengthening exercises.)

QUARTER SQUATS

Do quarter squats one leg at a time. Stand with your feet about shoulder-width apart, toes pointed forward. Hold on to something for balance, such as the back of a chair or a doorway. Extend one leg in front of you and bend the opposite knee, slowly lowering your buttocks about a foot, as if sitting down in a chair. Keep the lower half of your support leg perpendicular to the ground (don't let it go forward) so that you feel your hamstrings and buttocks working. Keep your knee centered over your foot. Hold, then return to start position. Start with two sets of 10 on each side.

LEG PRESS-UPS (BRIDGES)

These are great for building up your gluteal muscles and hamstrings. Lie on your back, bend one knee, and press the foot into the floor. Extend the other leg up and forward as shown. Press your foot down to elevate your buttocks and lower back. Start with three sets of 10, then switch legs.

Follow these rules and look forward to achieving a breakthrough in your running!

27

Building Rest Into Your Training

REX BAIRD, MEd, CSCS
Massage therapist and certified strength and conditioning specialist
at the International Academy of Neuromuscular Therapy

Successful running results from a balance of the science of training with the art of training.

To build balance into your training, you must understand that balance is a dynamic, not a static, concept. Imagine yourself as a tightrope walker trying to get from point A (where you start your training) to point B (a big race). Standing still is not the answer. You have to keep moving and adjusting your sense of balance if you want to reach your goal.

If you try to grind out too much work without planning enough rest, you'll lose your balance and fall off the training tightrope. When you have to climb back up and start over, you rarely reach your goal in time. In this chapter, you'll learn the core principles that will allow you to keep your equilibrium. You'll also learn how all this information fits together into a structured training plan. Finally, you'll learn to detect some early warning signs that will help you regain your balance before you slip into injury or over-training.

In principle, all athletic training is quite simple. You apply a stress, allow yourself time to adapt and recover, and then keep repeating the process until you've won the Olympic gold medal. In practice, nagging questions arise. Here are some of the questions you'd have to answer before running an interval workout:

What distance should I run? 200s? 400s? 800s?

Should I run all the same distances or mix them up?

How fast should I run?

How much recovery time will I need between repetitions?

Should I walk or jog between repetitions? How fast?

How many repetitions should I run?

What will I do if it's windy or hot?

If I feel subpar, should I gut it out?

How much warm-up and cool-down will I need?

How long should I wait before my next interval workout?

Although computerized programs are available to attempt to answer these kinds of questions, please understand that successful running results from a balance of the science of training with the art of training. You can rely on exercise scientists for cutting-edge training information, but you must learn to arrange this knowledge artistically in a format that suits your unique needs.

To help you achieve this balance, let's look at some basic principles stressed by running physiology experts like Tim Noakes, David Montgomery, and David Martin.

Law of Progressive Overload

The *Law of Progressive Overload* states that to maximize the benefits of a training program, the training stimulus must be progressively increased after the body has adapted. A 4:00 marathoner hoping to improve to 3:30 might gradually extend the length of his or her typical long run and slowly increase average weekly mileage. A 40:00 10K runner looking to run 39:00 (10 seconds per mile faster) would have to increase his or her intensity by learning to run interval workouts 10 seconds per mile faster.

An important part of overload is the relationship between volume and intensity. When Roger Bannister ran the first sub-4:00 mile, his usual workout was 10 intervals of 440 yards in 59 to 60 seconds with a two-minute recovery—a high-intensity, low-volume session. At the other end of the scale, when marathoner Bob Deines ran 2:22 (5:25 per mile) in 1969, his normal outing was a two-hour jog at a pedestrian 8:00 per mile—a high-volume, low-intensity session.

Learn the core principles that will allow you to keep your equilibrium.

© The Terry Wild Studio

Volume and intensity are the stimuli that we often think of first. But environmental factors such as heat, wind, hills, and altitude can also provide training stimulus. In 1977, Marty Liquori was training in Gainesville, Florida, for the World Cup 5K. The 95-degree temperatures and high humidity resulted in workouts so disappointing that Liquori almost decided to stay home. Factoring in the added demands imposed by the heat, Liquori's workouts were much better than he realized, and they produced an American record of 13:15. More obvious stimuli such as the hills and altitude outside Mexico City have also forged great distance-running success stories.

Exercise scientists tell us that volume and intensity are inversely proportional. In simple language, if you raise your volume significantly, you must decrease your intensity. If you raise your intensity significantly, you must decrease your volume. Remember environmental factors, too. Fifty miles a week on flat terrain during November is not nearly as stressful as the same mileage over continuous rolling hills in the heat of summer. The secret, of course, is to balance intensity (how hard you run) with volume (how much you run). We'll return to this issue later.

Most runners instinctively understand overload. Greater distance, more speed, and steeper hills leave the body with a message that's hard to ignore. Progression, however, is tricky. Runners are naturally ambitious and often impatient. The best advice is to make haste slowly. After completing a few of his track workouts at 59 to 60 seconds per lap, Bannister didn't suddenly decide he was ready to start cranking out 58s. He realized that even one second per lap was a big jump, and he knew that progress takes time, especially at the championship level. Small, gradual changes can be very effective for encouraging progress instead of forcing it.

Let's consider some options that Bannister might have used to increase his fitness gradually.

1. Complete the same workout with a slightly shorter recovery time.
2. Run 58-second laps (440 yards or 400 meters) but start with 4 and slowly build back up to 10.
3. Record the total running time for the $2^1/_2$ miles of 440s (400s), initially 10:00, and try to improve the total time slowly over the course of a few months.
4. Run 220s (200s) in 29 (58 seconds per lap), eventually move to 330s (300s) at the same pace, and finally try 440s (400s) at 58.

A common mistake runners make is trying to force progress in a straight-up, linear fashion. This approach is like trying to work seven days a week with no weekends or vacations. The body needs regular breaks to adapt to and consolidate its gains. A three-steps-forward, one-step-back plan works well for many athletes. A mileage increase might look like that shown in figure 27.1.

If this runner had tried to progress in a purely linear manner (adding two miles every week), he or she would have been logging 52 miles by week 11—probably an excessive rate of increase. Improvements in intensity would also respond to this stutter-step strategy.

It's tempting to keep applying the pressure when your fitness seems to be growing from week to week. Try thinking of your training as a long car trip. Accidents can happen if you're in such a hurry that you neglect to take periodic rest breaks. The stress of hard training is the stimulus that mobilizes the body to respond by becoming stronger. Many runners forget that this strength gain occurs not during the workout, but afterward, when the body is resting.

Also, one great workout doesn't necessarily mean that your fitness has just taken a quantum leap. Sometimes you'll have a good day that you'll be

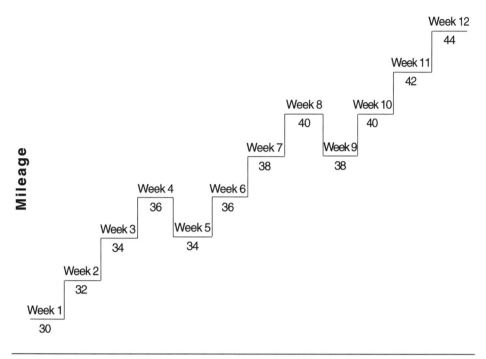

Figure 27.1   Example of a mileage increase.

hard pressed to repeat the following week. Knowing this, experienced runners often key their workouts to current race results. Running 400s at 5K pace or 800s at 10K pace are common choices of appropriate workouts. When your racing performance improves significantly, you can be fairly certain that it's time to advance your workouts accordingly.

Law of Adaptation

The *Law of Adaptation* is related to the Law of Progressive Overload. If you apply an appropriate workout stress (overload), your body will adjust by getting stronger (adaptation).

A hard workout at point A leads to fatigue at point B. At point C, you've bounced back to normal. And at point D (supercompensation), you've adapted to the stress and you're stronger than you were at point A. If you don't schedule another challenging workout, your fitness will eventually decline to where you started (point E). The secret is to apply proper stress at point D when you're most ready for it. In their eagerness, many runners don't wait long enough for full adaptation and supercompensation to occur. They never give themselves a chance to rise above their baseline. If you're not sure that you've completely recovered, rest an extra day to make sure you reach point D (point of supercompensation).

The time it takes to get from point A to point D depends on the magnitude of the stress or load. For a gentle fartlek workout, it might be 48 hours. For a marathon, it might be more than a month. Big stresses require long rests. The old rule of one easy day of recovery for every mile of racing is a good starting point for calculating your recovery needs. Listening to your body and carefully monitoring your reaction to various types of running stresses are, however, ultimately more valuable than following set formulas.

Law of Specificity

The *Law of Specificity* states that your adaptation depends on your overload. It is often stated as the SAID Principle—specific adaptation to imposed demands. We've noted earlier that Roger Bannister trained for the specific demands of a four-minute mile by running 10 quarter miles in 59 seconds. With this training, could he have completed a marathon in a respectable time? Probably not—his training was not specific to the demands of continuous running for hours at a time.

Keep the Law of Specificity in mind when you plan your training. If you were running the Boston Marathon, you'd be wise to practice running downhill. A 5K would require some training at race pace or faster. Preparation for a cross country race would involve training on uneven terrain. Your success in competition is often directly proportional to how well your training mimics the specific stresses of your target race. If you want to compete successfully, focus on a goal race, analyze the unique demands of that race, and then develop a customized plan designed to prepare you for the specific demands the race presents. You race only as well as you train.

As a rule, your training should become more specific as your goal race approaches. Many marathoners, for example, have found that doing medium-distance runs at marathon race pace is a more effective (specific) stimulus than the more traditional final-phase track work that would better suit a 5K or 10K athlete.

Law of Individuality

Although the Laws of Progressive Overload, Adaptation, and Specificity apply to everyone, they can't be implemented without considering the *Law of Individuality*. Each of us responds to overload in our own way and each of us adapts at a different pace. Steve Prefontaine and Kenny Moore both ran for Coach Bill Bowerman at the University of Oregon. Pre thrived on brutal interval workouts, often run several days in a row. Moore needed two or three days of rest after a track session. Both runners made the Olympic team.

Each of responds to overload in our own way and each of us adapts at a different pace.

© Caroline Wood/International Stock

Bowerman recognized their individuality and allowed their training to evolve accordingly.

The Law of Individuality is obvious but often ignored by coaches who must train a team of athletes or by runners who think a training program that worked for their heroes is right for them. Although we know we're unique, we sometimes try to duplicate the training of someone more gifted or experienced. The science of running lies in observing the principles we've discussed. The art of running lies in finding how to balance work and rest in a customized plan that suits our unique needs.

Laws of Realism, Gradualism, and Moderation

Even a near-perfect, individualized plan must observe the *Law of Realism*. I remember a runner named Ken who desperately wanted to qualify for the Boston Marathon in the days when men under 40 needed to break 3:00. He was eager, a good athlete, and was getting sound advice from his running buddies. After finishing a half marathon in 1:35 (7:15 pace), Ken pronounced himself ready to crack the three-hour barrier. When his friends pointed out that he'd have to run twice as far and 23 seconds per mile faster, Ken replied that carbo loading and adrenaline would carry him through. Instead, he struggled through a painful 3:28 and quit running.

Sadly, Ken's goal was actually realistic. With two more years of training, he probably could have broken three hours. He just needed to observe the *Law of Gradualism*. Although the goal of running is greater speed, the wise athlete models the approach of the tortoise, not of the hare. A plan that nurtures steady and slow progress will ultimately produce faster racing. Trying to force unrealistically rapid progress leads to disillusionment, injury, and burnout.

If observing the Law of Gradualism keeps your goals in balance, the *Law of Moderation* keeps your workouts in balance. A moderate workout provides the proper amount of overload, which encourages adaptation. In addition, it allows you to recover in a few days. A killer workout on Thursday before a Saturday race may impress your more sensible friends, but when they are crossing the finish line, you may be on the sidelines nursing a sore hamstring. In *Better Training for Distance Runners*, David Martin and Peter Coe offer advice that all runners should commit to memory: "The least amount of specific work required to achieve the best results is a powerfully effective training strategy." Sometimes, less is more.

Law of Variety

Let's imagine that you've put all the preceding principles together into the perfect training plan. Unfortunately, this perfection would last for only a few weeks. We need to consider the *Law of Variety*.

Strength and conditioning expert Charles Poliquin has coached athletes from 22 Olympic sports. "A training system," he says in his book *The Poliquin Principles: Successful Methods for Strength and Mass Development*, "is only as good as the time it takes you to adapt to it." As we've seen, when given enough time, your body will adapt to a workout stress. It grows stronger. Once this adaptation is complete, you need a new workout stress to trigger greater gains. So far so good. But your body will also adapt to your weekly training plan, and your progress may therefore stall out.

The solution, as modern coaches and sport scientists have discovered, is to arrange your training into several categories, each with a different emphasis. Arthur Lydiard was one of the first coaches to use this concept. His athletes would lay a foundation of relatively easy distance work and stamina. Then they'd focus on hills for a few weeks. Track work and specific race preparation came next. Each phase would build on the one that preceded it. This periodized approach builds balance into the program, and the athlete grows fitter by having to adapt to planned and sequentially changing stresses (see also chapter 5).

This systematic organization of your training is called periodization. The best thing about periodization is that it takes the guesswork out of training. When race day arrives, you're at peak fitness. You know you've done your homework. You know what pace you're capable of running. You're confident and eager to run.

Periodization takes the guesswork out of training. When race day arrives, you're at peak fitness.

To illustrate the power of periodization, we can examine the careers of two great runners, Ron Clarke and Lasse Viren. In 1965, Clarke ran a world record 27:39 10K on a cinder track without anyone to push him. In 1972, on a modern composition surface, Viren ran a 27:38 world record in the Olympic finals. You could easily argue that Clarke was the better runner. The track he ran on was much slower, and he had no real competition. But Viren won the gold.

During his incredible career, Clarke held world records at various distances between 2 and 10 miles. He never avoided competition. In fact, he seemed to thrive on it. He sometimes raced two or three times a week. He was racing at peak fitness, or close to it, year round. Unfortunately, Clarke never won a gold medal in the Commonwealth or Olympic Games. Less talented runners often seemed to run the race of a lifetime and steal Clarke's glory.

Lasse Viren on the other hand, won both the 5K and 10K finals in the 1972 and 1976 Games. Between Olympiads, Viren raced infrequently and often lost. But every four years—with gold medals on the line—Viren was invincible. He geared his training not for week-to-week or even month-to-month improvement. His periodized program spanned the four years between Munich and Montreal.

Few of us would be willing to devote four years to preparing for a single event. Peaking for an important race two or three times a year, though, is not only possible but also highly advisable. So if periodization is so effective, why doesn't everyone do it?

- First, the technical terms can be confusing. Instead of plotting microcycles, mesocycles, and macrocycles, most of us would be better off thinking of our training in terms of single workouts, weeks, months, and seasons.
- Second, periodization requires patience and discipline. Many runners have trouble keeping their competitive urges in check during workouts

or meaningless races. These eager folks are like the stand-up comic who tells his best joke first and has nothing left for a big finish.

- Third, periodization requires focus and planning. You need to choose a goal race, decide how much time you have to prepare, create a plan, and stick to it. Joining your friends for a track workout when you're due for an easy tempo run will only undermine your long-term progress.

- Fourth, you have to understand the practical aspects of how to structure a periodized plan. The schedules in this book offer you a great template from which to start. To keep the big picture in focus, consider this quote from German sport scientist Thomas Kurz: "A high intensity of training work, based on a previously done high volume of work, prepares the athlete for high sports results."

Notice the word *based* in that sentence. The high-volume phase, Kurz points out, brings slow, steady progress. If you've watched a house being built, laying the foundation seems to take forever. Once this work is complete, however, the rest of the house seems to take shape overnight. Likewise, after establishing a solid distance base, you can reach peak fitness quite rapidly—often in four to six weeks.

Remember the need for patience. Track work can bring rapid improvement, but as Kurz emphasizes, this progress is often unsteady and short lived. Think of your training as building a skyscraper. The broader the foundation, the higher you can reach. Lasse Viren's foundation took almost four years to build, and he reached Olympic heights that no one may ever again attain. Don't neglect your base.

Notice how periodization ties all the training principles into a neat bow.

Progressive overload. Each phase introduces a new stress to which you're not accustomed.

Adaptation. You plot enough time to respond to the overload.

Specificity. Each phase has a distinct purpose.

Individuality. You can adjust the span or the focus of each phase to suit your needs.

Realism. Assessing your total response to a number of different phases gives you a clear picture of your strengths and weaknesses.

Gradualism. Your plan's solid foundation gives you time to develop fully.

Moderation. Because each phase has a distinct emphasis and a time limit, you don't overdose on a particular kind of stress (e.g., distance, speed, hills).

Variety. You stay physically and mentally sharp because your training is always changing.

Incorporating these basic physiological principles into a periodized program will build rest and balance into your training. But sometimes even when you think you're doing everything right, telltale signs may be trying to warn you that something's wrong. Ignoring these signs can bring disaster—overtraining.

Avoiding Overtraining

Overtraining usually results from three simple mistakes:

1. Too much overload
2. Not enough recovery
3. A combination of the two

Some sport scientists consider overtraining a "disease" of the central nervous system because it can affect a number of bodily processes. Short-term overtraining is like a mild cold. If you arrest it in its early stages, you'll bounce back quickly. Long-term or chronic overtraining is more like mononucleosis—a serious imbalance of your entire body.

Your autonomic nervous system comprises two branches—the sympathetic and the parasympathetic. The sympathetic system excites your body and prepares you for action. Being involved in a fender bender would be a good example of what might trigger it. The parasympathetic system has an opposite, calming effect. Imagine yourself napping beneath a shady tree. These systems must work in harmony. Overtraining throws them out of balance.

It's helpful to distinguish between sympathetic system overtraining and parasympathetic system overtraining.

Sympathetic— caused by excessive intensity	Parasympathetic— caused by excessive volume
Slight fatigue	Abnormal fatigue
Trouble falling asleep	Trouble getting out of bed
Nervousness, hyperactivity	Listlessness, apathy
Elevated resting heart rate	Normal or below normal resting heart rate

A drop in performance, muscle and joint soreness, poor resistance to infection, and swollen lymph nodes may be common to either type of overtraining.

Generally, although not always, sympathetic overtraining is less severe and more easily overcome. The usual prescription is to eliminate intense workouts and just jog easily until you start feeling fresh. Parasympathetic overtraining is less common. It's seen more often in high-mileage runners and in sports like swimming and cycling in which large volumes of training are the standard practice. Because it takes more volume and a longer time span to become parasympathetically overtrained, more systems of the body become involved. The sympathetically overtrained runner might only have sore legs and a jumpy disposition. The parasympathetically overtrained runner might have sore legs, aching joints, a depressed immune system, and elevated stress hormones.

Never forget that competitive running is a stressful activity. Creatine kinease (CK) is a muscle tissue enzyme released into the blood stream by damage to the muscles. In an experiment, Rogers, Stull, and Apple (1985) found that runners who doubled their mileage overnight often had CK levels four times higher than normal. Postmarathon levels can reach 20 times greater than normal.

The best cure for overtraining is prevention. If you're feeling tired, pay careful attention to your level of fatigue early in your run. If it dissipates noticeably, you're probably OK. If your fatigue intensifies, stop running and walk home.

Unfortunately, no single reliable indicator of overtraining exists. We've seen that sympathetic overtraining usually raises your resting heart rate, whereas parasympathetic overtraining may actually lower it. If you looked at one only indicator in your car—the gas gauge—you wouldn't notice the blinking oil light, the squealing brakes, or the knocking engine.

Keep the physiological principles we've discussed in mind. Periodize your training plan. Back off at the first hint of overtraining. Remember that running well is like walking a tightrope. To keep your balance, you must constantly adjust your mix of work and rest. When in doubt, emphasize the rest. You'll experience a breakthrough instead of a breakdown.

28

Restoring and Resting Your Body

LINDA JAROS-OSGA
Sports massage therapist, certified personal trainer

REX BAIRD, MEd, CSCS
Massage therapist and Certified Strength and Conditioning Specialist
at the International Academy of NeuroMuscular Therapy

Easy days are there for a reason; they allow you to recover, adapt, and grow stronger.

Fill your bowl to the brim and it will spill
Keep sharpening your knife and it will blunt . . .
Do your work and step back.
The only path to serenity.

Although these words were written about 2,500 years ago by Chinese philosopher Lao-tzu, they highlight a concept that no successful modern-day runner can ignore. If you train too hard without a break, you'll lose your sharpness. Stepping back periodically is essential to making progress. As Vern Gambetta, athletic performance enhancement specialist says, "The key to success is not the work, but the rest." Of course, your training is important, but perhaps even more important to moving forward in your performance and enjoyment of running is what you do, physically and mentally, between your workouts. You must rest and recover for your training to have any benefit.

What's Involved in Rest and Recovery?

Let's start by outlining three broad categories of rest and recovery. Think of them as the three Ps:

Planning. "If you fail to plan, you plan to fail." Follow the training schedules in this book and adapt them to your needs. Remember that the easy days are there for a reason. They allow you to recover, adapt, and grow stronger. If your training plan is too ambitious, even the best recovery secrets won't bail you out once you realize you've overdone it. Be honest and realistic about your current level of fitness when you build your plan and plan recovery into your training (see chapters 26 and 27). As a rule, the harder your training gets, the more important restoration becomes. For example, it's not unusual for world-class athletes running 100 to 140 miles a week to receive a massage every day. For most of us, this is neither practical nor necessary. The important point is that as you increase training intensity, you build extra rest and recovery into your plan. You'll need it.

Physical restoration. Physical restoration, including active rest, restorative water activities, yoga, and massage, is the focus of this chapter. As you think about the big picture, though, you'll want to keep focused on the importance of other elements as well—good nutrition (chapters 13 and 23), sound sleep, and regular stretching (chapters 11 and 26).

Psychological restoration. Entire books have been written on psychological restoration. Whatever strategy you choose—sitting in full-lotus Zen meditation or just curling up with a good book—remember that your goal is to manage and reduce stress. Some activities may seem restorative, but perhaps really aren't. For example, surfing the Internet can relax your mind but may give you a sore neck and tight hip flexors from long hours of sitting. Pick an activity that leaves you refreshed both physically and mentally.

Although we have differentiated physical and psychological restoration for the purposes of discussion, we'll keep emphasizing throughout this chapter how they interact with one another.

A training plan that is too challenging will cause physical exhaustion and psychological burnout. Mistakes in the physical realm—fast food, late nights, no stretching—will undermine even a conservative plan. Ignoring the stress of a job deadline or a rocky relationship will soon make a 5-mile run on flat terrain feel more like a hilly 10.

Always keep in mind the words of Lao-tzu. Think of your life as a bowl. Fill it, but don't go overboard and spill it. Think of your training as a knife.

The harder your training gets, the more important restoration becomes.

© Tony Demin/International Stock

Sharpen the blade of your fitness but don't dull it with too much hard training.

Running a hard workout actually tears down the muscle fibers in your body. This provides the stimulus that mobilizes your body to adapt and improve its fitness. But if your body is going to respond to that stimulus by building up and growing stronger, it needs planned rest and recovery.

Our perspective of this topic comes from a combined 30 years of massage therapy practice. In that time, we have worked with elite runners, weekend warriors, and every level in between. The most successful of these athletes understand the need for rest, recovery, and balance in their lives. We feel that restoration is one of the most important aspects of training but one that is often overlooked. We hope that reading this chapter has piqued your curiosity about exploring the many restorative aids available to you.

Active Rest

We begin with active rest because it requires no special equipment or a therapist, just a commitment from you to respect your body and take active responsibility for your health. As Vern Gambetta points out, "When an athlete is accustomed to the stress of training, no activity at all is a negative shock to the system." So active rest is designed to work the muscles gently while giving the nervous system a vacation. For runners, active rest means getting rid of the aches and pains of hard training through any kind of gentle movement that increases circulation and relaxation. Runners can use it to stimulate recovery after a hard workout or as a total break from running after a long season or a particularly hard race. It sounds easy, but for most runners we treat, it's the most difficult aspect of recovery because it requires restraint!

Active rest is not cross-training. If you're a runner who typically trains for 45 minutes at a heart rate of 135, cross-training might be riding a bike for the same period and intensity instead of running. Active rest, on the other hand, would be pedaling easily on an exercise bike for 15 minutes in the evening to get the kinks out of an interval workout you ran that morning. You're not looking to improve your fitness; rather, you're trying to increase circulation, release stress, and calm your nervous system. For example, if you decided to cross-train by taking a spinning class (a group interval workout on a stationary bike), you would be relieving the pavement-pounding muscular stresses that running produces. But the intense demands that bike intervals create would still tire your legs and deplete your nervous system. A spinning class is certainly active, but it's not rest.

Research shows that for recovering between efforts on the track, easy jogging is more effective than complete rest because it promotes greater circulation. Likewise, gentle movement between hard workouts themselves will help you bounce back faster. Follow these suggestions for maximizing the restorative effects of active rest:

- Plan active rest sessions first rather than sticking them in randomly around your other workouts.
- Choose an activity that you enjoy, perhaps a walk in a park or on a beach so you can check out the scenery you usually pass on your runs. Investigate restorative water activities such as easy swimming and water running.
- Avoid high-impact or muscularly demanding activities (i.e., running, basketball, aerobics, stair climbing). Unless you're an advanced runner with years of high mileage under your belt, running is probably too stressful to be classified as active rest. Instead, try swimming, cycling, easy water running, walking, using an elliptical trainer, or cross-country skiing.

- Keep the intensity low—remember that you're just getting the kinks out. Sixty percent of your maximum heart rate would be a good upper limit.
- Keep the duration short (30 minutes or less). This is not a workout.
- Help yourself reestablish homeostasis—the natural state of balance among your body's many systems. Physical and mental stress can raise your temperature, blood pressure, and heart rate and can create a host of disruptions in your body chemistry and nervous system. Russian research reveals that scheduling an active rest session six to eight hours after a hard workout gives your body's normal recovery rhythm a boost just when it's starting to slow down.
- Get a massage on your rest day. Because massage is effective for calming the nervous system, we don't recommend working out soon after you get off the table. You probably won't feel like it anyway.
- Schedule psychological downtime (at least 20 to 30 minutes) after your active rest session. This is a perfect time for relaxing and doing mental activities that you enjoy (videos, chess, crossword puzzles, reading, meditation, etc.).

Too often, we see runners forced to take time off because of injury and fatigue. If you schedule the rest sessions into your weekly training schedule, you may be able to avoid prolonged downtime. This one is up to you!

Judi St. Hilaire on Rest and Recovery

"I battled an awful lot of injuries throughout my running career but learned to incorporate measures into my training program that would allow me to train and compete at a successful level. Pool running when injured, three to four days of tapering before races, physical therapy, chiropractic, and weekly deep massage were as much a part of my training routine as running. My career would not have lasted nearly as long as it did without them."
—Judy St. Hilaire, 1992 Olympian, 10,000 meters track

Massage

Most runners get a massage for two main reasons. First, they indulge themselves after a period of hard training that culminates in a big race—often a marathon. Second, they hobble in with an injury, hoping the massage therapist can fix them so they won't have to take time off from their training and racing.

We believe that a massage should be neither a postrace indulgence nor a quick fix. Instead, why not get regular massage as you prepare for the big race and reward yourself with injury-free training and perhaps even a PR?

We'll try to convince you with a quick list of what massage can do for you and your breakthrough. Massage will

- increase local blood circulation to the area being massaged;
- oxygenate the muscle, improving local metabolism and muscle function;
- release tight areas in the muscle (spasms, trigger points), allowing the muscle to elongate and relax;
- improve flow of lymphatic fluid, which transports cellular debris and is a key component of the immune-system function;
- interrupt the sensory feedback loop that can create excessive nervous impulses to the muscle, thus leading to overall relaxation, more economical energy expenditure, and increased circulation;
- encourage the formation of more functional scar tissue after an injury;
- moderate the buildup of thick, fibrous tissue and adhesions that may result from hard training; and
- establish a better balance between the sympathetic (fight or flight) and parasympathetic (relaxing) branches of the nervous system, thus leading to greater calm and a better ability to handle stress.

Some believe that massage can reduce delayed-onset muscle soreness (DOMS), which is defined as muscle pain and stiffness that develop 24 to 48 hours after hard physical exertion. But no credible evidence exists that massage can reduce the general aches and pains of DOMS, which is probably caused by microtrauma to the muscles, not by the buildup of lactic acid, which the body normally clears and reprocesses rapidly. Massage is a powerful tool, but mild exercise (i.e., active recovery) is far superior at clearing lactate. That's why your postworkout and postrace cool-downs are so important.

Finding a Good Massage Therapist

You may be wondering how to find a good massage therapist. Here are some hints:

- Find a massage therapist with whom you have a good rapport. For recommendations try fellow runners, coaches, and specialty running stores. Talk to physical therapists (PTs) and chiropractors who treat athletes. Many PTs and chiropractors have a massage therapist on staff.

- Check out large races and triathlons in your area. Many events offer postrace massage by trained therapists hoping to attract new clients.

- Make sure the massage therapist has experience working with runners.

- Make sure your massage therapist is connected with a network of other health-care practitioners (i.e., physical therapist, chiropractor, osteopath, podiatrist) who can handle problems that are not responding to massage. We make a practice of referring out if symptoms don't begin to improve after three sessions.

Finding a qualified therapist is essential, but to reap the full benefits, you must learn how to receive a massage. Here are some suggestions:

- Understand that in your body everything is connected. A flat foot may cause a sore neck. What you think is your problem (a sore hamstring) may really be only a symptom of something else (perhaps a misaligned pelvis).

- Don't detach yourself from your injured body by using negative labels like "my bad leg" or "my stupid plantar fasciitis."

- Don't judge yourself by saying, "I shouldn't have gotten injured." Adopt a let-go mindset on the table. Give your internal judge a vacation.

- Be prepared to experience soreness in unexpected areas during a massage. Pain can result from compensations. "I had no idea I hurt there!" is a common reaction on the massage table.

- Communicate what you are feeling to your therapist. You should be working together, not resisting each other.

- Don't take a no pain, no gain attitude toward your therapy session. Learn your limits on the table; this will help you know your limits in training and racing. If the session is too painful, that's a sign that your neurological system is overstimulated, which may slow recovery.

- Always hydrate before and after your massage session. Your body is about 60 percent water. If you're down a quart or two, you may get cramps during treatment. Dehydrated muscles resist change and limit the restorative effects of massage.

- You might not want to run right after getting off the table. Give yourself a chance to adjust to the changes that your massage has created and allow yourself to enjoy the greater sense of relaxation that you'll feel. There are no set-in-stone rules governing how long you should wait to run after a massage. If you listen to your body, it will tell you when you're ready. Don't be surprised if it tells you to take the rest of the day off.

How often should you get a massage? For many people it may depend on what their wallets will allow. If you can afford a massage from a professional every week or every other week, that would be ideal. If finances are an issue, you might try adult education courses on massage to learn self-massage techniques or learn to exchange with a training partner. Or think about bringing a licensed massage therapist to your running club to teach techniques to the group.

Yoga

When you think of yoga, what comes to mind? Many runners we asked made remarks like these:

"Isn't it just stretching?"

"Flexible people do yoga. I'm too tight!"

"Don't you just lie around for an hour in a semiconscious state?"

"It looks too hard; I'm afraid I'll get hurt!"

Do any of these reactions describe how you feel? We believe that consistent yoga practice is one of the best-kept secrets to help restore runners' balance of body and mind and reduce the injuries related to these imbalances.

Consistent yoga practice may be one of the best-kept secrets to help restore runners' balance of body and mind and reduce the injuries related to these imbalances.

So, what is yoga? The word literally means "union." Although creating flexibility through stretching is part of yoga practice, yoga encompasses much more—breath, focused intention, and balance. You do yoga movements in a slow and controlled manner so that your body has an opportunity to adapt to the stress of lengthening tight muscles. By letting your breath guide your movements—keeping it smooth and even—you can better know your limits. In other words, if your breathing becomes choppy or you find yourself holding your breath, stop, back off, and smooth out your breath, then continue. Perhaps you were pushing too hard. More is not better in yoga. Injuries while stretching happen when you disconnect your breath and consciousness from what you are doing. So, if you are inflexible, with patience and respect for your limitations you can safely increase your range of motion. This can translate to improvements or breakthroughs in your running performance.

A typical yoga class brings together various components (some that we have previously mentioned):

Postures or asanas. An almost infinite number of postures are practiced to help develop strength, flexibility, balance, and concentration. How long you hold the postures can add to the intensity of the practice.

Breath or pranayama. The vital component of breath helps to create flow and equanimity in the body and mind by having a calming effect on the nervous system. Regular breathing practices can increase lung capacity. Depending on your intention, you can use different breathing techniques for either energizing or relaxing. Breath further aids the flexibility process by creating internal heat, thereby helping muscles become more pliable and receptive to the demands of stretching.

Stillness or meditation. Learning to find stillness can help you focus and improve your recovery. Most runners are "on the run" much of the time. Learning to quiet the mind is valuable whether you are training and competing or dealing with the stresses of everyday life.

To help guide you on your yoga exploration, we sought the advice of Tom Gillette, teacher, writer, and respected lecturer in the yoga community. Tom is the codirector of Innerlight Center for Yoga and Meditation in Rhode Island. Here are answers to the questions asked by many runners with whom we spoke:

Q. There are so many kinds of yoga to choose from—what should I start with?

A. First, find a teacher with whom you feel a good rapport. Two kinds of yoga should be explored:

1. Vigorous, athletic, aerobic styles (which activate the sympathetic nervous system) such as ashtanga, power, vinyasa, and bikram yoga

2. Soft forms of yoga (which activate the parasympathetic nervous system), such as kripalu, shivananda, svaroopa, and restorative yoga

Q. How do I find a qualified teacher?

A. Teachers with substantial experience will be able to offer more help when problems arise. They will have more variations and modifications for individual body types. Teachers who have been teaching for only a year or two, however, can lead exceptional classes because they can be so enthusiastic.

Q. How often should I practice yoga to receive benefits?

A. To promote physical, mental, and emotional balance, ideally you should practice vigorous styles of yoga four to five times a week or soft styles three to four times a week. Hatha yoga will lead you to meditation. Sitting in stillness with a straight spine and a concentrated mind will give you a winning edge. Ironically, yoga and meditation are the antithesis of competition.

Q. What advice do you have to help athletes get the most from their yoga practice?

A. Keep competition out of your practice. Don't judge your experience. Practice patience.

Q. How long are yoga classes?

A. Most yoga classes last 60 to 90 minutes. Make sure the class includes 15 to 20 minutes of relaxation so you can secure its restorative benefits. This may be the most challenging part of the class for type A personalities, but it's what they really need from yoga! More important than the length of your yoga practice session is the consistency of your practice. Like any form of conditioning, the body needs repetition to adapt, open up, and make positive changes. So, if you have only 20 to 30 minutes to practice some days, it's better than no practice at all.

Restorative Water Activities

The restorative powers of water are not limited to passive activities like soaking in a hot tub or whirlpool. Active movement in the water (i.e., swimming, water running, or water aerobics) is a great restorative tool if you keep the intensity low. Of course, harder workouts in the water could qualify as cross-training, but remember that we're talking about active rest here. Water training eliminates the heavy gravitational forces that land-based activities can produce. Working in the water offers many benefits to the runner:

- Increased circulation to overstressed muscles, thereby preventing the stiffness that may occur between training sessions
- Support (buoyancy), reducing the stress on joints
- A safe, nonimpact environment that allows you to maintain your fitness without stressing an existing injury
- The opportunity to achieve stress-free range of motion in the spine and all joints

We recommend that you get in the pool once or twice a week to assist recovery. You may want to explore the various tools designed for water training, such as flotation belts and vests for water running and kickboards and noodles (flotation devices) to support you while you work the lower body. Your local YMCA or park district may provide these tools and instruction as part of a class. Of course, no equipment is necessary if you swim.

Remember to stretch and rehydrate after a recovery session of active rest in the water. Although water activities do not produce impact, you still need to stretch. In particular, the resistance of the water against the feet and thighs can tighten the calves and hip flexors, so stretch them out. And just because you're in the water doesn't mean you don't sweat!

Top 10 Tips for Rest, Recovery, and Balance

1. Schedule active rest sessions first.
2. Get a massage regularly, either from a professional or by exchanging with a training partner.
3. If symptoms of injury persist, seek the help of an appropriate health-care practitioner (i.e., physical therapist, chiropractor, osteopath, or podiatrist).
4. Explore yoga with an open mind; keep the competitor at home.
5. Check out restorative water activities to give your muscles and joints a break.
6. Drink plenty of water throughout the day to assist recovery.
7. Feed your body with healthy, nutritionally dense foods.
8. Learn from your mistakes—don't let injuries rule your life.
9. Take time to enjoy other aspects of life. Keep the balance.
10. Make sure you get adequate sleep for the amount of your training. Remember, the "rest" is up to you!

The hard and stiff will be broken.
The soft and supple will prevail.

Tao To Ching

29

Balancing Your Energies

JOAN BENOIT SAMUELSON
American and Olympic record holder in the marathon

Too much of a good thing, even training, is not the best way to go.

Many years ago, my brother, a physician in family practice, told me something that has resonated throughout my years as a runner: "Rest is the basis of all activity." This seemed like a total paradox at the time, but the older I get and the more experience I have as an athlete, the better I understand the intrinsic truth of his words.

Throughout this book you have discovered and rediscovered a number of ways to achieve a breakthrough in your running. You have read about training philosophies and racing strategies, you have studied conditioning and strength training, you have learned how to incorporate better dietary habits, and maybe you have even been inspired to try new running shoes or apparel. But until you have made a conscious effort to balance the energy you put into your training schedule with a life that is fulfilling and allows for ample rest and restoration, you will likely end up with an injury instead of a breakthrough.

Balancing Your Training Through Rest

My experience at the 1984 Olympic Marathon Trials will probably go down as one of the best illustrations of the value of rest in a training schedule. During a perfectly ordinary training run on March 17, 1984, I felt my knee snap. My injury required that I undergo arthroscopic surgery just 17 days before the marathon trials on May 12, 1984. At the time of my injury I felt I was very close to peak condition, but in hindsight it seems clear that I was peaking way too early for the trials that year. Surgery forced (or allowed) me to rest both my body and my mind 17 days before the trials, something I wouldn't have been able to do on my own then. Other than some swimming and a bit of work on a stationary bike, I was forced to rest for the two and a half weeks before this important race.

The result of that rest period is a matter of record. After winning the Olympic Trials Marathon in 1984, I went on to Los Angeles to win the first women's Olympic Marathon three months later in 2:24:52, a time that is still the Olympic record.

It no longer takes an injury for me to incorporate rest and recovery into my training schedule. Today rest is a component as important in my schedule as speedwork or a long run. As I get older, I find I need to take more time off or work more easy, light running days into my schedule. I still feel capable of delivering efforts and results similar to those of years gone by, but it takes me longer to recover between these efforts than it did when I was younger. For instance, I used to run twice a day, five or six days a week. Today I rarely run twice a day. Only if I'm training for a marathon do I even think about a double workout, and those usually occur on a day when I do a track workout.

And speaking of speedwork, earlier in my career it wasn't unusual for me to do speedwork two or even three times per week. Now once a week is sufficient for my training. In addition, I take at least three easy days after a race or a particularly hard workout. This is in definite contrast to my earlier career, when I could race or put in hard efforts every other day. Sometimes I even raced back to back on weekends!

Tapering (following a schedule of more rest and less hard training leading up to an important race) is important, although it seems to be as difficult for other runners as it has been for me. Like many of you, I have had a tendency over the years to test myself up until the last minute before a race. Almost every runner has a story about leaving their best races on the roads in training. Building extra rest into your schedule before an all-out effort can make a big difference in whether or not you achieve your breakthrough.

I define tapering as a period of the training cycle that lasts a relatively short time (which will vary from runner to runner) before a race or competition that allows an athlete to rest her or his body and decrease the levels of

Joan Benoit Samuelson on solo rest run.

© Photo Run

lactic acid in the muscles. Some runners use this time to hone their speed, but I find this counterproductive. Done properly, tapering is another way to bring balance into your training. I've found that too much of a good thing, even training, is not always the best way to go.

To keep in perspective the importance of rest, remember that once you reach a certain level of fitness in training, it can take up to a month to lose any significant degree of that fitness. Eminent exercise physiologist and coach Jack Daniels, PhD, had a difficult time convincing me of this at the time of my knee injury in 1984, but it has proved to be true over and over for me and for many other runners. A runner can train to the point of perfection and then defeat that training by not cutting back or resting early enough before the big event. Learn when to cut back on speedwork, long runs, tempo runs, and weight work to give your body the reserves it needs for a breakthrough performance. (For more information on tapering, see chapter 20.)

Rest Your Shoes for Better Performance

It has taken me years to perfect the art of choosing and breaking in new running shoes. I prefer to use a variety of training and racing shoes at any given time, for a couple of reasons. First, I find it easier to break in a new pair of shoes gradually. Rather than wearing out one pair completely and then going on to the next new pair, I like to have a number of pairs in various stages of wear. Introducing a brand new shoe too quickly can sometimes cause a significant change in how your feet hit the ground. And too much change can cause problems that result in an unnecessary injury.

It can also be a good idea to find more than one model of running shoe that suits you. Almost every runner has seen a favorite running shoe discontinued and had to scramble to buy up odd pairs around the country. While your favorite shoe remains in stock, try others to see if they work as well. That way you are never caught short.

Balance for Your Body: Cross-Training

The effects of cross-training for a breakthrough performance are discussed at length in chapter 12. Keep in mind that cross-training is also an excellent tool for creating balance, not only in your running but also in your life. Cross-training introduces you to alternative ways of getting in touch with your body and the world around you. Is it too cold and snowy for a safe run? Strap on your cross-country skis or snowshoes and get a great, fun, nonpounding aerobic workout. Take the family with you if you wish. Are the summer sun and humidity making you dread your next six-mile loop (or causing you to worry that it might even be dangerous)? Pack a picnic lunch and go to the beach, where you can swim and run for a mile or two on the sand. Are your shins starting to hurt from bumping up your mileage? Use a flotation belt and run in the pool. All these activities can help improve both your running and your attitude toward training. Some of them allow you to spend more time with friends and family, time that may be in short supply.

Though many runners discover cross-training after an injury, it is a wonderful way to promote overall strength and fitness. Water activities in particular are an excellent way of relieving sore muscles and maintaining flexibility by increasing circulation and range of motion, without the impact on the joints that other activities may involve. Cross-training allows you to take the burden of fitness off your legs and feet and use your upper body for cardiovascular conditioning. Strength training for the upper body can help runners balance a more highly developed lower body, leading to overall running efficiency. In terms of developing and maintaining physical balance to improve your running, the benefits of cross-training cannot be overstated.

Cross-training is an excellent tool for creating balance, not only in your running, but also in your life.

© Rich Cruse

A certain amount of cross-training has always been part of my life. Swimming, cross-country skiing, and biking are activities that I participate in regularly with family and friends. I can incorporate these and other sports into a training schedule if I have to augment or replace running due to injuries or time constraints.

Life's Balancing Act

All of us struggle to achieve balance in our lives. It seems that the harder we try to maintain balance, the more elusive it becomes. Women in particular, because they tend to assume the primary child-rearing and housekeeping responsibilities (often on top of working full time), have a tough time finding the balance they need for physical, mental, and spiritual health. As women, we need to be creative in finding ways to achieve balance while meeting the needs of our families and ourselves.

I tend to think that if we let it happen, balance will come to us naturally. The changing of the seasons is responsible for much of the balance in my life. The long, warm days of summer invite and encourage different activities than the cold, short days of a Maine winter.

Summer tends to be a spontaneous time of the year for me. I create extra long days by getting up earlier and going to bed later. My exercise habits change as well. With the natural rhythm of the seasons, I feel energized in the spring and summer. I often go out and experience one of those runs when I feel I could go on forever. During this time of year, I do a lot of gardening, which for me includes a lot of bending and heavy lifting. It is also a time when my family gets together to swim, hike, kayak, and just play.

I use the winter months to build strength. Normally I run only once a day. When I head to the ski slopes, I often do a three-sport day—cross-country ski, run, and downhill ski. In addition, winter is a time when I can incorporate water workouts into my training schedule. I do my water running and swimming workouts in much the same way that I would do a track workout, starting with a warm-up, doing intervals, and finishing with a cool-down. Although warm-ups and cool-downs are an essential part of any workout, you should tailor the specifics of a training regimen to meet your individual needs and time constraints.

Over the years I've discovered that working to achieve balance in my life becomes almost counterproductive. My motto has become "Go with the flow." I find that if I schedule things too far into the future, I become a slave to that schedule, even when it isn't working for me. A certain amount of spontaneity should take place during any given day on your schedule. For instance, when I was training for the 1996 Olympic trials, the schedule I had made out months earlier included a once-a-week track workout. Several weeks before the trials I came down with the flu. Had I been more flexible and less bound to my schedule, I would have seen the logic and benefit of skipping that week's track workout. As it was, I did the workout and had a terrible time. My performance that day played havoc with my head. I spent the next weeks trying to psych myself back up for the race. Taking one day off could have prevented weeks of mental distress.

If I take my cues from nature, from the world around me, I can follow the natural rhythms of my body and my environment. This isn't always easy to do, of course. Each of us struggles with the demands of career, family, and community. But one way to achieve balance in your life as well as in your running is to take time to listen to your body. Take time to listen to the natural world as well. Your body will give you cues by the way it responds to a scheduled workout. Don't hesitate to reschedule a run or workout so you can accommodate the energy level of your body and the emotional state of your mind.

I often tell people that before I had children I planned my day around running. Now that I am a wife and mother, I plan my running around my day. With the exception of a handful of world-class athletes, that's the way it is for most runners. We want to be the best possible runners we can be, yet it's also important to us to excel at our jobs, be full and loving members of our families, and serve our communities. That tall order takes patience, time, and effort.

It sounds strange, but frequently I find that the busier my schedule, the more balanced I feel. What I am doing is accommodating other interests that enable me to feel whole and complete. If it is on the schedule, somehow I manage to get it done. Setting a realistic schedule with enough time and flexibility for competing interests allows me to accomplish more. When I have a variety of interests and responsibilities, I seem to achieve balance more readily. Other runners have told me they feel the same way.

On the other hand, a schedule that is too light often encourages procrastination and boredom. I found that when I had an easy academic load in college or was injured or between seasons, I did the same thing every day without much inspiration or drive. I felt lethargic. These days, if all I had to do was run (a state I can hardly imagine!), I would tend to feel out of balance.

It is easy to lose sight of the richness of the world around us when we focus on one narrow goal or activity. Having a variety of interests will often add newfound appreciation for what running adds to our lives.

I learned the value of a variety of interests and experiences the hard way. When I was a junior in college, I accepted an athletic scholarship to run for North Carolina State University. Other than the hours I spent in the classroom, I lived, ate, studied, and traveled only with other runners and athletes. My life was one-dimensional.

During that year I contracted mononucleosis and became extremely sick. I believe I became ill because I was excluding healthy and interesting activities that would have made my life more complete and balanced. I also believe that an emphasis on running and fitness to the exclusion of all else is detrimental to both physical and psychological well-being.

That period of my life taught me a lesson that I carry with me to this day. When I am running or training, I focus with all the intensity I have. Then I let it go until my next workout. I try to apply that same concentration to my other activities throughout the day, whether I'm volunteering in my kids' classrooms, attending a board meeting, or working in my garden. It is important to focus on the task at hand. Some tasks require energy and hard work, whereas others require relaxation. We need to learn to balance tasks, too, and find that happy medium.

You Can Have It All

You can find ways to organize your life that will allow you to enjoy your family, your job, and your friends and still achieve a breakthrough in your running. The secret lies in how carefully and conscientiously you balance your energies. This accomplishment does not come about by chance. It requires an all-out effort that takes organization, determination, and flexibility. I can give you a few guidelines from my life:

- Know what you want to accomplish ahead of time. You might want to write down goals that are particularly important to you.
- Be flexible about how you accomplish your goals. Even the most meticulously made plans don't always work out the way we think they will. Running, like life, involves some flying by the seat of your pants.
- Make and stick to a schedule. You'll be more productive and find yourself enjoying a broader range of activities. We can modify the old maxim to read "Idle feet are the devil's workshop."
- Set priorities. Understand what is important in your life and what things make you feel good about yourself. Make sure those around you (family, friends, coworkers) know the important role that running plays in your life. At the same time, know within yourself the rank of running in your list of life priorities; for example, few parents would rank their running ahead of their children's health and well-being.
- Capitalize on the unexpected. Find ways to make use of unplanned free time. Don't let a change in plans throw you completely off your routine.
- Relax. Tomorrow is another day.

Achieving balance in your running requires that you examine many different aspects of your life. It is important that you balance the intense work of training with proper rest. Incorporating cross-training into your schedule will help you balance yourself physically as well as psychologically. Making running a part of a healthy and diverse lifestyle creates balance in the life you share with family and friends. The secret to a breakthrough running performance may well be achieving this overall balance in our lives.

Bibliography

Anderson, B. 1975. *Stretching*. Author

———. 1997. *Stretching at your computer or desk*. Bolinas, CA: Shelter

Anderson, B., and D. Bornell. 1984. *Stretch and strengthen for rehabilitation and development*. Palmer Lake, CO: Stretching, Inc.

Anderson, B., and S. Carlson. 1988. *Stretching for working America*. Palmer Lake, CO: Stretching, Inc.

Anderson, O. 1994. New study links stretching with higher injury rates. *Running Research News* 10:5-6

Benson, H. 2000. *The relaxation response*. 2nd ed. New York: Whole Care

Birch, B.B. 1995. *Power yoga*. New York: Fireside

Bompa, T. 1999. *Periodization: Theory and methodology of training*. Champaign, IL: Human Kinetics

———. 1999. *Periodization of training for sports*. Champaign, IL: Human Kinetics

Cerutty, P.W. 1964. *Middle distance running*. London: Pelham

Chapman, R.F., J. Stray-Gundersen, and B.D. Levine. 1998. Individual variation in response to altitude training. *Journal of Applied Physiology* 85:1448-1456

Cooper, K.H. 1995. *Faith-based fitness*. Nashville: Thomas Nelson

Cooper, P. 1998. *The American marathon*. Syracuse: Syracuse University Press

Costill, D.C. 1988. Carbohydrates for exercise, dietary demands for optimal performance. *International Journal of Sports Medicine* 8:1-18

Costill, D.C. 1986. *Inside running: Basics of sports physiology*. Indianapolis: Benchmark

Costill, D.C. 1980. Nutrition for endurance sport: Carbohydrate and fluid balance. *International Journal of Sports Medicine* 1(1):2-14

Couch, J. 1990. *The runner's yoga book*. Berkeley: Rodmell

Csikszentmihaly, M. 1990. *Flow: The psychology of optimal performance*. New York: Harper Collins.

Daniels, J.T., R.A. Yarbrough, and C. Foster. 1978. Changes in $\dot{V}O_2$max and running performance with training. *European Journal of Applied Physiology* 39:249-254

Farrell, P.A., J.H. Wilmore, E.F. Coyle, J.E. Billing, and D.L. Costill. 1979. Plasma lactate accumulation and distance running performance. *Medicine and Science in Sports* 11:338-344

Feuerstein, G. and L. Payne. 1999. *Yoga for dummies*. Foster City, CA: IDG

Goodie, R. 1984. *The Maine quality of running*. Portland, ME: Gannett Books

Hellemans, J. 1998. Hypoxic intermittent training pilot trial. Christchurch, New Zealand

Helmstetter, S. 1982. *What to say when you talk to yourself.* New York: Simon and Schuster

Jerome, John. 1998. *The sweet spot in time.* Halcottsville, NY: Breakaway

Kislevitz, G.W. 1999. A willingness to suffer: Ted Corbitt, a pioneer of ultramarathoning, recounts his ultra-amazing career. *Marathon & Beyond* Jan/Feb 3(1):66-75

Levine, B.D. and J. Stray-Gundersen. 1997. Living high-training low: the effect of moderate altitude acclimatization with low-altitude training on performance. *Journal of Applied Physiology* 83:102-112

Levine, B.D. and J. Stray-Gundersen, and G. Duhaime. 1991. Living high-training low: the effect of altitude acclimatization/normoxic training in trained runners. *Medicine and Science in Sports and Exercise* 23:S25

Martin, D. and P. Coe. 1997. *Better training for distance runners.* Champaign, IL: Human Kinetics

Milroy, A. 1998. The history of the London to Brighton race. *Ultramarathon World* [Online]. November. http://fox.nstn.ca/~dblaikie/uw-ldhst.html

Poliquin, C. 1997. The Poliquin principles: successful methods for strength and mass development. Napa, CA: Dayton Publications and Writers' Group

Rogers, M.A., G.A. Stull, and F.S. Apple. 1985. Creatine kinase isoenzyme activities in men and women following a marathon race. *Medicine and Science in Sports and Exercise* 17:679-682

Rusko, H.K., H. Tikkanen, L. Paavolainen, I. Hamalainen, K. Kalliokski, and A. Puranen. 1999. Effect of living in normoxia on sea level $\dot{V}O_2$max and red cell mass. *Medicine and Science in Sports and Exercise* 31:S86

Sjodin, B., I. Jacobs and J. Svedenhag. 1982. Changes in onset of blood lactate accumulation and muscle enzymes after training at DBLA. *European Journal of Applied Physiology* 49:45-57

Stray-Gundersen, J., R.F. Chapman, and B.D. Levine. 1998. HiLo altitude training improves performance in elite runners. *Medicine and Science in Sports and Exercise* 30:S35

Tanaka, K., H. Watanabe, Y. Konishi, R. Mitsuzono, S. Sumida, S. Tanaka, T. Fukuda, and F. Nakadomo. 1986. Longitudinal associations between anaerobic threshold and distance running performance. *European Journal of Applied Physiology* 55:248-252

Telford, R.D., K.S. Graham, J.R. Sutton, A.G. Hahn, D.A. Campbell, S.W. Creighton, R.B. Cunningham, P.G. Davis, C.J. Gore, J.A. Smith, and D. McA. Tumilty. 1996. Medium altitude training and sea level performance. *Medicine and Science in Sports and Exercise* 28:S124.

Unisports Centre for Sport Performance. 1999 and 1998. Intermittent hypoxic training trial studies (unpublished). Auckland, New Zealand

Wharton, J., and P. Wharton with B. Browning. 1996. *The Whartons' stretch book.* New York: Times Books

Index

Note: The italicized *t* following page numbers refers to tables; the *f* refers to figures.

About the Editors

Running Times magazine is the premier resource for dedicated runners. It offers cutting-edge advice on all facets of running, including training, nutrition, equipment, and sports medicine. It also provides comprehensive race results and listings of upcoming events. With a circulation of over 65,000, *Running Times* also offers insightful profiles of top athletes, and intelligent and witty commentary on the sport, making it a rewarding, inspirational resource for every runner or multisport athlete.

Editor-in-Chief **Gordon Bakoulis** is an elite athlete, coach, and publishing professional. For 17 years she has held editorial positions for such popular magazines as *Woman's Day*, *Glamour*, *Health*, *MS.*, *Working Woman*, and *Fitness Swimmer*, and has been a frequent contributor to many other sports and outdoor publications as a freelancer. She is the author of two books, *How to Train for and Run Your Best Marathon* (1993) and *Cross-Training* (1992). In addition to being an Olympic trials qualifier and a member of the Moving Comfort Racing Team, she has coached scores of runners and chaired the Road Runners Club of America Women's Distance Committee. Bakoulis resides in New York City.

Candace Karu is a writer and motivational speaker who lives in Cape Elizabeth, Maine. Formerly an advertising and public relations executive, Karu is now Editorial Director of *Running Times* magazine. She also conducts workshops and seminars on physical and mental fitness. A dedicated mid-pack runner, Karu is a veteran of 16 marathons. She is currently working with Andy Palmer, PhD, on a book project, *The Mind Is The Athlete*.

About the Contributors

A 1996 U.S. Olympic Marathon Trials qualifier with personal bests ranging from 2:19:25 in the marathon to 4:08 in the mile, **Randy Accetta** has written for *Running Times* and *Runner's World* magazines. Randy is the director of programs for Craftsbury Running Camps in Vermont, a board member of the Southern Arizona Roadrunners, and the Arizona head coach for the Leukemia Society of America's Team in Training program. Along with Greg Wenneborg, Randy coaches over 100 runners of all ages and abilities in The Workout Group in Tucson, Arizona. Randy teaches English at the University of Arizona, where he will complete his PhD in May 2000.

Stephen Anderson is a wellness consultant and personal fitness trainer specializing in worksite wellness programs, behavior modification programs, flexibility, and body mechanics. He has a Masters of Science, and Certificate of Advanced Study from Springfield College (1985). He is a member of IDEA, The International Association of Fitness Professionals, as well as the Reebok Professional Instructor Alliance and the National Wellness Association.

A six-time New Zealand Olympic qualifier who has been called the "winningest road racer ever," **Anne Audain** became an American citizen in 1995. She is the cofounder and race codirector of the Idaho Women's Fitness Celebration 5K in Boise, Idaho. She is also a frequent motivational speaker and is writing her autobiography with John Parker, Jr. Anne resides in Boise, Idaho, and Evansville, Indiana.

Rex Baird, MEd, is a massage therapist and Certified Strength and Conditioning Specialist (CSCS) who has been working with athletes of all levels since 1985. He is a staff member of the International Academy of NeuroMuscular Therapy and a member of the National Strength and Conditioning Association. As a competitor, he has an extensive background in track and field, distance running, and powerlifting.

Olympic gold medalist in the first women's Olympic Marathon (1984), **Joan Benoit Samuelson** is also the American record holder in the marathon (2:21:21). She is the founder of the Peoples Beach to Beacon 10K in Cape Elizabeth, Maine, and resides in Freeport, Maine with her husband and two children.

Roy Benson is a running coach, prolific author, *Running Times* contributing editor, clinic speaker, director of Roy Benson's Nike Running Camps, and coach of Marist High School boys' and girls' cross country teams. Roy resides in Atlanta, Georgia with his wife, Betty. He is a widely recognized expert on heart rate monitor training.

The editor of *Marathon & Beyond*, prolific running writer and editor **Richard Benyo** is also an accomplished ultramarathoner. He is the author of *Running Past 50* (Human Kinetics, 1998). Rich is the recipient of the 1998 Road Runner's Club of America (RRCA) Professional Journalist of the Year award.

Jacqueline (Jackie) Berning, PhD, RD, is an assistant professor at the University of Colorado at Colorado Springs, where she teaches nutrition in the Biology Department. She has worked extensively with collegiate athletes at the University of Colorado at Boulder as well as with professional athletes affiliated with the Denver Broncos, Denver Nuggets, and the Colorado Avalanche. Jackie is the staff nutritionist for the Cleveland Indians Minor League Baseball Teams and has been recently named National Media Spokesperson for the American Dietetic Association.

Jonathan H. Beverly is an accomplished freelance writer currently living in Brussels, Belgium. His writing credits include *Running Times*, *Runner's World*, and *Marathon & Beyond*. He's a long-time running coach with PRs of 34:36 for 10K and 2:46 for the marathon.

A full professor at York University in Toronto, **Tudor O. Bompa, PhD,** has authored numerous articles as well as several important books on physical conditioning including *Serious Strength Training*, *Periodization: Theory and Methodology of Training*, *Periodization Training for Sports*, and *Total Training for Young Champions*. His work has been translated into nine languages, and he has made presentations on training theories, planning, and periodization in more than 30 countries. Bompa lives in Sharon, Ontario.

As a certified kinesiologist, personal trainer, and advanced fitness appraiser, **Michael Carrera** has had the opportunity to work with a broad base of individuals ranging from amateur athletes to national level swimmers, figure skaters, marathon runners, and hockey players. Currently he is working with Dr. Tudor Bompa in the design and implementation of both fitness and sport conditioning certification programs.

Mark Conover was the surprise winner of the 1988 U.S. Men's Olympic Marathon Trials and competed in the Olympic Games in Seoul, South Korea. A cancer survivor, he is a frequent motivational speaker. Mark coaches the California State Polytechnic University track and cross country teams in San Luis Obsipo, California, where his lives with his canine companion.

The former national 5,000-meter champion with PRs of 15:41 for 5K and 32:40 for 10K, **Suzanne Girard Eberle, MS, RD,** is a registered dietitian specializing in sports nutrition. She is the author of *Endurance Sports Nutrition* (Human Kinetics, 2000). A *Running Times* contributing editor, Suzanne lives in Portland, Oregon.

Jim Ferstle is a freelance writer based in St. Paul, MN. He is a regular contributor to a variety of running publications, including *Running Times*, *Road Race Management*, and *Runner's World*. He was an editor for *The Physician and Sportsmedicine* and has written extensively on drugs in sport. His reports have appeared on the BBC, CBS's "60-Minutes," and the London Sunday Times. During the 1970s, he competed for Bowling Green State University, helping the team win Mid American Conference championships in track and cross country. Among his individual titles were the Central Collegiate Conference 6-mile and the Ohio State Relays 6-mile. After college he competed in road races, recording a PR of 2:22:45 in the marathon.

Tom Fleming is the coach of adidas Running Room in Bloomfield, New Jersey, a two-time winner of the New York City Marathon (1973 and 1975, and a twice second (1973 and 1974) and once third (1975) place finisher in the Boston Marathon. He has coached numerous athletes, including Anne Marie Lauck, Joe LeMay and Elaine Van Blunk.

Teresa Gibreal has worked in the fitness industry for 22 years and has been with Phidippides Running Store in Atlanta, for the past 10 years. As assistant manager, Teresa has been involved in product evaluation and employee training, as well as presenting seminars to running groups. A self-professed casual runner, she has completed two marathons. Teresa has a masters degree in physical education/exercise science from the University of Nebraska.

A *Running Times* contributing editor and 2:15 marathoner, **Jim Hage** placed eighth in the 1992 U.S. Olympic Marathon Trials and also competed in the 1988 and 1996 Trials. Jim is now a 42-year-old top-ranked age-group competitor who has maintained a running streak since July 16, 1982. He is the winner of two consecutive Marine Corps Marathons. Jim also writes frequently on running for *The Washington Post*. He resides in Lanham, Maryland.

Brooks Johnson has been a coach of runners of all distances since 1957, of Olympians since the 1960s, and of college teams at Stanford and California State Polytechnic University and elsewhere. Author of his self-published *Coach's Manual*, Johnson is currently serving as president of Strategic Resources Allocation Group in Orlando, Florida.

A freelance writer based in New York City and Santa Fe, New Mexico, **Heather C. Liston** has written numerous articles and columns for *Running Times* and is also a contributor to *New York Runner*, *Self*, *Fit*, *Women Outside*, and other publications. She is Director of Corporate and Foundation Giving for the Santa Fe Opera.

Linda Jaros-Osga has been in private practice since 1983, specializing in sports rehabilatative massage therapy. Her clients have ranged from elite athletes to weekend warriors. Among her client base have been Bill Rodgers, Joan Benoit Samuelson, Judi St. Hilaire, Pete and Chrissey Pfitzinger, Mark and Gwyn Coogan, John Treacy, Mark Carroll, and Amy Rudolph. Linda is also an educator for the continuing education of massage professionals and personal fitness trainers. Her focus in rehabilitation has been in functional training techniques including yoga, medicine ball work, pilates, and sports specific exercises.

Andy Palmer earned a PhD in sport psychology from the University of Georgia. He is a former 2:16 marathoner who competed in the U.S. Olympic Marathon Trials. Andy owns and operates Maine Running Camps in Bar Harbor, Maine, and coaches many individual runners. He is thrilled to be a part of this project.

Pete Pfitzinger, MSc, MBA, was the top American finisher in the 1984 and 1988 Olympic Marathons; he won the 1984 U.S. Olympic Marathon Trials. He is an exercise physiologist and the director of the UniSports Centre for Sport Performance in Auckland, New Zealand. Pete lives in Auckland with his wife Chrissey, a former New Zealand Olympian, and their two daughters. He is a *Running Times* senior writer and the coauthor of *Road Racing for Serious Runners* (Human Kinetics, 1998).

Kirk Rosenbach has been running for 25 years and is a member of the Atlanta Track Club's masters competitive team. He has been associated with the original Phidippides Running Store for 20 years and is a frequent lecturer on running shoe topics at Atlanta, Georgia area clinics.

Amol Saxena, DPM, is a podiatrist specializing in sports medicine at the Palo Alto Medical Foundation in Palo Alto, CA. He is a Fellow of the American Academy of Podiatric Sports Medicine and the American College of Foot and Ankle Surgeons. He has more than two dozen scientific publications, and has treated thousands of runners over the past 10 years. As an often injured college runner, he failed to reach his potential, but did manage a 32:02 10K. He currently is able to run 10Ks in the low 34's and marathons in the low 2:40's. He hopes to help as many runners as possible avoid the injuries he sustained.

Gregory Sheats has been doing foot and running shoe analysis since 1980 when he joined the staff of the original Phidippides Running Store in Atlanta, Georgia. His passion for running and long association with the leading running shoe designers and developers has lead to consulting and participating on numerous running shoe advisory panels.

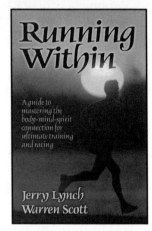

Producing Successful MAGAZINES, NEWSLETTERS and E-ZINES

If you want to know how...

Touch Typing in Ten Hours
*A few hours now will teach you a skill
that will be with you for life*

Improve Your Punctuation & Grammar
*Master the basics of the English language,
and write with greater confidence*

Getting Free Publicity
Secrets of successful press relations

Successful Seminar Selling
*The ultimate small business guide to boosting
sales and profits through seminars and workshops*

Quick Solutions to Common Errors in English
An A–Z guide to spelling, punctuation and grammar

howtobooks

Please send for a free copy of the latest catalogue to:

How To Books
3 Newtec Place, Magdalen Road,
Oxford OX4 1RE, United Kingdom
email: info@howtobooks.co.uk
www.howtobooks.co.uk

Producing Successful
MAGAZINES,
NEWSLETTERS
and E-ZINES

"Great ideas, practical help, and straightforward guidance...
a must-have for anyone planning their own publication."

CAROL HARRIS

howtobooks

Published by How To Books Ltd
3 Newtec Place, Magdalen Road
Oxford OX4 1RE, United Kingdom
Tel: (01865) 793806 Fax: (01865) 248780
Email: info@howtobooks.co.uk
www.howtobooks.co.uk

First published 2004

British Library Cataloguing in Publication Data.
A catalogue record for this book is available from the British Library.

Produced for How To Books by Deer Park Productions, Tavistock
Typeset by PDQ Typesetting, Newcastle-under-Lyme, Staffordshire
Cover design by Baseline Arts Ltd, Oxford
Printed and bound in Great Britain by Bell & Bain Ltd, Glasgow

NOTE: The material contained in this book is set out in good faith for general
guidance and no liability can be accepted for loss or expense incurred as a result of
relying in particular circumstances on statements made in the book. Laws and
regulations are complex and liable to change, and readers should check the current
position with the relevant authorities before making personal arrangements.

Contents

Appendices

Preface

When I launched my latest magazine, many people made comments about how 'brave' it was; many more asked questions such as: 'Where will you get contributions from?' or 'How will you let people know about it?'

I felt surprised by some of the things people said, because I felt that what I was doing was mainly common sense and not rocket science. However, on reflection, I came to think that, although much of it was commonplace to me, this was probably because I was taking for granted the experience and knowledge I had accumulated over the years. It then set me thinking that, if it wasn't just common sense, perhaps others could benefit from my making the information available to them. And that was how this book began.

This is not a book for the really experienced magazine and newsletter producer. If you have been running an established publication for many years, you will undoubtedly know all that is within these pages – and would almost certainly be able to add to it. If this is the case, I would welcome suggestions for anything else to include in a future edition of the book.

I hope, however, that if you are thinking of starting a publication, or if you have one for which you are already responsible, but which you would like to develop further, this book will give you some ideas and some practical help with your venture.

The chapters that follow contain straightforward guidance, in an easy-to-read format. You can access the chapters in any order you wish, depending on your need at any particular time. It is useful to re-visit some of the topics periodically, to check that you are still on track to meet your original objectives, or to consider how you may need to vary what you are doing in order to achieve new goals. Publications need to be re-evaluated on an ongoing basis, so they remain lively, focussed and relevant and the more attention you pay to doing this the more effective you will be.

I hope that, within these pages, you find many ideas for making your own publications a success.

Carol Harris

Acknowledgements

I would like to thank the following people for their help with this book:

Roy Elmore for the glossary and additions to the technical information. Paul Harris for some technical information and for reviewing the original draft. Roger Brooks and Martin Roberts for reading and making helpful suggestions. Members of the BACB Freelance Forum for ideas on resources and, in particular, Joanne Lawrence, John Player and Doreen Walford for reading the final draft and giving some useful additions to the text.

The photographs in Appendix 1 are reproduced by kind permission of Communicators in Business and Trident Photographic Services. They are full colour publications, but appear in this book in black and white only.

Introduction

What Kinds of Publications Are There?

It is useful to consider what differentiates various kinds of publication. Magazines and newsletters are referred to as 'periodicals', being produced as a series – over a period of time – as opposed to books, which are usually produced as one-off items, although some do form part of a series.

There are many kinds of periodical, including the following:

- newspapers
- magazines
- journals
- newsletters
- reports
- information sheets
- E-zines
- electronic newsletters

Each of these can be produced in a range of formats, frequencies, sizes and styles but, on the whole, each of the terms relates to a slightly different kind of product. Some of their features are discussed below.

Newspapers

Newspapers are topical and each issue tends to have a fairly short life – often just a day. They are usually printed on fairly cheap paper, have little or no colour (apart from supplements), are illustrated with photographs and carry advertising. They may be 'light' in style (often associated with 'tabloid' publications) or 'heavier' (usually 'broadsheets').

Magazines

Magazines tend to be fairly 'light' in content and writing style, and come out less frequently than newspapers. Weekly or monthly publication is common. They are often heavily illustrated and can have a variety of design features.

Journals

Journals tend to be associated with academic fields. They generally contain 'heavier' writing and longer articles and are often published at longer intervals – quarterly or bi-annually is common. Their design is often quite simple and they may have few, or no, illustrations, apart from charts, diagrams and tables.

Newsletters

Newsletters tend to be short publications – often just a few pages. They may be written for people within a particular interest group, rather than the general public, although this is not always the case. Newsletters are often produced by businesses for internal consumption, as part of an 'Internal Communications' (IC) function, or for their customers and clients. News-letters are often produced on a low budget and their appearance and size may reflect this.

Reports

Although some reports are 'one-off' publications, many are produced on a regular basis. Reports are generally produced to inform people about a particular topic of current or specialist interest. Reports are often produced within single organisations as part of operational management, but can also be published by other bodies for wider consumption, such as government reports on public services, reports on survey/market research findings and demographic trends/census reports.

Information sheets

Information sheets are usually very small publications, often just a single sheet of paper, designed to provide facts on a particular topic. As with reports, these may also be 'one-off' publications, or may be produced on a regular basis – and updated – as part of a wider communications process.

E-zines

E-zines are magazines that are produced electronically and designed to be accessed via e-mail or downloaded from the Internet. They are often shorter in length than printed publications, partly because it can be more difficult to read from a screen than from a printed page, and partly because most people use electronic media for speed of access and therefore value relatively brief material.

Electronic newsletters

Electronic newsletters are newsletters that are produced and sent by email, either in the body of the email or as an attachment. They are generally fairly short and are often produced partly for information and partly for publicity. Electronic newsletters frequently contain information on associated activities and may have links to other publications or websites.

Part One
Producing a Magazine

This part of the book contains information about magazine production. The chapters are sequenced as follows: they begin with the purposes and objectives of a magazine, continue with editorial functions and move to production functions and quality control.

Chapter 1
Identifying Your Audience: Considering Principles, Values and Ethics

Identifying Your Audience

It is important to identify your audience – and thereby your potential market – so that your magazine can be designed, promoted and distributed with that in mind.

There are two major categories of magazine:

■ **Consumer magazines**. These are aimed at individuals in the market for products, services or information.

■ **Business to business (B2B) magazines**. These are aimed at organisations wishing to know about the offerings of other organisations.

It should be apparent which of these categories your magazine falls into, although some magazines can serve both purposes.

There are also several groups of magazine readers, for example:

■ **Associates**. This includes friends, family, work colleagues, and so forth – people who are generally close contacts of the magazine's producers.

■ **Members of an organisation**. These are people within an established body, for example a club, association, professional body, business network or 'virtual' organisation. With most of these, people tend to meet face to face, but with virtual organisations, members generally communicate with each other by electronic means and do not have a physical workplace or other venue that they all attend regularly.

- **People within a geographical area**. This could be a village, a town, a county, a region, a country or an international area.

- **People in a 'functional' area**. This includes people who have something in common. They may share the same work sector – for example, engineers or hairdressers; engage in the same social activity – such as attendance at a leisure centre or a gardening club; be at a similar career stage – for example, school leavers or the self-employed, and so forth.

- **The general public**. This is a readership composed of anyone who is interested in the topic of the magazine, regardless of any of the above groupings.

It is worth considering each of the above categories and then deciding which of them apply to your own magazine. You can have several categories of reader, but do be careful not to make your desired readership too broad – if you try to appeal to the whole world, the chances are that you will lose focus, and potential readers will not understand why your publication is relevant to them.

Once you have determined your potential readers, you will have some idea of the potential size of your market; you can then decide whether to produce your publication for the whole of your market or to restrict the circulation size for financial or other reasons.

Considering Principles, Values and Ethics

People differ in their interpretations of the words 'principles', 'values' and 'ethics' – to my mind, principles are guides to action, values are the things that are important to a person and ethics are the codes of morality which people follow. You will probably have your own definitions of each of these concepts and you may simply think the terms are interchangeable. Whatever your opinion regarding the words themselves, there are a number of issues that result from the application of these concepts.

Together, these concepts are factors that govern the ways in which an activity is carried out and, in producing your magazine, you will probably find it helpful to explore your own beliefs about each of them, and the implications that follow from these beliefs.

Of course, the words themselves do not carry any inbuilt positive or negative connotations: a person can act from very commendable principles, yet the actions taken may have appalling consequences. In this chapter, however, I will assume that you wish to adopt principles, values and ethics that lead to beneficial results.

If this is the case, you may like to spend a little time considering which principles, values and ethics are involved in your desire to produce your magazine and in its actual production; for example:

Some principles might be:
■ to ensure balance in reporting and writing
■ to allow a 'right of reply' to material printed
■ to provide space for minority opinion

Some values might be:
■ to produce a high quality product
■ to remain independent in thinking and writing
■ to maintain open communications between people involved

Some ethical stances might include:
■ not printing incorrect, embarrassing, misleading or damaging material
■ not accepting inducements to print material
■ not publicly criticising competing publications

When you are clear about this kind of issue, you will find it much easier to decide on particular courses of actions and put your day-to-day activity into a broader, more significant, context.

Chapter 2
Producing a Business Plan

A business plan is an essential element of a commercial venture. If your magazine is not a commercial one, you may think this topic is unimportant; however, it is a useful exercise to produce a business plan so that you get all the relevant factors clear in your mind and can allow for any issues that arise.

Your business plan should show the various elements involved in starting up and running your magazine. It should include your objectives and desired results and your means of achieving them, the resources you need in order to achieve your results and the ways in which you will set about achieving them – in both the short and the long term.

It is good to keep your business plan as simple as possible, and you should take into account whether it is just for your own use, or whether anyone else will need to see it – for example, your bank manager, work associates or members of a committee.

Your business plan should be written clearly and concisely, so that each section can be read and understood by anyone involved with the business. It is possible to buy blank business-plan forms, which you can use as a basis for your own plan – a good place to find these is your local bank and they are also available from bookshops and stationery suppliers.

The Main Elements of a Business Plan

The main elements of a business plan are given here, although they do not necessarily have to be presented in the following order. *Note: You may find it easier to produce your plan once you have considered the information presented in the rest of the magazine section of this book.*

The main elements to consider are detailed below.

A brief summary of the business plan

This is useful as an overview, especially if the plan needs to be presented to other people who do not need the full details. Although the summary usually appears at the beginning of a business plan, it is usually written *after* consideration of all the elements contained in the plan, so you will probably find it easier to complete this section last.

The name and contact details of the publication and its producers

You should give the name of the magazine here. If the magazine is produced for your own organisation, you should give your own business name; if the publication is produced for another organisation you should name that too.

The purpose of the magazine, its scope and focus

This is the place to include your 'mission statement' – your major objective in starting and running the magazine. You should include some information on its aims and the nature of what you intend it to cover. It is useful to include any relevant historical information, such as the existence of any earlier versions of the magazine (for example, if it was created originally as a newsletter) or any previous moves by others to establish a publication in this particular field.

The format of the magazine

Here you can include some details of the number of pages planned, their size and the style of the magazine.

Any comparable or competing publications

If there are other publications in the field, a comparison of the features and advantages of yours with others can be helpful, together with any possibilities for collaboration. To check if any comparable publications exist you can ask at libraries, where they will have directories of publications or you can contact relevant associations or professional bodies or do internet searches.

Details of people involved in the magazine

You will need to include yourself here, and it is also appropriate to mention others with a major role in the venture. Perhaps you have an editorial team or board and maybe you have suppliers, such as designers or telesales agencies, whose services you use. If your business plan is designed to gain financial support from other people or organisations, the more information you can provide on the skills, expertise and track record of those involved, the better.

Your target readership

You should provide information on whom you expect to buy or read your magazine. You should also give details of any research you have carried out into potential readership/response to the kind of magazine you have in mind, including total market size and your estimated percentage share of the market.

Marketing

You should include information on how you will handle marketing and sales of your publication.

Financial information

This should include details of estimated income (e.g. revenue from advertising, subscriptions, sponsorship and reproduction rights) and expenditure (e.g. printing, postage, design, staff costs/fees) and any assets (both tangible, such as equipment, and 'intangible', such as intellectual property or trademarks). You should also include cash flow forecasts (when money is likely to come in and go out). It is also important to consider how the magazine will be funded until it is solvent, and whether any outside investment will be needed (including possible grants or lottery funding). A timescale for solvency is important – how long you expect it will be before the magazine breaks even or makes a profit. If the magazine is being produced for a not-for-profit organisation, it will be important to know the extent to which the organisation may need to support it financially.

Identification of any risk factors

You should consider any factors that could work against your magazine; for example:

- emergence of major competition
- growing too quickly for the resources available
- possible loss of funding
- competing time demands on the editorial/production team

Details of activities and controls

This should include information on the processes you will use to achieve results, and details of your accounting and other control systems. You don't need to go into too much detail here, but it is important to give a broad outline of the activities, systems and processes you intend to put in place. It is also worth estimating the time that setting up and running the magazine will take – remembering that it is likely to be more than you anticipate at first.

Future development

You should also consider how the magazine might develop in the future, and any new activities that might be associated with it; for example:

- production of other publications on associated topics
- expansion into different geographical regions
- merchandising associated with the subject area
- selling out to a larger publisher

Action planning

Finally, you should include details of major actions to be taken, the timescale for their achievement and any procedures you will establish to monitor and review your success and update your goals and activities.

This might sound like a lot of work and, if you are involved in the production of a very simple magazine, you might feel it is unnecessarily complex. However, the discipline of doing this thinking, even if you do not commit it all to paper in a formal way, will be of benefit and may well highlight issues and activities which might otherwise be overlooked.

Chapter 3
Carrying Out Research

Before starting production, it is useful to carry out some research. This chapter covers the reasons for conducting research and the main methods of researching.

Reasons for Conducting Research

There are three main reasons for doing research:

- to find out what appeals to your potential readers and what they are likely to buy or read

- to find out what any competitors are doing

- to locate resources

Let's consider each of these in turn.

Finding out what appeals to your potential readers and what they are likely to buy or read

If your magazine is for a particular interest group, it may be that you do not have to do any specific research, as you may know their interests, likes and dislikes before you start. For example, if you are starting a village magazine, a magazine for your company, or a magazine for a newly established voluntary organisation, you may well be doing so because you, or others, have already identified a need. Even so, it might be worthwhile carrying out a small amount of research to establish whether there is any alternative to setting up something new.

If you do need to find out about potential readers' needs, you can conduct some market research into this. Large-scale market research is very specialised and can be costly; however, small-scale research may just involve speaking to a few people in the relevant area and asking if they would welcome a new publication and, if so, what they would like to see in it and what they would be prepared to pay for it (if it is to be sold rather than given away). *If you need help with research, you can find a specialist in this area and a few sources of information on this are listed in the resources section at the end of the book (in Appendix 4).*

Finding out what any competitors are doing

If your magazine has competitors, it is useful to have information on them so that your magazine can be produced in a way that will attract readers to you, rather than lose them to other publishers. To this end, it helps to know the kind of material your competitors are producing, what their readership is, what their advertising rates are, and so forth. This is likely to be an easier task when you are dealing with commercial magazines than when you are concerned with magazines for small, non-commercial interest groups, because commercial magazines tend to have published data on their scope, circulation and finances. Even if data is not published, you can still contact the organisation concerned in order to obtain the information, or look to see if it has a website containing any useful information. *Places to find information on other publications are detailed in the resources section of the book (Appendix 4).*

Locating resources

To run your magazine effectively, you will need various resources, including finance, equipment, assistance and items to publish. To track these down you can speak to people in non-competing publications and search published data for information. There are many ways of sourcing goods and services at reduced costs, which is invaluable if you are working to a low budget. *You will find more on this in Chapter 12, 'Equipment and Resources'.*

Ways of Conducting Research

Look at published data

One source of information on commercially published magazines in the UK is BRAD (British Rates and Data). BRAD publishes details of periodicals, together with information on their circulation, scope and advertising costs – updated monthly. You can also check with professional associations, such as the Periodical Publishers' Association and the British Association for Communicators in Business, which should be able to give you information on their members' publications. Your local library should also be a good source of information in this area as they have a variety of directories of publications and publishing companies. *See the resources list for further contact details (Appendix 4).*

Ask within your particular sector
This might be an industry, a profession, a hobby, and so forth. People working within a sector will often be a good source of information and you could start by approaching professional bodies, clubs and associations.

Ask in your geographical area
This could involve checking with a local government authority or regional board. Local newspapers, libraries and information bureaux are useful in this context, as are local directories of various kinds.

Look on the Internet
This will be particularly useful if you are trying to track down electronically published magazines (e-zines), but will also give you useful information on printed publications. Search under key words, such as the topic the magazine covers, in order to gather information.

Attend relevant events
There are many events, such as trade fairs, conferences, exhibitions and seminars, in the publishing field. Attending some of these will help expand your information base and provide you with useful contacts for the future. The Resources List on page 151 gives professional bodies and magazines that can help you locate such events.

Chapter 4
Deciding on Style, Frequency, Format, Design and Circulation

Before making decisions on how your magazine will look and how often it will come out, you should consider how it is going to be produced. If you have only a very small-scale publication, you may find it adequate to produce it yourself, using desktop publishing packages on your own computer or, if the magazine is very small, even a typewriter. You can then do your own design and, when it is completed, you can print out and photocopy the pages and staple or spiral bind them. If, however, you are producing something more substantial, you will need to find suitable people, preferably professionals in the field, to work with you.

You will also need to consider whether your magazine is to be published in print only, in print with a copy put up on a website, or an electronic version too. The greater the range of methods, the more carefully you will need to think about design, and its co-ordination across the range of production.

Many 'do-it-yourself' designers produce material that looks fussy and complicated. To avoid this, go for simplicity and consistency throughout the whole publication – following the guidelines presented in this chapter.

Style

Style covers all those elements which give your publication its own, unique character. A good way of discovering your own style is to generate a list of adjectives and see which ones feel right for you. Here are some examples of style adjectives:

Accessible, friendly, high-powered, professional, current, informative, factual, academic, influential, readable, light, weighty, entertaining, leading, down-to-earth, provocative, campaigning.

Do any of these appeal to you? If so, which; if not, which other words would you select to describe the style you have in mind?

Another way of choosing style is to look at other magazines and see which of them come across in a way that seems appropriate for your own. You can then identify the elements of that style and incorporate similar ones when you produce your own magazine. It is useful to keep a scrapbook or folder with design elements you find appealing, such as the typefaces and sizes, the number and range of columns to a page, the amount of 'white space' around text and pictures, the use of lines and borders, the way in which illustrations are placed and so forth.

Frequency

You will need to decide how often your magazine will appear. Weekly or monthly is common for magazines, but there are other options too, such as quarterly, bi-monthly, and so on. Factors you should take into account in deciding frequency include the time you have available to work on the magazine, the cost of production, the amount of material you need to gather and the frequency of publication of any competing magazines.

It is helpful to have a set publication date (for example, the first day of a month), so that readers, contributors and advertisers know when they will receive their copies or when their material will be seen by readers.

Format

Page size

The size of your pages will affect the look of your magazine, its production cost and its readability. A large size may look impressive, but can be difficult for readers to handle and also difficult for them to scan with their eyes. Your magazine may also cost more to produce if you have a size that is not standard so that pages have to be cut down and offcuts wasted. A small size may seem economical, but may mean that your print size is very small and less readable – it may also look less enticing overall.

In the UK, standard A4 (297 × 210mm) size is easy and economical to produce so, if you are producing a low-budget publication, this may be the best one to select. As well as having standard size paper, it will also fit into standard size envelopes or polythene wrappers. Larger, or non-standard, sizes may require envelopes that are difficult to source or more costly to purchase and possibly more expensive to post. Also, many professionally produced advertisements are prepared in A4 size, or derivatives of this, so, if you wish to attract advertising, it is worth bearing this in mind.

In the US, American quarto (11″ × 8.5″) is a common size; this is a little like the old UK quarto size (10′ × 8″ page).

Having said all this, non-standard sizes can work well – currently a best-selling UK publication is *Glamour* magazine, which is a very small, unusual, size – but easy to hold and fit into handbags.

Number of pages

There are various points to bear in mind when choosing how many pages your magazine should have. You may want a large number in order to fit in a wide range of items, or just to make the magazine look more substantial. Alternatively, you may want a small number of pages so that it is easy to handle and quick to read. It is useful to spend time considering this at an early stage.

You will also need to decide whether to standardize the number of pages per issue, or to vary them according to what you can afford to produce and the amount of material you can generate or gather. If your magazine is funded by advertising, the number of pages in it will generally relate to how much advertising space has been sold: the more advertisements you have the more pages you are likely to be able to afford to produce. If your magazine is non-profit making you are more likely to be able (and need) to decide on a set number of pages per issue.

If you use a commercial printer for your magazine, remember they usually only print in multiples of four pages (and some in multiples of eight or more), so you should take this into account when deciding your overall page numbers. Also, if your magazine is being centre stapled, you will need to have an even number of pages in total (divisible by four) for this to work.

A large number of pages may look more impressive, and can give the impression of good value for money, but will take more work and more resources to produce. And some readers can actually be put off by the apparent effort required to read a very lengthy publication.

You should also remember, if your magazine is to be posted, that the more pages, and the larger page size, you produce, the more it will cost to send, unless you select flimsier paper to save on the weight.

Binding

Magazines tend to be either stitched (stapled) or perfect bound (glued). Both have their advantages. Stitching is usually cheaper and is the only sensible format for publications with only a few pages. For larger numbers of pages perfect binding is better, as it is easier to guillotine than bulky stitched pages, and easier to lay out the pages so that they all have the same sized margins once they have been put together.

Paper quality

There are various factors to consider here. Paper varies in weight, finish, opaqueness, bulk/substance, and so forth, giving different results. For example, gloss paper reflects the light more, and so may be more difficult to read, and very flimsy paper may show print through from one side to the other. When deciding which to choose, you should consider the issues that are important to you: image, feel, economy, durability, readability, and so forth. You might also wish to have the covers of the magazine in a heavier weight paper, or a different finish paper, to differentiate it from the inside pages. One way of deciding on paper, especially if cost is important to you, is to check what your printer uses regularly, or can get easily, as this may well reduce the costs to you. And if your publication is very small, you may find that the printer has 'left-overs' from a bigger job, which can be made available to you at an economical price.

It is impossible to give exact 'rules' for paper weight, as different papers of the same weight have different amounts of 'show through'. On the whole, 80gsm tends to be used for magazine production. You should be able to find an 80gsm paper that is acceptable, but may wish to go to 100gsm if the ones available to you show through text and illustrations too badly. You can also use lighter paper than 80gsm, but this is not recommended as it is very flimsy. It is also worth remembering that if you are using a computer printer to produce your publication, semi-glossy paper may not be suitable. Semi-glossy is all right for bubble jet but can damage laser printers as reflections come from the paper. For your information, this book is printed on 80gsm weight paper.

Design

Paper colour
White is conventional, but it is possible to print on different coloured papers. Coloured paper may well make production more expensive and it may not photocopy well, which could be an issue for you if you need to take copies of particular pages from time to time. You could choose to have white as your main colour, but have a section of the magazine in a coloured paper, but this may make it more expensive to produce. An alternative to coloured paper is to use a coloured ink, which can be applied as a background colour, or tint, to some pages, to give the appearance of different coloured sections.

Even if you decide on white, there are many 'shades' of white, so it is worth looking at what is available before deciding which will be most suitable for you. And if you have other printed items to go out with the magazine – for example, compliment slips or letterheads, then you may want to try to get them all to match up. This can be much harder to achieve than you might think so, if you are starting from scratch, it is probably best to select the magazine paper first and then fit the other, less expensive, items around it.

Print colour
Black on white is most conventional, but there are other options. If you print in only one colour then choosing a dark shade – blue, green, purple, magenta or brown for example – will allow you to use tints of that colour for illustrations or for background colour. If you did this with black, then all your illustrations would be shades of grey, which would not be as appealing on the whole. And if you selected a lighter colour in which to print, it would not show up as well on white paper, making it all more difficult to read and probably a bit insipid to look at.

It is also possible to print with 'reversed-out' lettering, so that the print is lighter than the background, as in white on black. Reversed-out lettering tends to be harder to read, however, so it is generally not a good idea to have large expanses of it.

You can also use 'spot' colour – one or more single colours to brighten up or highlight the text – or full colour, which gives the most flexibility to your illustrations. Each of these processes will add to your printing cost, so you need to make sure your budget is sufficient if you use anything other than single colour printing.

Number of columns

Another design element is the number of columns to a page. Having your type go right across a full page can make it very hard to read – it is easier to scan a narrower column width. Magazines often have two columns a page for articles and three for news. It is possible to have more than three columns per page but, unless you have an extra large format, this may look very 'busy'. A bit of variety in the number of columns is useful to add interest to your magazine, but you should not overdo this if you want it to look good. You should also remember that your column widths may determine the width of your illustrations, unless pictures deliberately take up different widths, with the text being wrapped around them. See illustrations on opposite page.

Print type and size

It is usually best to use one main typeface for most of your text. Different typefaces give different 'characters' to publications so, if you are not knowledgeable about this and you intend producing the magazine yourself, it is worth speaking to a designer about this particular element before you begin. An interesting aspect of typefaces is that many people believe that, if you are scanning documents into your computer, it can be easier for the machine to recognise fonts without serifs (typefaces with 'clean lines', rather than little squiggly bits in the letters). And some people believe that 'clean' fonts are easier for dyslexic readers to cope with. So there are various reasons for selecting one typeface rather than another and it is an area to which it is worth paying attention.

Most of this book has been set in a 'serif' typeface (Garamond) and in 11 point size. This paragraph, however, is set in a 'sans serif' typeface (Arial), although still in 11 point size. Very large or very small typesizes are harder to read than average size ones and 12 point is a commonly used size in publications.

When you use a 10 point size, particularly in a typeface that seems small – this sentence is an example of Times New Roman in 10 point – reading is likely to be more difficult.

Page with two columns of text

Page with three columns of text

Page with two columns of text in different widths

Page with different numbers of text columns in different positions

Picture in one text column

Picture in one text column

Picture across two text columns

Picture across three text columns

Picture embedded in two text columns

Examples of page layouts

And with a larger size (this sentence is Arial in 14 point), you will get much less text to a page, although it can look good for design purposes to use this kind of size in selected areas.

And emboldening print, as in this sentence (still 14 point but bold) makes the text stand out much more – the previous sentence is not bold, although its large size makes it appear so.

Finally, italics also stand out from ordinary type and can be useful to emphasize words or ideas and the space between lines (leading) can be varied to give different effects – the leading in this paragraph has been increased.

Illustrations

Illustrations can brighten up your magazine considerably. Illustrations come in many forms; for example, diagrams, line drawings, photographs, and so forth. There is also a wide range of graphic devices which can be used to add colour and form to your pages.

If you are producing your magazine personally, there are many instantly available graphics you can find in computer packages; however, many of these have been overused, many will not be entirely appropriate for your purposes and, unless you have considerable design talent yourself, it will be hard for you to produce something that is as good as a publication designed and illustrated by a professional. Also, if you use commercially available graphics they will not be unique to your own magazine. So, as a general rule, keep your design simple and uncluttered and avoid overuse of computer 'clip-art'.

Headings and 'signposting'

It is easier for readers to find their way through a magazine that has clear headings, page numbering and other devices to show where you are and what is coming next, than one that lacks these pointers. So do help your readers navigate your pages by assisting them with these elements.

'Modelling' design elements

Do remember the point made in the last chapter about keeping a scrapbook of design elements that appeal to you. Don't be afraid to mimic creative treatments that you like – the more you do this, the more you lean about design, layout and effective graphic presentation, and the easier you will find it to enhance the look and readability of your own magazine.

'Stylebooks'

If anybody other than yourself is involved in producing your magazine, it is useful to have a stylebook for reference. A stylebook is an explanation of the style elements used in the publication, for example, when to use capital letters or italics, what form of spelling to use if alternatives are possible, what size of headings and sub-headings to use, and so forth. The stylebook can be given to anyone involved in editorial or design work, and can then be followed to ensure consistency throughout the publication. *There are various stylebooks within the public domain – either free or available to purchase; two of them are shown below and their websites are listed in Appendix 4.*

STYLE GUIDES

Two of the best guides available are produced by *The Economist* and *The Sunday Times*. They are very different in approach and well worth studying. (See Appendix 4 for contact details.)

The Economist's Style Guide is based on its style book, written by John Grimond, which is given to all their journalists. You can access the *Guide* online or purchase a hard copy of it. Some of the topics covered in the *Guide* are: Abbreviations, Accents, Do's and Don'ts, Figures, Jargon, Punctuation, Spelling, Syntax, Titles. At the time of writing, *The Economist's Style Guide* section of their website also included a short quiz on writing style – this is well worth completing so you can assess your own knowledge and skills.

The Sunday Times' Guide is an online edition of *The Times Style and Usage Guide* and is aimed at helping people with grammar, spelling and names of organisations. To access elements of this guide, you simply click on letters of the alphabet and access a list of words beginning with that particular letter and advice on how to handle them in written material. There are also a few specific areas you can access individually – for example, sports writing.

Circulation

Finally, you will need to decide how many copies of your magazine to print. This will depend on various factors, such as variable costs and income and essential readers (e.g. your members if you are a membership organisation). In essence, the questions to consider are: 'How many do you anticipate will be required?' and then 'How many of these can you afford to produce?'.

Chapter 5
Editorial

If your magazine is very small, you may be able, or want, to produce it entirely on your own. If you are producing a more substantial publication, or have greater financial resources, you will probably need, or be able to use, the services of professional editorial staff.

Editorial staff are responsible for the content of the magazine. There is generally an overall editor, who makes major decisions about content and there may be sub-editors who also work with text and illustrations. Editorial staff also include writers and photographers who work with the content, rather than the production of the publication.

If your magazine is academic, or very specialised, or you wish to give it added credibility, you may choose to have an editorial board. An editorial board is usually composed of people who are prominent in a field relevant to your subject, or who have particular expertise in one or more specialist areas, or who have general experience in publishing. The board is there to support the editorial team, to give opinions on relevant matters and to lend authority to the publication.

If you do not have an editorial board, you may still wish to have some kind of review procedure – for example, sending articles on specialist topics to experts to 'vet'. This gives a second opinion – particularly useful where you may not have a good depth of knowledge yourself on a particular topic – and can also protect the editor from criticism for publishing contentious or inadvertently inaccurate material.

There is a range of activities that come into editorial work and some of the most important are considered below.

Researching
Depending on your subject matter, you may need to undertake research into various aspects, for example:

- whom to invite to contribute
- what has previously been published on a subject
- readership surveys

It is important to brief researchers well, so they can focus on exactly what is needed. There are many sources of information on conducting research, and readership surveys are a specialised form of research with which you would be well advised to seek professional help *(see Appendix 4)*.

Collating Information

If you can find people willing to take on the task voluntarily, or if you can afford to pay them to do so, you can have correspondents or column editors, whose responsibility it is to source and collate material for particular sections of the magazine. Some example of these are:

- diary editors
- book review editors
- news editors

By giving responsibility for these areas to different people, it spreads the editorial load and provides a variety of inputs and ideas.

Commissioning

This is the process of inviting contributions, or inviting specific people to provide defined items for publication. Material may be commissioned from people on a one-off basis, or you may have regular contributors, such as freelance writers or photographers, who produce items on a more frequent basis.

When you commission items, you should specify the following:

- the subject
- if text, the style and length of contribution you require
- if photographs or illustrations, the style and format you require
- the date by which material is required
- any fees or expenses that will be payable
- any travelling that might be required
- any other requirements

This subject is covered in more depth in Chapter 7 'Getting Contributions'.

Writing

It is usual for some material in magazines to be written by the editorial staff themselves and, if your magazine is very small, you may write most – or even all – of the material yourself. For other material, you should be able to get 'free' contributions in return for the publicity that is gained by the contributors. If you are publishing a commercial magazine, if you do not have your own in-house writers, you may commission freelance journalists to write for you. It is usual to have a column headed 'Editorial' in many magazines, and this is usually comments made by the overall editor, at the beginning of each issue, regarding current or topical issues.

Some issues to consider in relation to writing are:

- style of writing
- length of items
- variety of contributors

There is more information on writing skills in Chapter 8.

Interviewing

Part of the editorial process may involve conducting interviews for the magazine. Examples of interview topics are:

- interviews with prominent people in your field
- interviews with book authors
- interviews with creators of new products or services

There is more on interviewing skills in Chapter 8.

Editing

All material which arrives for publication requires editing. Editing means reviewing and revising, where appropriate, various elements, including the following:

- Writing style (e.g. is it formal or chatty; are items written in the first person or the third person?)

- Balance of content (e.g. are differing opinions put forward; is there a mix of opinion and fact?)

- Structure of content (e.g. do items have a beginning, a middle and an end; are logical numbering systems used?)

- Length (e.g. are items too long or too short; do their length fit with other items in the same issue?)

- Clarity (e.g. are items easy to understand and follow; are concepts and issues explained simply in straightforward language?)

To edit effectively you should go through the material, considering such issues and ensuring that the style and format of the magazine as a whole is in keeping with its objectives and reasonably consistent throughout. Be careful, however, not to radically alter people's contributions so that they simply reflect your own opinions or style of writing. Good editing is a skilled task and can make or break a publication.

Checking

It is important to check material, and substantiate facts, before your magazine is printed. Editing does serve this purpose to some extent but, in addition, it is useful to run some specific checks on all material produced. Because some of the checks may relate to sensitive issues, you may need a lawyer to advise you on them. Some checks that can be carried out are for:

- avoidance of libel
- avoidance of publication of confidential material
- avoidance of 'embargoed' material (material that may not be published before a particular date – usually relating to press releases)
- avoidance of copyright infringement
- accurate crediting of sources, authors and references

Proof-reading

Proof-reading follows on from editing and is a 'tidying-up' stage, where such things as grammar and punctuation are checked. Some of these things may already have been checked at the editing stage, but proof-reading gives a final check on them all. This is important, not just for the sake of convention, but because grammar and punctuation are essential aids to ensuring clarity and avoiding ambiguity. Proof-reading also acts as a second-line check on additional elements, as listed below. Proof-reading is a specialist skill and trained proof-readers are worth employing if your magazine is substantial, or if it is vital that its content is correct.

Some things that proof-reading can avoid are:

- duplication of facts
- mis-spellings
- missing words
- layout inconsistencies
- typographical errors

There is more on proof-reading in Chapter 8.

Publicising

Gaining publicity for your magazine is vital, unless you have a very limited circulation to a specific interest group that is well aware of the magazine's existence.

Some points it is worth remembering about publicity are:

- It brings your magazine to people's attention and keeps it there
- It can be used to let people know about specific features or offers
- It can make all the difference between financial viability and insolvency

There is more on publicity in Chapter 15.

Getting Advertising

Advertising is an essential element in a commercial publication and, even in a non-commercial one, it can help to add variety and interest for your readers.

Some things to consider about advertising are:

- how to balance advertising and editorial content
- what to charge for advertising
- what policy to adopt regarding advertising that may conflict with the principles of your magazine

There is more on advertising in Chapter 9.

Briefing Production Staff

Finally, it is the job of the editorial staff to brief the production team so that it produces what is required.

Some aspects of briefing are:

- giving clear objectives
- giving adequate timescales
- communicating as necessary until the job is complete

Briefings can be carried out by having meetings, sending emails, or in other ways, but it is important that a record is kept of what is said so there is no subsequent disagreement or confusion.

Chapter 6
Selecting and Organising
Topics and Items

Although you will have defined the field of interest your magazine will cover, you still need to decide the range of topics and the actual items to include and how to present them.

The range of topics your magazine covers will depend on the purpose for which you set it up. For example, if you produce a community magazine, the topics you cover are likely to be local and related to issues which are 'live' for your readers, whereas if you are producing a 'general interest' magazine, your topics may be wider ranging, including broader issues and items which may appeal to particular segments of your readership.

It is worth thinking fairly widely about your topics, as there may well be many that are not obvious to you initially. If there are other magazines, or books, in your field, they can be good sources of ideas for material.

Types of Item

There is a wide range of types of contribution you can include; these will relate to the kind of magazine you produce, the audience you reach and the issues you cover. Some types of contribution are considered below.

Articles

These are likely to be substantial contributions and what you include should be based on factors such as:

- the likely level of interest for the topic
- the number of pages you wish to allocate to the subject
- the overall balance of items within the magazine

The actual length of articles will depend on the style and size of your magazine. The 'average' person reads about 200–250 words a minute, and readers of most 'professional' magazines are likely to read at around 300–350 words a minute. This assumes that the text is set at around 10–12 point size; very small or very large typesizes become much harder, and slower, to read. And, of course, the larger the typesize the more space the article takes up in the magazine.

On the basis of 10–12 point typesize, an article of up to 1,500 words will be fairly quick to read, an article of over 2,000 words will be fairly substantial and likely to cover ground in more depth and an article of over 3,000 words is likely to be weightier and more suitable for journals, or one-off features, rather than regular magazine entries.

When considering articles for publication, you may print single articles on a topic, group several articles together or run a series of linked articles in consecutive issues.

Although topics for articles will vary, depending on your particular field of interest, some that are common to many publications are current issues, historical information, practical guidance and technical information.

When printing articles and some other items, it is useful to have a brief biography, photograph and contact details of each author (with their agreement) for reference at the end of the piece. It is also useful to have a short synopsis of each long article, either at the start of the article, in the contents listing or on a synopsis page, so that readers can scan through to see what is worth them reading in more depth.

Regular columns

These are features which run in each issue of the magazine. Regular columns tend to be shorter than articles and may be grouped together, or interspersed throughout the pages. Regular columns may be written by a single author, or you may have different authors contributing to a particular column in different issues. Regular columns may cover a wide range of matters, including advice and problem solving, regional issues and humour.

News

Depending on your subject area, there may be news items you can print; for example, recent developments in the field, information on prominent people, new products or services and relevant legislation. News items tend to give variety and, as they are often short, can help break up pages with longer items on them. You may also like to have a 'media' column, where you print summaries of news items carried elsewhere in the media; for example, in newspapers or on the radio or TV.

Correspondence

Most magazines have a correspondence column and this can be useful as a 'filler' item, as well as being an interesting area on its own merit. You may print single letters, have a whole page of correspondence or select short items from letters to give a variety of opinion. You may also have a series of letters on a particular topic if you can generate enough interest from readers to keep the topic going. Some specific reasons for including a correspondence section are:

- **Feedback**. When people write in, it gives you an idea of their opinions. Often feedback will let you know what people think of the magazine, or of a particular contribution or section, or of ideas you have put forward for reader comment. Feedback is vital if you are to keep your magazine relevant and attractive to its readership.

- **Debate**. Letters can produce an ongoing debate on topics or issues. This can give a sense of continuity and can also produce a wider range of opinions than may have been contained in an original contribution.

- **Interaction**. Having a correspondence column allows interaction between you and your readers, and between readers themselves. This tends to make the readership more of a 'community' and is particularly important where a magazine is offered to members of an organisation, or to those with strong affiliations to particular issues.

- **Variety**. Letters add variety to a magazine. Many readers look forward to reading them and to assessing the extent to which they reflect, or contradict, their own opinions.

- **Simplicity**. Letters are relatively easy to write, and some people find it more appealing to write a letter than compose an article. This can widen your contribution net considerably.

Editing letters

Although some letters may be usable in their original form, there can be reasons for editing them, for example:

- to make them a more appropriate length
- to take out sections that are not relevant
- to remove parts that are not factually correct
- to remove parts that are potentially libellous

On the whole, it is not regarded as good practice to re-write letters, although you may need to do a little light editing in order to correct spelling, grammar and punctuation. In some circumstances, however, even if a letter has been poorly written, you may choose to leave the wording exactly as it is, even if it is grammatically incorrect, perhaps indicating that the wording is as the author submitted it.

Do not be tempted to make up letters from fictitious readers, as this could backfire if you are asked for further information on them, or for people to be put in touch with them. It is, however, perfectly acceptable to invite a letter from a particular individual if you think it likely that that person will have an interesting point to make, where you want a balancing opinion to another point of view or where you want to encourage new people to contribute.

When including letters, you should check, before printing any contact details for correspondents, that they are happy for these to be included. It is usually acceptable to put a name and a geographic region, but do not put addresses, telephone numbers, emails, and so forth, unless the person has given permission, or asked, for these to be published.

Interviews

Interviews are often popular items and can come in many forms. You can include interviews with people who are prominent in your field, who have made a major discovery or originated a novel product or service, who are visiting from overseas or who are of interest for some other reason. Interviews may be conducted face to face, recorded over the telephone (with the agreement of the interviewee) or carried out by email or fax. *There is information on interview techniques in Chapter 8.*

Book reviews

If there are books produced on your subject area, they can be included in a review section. You can also include reviews of audio or videotapes, CDs, CD Roms, DVDs and software packages. You might also mention other relevant magazines in your field in this section, as long as you do not feel it would encourage your readers to leave you and subscribe to the other publications instead. If you would like to get books for review, you should contact the review department of relevant publishers, give them details of your magazine and ask to be put on their mailing list; when you find a book that you think would be relevant to your readers ask for one to be sent as a review copy. You should then send it to an appropriate person to review and, once the review has been published, send a copy of it to the publisher of the book. Before you send the copy for review, remember to take down details of the title, author, publisher, ISBN number, date of publication, number of pages, page size and price, as well as scanning in the cover (or getting the publisher to send you an image of the cover) to accompany the review. Publishers will also let you have photos and biographical details of authors and, if you wish, will often arrange for an interview with a book author as well.

Research reports

This is another useful area, especially if your magazine has an academic, or practical skills, bias. If you have the resources and contacts, you may want to commission, or produce, research reports yourself, otherwise you will need to find out what has been produced in your field. Establishing good contacts with colleges, research institutes, commercial companies with research departments, and so forth, can help you source this kind of material.

Advertisements

Advertisements are a source of revenue and also help give a variety of content and style in your magazine. You need to think about how much advertising you wish to carry, as too much can make the magazine look more like a catalogue and put readers off. It is also important that it is clear what is an advertisement and what is editorial material. There is a 'mid-way' term here, which is sometimes referred to as 'advertorial'; this means that an advertisement is combined in some way with editorial material, usually by an advertisement being accompanied by input from the editorial team itself – such items should really be marked as 'Advertising Features' to avoid misunderstanding or giving the impression that the magazine endorses the products or services featured in the advertisement. Chapter 9 deals with advertising.

Readers' offers

A readers' offer is something that is offered to readers of a magazine at a discount or with some other accompanying benefit. Some examples of readers' offers are:

- discounts on books
- low rate insurance
- free cinema tickets
- reduced rate hotel accommodation
- special prices on garden plants and furniture

Readers' offers can be of benefit all round: to the reader because they bring a clear benefit, to the publisher because they attract and retain readers and to the offering organisation as they publicise their products or services.

One particular readers' offer that many magazines feature is for reduced rate subscriptions to the magazine itself – this may be in the form of a reduction on the cover price, or an additional number of issues if a year or more's subscription is taken out. Another kind of offer is where a product, or a sample of a product, (for example, moisturising cream, chocolate, a diary, a small paperback book) is attached to the magazine (usually packaged with it in a polythene envelope or glued to it on an inside page). Although some of these offers tend to be found in expensive, commercially produced, magazines, the idea can be copied by others on a lower budget. *See Appendix 2 for examples of Readers' Offers.*

Events listings

This is a section which gives details of meetings, courses, conferences, exhibitions, social activities, visits, and so forth. You may run this as a simple list, or diary, or you may also have larger spaces available for advertisements of events. You can run events listings as a free service or you can charge for listings. *The chapter on advertising, Chapter 9, gives more information on this.*

Networking information

You may have a section that allows readers to contact each other in some way. For example, you may print details of regional networking groups, include requests for information and advice, promote email discussion groups, have a 'personal' column and so forth. You may also choose to run events at which your readers can meet; for example, social events, courses, workshops or exhibitions, although this is likely to be highly demanding of resources and very different from your publishing activities themselves. Be careful not to be taken off track by such activities, which can result in resources being diverted from your core activities too early.

'Snippets' and 'fillers'

These are any small items that are of interest to your readers; for example, quotations, news of forthcoming radio or TV programmes, humorous items, previews of forthcoming articles, local news items, 'personal' columns, items 'overheard' by readers, crosswords, competitions, horo-scopes, and so forth. These can be used to fill in space and lend variety to the pages. You can group snippets or you can intersperse them throughout the pages as appropriate, and they are very useful for filling awkward areas left over after installing major articles. It is worth collecting and filing such items so you always have a readily available supply to hand.

Examples of snippets and fillers

New European Internet Domain name
Via the European Commission, in March, European citizens, organisations and businesses were enabled to have '.eu' web sites and email addresses. Users will have the option of continuing to use their existing domains and also using a single EU domain name as well.

Poor usability of sites
In a survey of Christmas shopping carried out by ICONMEDIALAB, participants were given money to spend on gift items purchased online and were allowed to keep everything they bought during the test. Despite this incentive, a staggering 35% of participants could not purchase what they wanted because of the poor usability of the sites.

Some units of measurement
Time between slipping on a peel and smacking the payment
= 1 bananosecond
Basic unit of laryngitis = 1 hoarsepower
Amount you can dig in five hours = 1 back ache
1000 aches = a megahurtz
1 grandparental visit = 1 Nanover
200 Mockingbirds = 2 kilomockingbirds

Entrepreneurs

One in three people in England are currently running or considering starting, their own business, according to The Household Survey, a report conducted for the Small Business Service. Just under 6,000 people were surveyed, of which 18% were entrepreneurs, 12% were currently thinking about going into business and 70% were not interested in striking out on their own. A copy of the full survey and other reports in the SBS Research series are available at
www.sbs.gov.uk/research (website correct at time of writing)

Have you ever considered...?

If, as a study recently reported on by BBC Radio 5 shows, the human eye is capable of discerning between 8 million different colours, why does your, and my, computer have a basic capability of recognising 16 million different colours? Perhaps a computer expert could tell us. Also why, if the average adult human ear is capable of hearing a frequency range of between 20 and 15,000Hz (most speech being in the range 100-4,000Hz), are home hi-fi equipment CD players, etc., capable of outputting a frequency range from about 4Hz to well in excess of 20,000Hz? For the benefit of dogs maybe?

These items appeared in *Effecting Consulting* magazine.

Pictures

Most pictures in your magazine are likely to accompany other items, such as articles; however, you may wish to include photographs or other illustrations as items in their own right – for example, running a photographic competition or including a really interesting picture relevant to your subject matter. If you include photographs, they will need to be good quality and, if you receive them by email, at least 300dpi (dots per inch) for them to reproduce well. You should also remember that pictures take up quite a bit of space in transmission and unless you are on broadband they can be costly in connection time and hold up other incoming matter while they are downloaded.

There are many commercial suppliers of items such as crosswords, games and jokes, and there are also agencies that can supply you with news and other items. You can also search on the Internet for interesting bits and pieces and there is a range of websites that is likely to be really fruitful in this context. As sites change frequently, I have not listed many in this book, but you should be able to track them down fairly easily using standard search engines *(see Appendix 2)*.

Production information

This is information about the magazine itself. In this section, you can list the editorial and production team, give contact details, include guidance for contributors, print your advertising rates and guidance, and so forth. There is some information which there is a requirement to include, such as details of printers and ISSN numbers *(see Appendix 2)*. It is also useful to include some disclaimers, such as the editorial team not necessarily agreeing with the opinions of individual contributors and the publisher not being responsible for any consequences of articles being published. It is wise to take legal advice before putting such wording in your magazine.

Contents listing

If your magazine has more than just a few pages, it is helpful to include a contents listing. This can give topics and page numbers and may also include a very brief summary of what each major item contains. You may also want to include a note of some items, or features, contained in your next issue and this is a good aid to planning as well as being informative to readers and advertisers.

Presentation and Organisation of Material

Once you have made decisions regarding content, you can think about how items are to be presented.

There are no hard and fast rules about presentation, but it should fit well with your purpose, your style and your content. Some factors to take into account are:

- having a clear and interesting layout so that items can be found and read easily and willingly

- having a logical grouping of items so that any that relate to each other can be found together

- having a balance of items, so that the whole publication comes across as a coherent entity, rather than a collection of disparate sections

- having a consistent placing for regular items or features so that readers know where to find them

There is more on this topic in Chapter 4, 'Deciding on style, frequency, format and design'.

Selection and Rejection of Items for Publication

The editor's decision on what to include is usually final. If this is your first venture into publishing, you may wonder on what basis you can, or should, include or reject items; you may also wonder how to communicate rejection to hopeful contributors.

Inclusion should depend on the extent to which material meets your publishing objectives, which should have been stated in your business plan. You should also consider the overall balance of any particular issue. In addition to these two points, some criteria for selection or rejection are as follows:

- Is the item of interest to most readers, or to only a small minority of them?
- Is the item well written and structured, or is it rambling and hard to follow?
- Is the item an appropriate length, or is it too long or too short?
- Is the item balanced and factually correct or is it biased and misleading?
- Is the item novel, or does it duplicate material already published?
- Is the item informative or is it simply promotional?
- Is the item a useful follow-up to earlier contributions or is it irrelevant?
- Is the item relevant to a particular 'theme' or is it unrelated?
- Is the item generally acceptable or is it likely to give offence to some readers?
- Is the item original or is it plagiarising (using another person's material under your own name)?

If you have a list of criteria for acceptance, by definition you also have criteria for rejection; i.e. the contribution fails to meet one or more of your criteria. So, when rejecting an item, you can say why it has been rejected. Of course, some of the reasons are easier to communicate than others but, if you can accompany the rejection with some constructive advice, it makes it easier to accept. For example, you could say: 'If you submit this at half the length it would be more acceptable, because we don't have space for such long items', or 'We ran a very similar item to this last month, so it will be a while before we can cover this particular topic again'.

Chapter 7
Getting Contributions

A successful magazine relies upon the quality of its content. It is not vital to have a large number of pages, but it is important to have a regular supply of material that people will be interested in reading.

People producing new magazines often think it will be difficult to get contributions and wonder how to source them. However, it is actually quite easy to generate a regular flow of items as long as you prepare the ground well and then continue to manage the process. In order to do this it helps to know your field well, so that you can develop a wide network of people interested in contributing. If you are starting a publication in a field that is new to you, research into that field is an important first step in order to inform yourself about it and feel comfortable working within it.

There are four key factors involved in getting contributions and if you pay attention to these you will be able to attract a good range of items and a varied group of contributors. These factors are set out below.

Planning for the Future
You should think ahead several issues, so that you are constantly generating material for the future. If you do this, you are more likely to have an ongoing collection of items you can use. You don't have to put everything you collect into a particular issue and you don't have to give contributors a guarantee that their items will appear in a particular issue. 'Stockpiling' material for at least two or three issues ahead can give you a sense of security about being able to fill future issues and will be a help if, for any reason, you are unable to spend time collecting material for a particular issue of your magazine.

'Theming'
You can simply gather together an almost random collection of items for each issue, or you can 'theme' your issues, so that you have a particular

subject for part, or all, of each issue. Theming will allow you to seek contributions on that topic and make the issue more of a coherent entity.

It may be easier for you to fill space if you theme, rather than having continually to seek individual contributions on different topics. It may also be that, once you have one or two items on a particular theme, other contributors will be keener to add their own material to that issue.

Gathering Material

There are two main ways in which you can find material: using existing material and commissioning new material.

Accessing existing sources of material

There are many sources of material that you can tap into. Some of these will be free, while others may require payment. If you are on a low budget you will probably need to find free sources of information, but it is worth knowing about the others in case your financial situation changes. Some of the information sources you can access are considered below.

Websites

Whatever field you operate in, it is likely that there will be others working in it too. If you use the standard Internet search engines, you will be able to put in key words that will help you find out what others are doing. You must be careful not to breach existing copyrights *(see Chapter 20 for more on this topic),* but there is an enormous amount of free material available on websites generally. If in doubt as to whether items can be used in your publication, all you need to do is ask the owner of the site for permission. Some of the things you can find on websites are articles, useful hints, news items, information on new products, and so forth.

Press releases

You can ask to be included on the distribution list for press releases in your particular field of interest and this will produce all kinds of useful material that just pops through your letterbox (or comes to you via email) without you having constantly to ask for items.

To get on press release lists, all you need to do is contact the press office of any organisation you think is relevant and request that your publication is put on their press release list. You may need to qualify the request as they may well produce press releases on a range of topics and you may only be interested in particular areas.

Some organisations you can contact for press releases are local councils, manufacturing companies, trade bodies, professional organisations, sports organisations and charities.

The UK government issues press releases daily on a large scale and you can access these free through their website *(see Appendix 2)*. If you wish to be sent government press releases by mail, fax or email there is likely to be a charge for this, but if you are willing to search yourself on a regular basis you will be able to view them and select those of interest to your publication.

Internet discussion groups

There are numerous discussion groups that have regular postings and some of these also archive their postings and make it possible for the archives to be searched by key words. This is another useful source of material – either within the postings themselves or as a contact point for you to post requests for members of the group to send you items. You can find out about such groups in various ways, including approaching the information departments of professional or trade bodies.

Other publications

You may find it is worth reprinting material from elsewhere rather than using only original material. You will need to get permission to reprint items and, although this will often be given freely, there may be times when you have to pay a fee for this right.

Although it is good to use original material, there can be many reasons for using pre-published items. For example, the items may originally have been published in another country and your readers might not have access to them in their original form; they may have been published a long time ago and currently be out of print; or you may be unable to find anyone to write on a particular topic but have come across something suitable in another publication.

Commissioning new material

New material will usually be more appropriate for your publication as it is more likely to be current and readers will not have seen it before. There are lots of ways of obtaining new material and some of these are outlined below.

Asking people

If you think about your publication whenever you meet people, and then check to see if there is a topic about which they could write (or which they could illustrate with drawings, photographs, cartoons, etc.), you will find that you have an unlimited number of possible contributors. People are generally pleased, or even flattered, to be asked, and will generally co-operate if you ask them to contribute. Most people have at least one subject area in which they have a good deal of expertise; you just have to find out what it is and then find a link with your own publication. For example, if someone you know has just travelled to a particular region, bought a new computer, learned a language, read an interesting book or taken on a new job, there may be an article in the making.

Some people may believe they can't write well, or aren't sufficiently experienced, or informed, to do so. If you boost their confidence, they may well be motivated to contribute and then just need to use the appropriate skills in order to do so. You can help them with this by editing what they write, or by interviewing them (in person, on the phone or by email) if they really can't put pen to paper. Remember that most people seem happier to write about a specified topic than to think one up themselves, so if you brief your potential contributors well you have done half the work for them.

Also, remember to use networking skills when you are seeking contributions. If you ask people to let you know about other people they know, or to think of your publication when they are talking to people they meet, you will find you rapidly have an extensive network of potentially useful contacts. Used wisely, this can generate an enormous amount of material for you. And if you give talks, again remember to mention your magazine – this will also increase the number of people who know about it.

Notice what's around

Keeping alert to opportunities will really help your contributions flow. For example, scanning newspapers, listening to the radio, watching television and reading Internet discussion group postings will all acquaint you with people who are well informed on particular subjects. Often you will find that ideas for items come from seemingly irrelevant sources – it may just be a tiny snippet on a programme that sparks off a train of thought in you and leads to a really exciting piece of writing.

Once you have found the 'lead', all you need to do is contact the relevant publisher or producer, or respond to the chat group, asking if the person would be willing to contribute. You can also write to book authors, asking if you can use an extract from their book or if they will write a piece especially for you. Keep your eyes and ears open and you will find endless possibilities for contributions.

Liaising With, and Rewarding, Contributors

Maintaining good relationships with contributors is vital to success – they are the lifeblood of your publication and should be valued and cherished. So once you have found people to contribute, communicate with them effectively. Some of the things that they will appreciate are: knowing what your deadlines and publication criteria are (*see Chapter 10 for more on this*), knowing if and when their items will appear, being kept informed of any delays or changes to your scheduling, seeing proofs of their items if they are substantial or if you have made major editorial changes to them, being credited appropriately in the publication and being sent a free copy of the issue in which their contribution appears.

People have different reasons for contributing to magazines, for example:

■ They like writing.
■ They want to see their name in print.
■ They want to make a contribution to a cause.
■ They want the publicity.
■ They need to generate additional income.

All except the last of these are easy to handle, but the final one is more difficult if you are operating on a low budget. Although some publications pay contributors as a matter of course, others only pay in certain circumstances and some do not pay at all.

Some ways in which you can reward contributors are as follows:

■ **By paying them**. With a small publication, people are unlikely to expect payment and, even if they do expect it, they will usually understand the reasons why it may not be possible.

■ **By giving them publicity**. Adding their names, photographs and contact details to contributions or columns will give the authors some promotional space. Spare copies of the publication will also give them promotional tools they can use themselves.

■ **By giving them free copies of the publication**. Giving contributors a number of copies of the issue in which their item appears, or giving them a free subscription for a period of time, can be another useful reward. Make sure, however, if you choose this option, that the cost of providing these copies does not exceed what it would have cost if you had paid for the contribution in the first place.

Contracts

Finally, it can be useful and, in some circumstances, essential, to have a written contract for the provision and acceptance of contributions. In principle, if you publish guidelines for contributors, these are likely to be upheld as the basis of an agreement between you and them, but there are some specific points that could usefully be put into a contract, including, for example, the contributor recompensing you for any claims made against you as a result of material contained in their contributions. While it is unlikely that issues of this kind will affect very small publications, it can be useful to take legal advice in this area, or at least read something that will inform you better on these topics. If you join one of the professional associations listed in Appendix 4, such as the National Union of Journalists, they will be able to give you further information on this subject and tell you how to insure yourself against possible litigation in this area. *You will find more about this also in Appendix 4.*

Chapter 8
Writing, Interviewing and Proof-reading Skills

There may be occasions when you need to write contributions for the magazine yourself. If you have a wide range of contributors this will be less important, but it is an important skill to have if needed. There is probably no substitute for a good course on these topics, but here are a few basic points to give you a grounding.

Writing Skills

Some of the key points to remember are considered below.

Relevance

Make sure that what you write is relevant to the topic. You should keep to the point and help your readers to understand why what you are writing is relevant. Avoid going off at tangents and make sure that any examples or anecdotes are clearly related to the main direction of your writing.

Clarity

Make your writing clear so that it can easily be understood. There are measures of clarity, such as the FOG index; these indicate that the shorter your sentences and the fewer syllables your words have, the easier your text is to read and understand. You can check this for yourself by looking at a variety of magazines, selecting a 'typical' article from each one, and then taking three separate sentences from each article. Count the number of words the three sentences contain in total and multiply that number by the number of words the three sentences have that contain three syllables or more. This will give you a numerical figure. Compare the final figure for each of the publications you have selected – the lower the figure, the easier it should be to make sense of the writing.

Brevity

Make your writing reasonably short and succinct, unless you are producing something that needs particularly lengthy, or in-depth, construction. The more technical, or academic, your magazine is, the more scope you will probably have for longer writing.

Structure

Make sure that the items you write have a beginning, a middle and an end – this may sound obvious but people do not always follow this practice. The beginning should introduce the topic, the middle should explore it and the end should review, sum up or provide conclusions. You should also show the connection between points as they occur, by referring back to the overall purpose of the piece and by using linking phrases and sentences to show the direction you are taking.

Style

Make sure you adapt your writing style to the kind of magazine you are producing. Refer back to the chapter *(Chapter 4)* on selecting a format and check that the words you use to describe your magazine are echoed in the writing style you select. As a brief reminder, some styles are:

- chatty
- serious
- motivating
- down to earth
- campaigning

Interviewing Skills

Some key points here are considered below.

Arranging the interview

You will need to agree with the interviewee that they are willing to be interviewed. You will also need to find a mutually convenient time for the interview to take place.

Selecting the environment

You will need to find a suitable place, without interruptions, if you are meeting face to face, or somewhere quiet if you are conducting the interview on the telephone. You can also conduct interviews by email but, if you do this, you should make sure that you are correctly 'interpreting' what the interviewee says – without accompanying voice patterns and tonality, or 'body language' you may read the responses in an inappropriate way.

Planning the interview

It is helpful to plan the main points you would like to cover. This will help you structure what you ask and will enable you to give the interviewee an idea of the topics you wish to cover. Some possible topics are:

- historical information
- biographical information
- technical information
- opinions and attitudes
- new developments
- controversial issues
- issues of specific relevance to your readership

Deciding what to ask

You may plan to ask some specific questions, but it is also helpful to formulate questions as you go along, depending on the responses you are getting from the interviewee. Remember:

- to be aware of any sensitive issues

- to avoid questions which 'lead' the interviewee; i.e. make the person more likely to give a particular response

- to avoid questions that are discriminatory

- to consider a range of question types (for example 'closed' questions to elicit facts – e.g. 'Where did you study?'; 'How long were you there?', 'open' questions to elicit opinions and exploration – e.g. 'How did you handle that situation?'; 'What were your reactions to the proposals?')

- to include questions that are particularly likely to interest readers

- to make your questions interesting and varied

- to allow the interviewee to come across as a person

Recording the discussion

You will need to have an appropriate way of recording your interviews. You may choose to make notes, but if you do not do shorthand in some form it may be hard to get all the important points down. You may tape-record the interview (as long as you have the interviewee's permission to do so), but this then means going through the entire interview again in order to extract the elements you want. You may have an assistant who can make notes, or operate a recording device, while you conduct the discussion, but you cannot be sure that another person will take down the key points as you perceive them. Whichever method you choose will have advantages and disadvantages, so you can only select the one that you think will work best in the circumstances. If you do choose to use a mechanical recording device, do make sure it is working properly and that you have an adequate supply of batteries, tapes or other items as required.

Writing up the interview

It is good to write up the interview as soon as possible after conducting it, so that any points made will be clear in your memory. Even if you do a draft and edit it later, this is better than leaving it until you are no longer sure what was said or what point you wished to remember.

Checking with the interviewee

It is useful to send the interviewee a copy of the final interview text. You should agree in advance whether the interviewee has any right of veto or amendment regarding your text, otherwise the only purposes of sending are to check for accuracy and give the interviewee sight of it before publication.

Proof-reading Skills

Proof-reading is important if your magazine is to look professional; it allows the following things to be checked:

- Spelling
- Grammar
- Punctuation
- Layout

When proof-reading, make sure you look carefully at each word – 'Seeing' and 'hearing' each word is helpful and some people proof-read sentences backwards, which they say helps them to see individual words more clearly!

Look for mis-spelled words, inappropriate punctuation, words and sentences inappropriately split ('orphans' and 'widows' if odd letters or words are split off from others), consistency of fonts, sizes and styles of headings and consistency of writing style. If you are 'marking up' copy for someone else to alter, you need to learn the correct signs to use and you can find these in books on the subject (some of the more common ones are shown below).

Proof-reading can be assisted by spell/grammar checking software; however, computers do not always pick up every error or check for ambiguity. Also, much of this software is American and therefore does not always allow for other forms of the English language. And sometimes computers can be counter-productive as they may automatically substitute a quite inappropriate word for one you have written, and this may not subsequently be noticed before publishing.

As well as checking straightforward things such as spelling and punctuation, if proof-reading is done by someone other than the person who has written the material, it also gives another perspective on what has been written. This is useful, as it can help you confirm that the writing is clear, understandable and meaningful. It is also useful to have a second opinion on any potentially contentious contributions, or parts of contributions and, if you have taken out insurance *(see Chapter 20)* against libel, your insurance company may insist that material is read by a legally qualified person in order to avoid possible litigation.

Proof-reading is a specialist activity and you would be well advised to leave it to a person who does it professionally. This may be costly, but should give you a high-quality result. If you ask a non-professional to proof-read for you, you need to be sure they are capable of doing the job.

It is also important to brief your proof-reader appropriately. Some proof-readers will try to change the language used, as well as correcting typing or grammatical mistakes. This can result in words being used that may change the meaning, the style or the construction of the writing. If this is done, you may need to check with the original author that the corrections are acceptable; it depends on what agreement you have with contributors as to how much editing is permissible. And, if much editing is done, you may want to send proofs to contributors, both as a courtesy and as a safeguard to you, before going to press.

Finally, consider when proof-reading will be done. You may wish to get items proof-read singly, or you may want to send the whole publication to be proof-read at the same time. Each has its advantages. It is administratively easier to send it all at once, but it may take longer because your proof-reader has a larger volume of material to go through at one time.

There is a professional body for proof-readers (The Society of Editors and Proofreaders) and that is the place to find a qualified person if you need one: (*see Appendix 4 for their contact details*). The Society also has a Style Guide on their website, covering topics such as proof correction marks.

Instruction	Textual mark	Margin mark
Change to capitals	The government	=
Change capitals to lower case	The Prime (MINISTER)	≠
Start new paragraph	are ready. The new manager is	⌐
Close space between characters/words	The book case	◠
Transpose characters	letter form	∏
Insert new matter	The/gold rings	five /
Delete	See the appendix.	♂
Insert a full point	I have finished/	⊙
Insert apostrophe	The childs toys	⸲

Examples of proof correction marks.

Chapter 9
Sales, Advertising and Sponsorship

Unless you are producing a magazine that is completely subsidised by the organisation for which it is produced, you will need to have a plan for raising income.

There are different ways in which you can generate funds, for example through paid advertising, sponsorship, donations, subscriptions, sales of single issues, etc. This chapter will concentrate on three main sources of income:

- sales
- advertising
- sponsorship

Sales

If you are not functioning as a not-for-profit business, you will probably need to raise income through sales of your magazine and possibly associated products and services, including your mailing list. And even if you are not-for-profit and your magazine goes free to staff or members, you may wish to sell additional copies to others outside your organisation.

Ways of raising finance through sales

There are various ways of selling magazines and some of them are as follows: You can include details of the cost inside each issue so that those who would like to receive it can send you the appropriate sum. You can advertise it in various ways, for example in relevant local, national or trade papers. You can ask existing purchasers or subscribers to publicise it to other people they know. You can ask local shops if they are willing to stock it – preferably on a 'sale or return' basis or for a commission on sales. You can promote it on your website, or via email networks and you can ask others to mention it in their own emailed newsletters.

Although you can sell single issues of your magazine, it is more effective – and administratively simpler – to sell annual subscriptions and you may wish to offer a free trial issue, deferred payment, a discount for an annual subscription, or something like fifteen copies for the cost of twelve if people take out a subscription with you.

You can also offer your mailing list for rent (either on a one-off basis, or for a particular period of time). If you do sell your mailing list, you must make sure that names are only included of people who have indicated that they are happy to receive mailings from other people or organisations, and you should also decide whether you will provide the names as sets of labels or on a database. Although there is no easy way of ensuring that purchasers of mailing lists do not use the list for more than the occasions they have paid for, a good principle is to include 'sleepers' in the list; sleepers are names and addresses that are put there simply as a check on when the list is used – if the list is used on unauthorised occasions the sleepers will receive a mailing and you will then know that another mailing has been sent out by the purchaser (or by someone who has used the list without payment at all).

Payment handling processes

If you are going to sell copies of your magazine, you will need to consider what processes to use – cash sales at retail outlets, cheque payments, credit card payments (face-to-face, on the phone, on receipt of a form or on-line) or standing orders/direct debits are common methods.

If you wish to have debit/credit card or standing order/direct debit payments, these require arrangements with banks or merchant services and can involve you in some up-front costs, as well as the loss of a small percentage on each transaction with some of the services. You may also have to wait several weeks to receive your money if dealing with some credit card services.

Setting a price for your magazine

You will need to consider what to charge for your magazine and this can reflect its apparent value to readers, market rates for similar publications, and the extent to which you are willing to be flexible in order to attract income. It is possible to have one price as the 'cover price' – i.e. what is printed on the magazine itself, another price for annual subscriptions (or longer periods) and another price for 'discounted' subscriptions (e.g.

introductory offers, special rates for particular reader groups, and so forth). It is useful to look at rates charged by other publications when doing your initial research, although you should be aware that the cover price is not always what readers pay for the publication.

Advertising

As well as generating income, advertisements serve a wide range of other purposes – let's just consider these before moving on to ways of using advertising to raise funds:

- **They add variety**. Advertisements break up the editorial copy. They do this in various ways; for example, they may be different in *style* from the text of the magazine and they may be different in *content* if they cover areas not specifically included in editorial items.

- **They provide information**. Advertisements give readers useful details regarding products, services, and so forth. Although generally designed to produce benefits for the people and organisations placing them, they often contain useful information which can have value both to potential purchasers and to others interested in issues and trends relating to a particular topic.

- **They act as promotion**. You may include advertisements for the organisation that produces, or sponsors, your magazine; this will help gain attention and carry their messages to a wider audience.

What is an advertisement?

You may think your magazine does not need advertising, or that it would somehow make it seem less 'serious'. Even if this is the case, there are many items carried by magazines that have an element of advertising, although they may not be regarded as pure advertising, or may not be charged for. Here are some items that could be considered as advertising:

- for sale and wanted columns
- job-seeking enquiries
- personal contact columns
- requests for information
- details of events
- book reviews
- readers' offers
- product advertisements

■ service advertisement

All of these provide benefits to people seeking information, advice, assistance, products or services.

How advertising can be carried
There are different ways in which you can handle advertising material. For example:

■ You can print it in the magazine itself.
■ You can publish it on a website.
■ You can include it as printed inserts ('loose' sheets you include with the magazine).
■ You can email it to readers who have indicated they wish to receive such material.
■ You can put it on products that are associated with the magazine (for example publicity material, free gifts and so forth).

Generating an income from advertising
Advertisements are an excellent way of increasing your income; however, there are various factors to take into account when you take advertising. These are considered below.

Setting advertising rates
To set your advertising rates you should work out your costs, decide how much profit you need to make and fix the rates accordingly – although still in line with general 'market' rates for your kind of publication. Some of the factors that can affect your advertising rates are the following:

■ **Your circulation**. The larger this is the higher rates you will be able to charge advertisers.

■ **Whether you print in black and white only, 'spot' (single additional) colours or full colour**. These have different costs.

■ **How long you have been in existence**. A new magazine may find it harder to attract advertisers and you may need to offer lower rates as an incentive to advertise.

■ **Whether or not you receive advertisements in a final form – as an email attachment, on a disk, as film or finished artwork**. If advertisements come in as text only and you have to get them into usable form, this could involve a lot of design time and – unless you do it yourself – paying a graphic designer. So your advertising rates need to relate to 'finished' copy, with additional charges being levied if you have to provide design services to advertisers.

Charging for advertising

Assuming you do not offer advertising as a free service to your readers, you will need to decide what to charge for space in your magazine. There are various options:

- commercial rates
- discounted rates
- 'semi-free' advertising
- free advertising
- 'contra' deals

Let's take each of these in turn:

- **Commercial rates**. This means charging advertisers rates which:
  - cover your costs and provide adequate income/profit for the time, effort and resources you devote to them. To do this you will need to work out what your costs are – both direct (for example, purchases) and indirect (your own time and effort) and then assess how much you wish to make in addition.
  - are comparable with market rates for similar publications. To do this you will need to find out what others are charging. If you ask for a media pack (usually a copy of a magazine, its advertising rates and some information about the size and nature of its circulation) or a rate card (the magazine's advertising rates) you will obtain this information – although you may find that some magazines do not wish to send this to their competitors. You can also look in BRAD *(British Rates and Data – see Appendix 2)* which gives advertising rates for publications that are listed in it.

- **Discounted rates**. It can be helpful to allow some space at reduced rates. You may do this as a service to people and organisations on low budgets, or you may do it as a deliberate tactic to increase your advertising revenue – either to increase its volume or to give the discounts as an incentive for future, or bulk, advertising space purchase.

Discounted rates can be helpful in circumstances such as the following:
–   You want to offer an inducement to begin advertising.
–   You want to offer an inducement to continue advertising.
–   You want to attract advertising that might otherwise have been placed elsewhere.
–   You want to fill space that might otherwise not generate an income or would simply be empty.
–   You want to reward the loyalty of regular advertisers.
–   You want to offer reduced rates (or even free advertisements) to people or organisations prepared to promote your magazine in return (often referred to as 'contra' deals – *see the section after next)*.

If you do discount the cost of advertising, you can do it in various ways, for example:
–   reducing the price of a single advertisement
–   reducing the price of a series of advertisements if they are booked (and preferably paid for) at the same time
–   reducing the price of one or more subsequent advertisements if the first one is booked at full price
–   reducing the price of a repeat advertisement where there are no changes to the material supplied
–   reducing the price of advertisements for a selected group of advertisers (for example, members of an association)
–   allowing an extended period before invoicing, or extending the period allowed for payment, so the advertiser gains cash-flow benefits
–   discounting the price of advertising if payment is received in advance or within a specified period.

Many advertisers will expect reduced-rate advertisements and if you have advertising placed through an advertising agency they will expect discounts so that they can make money through selling space to their clients at a higher price than they buy it from you.

■ **'Semi-free' advertising**. This can be another useful inducement to advertisers. Some ways of using this process are to:
–   offer a free second advertisement – in either the same, or a subsequent issue, if the first one is paid for in full
–   offer 'advertorial' – whereby a paid advertisement is accompanied by free editorial text on the features or benefits of the item advertised

–   offer a free listing or small advertisement to people who subscribe to the magazine

■ **'Contra' details**. This is a common feature of magazine production and is an arrangement whereby you and another person or organisation enter into an agreement to mutually promote each other's products or services, or reciprocate in other ways. To use contra arrangements, you need to have something of benefit that you can offer. Here are some things you may have that others could value:
–   free (or reduced cost) advertising space – in the body of the magazine, as loose inserts or on your website
–   website links – where you provide a link from your website to the other organisation's site – the link may just be their website address or may be accompanied by information about their products or services
–   mailings to your database (or provision of a single set of subscriber address labels) – as long as the people on your database have agreed to have additional mailings from third parties. *(See also section on sale of mailing lists earlier in this chapter.)*
–   use of resources (for example, sharing administrative help, office space, design facilities and so forth)
–   exhibiting (or distributing) material at each other's events
–   readers' offers – where a supplier gives you products or services to offer your readers and you benefit by having an inducement to readers to buy your magazine

Volume of advertising

It is important to consider the volume of advertising your magazine will carry. Too much and it may look like a catalogue, too little and it may fail to cover its costs. Once you get more than half of the pages containing advertising, it usually looks less like a magazine and more like a pure advertising publication.

Placing advertisements

The placing of advertisements has an impact on both the appearance of the publication and the ways in which readers respond to the advertisements themselves. Here are a few points about placement:

- Advertisements placed on right-hand pages often stand our more than if they are placed on left-hand pages, but you also need to remember that right-hand pages are usually easier for people to read, so your articles will be more attractive if they are placed there. It is, therefore, a choice you will need to make as to whether the advertisements or the editorial text should be given prominence.

- Half-page advertisements tend to be more noticeable if they are placed with editorial text than if they are placed in pairs on one page competing with each other for attention.

- Placing advertisements with text on the same topic is likely to be useful to both readers and advertisers.

'Marking' of advertisements

Advertisements can sometimes look like editorial material, especially if they have a lot of text in them. In such cases, it is a good idea to mark them with the words 'Advertisement' or 'Advertising Feature', so that readers do not think they are editorial comment.

Attracting advertising

You may choose to find advertisers yourself, but it can make sense to use specialists to help you in this task. If you choose the latter course of action, there are many people and organisations working in this field. Two options are:

- telemarketing/telesales, where you have people contacting potential advertisers by telephone in order to sell advertising space for you

- advertising/PR agencies, which will handle a total campaign for you, selling advertising as part of the overall approach

Both of these options are likely to cost a good deal, unless you can find an agency willing to act for you on commission only (taking part of the advertising income they generate) or at a low fee for each organisation they contact on your behalf, or at a low retainer plus a higher rate of commission on sales. Selling advertising space is a specialist activity – and selling magazine advertising space is even more specialised – and just because an organisation does telesales does not mean they will be good at selling advertising space for you. So check their field of expertise and their fee structure before undertaking this kind of relationship.

Sponsorship

Another way of generating income for your publication is through sponsorship. Although sponsorship is often considered as applying only to high-profile activities – for example, sports, the arts, academic studies, and so forth, it can be used effectively by small magazines. Some aspects of sponsorship that you might like to consider are discussed below.

Who might sponsor your magazine?

There are several options here, including the following:

- **Local firms**. These might be interested in subsidising the production of one issue of a local publication in return for information on themselves being distributed in, or with, the magazine. A sub-set of this kind of sponsorship is when you do a feature on, for example, a local event or activity, and businesses in the area take small advertisements around the text supporting that feature in the magazine.

- **Organisations related to the topic of a feature in the magazine**. For example, if you run a feature on small business development, you may get support from suppliers of IT systems, finance agencies, telephone companies, and so forth.

- **Firms operating in the field on which the magazine is focussed**. As an example, if your magazine is to do with healthy living, you might get support from manufacturers of exercise equipment, organic food or stress management music.

Which elements might be sponsored?

Sponsors will have differing views on what they wish to sponsor; some options are:

- the whole publication
- selected issues of the magazine
- selected features, such as a supplement or a feature series
- particular aspects of production, such as postage costs, administrative help, photographic services or purchase of computer equipment
- associated events, such as an exhibition, a press lunch or a workshop

What forms may sponsorship take?

Sponsorship may come in the form of financial support, but this is not the only way sponsorship can take place; here are some possibilities:

- money – provision of funding, either for general or for specific purposes
- assistance – provision or secondment of people to assist with work
- equipment or materials – provision of major or minor items to help the business run
- Publicity – provision of promotional items or activities

Attracting sponsorship?

There are many publications dedicated to this topic and there are also professional associations involved with the subject of attracting sponsorship. Sponsorship generation is a professional field and you may well benefit from the services of someone who specialises in this. It could be expensive, however, although you might find someone prepared to work for you on a commission basis. *You can find references to sponsorship-related bodies in the resource list of this book (Appendix 4).*

Grants

As an alternative to sponsorship, you might consider trying to get a grant for your magazine. This is more likely to happen if you run on a not-for-profit basis. You can find out about grants – both national and international (e.g. European funding) through local business centres or information services.

Credit Control

When you are dealing with invoicing or other forms of financial transaction, there may be occasions (probably rare, but possible nonetheless) when creditors do not hand over the money. In such cases you will need a procedure for dealing with the relevant people or organisations – you can do this in person, or engage a professional in debt recovery to help you; there are organisations called 'Factors' which will 'purchase' your debts at a discount and then recover the money themselves. Otherwise, you will simply have to write off the occasional bad debt as a business expense.

Chapter 10
Guidance to Contributors and Advertisers

People who write for you, or who take advertising in your magazine, need to know what you require from them. It is helpful to have two sets of information – one for contributors and one for advertisers. You can include some of this information in the magazine itself, you can include it in printed documents that can be sent to people, you can have it as an attachment to be sent with emails and you can include it on your website. *Some sample guidance documents are given in Appendix 3.*

Guidance for Contributors
Some of the information that you should consider providing for contributors is detailed below.

What kind of contributions you welcome
This should outline whether you take articles, letters, book reviews, news items, events listings, photographs or other illustrations, and so forth.

Your copy dates
Copy dates are the dates by which material should be sent to you for inclusion in the magazine. You may want to have the same copy dates for editorial material and for advertisements, or you may accept advertisements later than other copy. You will need to decide whether you can allow any leeway on these dates, because copy often arrives late and you should have a policy for dealing with this. Advertisements that are late can cause problems but, as they generate income, you may wish to deal with late arrivals more leniently than late editorial material.

The length contributions should be
The average person reads around 200–350 words a minute, given a type size of 10–12 points. Assuming an average A4 size magazine page contains about 900 words, it will take around three minutes to read. The longer each item

is, the fewer items you can get into the magazine, so you will need to decide if you want a small number of long items, a large number of small items or a mixture of the two – and then invite contributions accordingly. For magazines, a combination of short and longer items works well, as it gives variety and is not too demanding in terms of the time it takes to read. When inviting contributions, you should specify how many words they should contain, not the number of pages they should take up. You can be flexible with type sizes (either increasing or decreasing them) and with 'leading' (the spaces between lines of type) if you need to make items fit particular spaces.

What additional material is required
This is particularly important for longer contributions, when you may wish to ask for photographs of or biographical/promotional information on the contributor, additional illustrations, references, and so forth.

How to credit sources
Many contributors refer to material which has originated with other people and you need to give them an indication of how to credit such sources. For example, articles may contain references to other published works, to the ideas of third parties or to personal correspondence. In such instances, the principles of 'intellectual property', 'copyright' and 'trademarking' are relevant. Very simply, these principles mean that you cannot use another person's ideas, or reprint text, without permission – there are exceptions for some purposes, such as book reviews, but this is a serious issue that needs proper consideration. If you wish to be safe, you should read further on this topic, or take legal advice. *See the resources list for more information on this (Appendix 4).*

Who retains copyright
Copyright is the term used for 'ownership' of published material. Normally the person who creates such material owns the copyright. However, it is possible for copyright to be transferred to others – for example, if an employee writes something on behalf of an employing organisation it may be that the copyright belongs to the employer. You need to specify whether you wish to take ownership of material printed in your magazine, whether copyright will remain with the authors or whether you will both have rights over material produced. For example, you may wish to retain the right to reproduce items again – perhaps in compilations of extracts from the magazine – or the right to publish items in different forms – for example on

your website. Again, this is a complex issue on which you should obtain proper professional advice. You will also need to ensure that contributors to your magazine confirm that there are no other, pre-existing, copyrights on material they send to you or that, if there are, they have permission to include such material in their submissions to you.

What format you require

This will depend on your magazine but, as a guide, editorial items should be word processed or typed, double-spaced with wide margins and in a sufficiently large type size to be easily readable. With the advent of word processing it is much easier to edit on arrival so, if material does come in another format, it should be relatively simple to adjust the type size, margins and other formatting features. You should also specify the form in which you wish to receive contributions. For example, you may wish to receive items by email, fax, post, on disk or CD Rom. You may wish to have items sent in Word format, as PDFs or in other formats. You may wish to have 'camera-ready' artwork or film, and so forth. Being clear about this will save time and avoid unnecessary work.

Where copy should be sent

You may wish material to come to the editorial office or to be sent direct to a designer or printer, depending on the items and timescales involved. If material is to be sent to anyone other than you, you should make sure the recipients are told to expect it and the senders are told to label it accordingly and give their contact details in case of problems or delays.

Guidance for Advertisers

Some information to consider providing in this context is set out below.

Specifications

Advertisers will usually need specific technical information to be provided to them – usually referred to as 'mechanical data'. It is helpful to supply this information on a printed form, covering items such as the dimensions of the page, the area on each page – or part of a page – that can be used for type or illustration, availability of colour printing, resolution (quality) of photographs or illustrations required, special positions available for advertisements, and so forth. If you are able to originate (design and lay out) advertisements on behalf of advertisers, you should say so, and give any costs involved, and you should also indicate your terms and conditions for advertising. *An example of advertising terms and conditions is given in Appendix 6.*

Format

As with editorial material, you will also need to tell advertisers whether to send you material by email, on disk or CD Rom, by fax or post. You will need to know whether they are sending you text together with instructions for layout, finished art work, a PDF file or film. Any material coming to you, or to your designer or printer, should be adequately labelled and give contact details for the sender. There are occasions when queries arise, material gets mislaid or damage occurs to packaging or contents, and it is important to be able to identify and respond to items that are sent.

Payment

You will need to tell advertisers what your rates are, assuming you charge for including advertisements. You can print your rates on the advertising form – or 'rate card' – and this should be updated as appropriate. It is usual to charge higher rates for special placements (for example, a right-hand page, a cover or next to a specified item of editorial), and lower rates for repeat advertisements. You may want to ask for pre-payment with bookings, or you may be happy to invoice or to use pro-forma bookings. You will also need a system for recording and controlling advertising bookings, arrivals, handling and payments.

General Advice to Contributors and Advertisers

Restrictions on acceptance

You should reserve the right to refuse items that are unsuitable, do not comply with statutory requirements, arrive late, are in an incorrect format, are not accompanied by a specified form, are not pre-paid, and so forth. It is also useful to say that you reserve the right to refuse items without giving a reason, although you should be prepared to justify your action should you be challenged on this through a court, tribunal, trading standards authority or similar body. You should also indicate that you do not accept responsibility for loss or damage arising from error or inaccuracy in printing or other forms of publication, or for omission of items, or for the consequences of such errors or omissions. Again, the wording you use should be checked for clarity and legality.

How items will be reproduced

You should indicate whether items will simply appear in a printed magazine, will be re-printed elsewhere, will be distributed electronically or put on a website, and so forth. Again, this is a technically complex area and you are advised to get professional advice before giving contributors guidance of this sort.

The date for copy to arrive

You need to allow plenty of time between arrival of copy and completion of editing. For a small publication, a month should be adequate, but this period may lengthen considerably for more substantial publications. You may decide to allow late arrivals, but bear in mind that you will be unable to complete final editing and layout until you have all the material in your hands. You may decide to accept advertising copy later than editorial copy and this is often easier as, if advertisements come through an agency, they are likely to be in a form that requires no work on your part apart from passing on to a designer or printer to incorporate in the magazine as a whole.

Chapter 11
Production

In conjunction with editorial, a magazine needs production processes and staff. Again, if your magazine is very small you may be able to do all the production work yourself, but if it is more substantial you will need assistance. Production staff are involved in the process of the magazine being produced and, although under editorial direction, production people are the experts in how to create the finished product.

Production includes design and print and, if your magazine is printed, you can choose whether to have a separate designer and printer or whether to get a printer to do the design for you as well. There can be benefits either way. With separate people you can make sure you select the best you can find in both fields; with a combined team you can hope to gain more collaboration and consistency in the production job.

There are various ways of finding people to produce your magazine. You can ask people you know, as they may well have good contacts in this field. You can look at directories and websites dealing with print and design. You can look at other magazines you think are well produced and then contact their production teams to see whether they use external contractors themselves or contract out their own services to others. You can also go to the relevant professional associations or trade bodies to source suppliers – and you can find details of these in trade publications or local libraries and information bureaux.

We will now consider some of the tasks involved on the production side.

Design
The overall design and layout of a magazine is intrinsically bound up with its purpose and style. As well as text, magazines contain a wide range of graphic elements, including photographs, drawings, diagrams and other illustrations, together with typefaces/sizes and the use of 'white space'.

The design function involves creating the physical appearance of the magazine, and it is part of the design function to ensure that all the elements mentioned above enhance and support the text so that the magazine overall is a coherent and attractive product.

The term used for the creation of design elements is origination and some aspects of design are as follows:

- ensuring design elements contribute to the overall purpose of the magazine
- aligning text and illustrative material
- ensuring that design elements contribute to readability and comprehension
- selecting paper type and size

If the magazine is part of a range of documents, it is likely to be important that they all have the same style. 'Corporate identity' is the term used in business for consistency of appearance and image.

Printing

Printing involves producing multiple copies of the original text and illustrations. At the most basic level this may simply mean photocopying, or printing copies on a computer printer. Normally, however, printing is done by specialist services.

It is possible to get printing done at 'print shops', which are usually high street services that undertake a limited range of print jobs rapidly and at low cost. For anything other than the most basic magazine, however, it is best to go to a specialist printer, who can also advise on design and on paper selection if you do not have the services of a designer of your own. If you have a magazine with a large circulation, it may be most economical for you to print overseas as this can result in very substantial cost savings.

Some aspects of printing to consider are the following:

- **How many copies you need.** This will determine the process you use (remember that, with commercial printers, very small print runs tend to cost more, proportionately, than longer runs, but also consider where you will store additional copies if you have many more produced than you need immediately).

- **Whether you need single, 'spot' or full colour printing.** Some printers are more economical for one or other of these.

- **What quality you need.** Again, some processes will provide better results than others.

- **Where you can get the best value for money.**

Finishing

Finishing is usually done by the printer and is the process of making up the printed sheets into the final publication; i.e. cutting to size, collating, binding, and so forth. Sometimes, however, printers will send the printed sheets to another specialist house for finishing, especially if the printer is a small one and uses a 'trade' finisher, with equipment that the printer cannot afford themselves.

Packing

Packing is simply putting the magazines (and any accompanying inserts) into boxes to deliver to the publisher of the magazine, or into envelopes or plastic sealed wallets to deliver straight to readers/subscribers. Again, it may be more economical to use professional packing services, depending on the quantity of copies to be produced and distributed.

Distribution

Distribution is the process of sending copies to readers, contributors, advertisers and others. This may also be done by the printer, finisher or packer, or it can be done by the publisher. It is worth comparing the relative costs of each method before making a decision on which course to take.

Costs of distribution can vary enormously – both in relation to handling and to postage costs. There are ways of sending bulk supplies to readers and some publications use overseas mailing houses which can save enormously on postage costs. *Chapter 13 deals with distribution.*

Selecting production services

If you are just starting up and do not have in-house staff, you will need to find suitable and affordable services. Some factors to take into account are considered below.

Cost

Cost is likely to be a major factor for most magazines. Because of the cost implications, it is worth getting several quotes for the work you need before making decisions on suppliers. Design and print costs can vary considerably, depending on a variety of factors, such as the reputation the people have, how much they need or want the work and whether they are geared up for small or large-scale production.

Relationships

Another factor to consider is how well you relate to the people providing your services. You may have the 'best' production team in the world but, if you don't get on well with them there may be difficulties. If you are going to have a long-term relationship with suppliers you should do your best to select suppliers who seem to have a similar approach, values and ways of working to yourself so that you can work with them on both a personal and a professional basis.

Locality

Having suppliers who are close by is not essential, but it can be helpful as it may save money on transport of materials and is easier if you need to visit to check things as they are being produced. So much business is now being done electronically that it can be as easy to have people working for you on the other side of the world as in the next street; however, there are still some advantages to proximity.

Quality of service

This includes elements such as reliability, meeting deadlines, following guidelines, and so forth. You can develop your own quality measures and should bear in mind that the quality of service to you ultimately affects the quality of your own services to your readers, subscribers and contributors. Also associated with quality is the technology that is used, and you should check that your suppliers have the equipment and the experience to work in the way you want. For example, can they accept material directly from a computer by email or do they need a disk, film or PDF file sent to them? Do they work with Macs or PCs or both? Is your computer's operating system and software compatible with theirs? Finally, check that they can work to your deadlines, especially if you know they are likely to be tight ones.

Approach

It is particularly important, when using design services, that you check that they can work in the style and manner you require. A good designer will be able to work in a variety of styles, but will still have their own preferred ways of doing things. So, before making a decision, try to find someone who has done similar work before and can show you examples of material.

Working with your team

If things are to work well, there are some points to remember and discuss with your suppliers, and these are dealt with below.

Clarify responsibilities

You should agree who will be responsible for what, so people know what they, and others, will be doing. You should avoid overlaps of responsibility and gaps in responsibility – in this way everyone should have a defined role and every task should have a manager or 'owner'.

Have agreed schedules

You should agree a production timetable which is attainable on both sides. You can start with the present time and work forwards, or you can start with the desired publication date and work backwards. Either way, you should end up with a properly timed schedule, showing each stage of the production process, its manager, its activities and its timescale. *(There is more on this in Chapter 14 'Project management'.)*

Have agreed procedures

Agreed procedures are as important as agreed schedules. It is particularly helpful to ensure that material is supplied in the required format – e.g. on disk, electronically, as film, or as high resolution PDFs. Pages should be produced singly or in 'printers' pairs'. You will also need to ensure that 'impositions' are provided – either hand-drawn sketches or computer files showing what is meant to be on each page. It is also important that proofs are supplied and returned in good time. Having a set procedure for each element of the production helps keep to schedule and avoids disagreements regarding who is responsible for what, and when particular tasks should be done.

Communicate effectively

When you have others working with you, whether on a paid or a voluntary basis, you need good communication systems for briefing them and for interacting with them, and it is particularly important to have good communication channels and procedures if there are several parties to interactions. In this way, you can ensure common understanding and a team approach to activities. In particular, if you have separate designers and printers, you should establish whether they deal directly with each other or via you or another member of your staff. This is important in order to avoid confusion and the possibility of tasks not being done because each person thought someone else was doing it – in such a case you could well end up as 'piggy in the middle'. In order to communicate well the following things are useful:

- meeting on a regular basis with your associates, suppliers, agents, volunteers, editorial board, etc.

- letting people know what you expect from them and telling them in good time of any changes to requirements; being clear and explicit and keeping in touch without pestering

- having agreed schedules/areas of responsibility, copied to everyone who needs to know, and providing sufficient scope for people to respond flexibly to changes in circumstances

- finding out what motivates the people with whom you deal and bearing this in mind when interacting with them

- letting people know how you think they are doing and giving others opportunities to give you feedback on how your relationship with them is going: both positive and negative feedback can be helpful as long as they are directed towards a result

- keeping records of discussions and action points

Chapter 12
Equipment and Resources

Whatever sort of magazine you are producing, there will be various kinds of resource you need. This chapter will cover three different sizes of magazine:

- small-scale self-produced
- larger-scale self-produced
- commercially produced

Small-scale, Self-produced Magazines

At this level, you can probably get by with a word processor (or even a typewriter if you are not yet in the electronic age), a telephone and an effective filing system. You can get your magazine photocopied locally and you can distribute copies by hand, giving them out at meetings, popping them through letterboxes or posting them in the normal way.

If you are working to a very limited budget, it is worth exploring the many sources of discounted, or second-hand, items of equipment. You can find out about these in a variety of ways, such as:

- scanning local newspapers or websites or checking out electronic auction sites such as Ebay and Loot (*see Resources List in Appendix 4*)

- reading 'for sale' columns in the trade press

- looking for auctions or disposals of bankrupt stock (there are magazines devoted to such sales, often read by people wishing to find cheap supplies of stock to trade in and you can find out the names of such publications through your local library)

Larger-scale, Self-produced Magazines

If you produce your magazine on a larger scale, but it is still produced entirely, or mainly, by yourself, then you will need more in the way of resources.

A computer

This will be your main production tool. It will be useful if your computer has the following capabilities:

■ **Word processing.** Nowadays, this is the only practical means of production for anything other than the most basic document. Word processing will enable you to type, store, manipulate and retrieve your text. *Word* from Microsoft is the commonest word processing package and *Word Perfect* from Corel is another option.

■ **Page layout and design**. There are various software packages available that allow you to produce your text in the form of a laid-out page. The simplest thing is to use a basic word processing package, such as Word; if you want something that will do a more sophisticated job you could use *PageMaker* from Adobe, *Microsoft Publisher* or – more economical – *PagePlus* from Serif. Many professional designers use *QuarkXpress* and, although it is expensive, it can be useful to have access to this software, especially if you have to make last minute editorial changes.

■ **E-mail.** This will allow you to communicate with relevant people, such as contributors, readers, subscribers, suppliers, and so forth. The most commonly used e-mail package is *Outlook Express* from Microsoft, which comes as standard with any PC that has *Microsoft Windows*. A similar product is *Outlook* which comes with *Microsoft Office* and has many additional functions useful to a prospective magazine publisher. *Excel* can be used as a simple substitute, and it is also worth checking out the contacts and scheduling functionality of *Outlook* (not *Outlook Express*). It is worth getting a fixed-price package for your Internet access, rather than a pay-as-you-go one, as research may take longer than you think. Many packages allow you several email addresses, so you can direct incoming and outgoing messages to particular people or computer folders such as 'editor@...'; 'advertising@...'subscriptions@...' and you can register a domain name inexpensively, which will give you an address, without necessarily having to set up a corresponding website. Finally, broadband/ISDN access is also useful if you need to send or receive lots of images, such as photographs, that can otherwise take up a lot of computer/telephone connection time. *(See also the section on telephone lines later in this chapter.)*

■ **Database access.** If you plan on keeping any records, a database will be important – as it is for the management of any major project. Some of the things you may wish to record are contributors' contact details, the contents of each issue of the magazine, time scales for production, actions to be progressed, and so forth. *Access* from Microsoft is a commonly used database package which will cope with this kind of material.

■ **Accounts packages.** You may want to have the option of running your own accounts on computer, particularly if your magazine is a subscription-based one and you need to keep a database of people subscribing, magazines sent out, payments due and made, and so forth. Accounts packages suitable for small magazines include *QuickBooks* from Intuit and *Sage*. When installing such packages, it is worth looking ahead to anticipate any major developments in your publication as some packages are quite limited in their applications and you may find in the future that they cannot do all the things you would wish for.

■ **Internet access.** It is useful to have Internet access so you can search for material and contacts relevant to your magazine. There are many search engines (*see comments in Appendix 7*) that will help you locate material and it is worth experimenting to find the best one for your purpose. Remember with the use of both the Internet and emails that you will need effective virus protection software on your computer.

A printer

A printer is essential if you are to produce material which is copyable, or if you wish to make good multiple copies. There are various kinds of printer, including inkjet and laser. If you are going to print your magazine in colour, a colour printer will also be essential.

A scanner

A scanner is helpful, both to scan in non-text items, such as photographs or diagrams, and also to scan in text by OCR (Optical Character Reading/Recognition software), if you need to work with material that is unavailable in electronic form. OCR software is often supplied with a scanner. Without a scanner, a good deal of re-typing may be required. Some colour printers are also available with interchangeable scanning heads, but a stand-alone scanner will give you more flexibility.

A fax machine

Many people still send messages by fax, and this can be a useful way of receiving contributions from people without email. You may have a 'stand-alone' fax machine, or this facility can be run from your computer. Using plain paper in a fax machine is more expensive, but it does result in pages that can be retained for a long time, unlike the flimsy, shiny heat-sensitive paper on rolls, on which the print fades fairly rapidly.

Telephone lines

You will need a phone for everyday contact, and it is also useful to have a separate line for your email/Internet/faxes, so you don't put your regular phone line out of action when you are working on the other equipment. It is worth searching around for cost-effective telephone services, as there are many discounted ones on the market. Some services give you free Internet access; they use a normal modem and are an economical way of extending your communication links.

If you require faster data transfer, however, you will probably need services such as broadband and ISDN (if these are available in your area). These services are more expensive than standard telephone lines, but do really speed up your activities; for example, when sending files to your printing company (although an alternative is to send material to your printer on disk). Such services require some extra software and/or hardware on your computer before you can use them. With broadband and ISDN you can use the Internet and the telephone at the same time, saving you the cost of two separate telephone lines.

A photocopier

You can choose between buying or renting a copier. You will need to consider service arrangements, as faults can be costly to rectify without a regular maintenance and service contract. Copiers vary considerably in the facilities they offer, from simple copying to collating, stapling and so on. Copiers tend to take up quite a bit of space, and can be noisy, and the older ones tend to emit fumes, so you need to place them carefully and ensure there is no health hazard if you are buying an old second-hand one. Most fax machines will also work as copiers, but will mostly not copy anything thicker than one sheet of paper at a time.

You can also use your computer scanner to copy items and this also has the advantage of providing you with an electronic copy for future reference; however, this is likely to be too time consuming for a large volume of copying.

You may wish to photocopy your entire magazine, rather than print copies from your computer. Whether or not you do this will depend on factors such as:

■ whether you already have a printer or photocopier and, if not, what it would cost to purchase or lease one (including the cost of any service contracts), compared to the cost of using a commercial photocopying service

■ how many copies you will need, and how often

■ how quickly you need the copies produced

■ whether you need copies collated by machine or are prepared to do this process by hand

A franking machine

It may be useful for you to have one of these if you need to post substantial numbers of your magazine; it is simpler than putting stamps on each item. If you need to send out very large quantities however, say 1,000 or more at a time, then you will probably be able to arrange for your local post office to accept pre-payment and frank them for you, and possibly even collect them as well, which will be a great saving in time and effort. There are also substantial cost savings to be made through bulk mailings and you can find out about these through your local postal and courier services, such as Parcel Force in the UK. If you want to pay for large numbers of stamps, or franking, at a post office, you can get a post office card, which gives authority to them to accept a cheque from you up to a high limit – otherwise you may find that a personal cheque guarantee card is insufficient for the volume you need to deal with.

Working space and storage

You will need to think about the organisation of the area in which you will be producing your magazine. You will probably need more surface space than you think in order to handle items, look at page layouts and so forth, so it is a good idea to put as much material as you can on shelves and storage units, freeing work surfaces for everyday use. It is also important to have good seating, lighting, heating and ventilation for a space that is in constant use.

Assistance

Finally, you will need to consider the possibility of enlisting voluntary or paid help with your magazine. If it is for a small interest group, you will probably be able to find people to help on a voluntary basis, as long as you explain to them clearly what is involved, brief them fully and help them become enthusiastic about the project. Paid help will give you many further issues to consider, such as possible tax and insurance commitments (and you will, in any case, have to consider insurance if you have other people working at your premises, or on your behalf – including the use of their cars on your behalf, even if you are not paying them directly). If you wish to explore the possibility of assistance, it is worth speaking to your local employment service as there may be grants available to you to assist with this (there may also be grants available for capital expenditure).

Commercially-Produced Magazines

If your budget will allow you to have your magazine designed and printed commercially, you will need to do less of the production work yourself. However, you will still need most of the facilities mentioned in the previous section as you will need to communicate with people, keep records and accounts, and so forth.

It is worth keeping up with developments in technology, so you can take advantage of those which will keep your publication in the forefront of progress. You may also need to consider employment issues and, if you don't already have this experience, think about getting some training yourself in managing staff.

Final points

Remember that some of your major resources are your own time, health and relationships and build consideration of these into your planning.

Chapter 13
Distribution

An important aspect of magazine production is how to dispatch copies to your readers. If your circulation is very small and very local you may be able to hand copies to people personally, put them through letter-boxes or give them out at meetings. Otherwise you will have to find different methods of distribution. Some options are considered below.

Methods of Distribution

Post out in bulk

You can do this yourself or you can take on additional helpers to handle the dispatch. For small numbers you can just put stamps on and post them; for larger numbers you can frank envelopes, and for even larger quantities your post office will be able to frank them for you – and may also collect from you, although they will usually want pre-payment or for you to establish a regular account with them. In addition to standard postal services, there are many less expensive options to consider. Bulk mailings can save money, carrier services are useful for large quantities to single addresses and there are some services that are, strangely, cheaper if you can get your copies to countries overseas to distribute from there. It is well worth exploring options before making a final choice.

Ask your printer to dispatch it

If you have printers producing your magazine, they may well be able to put copies in envelopes, or 'polybags', together with any inserts you may have to accompany them – advertisements or your own additional information. They will probably be able to purchase supplies of envelopes or polybags in bulk at better rates than you can. If you take this option, you will have to decide whether to let them have your mailing list to print recipients' names and addresses from, or supply them with pre-printed labels each time an issue is sent out.

Ask a specialist mailing house to dispatch it

Although it involves another organisation handling the magazine, it may be more economical for a specialist mailing house to handle the distribution for you. Your printer can send it to them direct and may even have their own links with a distribution service you can use.

Send bulk supplies to other bodies to distribute for you

Another useful way of circulating your magazine is to send copies to other organisations with access to readers; for example, overseas organisations working in the same field, large companies or networking groups. In this way you can save on the mailing costs you would incur if you sent each copy directly to individual readers.

Use electronic means

Whether or not your magazine is produced initially as an e-zine, you may want to circulate some electronic copies of it. You can do this as direct email attachments to named recipients, or you can email or send a disk or CD Rom to another organisation to print out at their location. If you choose the latter of these, you will need to consider having a licence agreement with this organisation in relation to their reproducing the magazine. And, if it is reproduced elsewhere, you will also need to consider how, if at all, you ensure quality standards when the control of reproduction is out of your hands.

Free Copies

It is worth remembering that you will probably need to give away some copies of your magazine free and to allow for this in your costings and print runs. Some reasons for giving free copies are the following:

- **Press/media copies.** You can send copies to selected publications or other media for information and to alert them to possible news stories relating to the magazine.

- **Library copies.** You can send copies to selected libraries for reference.

- **Review copies.** You can send copies to relevant people/organisations for review. It is useful to send the Library Association copies for inclusion in its reviews of new publications.

- **Exhibition copies.** You can give copies to visitors if you have a stand at exhibitions, although you might want to make some charge, say a 50% reduction in the cover price, if you do this in large quantities.

■ **Talks/workshops copies.** You might want to give copies to people who attend talks you do or workshops run by yourself, or third parties, on subjects relevant to the field covered by your magazine.

■ **Contributors' copies.** You will need copies to send to people who have contributed. Usually a single copy will be sufficient, but some people will want more and you can decide how many you can afford to give away. You will also need to decide what size of contribution merits a free copy.

■ **Advertisers' copies.** You will need copies to send to anyone placing a substantial advertisement with you – these are called 'Voucher Copies'. If someone places only an events listing or a small classified advertisement, it is unlikely to be economical for you to give them a free copy in return.

Remember to distribute copies in good time and to keep to your stated publication dates unless there is an exceptional reason for not doing so. And if you have spare copies left over, it is useful to use them for publicity purposes by giving them away free, rather than having them take up space and become out of date.

Chapter 14
Project Management

This chapter pulls together the various tasks involved in magazine production and gives you some suggestions for systems and procedures which will help you manage your activities. The chapter is split into two parts – project management *processes* and project management *tools*.

Project Management Processes

The following topics, which have already been covered in the book, are the major areas of project management activity on magazines:

- managing finances (Chapter 9)
- publicising your magazine (Chapter 15)
- managing contributions (Chapter 10)
- managing advertisements (Chapter 10)
- handling production activities (Chapter 11)
- communicating with people (Chapter 11)

Let's take each of these in turn and consider the processes you can establish to manage them.

Managing finances

This is a complex area and you will need to decide whether to keep manual or electronic records, or both. It is worth discussing financial management with someone qualified in accountancy or bookkeeping if you do not have expertise yourself in this area.

Publicising your magazine

It is worth keeping files on publicity activities. An example of files you could keep on this topic are:

- general publicity campaigns
- sources of publicity
- publicity to be conducted for the current issue

■ past publicity
■ ideas for future publicity

Managing contributions

It is important to have a good system for recording and dealing with contributions, otherwise your content will be in disarray.

The simplest method to adopt is to have a single folder for each issue of the magazine; it is useful to have this both in a manual system (e.g. a filing cabinet) and electronically (as a computer file). It really is worth having manual files as well as computer ones because, if your computer is out of action, or you get a virus which destroys your files, you still have a hard-copy back up, and also some items may be easier to hold manually – for example, if you are sent a large report from which to extract items for publication.

Within each manual file, it is useful to have a clear plastic folder containing everything relating to a particular contribution. To start with, each folder might just have a piece of paper with a note of an idea for a contribution; it could then progress to having details of possible contributors, notes of conversations and progress made, draft contributions and final versions of the item. You can also indicate which items need sending to contributors as proofs before printing. If you label each folder, or tag it in some way, it will be easier to see at a glance what each one contains. (There are now bright labels available, which can be stuck to papers and peeled off when necessary, that really help with this – they are also useful for proof-reading and marking up copy. The labels are a development of PostIt® Notes and the best ones to get are about two inches long and half an inch wide, in a range of bright colours.)

Remember to discard earlier drafts as they are superseded by later ones, otherwise you could find your files bulging with irrelevant papers. And if you decide a particular contribution will not be going into a particular issue, you can move it elsewhere, for example into the file for your next issue, or into a pending file.

Once the issue has been published, you can discard most of the contents of the manual files, making sure you do keep any items which you think you could need again in the future.

As well as the single issue files, it is useful to have a general file for ideas for future issues. It is also useful to have separate files for items such as book reviews, reader correspondence, contact details, and so forth.

If you keep electronic files on your computer, make sure you have a system for giving them names you will remember. It is useful to put incoming editorial material into Word files, so you can edit them, and it is helpful to keep separate folders for each issue of the magazine, with a contents listing in each issue's folder so you can keep track of what you are expecting, what you have received and what has been completed or sent to design or print.

Managing advertisements

As with contributions, it is useful to have files for each issue, showing what advertisements are expected, have arrived or are still being dealt with. You can also have a general file for possible future advertisers; either ones you intend to contact or ones who have expressed an interest in taking advertising space in the future. You can also show which advertisements have been paid for, which ones are repeat advertisements or part of a series, and which ones need to be sent out as proofs before printing. If you can use a spreadsheet, you can produce one with records of all your advertising on – showing potential contacts, contact details, dates of contacts made, results of discussions, actions pending, booked advertisements, copy received, advertisements printed, invoices sent, etc.

Handling production activities

Keeping track of production is vital, especially if you publish on a specific date rather than just during a particular time period. Some things you will need to keep records of are:

■ copy deadlines for both editorial and advertising
■ progress on incoming items
■ dates to get your publication to your designer and/or printer
■ dates for distribution

You will also need to keep track of supplies so that you do not run short of materials for anything you produce yourself (for example photocopying paper, ink cartridges, envelopes, and so forth).

Communicating with people

Last, but not least, you will need a system for ensuring you communicate with the relevant people and keep records of some of those communications. Some things you may wish to record are:

■ dates on which you commissioned articles or book reviews
■ any extensions to copy deadlines you have agreed with people
■ forward dates on which you need to telephone or email people
■ any current issues or problems with which you are dealing

Project Management Tools

There are various ways in which you can monitor your progress in projects; these tend to be split between manual and electronic methods.

Manual methods

Some useful methods are:

■ having a wall-chart showing progress and activities
■ having a card file index giving details of particular activities
■ using a diary to record actions and anticipated events

Electronic methods

Some useful methods are:

■ using project management software to record progress

■ having an electronic diary system to give you reminders of actions to be taken

■ having a list of items and actions in each computer folder, so you can see with each of them exactly what you are expecting and what you have received

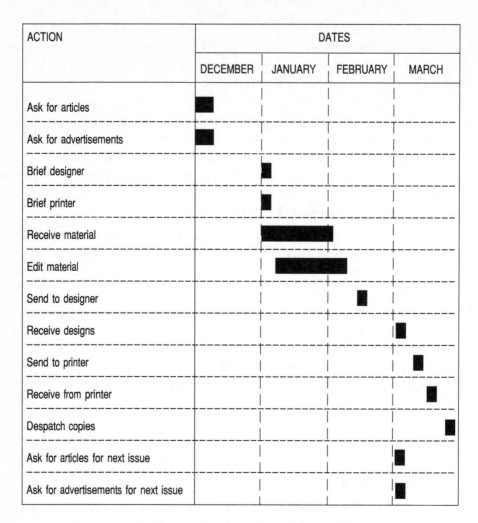

ACTION	DATES			
	DECEMBER	JANUARY	FEBRUARY	MARCH
Ask for articles	■			
Ask for advertisements	■			
Brief designer		■		
Brief printer		■		
Receive material		▬▬▬		
Edit material		▬▬▬		
Send to designer			■	
Receive designs				■
Send to printer				■
Receive from printer				■
Despatch copies				■
Ask for articles for next issue				■
Ask for advertisements for next issue				■

Simple example of a project planning chart

Chapter 15
Publicity

In most cases it will be important for you to publicise your magazine so that people get to know about it. If you are producing it for a very small group of people, then little publicity will be needed, but in most other circumstances you will need to consider the best ways to communicate what you are doing.

There are two main stages of publicity:

- before you launch
- once you are in production

Pre-launch publicity will alert people to what you are offering and post-launch publicity will keep your presence visible.

This chapter covers the *reasons* for doing publicity and the *methods* of generating publicity.

Reasons for Publicity

There are many reasons for attending to publicity:

- **To inform people.** Publicity helps people become aware of your existence, your aims, your scope and style, your cost, your frequency, your progress, and so forth.

- **To generate an image.** Publicity helps people become aware of how you wish to be perceived – and to link this perception with a desire to read, advertise in or otherwise be associated with you.

- **To generate anticipation.** Publicity helps generate a keenness to see and read the magazine. By letting people know what is coming, they can be geared up to buying the magazine and reading it.

- **To generate enthusiasm.** Publicity can produce initial, and long-lasting, enthusiasm for your magazine.

- **To attract contributions.** Publicity can bring your magazine to the attention of potential contributors, either directly or through third parties who mention it to others.

- **To attract advertising.** Publicity can bring your magazine to the attention of potential advertisers – again either directly or through intermediaries/agencies.

- **To attract readers/subscribers.** Publicity can attract readers/subscribers through the points mentioned above and also directly, through specific invitations to purchase individual copies or subscriptions.

- **To maintain a presence.** Publicity can keep you in people's minds over a period of time.

- **To communicate changes.** Publicity can help your 'stakeholders' (readers, advertisers, contributors, suppliers, etc.) understand what you are doing and how and why you are doing it.

Methods of Generating Publicity

Here are some methods of generating publicity:

- **Word of mouth.** Talking to people spreads the word. It is said that anyone in the world can be accessed via a chain of only five or six contacts – i.e. you speak to someone, they tell someone else and so on. And word of mouth tends to be good because you can communicate your enthusiasm directly and this enthusiasm can easily be spread.

- **Paid advertising.** You can advertise your magazine in this way, which can be useful but may be costly. There are various ways in which you can advertise – for example in newspapers, other magazines, on the radio or television, on the Internet, on posters and so forth.

- **Free, or low-cost, advertising.** Cards in local shops or supermarkets, flyers in leisure centres or garages, leaflets through letterboxes or on car windscreens – there are a range of ways of advertising without high costs. However, some of these methods are not permitted in particular countries, so check any local restrictions before you use these techniques.

- **Direct mail.** Mailing people directly (mailshots) about your magazine is good, but will incur the cost of printing the information, buying envelopes and stamps and possibly purchasing a mailing list. If you are going to use direct mail, you need to be certain that you have access to a relevant, and up-to-date, list of potential purchasers, subscribers or advertisers. There are many organisations that sell mailing lists, or you can generate your own by using published directories, available from local libraries or from organisations in the field you serve – for example professional bodies if your magazine is for practitioners of a particular discipline, trade associations if you are going out to businesses, local authorities if you are aiming at community groups, and so forth. You can also download lists from certain Internet sources.

Do check that there is no restriction on direct mailing to people on lists you source yourself, as some organisations – professional bodies for example – state that their lists are for members' use only and are not to be used for unauthorised mailings.

Direct mail can produce very limited results – often only 1%-2% response rates although, if you make sure your lists contain people who have already been in the market for similar or complementary products, responses could be higher. There are direct mail specialists who can handle this process for you, but you will need to have an appropriate budget to fund this if you are using commercial services.

You should also be aware of the existence of mailing preference services, which keep lists of people who do not want to receive unsolicited mail, faxes or emails and you should also be aware of the fact that certain unsolicited approaches are, or are becoming, illegal in certain countries. In the UK, new legislation has made 'spamming' – sending unsolicited electronic messages to people, illegal (although this only applies to private individuals, not businesses).

■ **Public relations/media contacts/press releases.** Public relations is the process of keeping your existence and activities in the 'public eye'. In practice, it means maintaining good relationships with your 'audiences' and 'stakeholders' – which may be the general public, a small segment of the community or specific people and organisations. Making contacts with local media representatives is a good way of publicising your magazine. You should make sure you know who your local newspaper and radio journalists are and keep them informed of your activities. Send out press releases too to keep them alerted to what you are doing (*see Appendix 10 for an example of a press release*).

One good way to improve your public relations is to produce a good story about your magazine, perhaps something amusing that happened when it was being produced, or news of a feature on – or by – a local personality. You can also run a competition or make a special offer that is newsworthy. And keep the news coming – don't rely on one single approach to do the whole job.

■ **Contributors.** Anyone who contributes to your magazine probably has useful contacts and their own publicity network, so tap into these wherever possible. There are many ways in which contributors can help promote your magazine – for example you can give them spare copies of their own printed contributions to pass on to others, you can ask them if they will give one or two spare copies of the entire magazine to their own friends or colleagues, you can ask them to mention the magazine or give out copies when they are doing talks, and so forth. This is a very useful method of publicity as your contributors are likely to be willing ambassadors for you – partly because in promoting your magazine they are giving their own input to it more exposure.

■ **Exhibitions.** Having a stand or table at exhibitions or conferences, or even in a local supermarket, will get your magazine noticed. Take some free samples, or some flyers showing sample covers or pages and listing the benefits of readership/subscription. Talk to people who visit your stand and find ways of getting them to publicise the magazine for you. Offer reduced rate subscriptions to anyone signing up there and then.

■ **Sponsorship.** Sponsoring events can be useful in publicising your magazine, as long as you can afford to be a sponsor. For example, a community magazine could sponsor a local person in a charity run, while a professional magazine could sponsor – or part sponsor – a conference, award a bursary for a student to attend a training course or give books to student who have limited funds (*also see Chapter 9 on sponsorship*).

■ **The Internet.** You can promote your magazine through the Internet – a rapidly growing form of publicity. This can be done by having your own website, where you can explain what you publish, give extracts from your magazine and include details of how to subscribe or receive a sample copy. You can also have links from other sites to your own site and you can arrange for your magazine to be mentioned on other relevant sites. If you do have a website, you should seek guidance on how to get it listed most effectively on search engines so it has maximum exposure to its desired audience (*see also Appendix 8 on setting up a website).*

■ **Other promotional/incentive producing activities.** There is a wide range of promotional techniques that can be used to promote magazines, as much as other types of product or service. Some techniques are:

- producing badges, T-shirts, mouse mats and marker pens with your name, logo and contact details on
- getting skydivers to hold banners with your name
- having people walk up and down with placards
- producing calendars and Christmas cards with your details on
... and so on.

The only limits are the imagination and your purse! If this interests you, the promotion 'industry' is a growing one and there are several magazines and trade fairs devoted to it *(see Appendix 4 for more on this)*.

And finally... remember – it is important to keep your publicity going: the more people see you the more they will have you in mind.

Chapter 16
Readers' Surveys

As a magazine publisher, it is important for you to keep in touch with your readers, so that you can monitor their opinions and expectations and keep your magazine appealing to them.

Reader surveys can help you keep in touch with how your readers think and what they want from your magazine. Some of the things that surveys can provide information on are:

■ your readers' characteristics ('demographics'), including age, income group, location, job type, interests, activities, and so forth

■ your readers' opinions on items you publish

■ your readers' reactions to, or interest in, particular advertising features

■ your readers' responses to new design features in the magazine (page layout, typefaces, etc.)

■ your readers' purchasing behaviour (what they buy – for example, other publications, cars, computers, food, holidays, clothes, etc.) and purchasing power (budget size and frequency of purchase)

This chapter will cover two topics: survey types and survey techniques.

Survey Types

Questionnaires – included on your subscription application and/or renewal forms

With this type of questionnaire, you can ask people about such things as their geographical location, their jobs, their income, their areas of purchasing responsibility, their interests, and so forth. You can also ask them what kind of features they would like to see in your magazine. This kind of questionnaire is commonly used for controlled circulation (free-distribution) magazines, where a database of readers is maintained – and often sold to third parties (only including the details of people who have agreed to information on themselves being disclosed to others).

Questionnaires – inserted into the magazine

The reasons for this format are the same as with the preceding category – the only difference is that they are included with the magazine for all readers, not just sent to new and renewing subscribers.

Questionnaires – sent by email to readers

These are becoming increasingly popular and there appears to be a growing willingness for people to complete them as they tend to be easy and quick and do not involve posting an envelope.

Telephone surveys

With this type of survey, a sample of people is selected to contact. It is important to note, however, that people may have expressed a preference not to receive unsolicited telephone calls, and so telephone surveys may be best kept as an option on a questionnaire form, where you ask whether the person would agree to a future telephone call and, if so, to indicate this on the form. If, however, a person has already given you their telephone number, it is likely to be acceptable to make this kind of call.

Readers' advisory groups, panels or 'focus groups'

These are samples of readers, potential readers, or other interested parties, who are approached from time to time for their opinions, reactions and ideas. With such groups it is possible to make periodic assessments of opinions and behaviour, try out new ideas and get feedback on an ongoing basis.

Correspondence columns and 'readers' corners'

These encourage debate and are other ways of gauging opinions, although they are only likely to give a narrow sample of readers' opinions.

Feedback

Inviting feedback on the magazine as a whole, or on particular sections or items, is another useful way of gathering information, but is likely to produce a much more limited response than a targeted survey. A simple way of inviting feedback is through the editorial column of the magazine itself, but often such invitations have disappointing responses.

Survey Techniques

Conducting surveys is a specialised process and, if you want to do anything more than a very basic fact-gathering exercise, you would be well advised to enlist the services of a professional in this area. There are a number of publications on survey techniques *(see Appendix 4),* which go into a good deal of depth on the topic. The following points simply outline some of the issues you will need to consider.

Incentives

Response to printed surveys tends to be very low – it may well be less than 5% of those invited to respond, so it is important to do whatever you can to increase your response rate. One way of doing this is to offer an incentive to complete your questionnaire.

Examples of incentives are:

■ a free gift
■ a reduced-rate subscription
■ entry to a prize draw

Timing

Surveys should not be conducted too frequently; if they are, readers may well become bored, irritated or fail to complete them. Once a year is probably about the maximum for a good general survey, although you could conduct 'mini surveys' on specific topics more frequently. Some good times to do a survey are when you have a new development in mind and you want to test opinion towards it, or when you need more information about your readership in order to monitor trends. You might also wish to do a survey in order to assess readers' possible responses towards potential advertising campaigns.

Length

It is impossible to give 'rules' for this, but it is generally good to keep the length of your survey reasonably short, so that it can be completed in a few minutes. If it is likely to take more than five minutes or so to complete, you can include a note saying that it will probably take a particular length of time to complete and giving reasons for producing a questionnaire of that length.

Questions

There are many topics for questions and also many questioning techniques. Some of the issues to consider are:

- **in which order to place questions**

- **the kind of rating scale to use for responses** – for example, numerical ratings, preference scales, alternatives to choose between, and so forth

- **the manner in which you invite responses.** It is important to keep your language neutral and avoid 'leading' your readers. There is much scope for bias in questionnaire design and it is a subject that needs to be handled carefully. Of course, surveys are sometimes designed with the intention of producing a biased response, but this raises major ethical issues.

- **The reasons for including particular questions.** You should make sure there is a justifiable reason for each one and that they do not conflict with privacy and anti-discrimination legislation.

Analysis

Responses to surveys have to be analysed. If you consider this at an early stage in the process it will make the task easier. For example, having questions with 'fixed choice' options, where the reader only has to tick a box or put a mark on a scale, makes the survey easier to analyse than one with 'open' questions, where you invite a written answer. In the latter case you subsequently have to spend time placing the responses into categories.

Publication

Finally, you should decide whether to publish the responses to your survey or whether simply to use them to inform your own decision-making processes. The results of some surveys will be of interest to your readership, while the results of others might not. There may also be an expectation that, if you invite responses, you will let people know the results, so there are various factors to take into account in considering whether or not to publish survey results.

As a last point, you might consider doing a joint survey with another body or with an advertiser. This could generate funds for you, if part of the costs were met by the other party, but there are issues regarding confidentiality, administration, and so forth, if you take this course of action.

Chapter 17
Ensuring Quality and Identifying and Dealing with Problems

Preceding chapters have covered specific aspects of magazine production; this one considers the question of overall quality and how to handle occasional problems that may occur.

Ensuring Quality

Whatever kind of magazine you produce, it is likely to be better valued if people perceive it as providing quality. To achieve this, there are several areas to consider and they are outlined below.

Appearance

This is about paying attention to how your magazine looks. Is it printed on good quality paper, which doesn't show print through from the page behind and isn't too reflective? Is it easy to read, with an adequate print intensity? Is the design pleasing and appropriate? Are the illustrations relevant and interesting?

Feel

This is about the tactile sensation your magazine creates. Does the magazine feel good to touch and handle? Is it a good size to handle and easy to hold up when reading? Is the paper a good weight – not too flimsy or unnecessarily heavy and stiff?

Content

This is about the material contained within your magazine. Is the content appropriate for the readership? Is there a good, balanced, mix of items? Is there a variety of topics and issues? Are the contributions of interest to those reading it? Are items topical and up to date? Are there new features from time to time?

Editing
This is about how your magazine is written and monitored. Is it well put together? Is it properly proof-read for typing, spelling, punctuation, grammar and layout? Are contributions appropriate in length and style?

Efficiency
This is about how well your magazine achieves its objectives. Does it appear on time? Is it well packaged, so that it arrives in good condition? Are enquiries from readers, contributors, advertisers or others responded to in good time, pleasantly and helpfully?

Expectations
This is about people's opinions of your magazine. Does the magazine go beyond what people might expect? For example, does it give excellent value for money, does it have exciting offers or discounts, does it produce special supplements or editions, do its staff respond quickly and effectively to enquiries?

Development
This is about future progress. Does your magazine continually review its effectiveness? Does it keep in touch with, and respond to, its market? Does it maintain a lively and stimulating content? Does it have other plans for future development?

Identifying and Dealing with Possible Problem Areas
On occasion, you may run into difficulties when producing your magazine. How these difficulties are handled will affect the magazine's success. This section deals with possible problem areas and ways of dealing with them.

Misunderstandings
Sometimes there are misunderstandings between people involved in magazine production. Often these misunderstandings are to do with words used. For example, what does the word 'soon' mean: does it mean quickly, tomorrow, in half an hour, in five minutes? What is meant by 'Can you?': does it mean 'Please do this' or does it mean 'Is this possible'? Avoiding misunderstandings completely may be impossible, but working to minimise them is important.

One area in which misunderstandings often occur is in instructions for printers. A common area for confusion is to do with colour printing. When a colour is specified, it may appear differently in the completed product, depending on factors such as:

- the paper used
- how much ink is put on the rollers
- whether a tint is used
- whether spot or full colour printing is used

Often results involve a degree of trial and error and it is useful to know about possible areas of difficulty in advance, so that problems can be anticipated.

Delays

On occasion, delays occur. These can happen when contributions or advertisements arrive late, when design or printing takes longer than expected, when editing or proof-reading is not done on time, when postal delays occur, and so on. You cannot always prevent delays, but it is important to have a policy and procedure for dealing with them. Important elements of this are:

- letting relevant people know that a delay is likely, or has occurred
- considering alternative courses of action
- having a stand-by procedure

Errors or inaccuracies

Another problem area is to do with mistakes. Some common mistakes are:

- typing or spelling mistakes (for example getting a contributor's name wrong, or printing an incorrect date for an event)

- factual mistakes (for example, quoting incorrect statistics or crediting the wrong person as a source)

- omissions (for example, leaving contact details out of an advertisement or leaving a diagram out of an article), and so on.

Not only are errors and inaccuracies misleading, they can result in embarrassment or loss of income for the people on whose behalf the information has been printed; in extreme circumstances it could lead to you being sued, so it is vital to avoid mistakes wherever possible.

Unauthorised use of material

It is possible to find that material you have printed legally 'belongs' to another person. Often when this happens it is purely in error, but sometimes it arises from direct plagiarism (effectively stealing) of another person's material. Even failing to credit a source of information could result in what you print being regarded as unauthorised. It is not always practical to check every item contained in every contribution for prior ownership, but you should at least ensure that contributors know they should credit where relevant and avoid unauthorised use of another person's work.

Offence

Sometimes people take offence at items contained in a magazine. There can be a number of reasons for this, for example:

- language used
- pictures printed
- opinions expressed
- lack of balance

And, at the extreme, people may consider they have been libelled because of something printed about them, possibly resulting in litigation. So it is important to think through the possible implications of items you publish.

Unwanted communications

Another problem area is when people are contacted without their permission. This results in 'junk', which is a term that applies to posted items, faxes or electronically transmitted material (in the latter case it is referred to as 'spam'). In some countries it is illegal to transmit information that has not been requested, so do take as much care as possible only to circulate people with information they actually want to receive. In the UK there is a range of 'preference services' that people can register with if they do not wish to be sent unsolicited communications, and the law regarding this kind of correspondence has recently changed so that unsolicited electronic messages to private individuals (although not businesses) have been made illegal. Also, at the time of writing, there are serious concerns that the Internet could well be totally incapacitated by the growing use of spam, to the detriment of users worldwide, so this is a major area of potential problems.

Some Ways of Dealing with Problems

If problems have occurred, involving other people, there are a number of steps that can be taken. Some are set out below.

Apologise

If others are involved, apologising, directly to the person concerned and/or in print, can help. An apology does not change the original situation, but may well alleviate discontent and prevent further aggravation from occurring.

Rectify

Correcting a mistake also helps. For example, spotting errors in time to rectify them and printing corrections where an error has occurred, will be beneficial. Not all readers will see the correct information when it is re-printed, but it is better than leaving the original mistake totally uncorrected.

Compensate

In some cases it may be necessary to compensate people for errors and omissions. Some ways in which this can be done are:

- re-printing an incorrect advertisement free of charge, or at a reduced rate
- refunding charges for incorrect advertisements
- giving additional free copies of the magazine to anyone whose work has been subjected to an error

It is always worth offering compensation that is worth more to the recipient than to you; for example, putting an advertisement again in free of charge is likely to be less costly to you than refunding the original payment.

Part Two
Producing a Newsletter

The first part of this book has focussed on magazines; this next part deals with newsletters. Newsletters tend to be short publications – often just a few pages. They may be written for people within a particular interest group, rather than the general public, although this is not always the case. Newsletters are often produced by businesses for internal consumption, as part of an 'Internal Communications' (IC) function, or for their customers and clients. Newsletters are often produced on a low budget and their appearance and size may reflect this.

Chapter 18
Newsletters

Of course, much of what I have written already applies to newsletters, but there are also differences, so I would like to briefly cover the main areas contained in the part of the book that deals with magazines, showing any points of difference where they occur.

Purpose and objectives

When producing any publication, you need to be clear on your purpose and objectives. The purpose of both magazines and newsletters can be similar – i.e. to inform, educate, influence, entertain, etc. Also the objectives can be similar – i.e. to achieve a particular level of circulation, to achieve a particular level of financial return, to achieve a particular standing in the marketplace.

However, whereas with a magazine you will probably need a detailed business plan, with a newsletter this may not be necessary as it is generally a much smaller scale activity. You will, however, still need to know much of the information that a business plan would contain – for example, your purpose, your target audience, your format, whether there are any competing newsletters, how you will promote your newsletter, what it will cost, how you will produce it and any possible problem areas or obstacles to overcome.

Research

You will need to do research with a newsletter, just as with a magazine, but this may be a bit harder to achieve, as newsletters are often less 'public' than magazines.

A good way of researching newsletters is to see if there is a professional or other focal body for the area of activity in which you will be engaged and then ask them if they have a library or information department that keeps archives of newsletters in the field.

Alternatively, you could contact individual organisations in your field and request copies of their own newsletters – for example, environmental groups, sports bodies, hobby groups, manufacturing companies, and so forth. Usually organisations are only to happy to oblige with such information.

A further way in which you could get information on newsletters is to see if your local library can point you in the direction of sources of information on them – this is always a good starting point for research and most library staff are very helpful and knowledgeable.

You can also carry out Internet-based research and look at other organisations' websites where you are likely to find PDFs *(see Appendix 24)* of their own newsletters. You can then compare yours with theirs (or your ideas with their practices) and you can also contact their editors, who will usually be very helpful and informative.

Style, frequency, format, design and circulation
The same principles apply as with magazine production, except that as newsletters are shorter and more informal, and probably appear more frequently, they need to be simpler in style and appearance.

Have a look again at the first page of Chapter 4, where you will see the words that are used to describe different kinds of style, and see whether any of these are appropriate for your newsletter or whether anything different applies. Then consider the other elements, such as frequency, size, colour, print type, headings, and so forth.

Illustrations are likely to be very limited in a newsletter, but you can have some. Often the most suitable form of illustration for a newsletter is a line drawing, but you can use photographs, charts and other graphic devices, although if you are photocopying your newsletter you should avoid over-complicated devices or dark photographs that may not photocopy well.

Editorial and production
This whole area is likely to be very reduced for newsletters, compared to magazines. Fewer editorial staff are needed for newsletters, and production may well be carried out by the same people as produce editorial content – although it is important to have good design facilities if you want your

newsletter to look professional and readable. Details of editorial and production activities can be found in the earlier chapter on these topics and if your newsletter is substantial, then you can follow the guidance given there. If, however, your newsletter is quite small, you will simply need to ensure that it has relevant content, is produced on time, is clear and understandable, and is produced in a way that fits with your budget and design requirements. Don't be afraid to edit material sent in, even if it is from voluntary contributors: concise, well-targeted articles do raise enthusiasm and, as many contributors are not professional communicators, their submissions can frequently require editiorial input.

Equipment and resources

Again, equipment and resources needed are likely to be much fewer with newsletter production. You will find it easier to produce if you have a computer; this will also help you manage your database of readers and – if relevant – advertisers. If you are considering very small-scale production, a photocopier may be adequate for producing copies for your readers, otherwise you will need the services of a suitable printer.

Selecting and organising topics and items

For a newsletter, this is likely to be a straightforward task. Newsletters should be clearly focussed on their field of activity and, therefore, topics and items are often self-selecting.

Newsletters carry NEWS, so this should be your main concern. What counts as news will vary from one publication to another, but generally your items should be informative, topical, relevant to most of your readership and within the time-frame of your publishing schedule – there is nothing worse than news that arrives too late to be of use – particularly information on events that have already occurred by the time the newsletter reaches its readers.

Most items will need to be quite short in a newsletter – whereas a magazine article is often upwards of a thousand words, and may be several thousand, very long items would be out of place in a newsletter. On the whole, if you can keep your items to under five hundred words, this works well in most newsletters. You can have an occasional longer item, but this will restrict the space you have available for other things.

Good items for newsletters are:

- news relating to your area
- events listings
- letters about relevant topics
- information on useful products and services and links to useful websites
- reports on activities carried out by people in your readership group
- networking information
- 'snippets' and 'fillers'
- advertisements

Getting contributions

With newsletters, this is generally straightforward – your most likely contributors are:

- yourself
- others in your 'community' of readers
- people wishing to contact others in your community

Once you have established your likely readers, these are the ones to approach with requests for contributions. Apart from this, do follow the suggestions in Chapter 7, 'Getting Contributions' – as many of the same principles apply.

Writing and interviewing skills

Much of this is the same as for magazine production, but with newsletters, writing generally needs to be more focussed, 'snappier' and more concise. It is useful to look at a range of other newsletters before you start yours, so you can get a feel for the kind of writing styles they have, and an Internet search is useful in this context.

Proof-reading

Exactly the same advice applies to newsletters as to magazines – make sure you do proof-reading effectively in order to produce a quality publication.

Advertising and sponsorship

Again, similar principles apply to advertising as to magazines, and sponsorship may be easier to get for a newsletter than for a magazine. Certainly with 'local' newsletters, such as village newsletters or club newsletters, you may find sponsors in some of your readers, local businesses, relevant suppliers, and so on.

Often an individual or a business will sponsor a whole edition of a newsletter – for example, covering the cost of printing or distribution, or you may have sponsors for each of these activities for a whole year. Sponsorship may also take the form of assistance, such as providing help with putting newsletters into envelopes, putting them through letterboxes or giving materials such as envelopes or photocopying facilities.

Advertising may be more difficult with a newsletter, because many newsletters have only a limited circulation, but it is possible to attract advertising if you are operating within a 'niche' market or in a local area that particular advertisers wish to target.

Guidance to contributors and advertisers

Again, this is similar to guidance to magazine contributors and advertisers, but on a smaller scale. You may have to be stricter with copy deadlines with a newsletter, as newsletters often come out more frequently than magazines, giving less time for the collation of editorial and advertising elements.

Distribution

Newsletter distribution tends to be easier than magazine distribution as they are often smaller and therefore easier to handle and lighter and less expensive to post.

Publicity

Newsletters often function within more of a closed community than magazines do, so they can be easier to publicise. Many newsletters are for employees of a business organisation or membership body, who receive them automatically, therefore removing the need for publicity to the majority of readers. If you do need to publicise your newsletter, a good way of doing so is through existing readers; this is inexpensive and effective and all you need to do is ask current readers to recommend, or pass on, their newsletter to someone else. These new people can do the same in turn, potentially growing your readership base substantially. You can also publicise newsletters on the Internet, either through your own website, via emails to people who are happy to receive communications from you, or through third parties.

Readers' surveys

This is not such a common practice with newsletters as with magazines, but there is no reason why surveys cannot be carried out for newsletters. The same guidance will apply as in Chapter 16 on reader surveys.

Principles, values and ethics

This is an area that may also not be considered as much with newsletters as with magazines, but the same issues arise with both.

Dealing with problems

There are likely to be fewer problems with newsletters than with magazines, because of the smaller scale of activity. Some problems that can arise specifically with newsletters are:

- missing schedules, as newsletters are less substantial publications than magazines and people do not always take them as seriously. However, if you take yourself seriously as an editor, contributors should respond. Set clear deadlines, give reasonable amounts of time to respond to them and chase copy well before the final date. Also remember that if people understand the whole production process – what the deadlines are and when the readers will receive their copy, they are likely to respond better – understanding the whole process is really helpful to them. As a last resort, some publications 'name and shame' in a mild way, by publicly naming and thanking those who sent their copy in before the deadline

- filling space 'for the sake of it' in order to comply with a frequent production schedule

- adopting too serious or heavy a style, more fitting to a weightier publication

- sending newsletters to recipients who do not wish to receive them and subsequently complain – i.e. being a 'junk mailer'

Ensuring quality

The main ways of ensuring quality with newsletters are to:

- make sure they keep closely to their stated aims
- keep them topical and relevant
- proof-read diligently so that information (especially dates, contact details and advertising matter) is always accurate

Project management

As with magazines, it is vital to have systems and procedures for getting your newsletter out on time and in accordance with your goals. Make sure everyone involved knows their roles and responsibilities and is capable of fulfilling them and keep them updated on deadlines. When people understand the whole picture, they are more likely to respond well. Finally, it's important that you update your methods and activities to ensure that you have an effective and developing newsletter.

Part Three
Producing Electronic Publications

Electronic publications are publications that people receive via their computer. The most common ways of receiving such publications are 1) by reading or downloading material that appears on an internet website and 2) by receiving them as emails or attachments to e-mails. A term commonly used to describe electronic publications is e-zines, but I am going to use this term just for electronically produced magazines, and I am going to refer to the newsletter equivalent as electronic newsletters (EN for short).

Chapter 19
Electronic Publications

1. Electronic Publications in General

Electronic publications are becoming more and more common as web-based/online publishing increases as a sector. It is easy and fast to publish online and the costs are very much lower than for conventional printed publications. Because of this, many people and organisations are relinquishing some, or all, of their conventionally produced publications in favour of electronic ones.

As an example, many catalogues are currently produced online as well as in printed format, and many suppliers of goods and services also offer online purchasing (for example, books, clothes, food, travel tickets, hotel accommodation, and so forth). And all the major daily newspapers have on-line versions on offer.

Although electronic publishing is straightforward, online publications are not always of high quality, as many people think they do not need to be as stringent with their writing, or believe that they can do wonderful graphic design simply because their computer has a software package that can be used for this purpose. So, if you are considering online publishing, you will need to think through your objectives, resources and capabilities before starting.

Although many aspects of magazine and newsletter production are similar in both printed and electronic publications, there are some notable differences, in particular the following:

- writing style
- graphic elements
- timescale
- readership
- online marketing

Let's consider each of these briefly.

Writing style

I am assuming that your publications are going to be read on screen. If they are simply meant to be downloaded, printed out and read subsequently, they are effectively equivalent to a publication that was originally produced in printed form, in which case many of the comments that follow here are irrelevant. However, if the text is mainly intended to be read on a computer screen, it is important to remember that most people find it slower reading material on screen than reading it on a printed page held in front of them. This means that their tolerance for large volumes of text is much diminished when they have to access it via their computer. So the writing style for this purpose generally needs to be clear, concise and lively, or people will lose concentration and interest. Of course, writing should normally be all of these things anyway, but it is even more important with on-screen material.

Graphic elements

Columns

Having columns, rather than text going right across the page, can look inviting, but if you do this you must make sure that it is readable. If your articles are long, it may be hard to read if people have to keep scrolling up and down to follow the same article across different columns – and this is compounded if you have set your margins so that they are wider than a screen width and people have to keep moving the page to get to the end of lines. This is impossible to do for any length of time. Text going right across a page is simpler, but long lines are generally difficult to read, so you have to assess which format is best for your content and your readers. If you are going to have columns, it helps if most of your items are short and take up only one column width each. One option is to have columns of different widths – one wider and one narrower, so that the main items can be printed in the wider columns, and shorter pieces, or accompanying notes, in the narrower ones.

Typefaces and sizes

If your text does go across the whole page it needs to be in a reasonably large (but not too large) type size and in a clear typeface, otherwise it is, again, difficult to read. A good principle is to use a 12 point 'sans serif' *(see Glossary, Appendix 3)* typeface, such as Arial, which is clear and easy to absorb.

Illustrations

A wide range of graphic elements can be used on-screen, but you need to take care that they don't take a long time to download. If you have large photographs embedded in an email, animated elements on a website page or very high definition illustrations, these can take a good deal of time to arrive. This is fine if the recipient is on broadband, but otherwise may irritate people because of the length of time it takes before they can access the material and it can also happen that telephone links are broken during lengthy downloading, thus wasting time in re-accessing the information. Having a lower resolution to photographs and other graphics will reduce the time taken to download – such illustrations will not print out as clearly as ones with a higher resolution, but they will look perfectly acceptable on a computer screen.

Timescale

It is much easier to produce electronic publications frequently than it is to produce printed publications. This is because design is done as part of the early production stage and the publication does not need subsequently to be sent to a printer or distribution house for further processing.

An electronic publication, therefore, can easily come out weekly, probably in a shorter version than a printed publication, but also probably in a more up-to-date version because of the shorter production time involved.

Readership

It is generally easier to build a readership base with electronic publications as they tend to be less expensive – and often free to the reader – and because they are easier to publicise through email networks.

Electronic publications should not be sent to unwilling recipients, otherwise they will be classed as 'spam' but, once a recipient has been identified, delivery is straightforward and simply requires a short computer entry to be made.

Online marketing

Electronic publications can, themselves, be marketed online and they can also contain online marketing for other products and services.

One excellent way of marketing online is through what are called 'Affiliate Programmes'. Affiliate Programmes involve the use of other people to market your products or services. The way they work is as follows: you contact other people with an offer. The offer is usually that, if they mention, or promote, your products or services on their own websites, in their own electronic publications or as footnotes to their emails by including a link to your website, when people click through to that link (or, less commonly, mention they are an affiliate in an email to you) and then pay you money for a product or service, the person whose site included the original link will receive a commission on the money you are paid. This is a very effective way of marketing and can boost your sales enormously.

2. E-zines

E-zines may be defined as electronically produced magazines. There are two ways of producing such publications; the first is to place a copy of a printed magazine onto your website; this will usually be in PDF format (*see Glossary, Appendix 3);* the second is specifically to design the magazine for on-screen consumption. In this section I will deal with the latter of these two – magazines designed specifically for on-screen reading.

Size

Because it tends to be harder to read on-screen than from a printed page, it is usually best to keep e-zines relatively short.

Typefaces and sizes

Again, because of the difficulty of reading on-screen, typefaces do need to be clear and typesizes adequate to cater for those with less than perfect vision.

Graphics

A wide range of graphic devices can be used in e-zines but the same principles apply as with printed magazines – keep them uncomplicated and avoid over-use of commercially available 'clip-art', which can make them look unoriginal.

Format

PDF format is a good one to use; this retains the printed format on the web and makes it less likely that people can make alterations to your work. It is possible to alter PDFs, but it requires special software.

Content

As with any magazine, you will need to generate editorial copy; however, there are also other options for e-zines. There are many free articles available to download from the Internet and these can be accessed from many websites (check before using them that they really are available for re-publishing).

It is worth having a really enticing article at the beginning of the e-zine; unlike printed magazines, where people flick through the pages, often beginning at the back, if the start of an e-zine is not attractive the rest of it may never be read.

The same principle applies to the beginning of articles where, if the first line is really enticing, readers are more likely to continue with the rest of the article. It is also important to have really good headlines and sub-heads, which help draw readers in. Headings can incorporate an interesting item from the following article, and can include words that create an emotional response, and can also indicate the benefits to be gained from reading the article. Some words that have been shown to be effective in gaining attention in headlines for articles, reports and letters are: 'Now', 'You', 'Free', 'Secrets', 'Discover', 'How to'.

Security

Once an e-zine is on the Internet it is impossible to prevent it from being copied and sent to other people. However, the same applies to printed publications which can be photocopied quite easily. You can include a statement to the effect that unauthorised reproduction or distribution is prohibited, but this can be very difficult to enforce. However, there is software that enables you to 'hide' elements within images on the web so that if you find they have been used elsewhere you can identify that they 'belong' to you (this process is called steganography).

Cost

An e-zine can be charged for or sent free, depending on whether you are running a commercial business or not. If you do charge, you may consider arranging online payment, although this will require setting up an account with one of the services through which you will have to operate such payments, and this will cost you an upfront fee plus a percentage of each transaction. It does, however, make it simpler for people to subscribe to your e-zine. There are some useful ways of encouraging people to subscribe to e-zines; these include reduced rates for an initial period, additional issues in return for payment by standing order or direct debit, or asking for a deferred payment that is only actioned after a particular period of time – for example, one to three months after subscribing, so that the subscriber can get used to the publication before finally committing money to it.

Method of distribution

You can send your e-zine as an attachment to an email message or you can direct people to your website where they can find the e-zine (in which case it is useful to do a reminder to people each time an issue comes out so they know a new one has arrived on your site). If you send your e-zine as an email attachment, you need to consider its file size and how long it will take to download. If recipients are on broadband, this is not such an important factor but, for those who are not, a large file size can take a very long time to download and the recipients are also at the mercy of telephone line 'blips' while downloading, which result in disconnection and the need to download all over again. If you simply put the e-zine on your website, people can then choose just to read it online, or to print out single pages as and when they choose. You should also consider the time it takes for people to get into your site to view your e-zine and this will relate to your design elements – lots of fancy graphics and moving elements will add substantially to the time taken – and there is evidence that after fifteen to thirty seconds people tend to lose interest and give up if they have not yet accessed the material for which they are searching.

Advertising

You will need to consider whether you will take advertising in connection with your e-zine. If you do, this can take various forms:

- The first is advertisements included within the body of the e-zine itself – these can be designed along with the rest of the text, or artwork provided by advertisers can be slotted in.

- The second is 'banner' advertisements, which are small advertisements that can appear on your website close to the e-zine, but not inside it.

- The third is web links that, again, can appear on the website associated with the magazine but not inside it.

■ The fourth is 'pop-up' advertisements, which are moving features that generally appear on screen in front of the e-zine and which have either to be read or deleted by people before they can get to the content of the e-zine itself. Pop-ups can irritate many people and, while they are undoubtedly attention grabbing, they can be counter-productive – so use them with discretion. You will also need to decide what to charge for advertising and this will depend, as it does with printed publications, on your total readership, the size of the advertisement and other similar factors.

Monitoring your readership

There are various ways of checking on who reads your magazine – but this only applies if it is available on your website rather than as an email attachment. One way of checking is to monitor the number of 'clicks' you receive – and this can be to a site, to a page or to an item. Another way is by using what is called a 'cookie', which is an electronic data file that can remember how often a person visits a site (people can, however, turn cookies off in their browsers, so this may not always be an entirely accurate process).

3. Electronic Newsletters

Electronic newsletters are newsletters specifically designed for on-line receipt and reading. These are now becoming very common and are a useful business tool and also a good commercial prospect. In this section I will cover some of the main aspects of producing electronic newsletters.

Title

It is important to have a name that invites people to read the newsletter. Thinking about your overall purpose and approach will help you select a name and it is important, where possible, to make the name reflect the benefits that readers will get from subscribing to your publication.

Frequency

Because of the ease with which ENs can be produced, it is tempting to bring them out very frequently. However, monthly, fortnightly or, at most, weekly is about the maximum that most people can cope with receiving an EN. Less often than monthly means they are less likely to contain topical news, and more often than weekly means recipients are likely to go into overload and not bother to read them. However frequently you do produce your EN, if you find you cannot keep to your schedule from time to time, it is worth letting subscribers know that there will be a longer gap and when to expect you back; this will keep them involved, and save them having to contact you to find out what is happening.

Timing

Some people consider that there are optimum days of the week on which to send out ENs. This may be so in general terms, but for individuals the 'best' day can vary. Mondays are probably not good days for most business people as they will probably be returning after a weekend to lots of other messages and unfinished work; similar points could be made about Fridays, when people are likely to be trying hard to complete all their urgent work before leaving for the weekend – unless they are very efficient, in which case Friday afternoons may be good times for them when they are beginning to 'unwind'. This means that mid-week is probably best for the majority of people.

Length

Short and concise is the aim with most ENs. Lengthy articles are generally not advisable, although one main item each time is usually acceptable. A good length for an EN is probably around 1,000 to 1,500 words (two or three 'pages' of text): this is straightforward to read and sufficiently short to retain most people's interest. It is also important to keep your EN relatively small in terms of file size so that it does not take too long to download – and some people think they should be kept below 24kb in size to avoid some ISPs (AOL in particular) converting them into attachments which may then be discarded by some recipients. One way of keeping your EN short is to provide links to items elsewhere rather than printing them in full in the EN itself. For example you may provide a link to your website where more in-depth information can be located, or you may provide a link to an advertiser or to an events organiser.

Topics

Although you could have several different topics in an EN, it is probably more effective to focus on one main 'theme' in each issue.

Content

In order to generate content for an EN you can follow the general guidelines given in Chapter 6. There are many different kinds of content that can be included in ENs; some good ones are:

■ up-to-date news
■ tips and ideas
■ contact details for useful products, services, people and organisations.

If you are running a commercial organisation, you can use your EN to generate more business. This tends to work well when you don't simply use the EN as a promotional tool, but mainly include articles and tips that are useful to your readers. And the more focussed your items are, and the more they are used to produce specific results – such as informing people about the benefits of a particular product or service – the more effective they are likely to be. Using an EN in this way is often more effective than conventional advertising and is an excellent way of keeping your name and activities in front of your potential customers or clients. Finally, if you allow your own personality and style to come through in your EN, it is likely to be attractive to readers as it becomes more of a person-to-person interaction, rather than a detached information document.

Archiving content

When you produce a regular EN, it is useful to arrange for an archive so that readers can refer to earlier items, and new subscribers can search for items published before they 'joined'. This can be done by filing them on your website, and also having an index by which they can be located.

Charging

Whether to charge for an EN is an issue that faces many publishers. On the whole, people are not willing to pay for a 'standard' EN, and asking for a payment is likely to deter the majority of your potential readers. It is, however, possible to charge for advertising within your EN, or for web-links from it, or for sponsorship of a particular issue, or – if your EN is sufficiently specialised and valued by your readers – to charge for the newsletter itself. And if you have subscribers who are happy for their details to be passed on to third parties, you may also be able to sell your mailing list to advertisers.

Format

Because formatting may be changed when sending from one computer to another, as the settings on the recipient's browser may be different, as may the operating system on the computer (e.g. Windows or Mac), it can be a good idea to put in a carriage return at the end of each line, rather than simply allowing the computer to automatically 'wrap round' lines – this should ensure that the recipient receives the text in the format in which you sent it. This also means that your right-hand margins will not be 'justified', but this, in any case, is better for most newsletters as it gives a more informal and personalised feel. It is also useful to look at your EN on different browsers *(see Glossary, Appendix 3)* and monitors to check how it comes across – this is particularly important with ones that are produced as web pages. You can download the major browsers free from their companies' websites and then use them to check how your EN looks when different people receive it.

When considering format you should also think about the form in which to produce your EN:

■ The simplest form is to have it as the body of an email – this is simple, although design features will be very minimal; it does have the advantage of not including an attachment, so that readers who dislike having to open attachments are more encouraged to look at what you have sent them. Email newsletters are fast to download and quick to produce.

■ The next two options for ENs are files produced either as RTF (Rich Text Format) or HTML (Hypertext Mark-up Language). RTF is a simple format, which is used to produce text without elaborate graphics. HTML is more sophisticated and is used to produce web pages. With HTML it is possible to have an index of items at the top of the newsletter with the facility for readers to click on any one of them and be taken straight to that particular item – an invaluable feature in a newsletter of any substantial length. Of course, to use some of these features it is necessary to be connected to the Internet, which not everybody wishes to do just to read a newsletter. In case you have some subscribers who do not have the facility to read HTML pages, it may be worth offering them RTF as an alternative. To produce your newsletter on a word processor in either RTF or HTML, just go to 'File', then 'Save As' and select which of the two formats you want.

■ The next choice is to produce your EN only on your website, so that people have to view it there – this means they have to take the initiative in order to view it and also have to be online to do so; however you may get more readers in this way through people coming across your newsletter when searching the web.

■ Finally, you can produce your EN as a PDF, which is probably an over-complex way of producing and sending what is actually a simple kind of publication. Also, with PDFs people need special software in order to read them and remember too, that if you have large PDF files, or other large attachments, they may take a good deal of time to download and some ISPs limit the size of attachments that may be sent and therefore will not forward these to people.

Getting subscribers

There are various ways of getting subscribers to ENs; these include:

■ sending people emails inviting them to subscribe (avoiding 'spam' as mentioned elsewhere in this book and remembering that 'harvesting' – searching the Internet for email addresses and then collating these into a database and selling them on – is illegal in many areas)

■ having a page on your website where people can subscribe

■ asking existing subscribers to forward their issue to other people

■ buying mailing lists (an expensive option that is probably the least recommended way of building a list; also mailing lists are often out of date as soon as they are produced so a lot of wastage can occur)

■ publicising your newsletter in other people's newsletters

■ getting on a electronic newsletter-promoting directory (e.g. New-List.com)

■ offering incentives to subscribe (free reports on relevant topics can be attractive – these can be produced by you, or acquired free, or at low cost, from other sources)

■ including reference to the newsletter (and also possibly a link to your website for subscription) in your email 'signature' – the text at the bottom of emails where you give a bit of publicity and contact details for your activities). You can also mention your newsletter on your business cards and any other appropriate stationery

How to subscribe

It is important to give people the opportunity both to subscribe and to unsubscribe. Although you can rely on people just asking for a subscription, it is often better to ask them to confirm that they have requested the subscription. It is not unheard of for others to request subscriptions on behalf of people who do not want them; it is also possible for people inadvertently to subscribe to publications they do not want. By giving them the opportunity to decline – or to unsubscribe once they have subscribed – you can save problems caused by unwanted subscriptions. You can obtain software that allows you to offer subscription options – use a search engine to find the best ones for you. There are three wasy to invite subscriptions:

- The first is simply to send an email inviting people to return the email if they wish to subscribe. (It is, in any case, worth having an email 'signature' on all of your e-mails, whether to do with the newsletter or not. An email signature usually contains your name, contact details and a short message, and you can include in it details of your EN, plus a link to your website where people can find out more or subscribe.)

- The second is to invite them to go to your website and then click on the invitation to subscribe, when they will find an automated email comes up and they just have to put the word 'subscribe' in the subject line or click the 'subscribe' button.

- The third is to invite them to visit your website and complete a subscription form there.

The last of the options gives you more information about your subscribers; the other two simply give you their email address; however, setting up forms can be complex and is more of a task for potential subscribers to undertake, so you need to consider carefully which option to go for. When directing people to your website it can be useful to do it via 'deep linking', whereby they are directed to a specific subscription page within your website, rather than just the home page. And remember to include an email address on your web site so that if something goes wrong when a person is trying to subscribe, they can contact you for assistance. Finally, avoid making too many answers compulsory on your form, or you might lose some of your potential readers.

Incentives for subscribing

It can be useful to give people an incentive to subscribe to your EN. Offering a gift is one option and a simple gift is a report or an 'e-book' that can be sent to them as an attachment or that they can download from your website. You can produce such items yourself or obtain them elsewhere – many are offered free of charge on other people's websites. Another way of doing this is to invite people to request the report or e-book and, on its front page, include a form inviting the reader to subscribe to your EN through an auto-responder (an automated response mechanism for dealing with subscription requests and other similar communications). Doing this builds what is called an 'opt-in' list or a 'sub list', which is a highly targeted list of people who are definitely interested in what you have to offer.

How to send

If you have a substantial number of readers/subscribers, it is easiest to send all copies at once, by having a full list of all the subscribers which is activated as a group (to do this you can set up a mailing group which contains names of recipients – your 'help' text in your email package will give you information on how to arrange this kind of group). You have to be careful with this approach, however, as some ISPs reject multiple mailings as suspected spam. You also have to be careful to keep individual recipients' details confidential so, if you are sending multiple copies in one mailing, they should all be 'BCC' (Blind Copies, where recipients are not made aware of the identities and contact details of others receiving the newsletter) – your email software package will give you ways of doing Blind Copies. It is worth asking your own ISP what is the maximum number of recipients they will allow for a single mailing.

It is also worth using an email merge package in order to personalise your message to recipients; this requires a database in conjunction with the usual email software and you can then include subscribers' names on each individual newsletter.

Choosing an ISP (Internet Service Provider)

When producing an EN it is important to sign on with an ISP that serves your purpose. Amongst other things it is important that the ISP has a fast server-response time, will allow you to send the number of copies you require at one – or in a small number of – mailings, gives good support in case of computer breakdown and has other facilities that enable you to service a subscriber-base effectively.

Gaining additional benefits

There are various ways of using your EN to gain further benefits and one of these is to collate some of the items that have appeared in them and produce them subsequently as an e-book or a printed book. This gives the items further exposure and can generate additional income for you or your organisation. If other people have written any of the items you will have to have their agreement before incorporating them in any additional publications in this way.

Part Four
Additional Information

Chapter 20
Additional Items

In this chapter you will find some additional items that merit attention. Some of the following points refer only to the UK, so if you are elsewhere, do check what pertains in your own country.

Numbering of periodicals

There is a requirement for all published books and periodicals to have an 'official' number printed on them. This helps people find your publication if they wish to obtain copies, as it can be looked up, by its number, at places such as bookstores, and enquirers can then find out who publishes it, how often it comes out, what it costs and where it can be obtained. The numbering system for periodicals is called the ISSN – International Standard Serial Numbers. *To obtain an ISSN number, see the contact details in the resource list (Appendix 4).*

Bar coding

If your magazine becomes really successful and you are able to sell it through a wholesale distributor, or through retail outlets, it will be necessary to have a Bar Code printed on the cover. Once registered, your individual bar code can easily be originated in a number of readily available graphics programmes for use on your magazine. *See the resource list for details (Appendix 4).*

Advertising rates

In the UK, advertising rates are listed in BRAD *(see also section on advertising). To be listed in BRAD, which will help let potential advertisers know about you, see the contact details in the resource list (Appendix 4).*

Audited circulation

It is possible to have your circulation officially audited, which then gives potential advertisers a statement about how many people read your publication. It can be expensive to do this, but is likely to bring additional advertising revenue as a result. *To find out about auditing you should contact the ABC, whose details are given in the resources list (Appendix 4).*

Data protection

There are requirements about what information can be held on people and what has to be disclosed on request; some information has to be registered officially. As a magazine publisher, you may need to register if you hold personal information on people. *To find out, contact the Data Protection Office listed in the resources section (Appendix 4).*

Website

It will help your publicity, and your general image, if you have a website for your publication. A website can be set up relatively easily and the cost will depend on how sophisticated it is, who designs it for you and how often you need it changed. *For information on web design, see Appendix 4.*

Membership of professional bodies

As a publisher, you may wish to join a body that can represent your interests, provide you with information and advice, give you accreditation and so forth. The PPA (Periodical Publishers Association) is a body that can do this. The British Association of Communicators in Business is another possible body for you to consider. You may also be eligible to obtain a press pass if you are a recognised journalist or publisher and this can entitle you to entry to events you attend in a professional capacity. *Details of the above bodies may be found in the resources list, Appendix 4.*

Insurance

You should have insurance if you are in the publishing business. Some types of insurance that could be relevant are professional liability/indemnity, libel and public liability. You might also want to consider health insurance if you are producing the publication on your own and wish to have assistance with the cost of providing alternative services if you are ill and unable to work. You can get quotes for insurance from a wide range of suppliers and, if you are a member of the PPA *(see preceding paragraph),* you will be eligible for their group scheme after any specified qualifying period.

Writing and publishing skills

If you are not already a trained journalist or manager, you may need training in some specialist skills. Some areas in which you could train include:

- writing
- editing
- interviewing
- design
- PR
- sales and marketing
- finance
- website design.

The professional bodies run courses on many of these areas and you can get information on them through the contact details given in the resource list, Appendix 2.

Box number

While it is important to publish contact details for the magazine, so that contributors, advertisers and readers can find you, you may wish to have a box number rather than give a full postal address. *To find out about this, contact your local postal service.*

Legal issues

Copyright and intellectual property rights have already been mentioned earlier (Chapter 20) and, in the UK, copyright is automatically 'owned' by the author/creator of an item, unless a specific agreement is made to the contrary, but you may wish to have a statement within the magazine or newsletter re-iterating the copyright and intellectual property rights position of you as the publisher and contributors in their own right. Other legal issues that you should be aware of include contractual arrangements (what contracts, written or implied, you have with contributors, suppliers, employees and others) and libel, defamation and slander (being careful not to print, imply or say, incorrect facts about people).

UK anti-SPAM regulations

It is now a criminal offence to send spam to individuals; spam is defined as unsolicited electronic messages. The new laws came into force in the UK on

11 December 2003 and are: The Privacy and Electronic Communications (EC Directive) Regulations 2003. Statutory Instrument (SI) number 2426. Under this law, companies have to get permission from an individual before they can send emails or text messages, but the law does not cover business email addresses. (The anti-spam group 'Spamhouse' has criticised the Government for excluding work addresses in this legislation.)

Chapter 21
Summary of Key Points and Action Planning

This book has covered a range of factors involved in magazine and newsletter production. I hope it has given you some of the tools required to produce your own publication and has encouraged you to explore further the advantages and benefits of this field of activity.

In conclusion I would like to summarise what I believe are really key points and then give you a way of taking your development further:

Key Points

■ Set objectives, targets and standards and then focus your efforts on working towards them.

■ Ensure that you, and others, have clearly defined roles and activities, that skills are constantly updated and that everyone is kept informed of relevant issues and activities.

■ Set up effective systems and procedures and make sure they are monitored and reviewed.

■ Deal with problems quickly and effectively.

■ Constantly review your activities and keep developing to retain interest and results.

Action Planning

If you have found this book useful, it would be good to continue your learning and development through a personal action plan. An action plan is simple to produce and need only consist of a sheet of paper (or computer file) with a number of columns on.

■ The first column can be used to write down activities which you would like to undertake; for example, I intend to find some websites with material I can use in the magazine; I intend to read more about English usage; I intend to improve my design skills.

■ The second column can be used to associate a timescale with the activity; for example, I will undertake this over the next two weeks; I will spend a day a month on this; I will have completed this by the end of March.

■ The third column can be used to indicate any resources you need for the activity; for example, I need a budget for training; I need more time to do some reading; I need someone to give me feedback on my interviewing skills.

■ The fourth column can then be used to detail your progress and results; for example, I have added a further ten contributors to my list; I have set up files for the whole of next year's issues; I have improved communications with my team by having weekly meetings which are recorded, with each person having identified action points to deal with.

Having this kind of action plan will allow you to set goals and monitor your progress and, if you have a team of people working with you, you might like to suggest to them that this could be a helpful process for them also.

And, as a final point, I would like to tell you about two publications I came across in recent years. The first was a small, family-owned, business that started an information-based newsletter. They ran on a small budget, grew in line with their resources, produced a publication that was very unassuming in appearance and, by focussing on what their readers wanted, and needed, became extremely successful. The second was a high-profile magazine, set up by professionals, with substantial financial backing. They had a large readership base, sent out a high number of free copies, extended into various ancillary activities to complement their publishing and, within a relatively short space of time, went into receivership. There are no guarantees in publishing – it can be a risky business but, if approached sensibly – with a clear focus on satisfying readers' needs and wants and a practical concern for financial management, you can produce an excellent publication that is both highly regarded and financially rewarding. I wish you every success in your venture.

Appendix 1

Examples of Award-winning Magazines and Newsletters

The publications featured here are winners of the British Association of Communicators in Business Awards (Europe's biggest business communications competition). They are full colour publications, but appear here in black and white only. The photographs are reproduced by kind permission of Communicators in Business and Trident Photographic Services.

BOC Focus for BOC Gases

Hub Bub for Unilever Best foods

Dataday for Metering Services

The Business for BT Retail

Spirit, for GlaxoSmithKline
Values Voice, for Co-operative Insurance Society
The Magazine, for Mitchells & Butlers

'ECR Europe' for ECR Europe
'People Power' for UNIFI Communications
'Cruel Summer' for The Source, AWG
'Green card offers entry kit into National Assembly 2002' for Red Cross Life
(British Red Cross)
'The life and crimes of Brixton' for Metline (Metropolitan Police)
'Record drugs ring busted' for Portcullis, HM Customs & Excise
'How we foiled plot to kidnap Posh' for The News, News International

Appendix 2

Examples of Readers' Offers

The following offers appeared in *Effective Consulting* magazine.

READER OFFER:

WORTH £195!!!

FREE EXECUTIVE SUMMARY AND BENCHMARKING OPPORTUNITY

Readers of *Effective Consulting* and visitors to its website can get a free eight-page Executive Summary of 'Winning New Business in Management Consultancy... the Critical Success Factors' by e-mailing their name, consultancy and postal address to policypubs@kbnet.co.uk — If you'd prefer to buy the full report, send a cheque for £195 to Policy Publications, 4 The Crescent, Bedford MK40 2RU.

(There's a money-back guarantee if you return the report in resaleable condition within seven days of receipt). If you buy the report, you will be offered an opportunity to benchmark your consultancy against the others on the *Policy Publications* database confidentially and **FREE OF CHARGE, SAVING THE USUAL £195.00 FEE**.

This offer appeared in *Effective Consulting* magazine

These offers appeared in *Effective Consulting* magazine

Appendix 3

Glossary

Here is a selection of terms that are commonly used in magazine/newsletter production:

Ampersand The correct term for the character &.

Auto-responder Software that sends automated replies to messages.

Bitmap A digital image that comprises rows of dots, either square or rectangular, in a regular grid pattern.

Bleed If a background colour or image is to run right to the edge of a printed page, an additional 3mm to 5mm of image is allowed on the three sides beyond the dimensions of the page when trimmed (guillotined).

Bromide A positive image produced by an imagesetter output on white photographic paper rather than clear acetate film.

Browser A tool for reading web pages.

Bureau An independent service provider where you can send Postscript files to be output on an imagesetter.

Burning (a CD) Downloading data to a CD-R or CD-RW with a computer's CD writer function.

CD-R (Compact Disc – Recordable). A CD on which data can be stored and read.

CD-Rom (Compact Disc – Read Only Memory). Most software and clip-art will be supplied on this form of CD. You cannot download your own data onto these.

CD-RW (Compact Disc – Read Write). A CD on which data can be stored – and then can be subsequently overwritten as on a hard disk or floppy disk.

Clip-Art Graphic images, illustrations, cartoons, etc., that are available with many computer programmes; these can be purchased on CD-Rom, or obtained free on the internet.

Colour Separation Separation of colour images into the four basic colours used by colour printing machines (see CMYK).

Commercial 'A' The correct term for the character @.

Cookies A small file, held on your own computer, which can give information about your activities to the owner of another website (for example what you have previously purchased from their site).

Copy Any material supplied for articles or advertising in the magazine.

CMYK (Cyan-Magenta-Yellow-Black). The four basic colours used for printing in full colour.

Digital Printing Relatively recent technology that allows commercial printers to accept computer-generated files (such as PDFs) and enables printing without the need for intermediate filmwork or printing plates.

DPI (Dots Per Inch). A standard measurement of output resolution used by scanners etc.

DTP (Desk Top Publishing). In-house origination and printing/publishing of any documents using one's own computers, printers, etc.

DVD (Digital Video Disk). Used for recording moving images, such as films.

EPS (Encapsulated Postscript). An EPS file can be made from a variety of software and can contain comprehensive text and image information for transfer to a wide range of other software applications.

Ellipsis In typography, a row of dots thus... – used to indicate unprinted words (sometimes called 'dot leaders').

Emulsion Down See RRED.

Emulsion Up See RREU.

Filter Computer software that alters images and text to produce special creative effects.

Flatbed Scanner A device for scanning any flat original photograph, artwork, text, etc., that produces a digital image for use in a computer.

Filmwork For much commercial printing, positive or negative acetate filmwork is produced via an imagesetter in order to make the printing plates.

Folio Page number.

Font The complete set of characters, accents and symbols for any individual typeface. Serif and Sans Serif are the two main groups.

GSM (or gm2) Grams per square metre – a way of indicating the weight of paper; in the US weights are indicated in pounds, not metric measurements.

Gutter The white space between columns of text.

Halftone To give the effect of a normal (continuous tone) photograph, dots of different sizes are used to produce the printed image. For general magazine use the most common designation for such images will be a

'Screen Size' of 150 lpi (lines per inch). Very fine quality printing will use 200 lpi and some newspapers use halftones as coarse as 60 lines per inch. Colour photographs are printed using four superimposed half-tones (C + M + Y + K), each screen being at a different angle to eliminate patterning. (See also Moiré.)

Greyscale A monochrome digital image that uses 256 levels from solid black to white with 254 decreasing levels of grey in between.

Imagesetters High quality digital printers used to produce filmwork (negative or positive) and bromides, from Postscript files, for use in the production of printing plates for commercial printing presses.

Imposition Pages arranged in multiples for printing so that they are in the correct sequence when the magazine is finished. (See Printer's Pairs.)

Imprint The publisher's and printer's details (usually found near the beginning of the magazine).

ISDN (International Standard Digital Network) Special digital telephone lines for carrying data.

ISP Internet Service Provider

JPEG (Joint Photographic Experts Group) One of the most widely used formats for rapid transmission of digital image files – they can be compressed to as much as one-hundredth of their original size.

Kerning Adjusting the spacing between typeset text. This can usually be pre-set if required.

Keyline A line (usually thin) around a halftone or graphic image or patch of colour.

Leading (Pronounced 'Ledding') The spacing between lines of type – usually expressed in 'points' (See pt). This text is 9pt type that is 2«pt leaded, i.e. has an additional 2«pt space between each line of type. Its correct designation is 9pt on 11«pt Helvetica Medium – usually written as: '9/11« Helvetica Med.'

LPI (Lines Per Inch). See 'Halftone'.

Marked up copy Text that has letters or symbols written on it as instructions to printers – often from proofreaders. Some things that can be indicated in this way are whether to put letters in upper or lower case (capitals or small letters), when to indent sections of text, how to correct a typing error, when to embolden words, what size to make a heading and when to use italics.

Mechanical Data The technical information relating to the make-up and production of your magazine that is required by advertisers in order to prepare their advertisements to be compatible with your magazine.

Moiré (Prononced Mwah-ray) Poor registration, or halftone separations produced at the wrong angles, can cause the ink dots to produce visible patterning, or Moiré effect, on the printed image.

Monochrome Single colour (printing) – usually black.

Neg Negative film (clear image on a black background).

PDF Portable Document Format. An Adobe file format that allows proofs to be transferred worldwide across computer networks (and email etc.) for reference, proofing and printing.

Perfect Binding Pages are glued into a spine.

PMS Pantone Matching System. A colour-matching system widely used by designers and printers. A PMS colour swatch booklet is invaluable for reference to anyone producing printed material in colour.

Positive (Often called 'Pozzy') – positive film (black image on clear film).

Printer's Pairs A magazine's pages are printed in pairs. For example, for a simple stapled 48-page magazine, page 48 will be printed alongside page 1. On the back of this will be printed page 2 alongside page 39. Odd numbered pages will always be on the right-hand side of a pair and even numbered pages on the left.

pt (Point) Typefaces are measured in 'point' sizes. This text is set in 11pt type. The section heading is in 30pt type.

PS Postscript. The Adobe computer language that enables computer page files to be converted into the formats used by imagesetters to produce filmwork for commercial printing. (See Imagesetters.)

Rate Card A printed list of mechanical data and prices for the various sizes of advertisement in your magazine.

Registration The correct positioning of one printed colour on top of another in colour printing. Also the correct positioning of the image on the reverse of a printed sheet.

Registration Marks Cruciform and/or circular marks outside the page area which allow the printer to achieve accurate superimposition of colours on the sheet.

Resolution The amount of information that a digital image can accept and then reproduce. The higher the resolution, the greater the detail. Web images have a resolution of 72dpi. Good quality colour printing needs images to have a resolution of a minimum of approximately 300dpi (although for printing purposes, bitmap images need a resolution of approximately three times that of greyscale and CMYK).

Reversed See WOB.

RGB (Red – Green – Blue). Most flatbed scanners scan in these three colours only. These can be used for DTP, but digital images thus produced have to be converted to CMYK in a programme such as Adobe Photoshop before colour separation and commercial printing. If an RGB image is left un-converted in a file that is to be printed in full colour (CMYK), it will only reproduce as a black halftone.

RRED (Right Reading Emulsion Down). Filmwork produced with the sensitive coating that contains the image on the underside of the acetate when viewed to read correctly.

RREU (Right Reading Emulsion Up). As above but with the coating containing the image on top.

Saddle Stitching Mechanical stapling.

Scanner See 'Flatbed Scanner'.

Screen Size See 'Halftone'.

Separations The individual files or filmwork used to produce printing plates for commercial colour printing. See 'Colour separation'.

SPAM Unsolicited electronic messages.

TIF (or TIFF) Tagged Image Format File. The most commonly used format for photographs, illustrations etc. They can be used for Bitmap, Greyscale, RGB or CMYK images.

Tint A reduced strength application of any colour – always expressed as a percentage of the solid colour. (The word 'Glossary' in the heading for this section is printed in a 50% tint of black.)

Trim Marks Small lines at each corner of the printed sheet that indicate the correct place where the sheet should be trimmed (guillotined).

Twin Wire Stapled with two staples in the spine.

Typeface The manufacturer's style name for a font. This text is set in 'Garamond'; the section heading is set in 'Libre Sans Serif SSI'.

WOB White out of black (i.e. 'reversed out' lettering, where the letters appear in white on a black background).

Work-and-Turn (Or Work-and-Tumble). Printing the back and front images of a leaflet side-by-side on half the print run required, then turning the printed sheets over and printing the other side. The total quantity is achieved when the printed sheets are cut in half.

Appendix 4

Resources List

Professional bodies/membership associations

The Periodical Publishers Association (PPA) Queens House. Trade association for publishers. This organisation runs many useful courses and workshops for small magazine publishers. 28 Kingsway, London, WC2B 6JR. Tel: 020 704 4166 Fax: 020 7404 4176
Email: info1@pppa.co.uk

The Publishers Association. The leading trade organisation serving book, journal and electronic publishers in the UK. 29B Montague Street, London, WC1B 5BW Tel: 020 7691 9191 Fax: 020 7691 9199
Email: mail@publishers.org.uk Website: www.publishers.org.uk

The British Association of Communicators in Business (BACB). Suite A, First Floor, Auriga Building, Davy Avenue, Knowlhill, Milton Keynes, MD5 8ND Tel: 0870 121 7606 Fax: 0870 121 7601
Email: enquiries@cib.uk.com Website: www.cib.uk.com
Courses, conferences, publications, advice, awards, etc. Excellent short courses for those new to editing and other forms of communications. Freelance Forum from which you can source assistance, or join as a networking and support group.

UKNEPA – Newsletter and Electronic Publishers Association. An international organisation for newsletter producers.
Website: www.newsletters.org

The National Union of Journalists (NUJ). Union for those involved in publishing/writing. 308 Gray's Inn Road, London, WC1X 8DP.
Tel: 020 7278 7916 Website: www.nuj.org.uk

The Chartered Institute of Journalists. 2 Dock Offices, Surrey Quays Road, London, SE16 2XU Tel: 0207 252 1187
Email: memberservices@ioj.co.uk
Website: www.memberservices.co.uk

The Society for Editors and Proofreaders, Riverbank House, 1 Putney
   Bridge Approach, Fulham, London, SW6 3JD. Tel: 020 7736 3278
   Email: administrator@fsep.org.uk Website: www.fsep.org.uk

Other useful bodies

ISSN Agency. Wall Mead House West, Bear Lane, Farnham, Surrey, GU9
   7LG Tel: 01252 742590 Email: isbn@whitaker.co.uk
   Website: www.whitaker.co.uk/isbn.htm

Bar Coding. E Centre UK, 10 Maltravers Street, London, WC2R 3BX Tel:
   020 7655 9000 Fax: 020 7681 2290 Email: info@e-centre.org.uk
   Website: www.e-centre.org.uk

Data Protection. Office of the Data Protection Commissioner, Wycliffe
   House, Water Lane, Wilmslow, Cheshire, SK9 5AF Tel: 01625 545745.
   Email: mail@@dataprotection.gov.uk
   Website: www.dataprotection.gov.uk

BRAD (British Rates and Data). Details of advertising rates for British
   publications. 33-39 Bowling Green Lane, London, EC1R. ODA Tel:
   0207 505 8000 Fax: 0207 505 8264 Website: www.intellagencia.com

British Library. *Copies of all publications with ISBN/ISSN registrations
   should be sent here*. The Legal Deposit Office, The British Library,
   Boston Spa, Wetherby, W. Yorks, LS23 7BY Tel: 01937 546267
   Fax: 01937 546273 Email: legal-deposit-serials@bl.uk

ABC (Audit Bureau of Circulations). Certification, information and
   watchdog activities. Saxon House, 211 High Street, Berkhamsted, Herts,
   HP4 1AD Tel: 01442 870800 Fax: 01442 200700
   Email: abcpost@abc.org.uk Website: www.abc.org.uk

Plain English Campaign. PO Box 3, New Mills, High Peak, Derbyshire,
   SK22 4QP Tel: 01663 744409 Fax: 01663 747038
   Email: info@plainenglish.co.uk Website: www.plainenglish.co.uk

Trade events

The National Incentives Show. London and the National Exhibition
   Centre, Birmingham – December of each year

Training organisations

Management Magic. Pentre House, Leighton, Welshpool, Powys, SY21
   8HL Tel: 01938 553430 Fax: 01938 555355
   Email: management.magic@border.org.uk Websites: www.border.org.uk
   and www.effectiveconsultingmagazine.com Training in a range of

personal and business skills including magazine and newsletter production

Website designers
Border Management and Training. Pentre House, Leighton, Welshpool, Powys. SY21 8HL Tel: 01938 55330 Fax: 01938 555355 Email: info@border.org.uk

Survey providers
TFI Survey. Internet and paper-based surveys. 41 Green Lane, Northwood, Middlesex, HA6 3AL Tel: 01923 827095 Email: tfisurvey@btopenworld.com

Useful publications and websites
Brad (British Rates and Data). Details of advertising rates for British publications. 33-39 Bowling Green Lane, London, EC1R ODA Tel: 0207 505 8000 Fax: 0207 505 8264 Website: www.intellagencia.com

Whitaker. General resource book, with details of addresses of institutions, heads of organisations, country information, etc. Annual. Stationery Office. ISBN 011 7022 799

Willings Press Guide. Information on periodicals and newspapers, under categories, e.g. geographical areas, topics, etc. Annual. ISBN 095 089 0251

Benn's Media Guide. Similar to Willings ISBN 086 382 5079

The Handbook of Internal Communications. Edited by Eileen Scholes. Gower, 1997. ISBN 0 566 07700 0

The House Journal Handbook. Peter C Jackson. The Industrial Society, 1976. ISBN 0 85290 135 6

The Handbook of Communication Skills. Bernice Hurst. Kogan Page, 1991. ISBN 0 7494 1840 0

Making the Connections. Bill Quirke. Gower, 2000. ISBN 0 566 08175 X

Editing for Industry. Charles Mann. Heinemann, 1974. ISBN 04 349 1200X

Public relations, Writing and Media Techniques. Dennis Wilcox. Longman, 2001 (4th edition). ISBN 032 107 0143

The Economist's Style Guide. See: www.economist.com (Partly available on-line and also as a printed publication)

The Sunday Times Style Guide. See www.thesundaytimes.com

Writers' and Artists' Yearbook. A&C Black, 2003. ISBN 071 366 659 5

Keeping up the Style. Leslie Sellers. Pitman Publishing, 1975. ISBN 0 273 00075 6

English for Journalists. Wynford Hicks. Routledge, 1999. ISBN 041 517 0087

Writing for Journalists. Wynford Hicks. Routledge, 1999. ISBN 041 518 4452

Oxford Dictionary for Writers and Editors. OUP, 2000. ISBN 01986 62394

The Penguin Dictionary for Writers and Editors. Bill Bryson. ISBN 0670837679

Essential English for Journalists, Editors and Writers. Harold Evans.

The New Fowler's Modern English Usage. Edited by R W Burchfield. Clarendon Press, 1996. ISBN 0 19 869126 2

You Have a Point There. Eric Partridge. Routledge, 1978. ISBN 041 505 0758

Usage and Abusage. Eric Partridge. Penguin Reference Books, 1963. ISBN 0837 124 662

The Complete Plain Words. Sir Ernest Gowers, TSO 1987. ISBN 014 051 1997

The Synonym Finder. J I Rodale. Rodale Press (USA), 1979. ISBN 0 87857 243 0

The Concise Oxford Thesaurus – A Dictionary of Synonyms. Compiled by Maurice Waite, BCA, 2002. ISBN 0968 0453 X

The Essential Law for Journalists. Butterworths Law, 2003. ISBN 0406959498

Networking for Success. Carol Harris. Oak Tree Press, 2000. ISBN 1 86076 161 5

The New Diary Tristine Rainer and Jeremy Tarcher, 1979. ISBN 087 477 1501

Incentive Today, 3rd Floor, Broadway House, 2-6 Fulham Broadway, London SW6 1AA. Tel: 020 7610 3001 Website: www.incentivetoday.-com

New-List.com: notifies subscribers of new email lists on any topic.

Ezine-Tips.com: a source of free information for email newsletter publishers.

Government website for press releases: www.gnn.gov.uk

General web auction sites: www.ebay.com www.loot.com

Appendix 5

Guidance to Contributors

As an example of information you can provide to people who write for you, this is the guidance originally given to contributors to Effective Consulting magazine.

Effective Consulting welcomes contributions. When submitting items, please bear in mind the following guidelines:

Acceptance of all items is at the discretion of the Editor and there will be no guarantee that editorial material submitted will appear in the magazine or in any particular issue of the magazine.

Articles should be a maximum length of 2,000 words and should be original, unpublished work.

Articles should, where possible, be accompanied by a photograph of the author and any other illustrations appropriate to their topic (we can arrange for illustrations if required), plus brief biographical/promotional information on the author. Please note that if photos/illustrations are E-mailed they should be 300dpi jpg. Items sent by post will only be returned if they have labels on the reverse side with the name and address of the person supplying them.

Any materials submitted are entirely at the owner's risk.

Pentre Publications will retain copyright of all items submitted. Authors may re-use their own material which has been published by Pentre Publications on condition that, if it is republished, it is accompanied by the words: 'First published in Effective Consulting magazine'.

Any items accepted for publication may, at the discretion of the Editor, be:

- Placed in any issue of the publication

- Placed on the web or otherwise distributed electronically to subscribers

- Reprinted elsewhere (eg in monographs/collations of previously published Effective Consulting material)

There must be no pre-existing copyright restrictions on work submitted and acceptance is based on this premise.

Sources/references should be quoted wherever possible.

While every care is taken to ensure the accuracy of information published, the Editor and Publishers of Effective Consulting can accept no responsibility for loss or damage, or consequences thereof, caused by error or inaccuracy in the printing, late publication or omission of any editorial or advertising material.

All items should be submitted by E-mail to: editor@effectiveconsulting.org.uk or on disk to: Pentre Publications, Pentre House, Leighton, Welshpool, Powys SY21 8HL.

No material from Effective Consulting, may be reproduced in part, or in whole, without the written permission of the Editor.

Appendix 6

Terms and Conditions of Advertising

*Here are some examples of information you can provide to advertisers –
again from* Effective Consulting *magazine.*

Booking must be made on the appropriate booking form, unless otherwise
agreed.

Copy must arrive by the stated copy date.

Advertisements must conform to the mechanical data requirements stated
on the booking form. Any additional origination work required will be
charged for.

Advertisements must be pre-paid at the rates stated on the current booking
form, or a pro-forma invoice should be completed.

Advertisements must comply with any current statutory requirements.

Advertisements will appear in both printed and electronic versions unless
otherwise agreed.

Unless a premium position has been requested and agreed, siting of
advertisements rests with Pentre Publications.

Pentre Publications retains the right to decline, or to request amendments
to, any advertisement which, in its opinion, is unsuitable for the
publication.

The Editor and Publishers of Effective Consulting can accept no
responsibility for loss or damage caused by error or inaccuracy in the
printing, late publication or omission of any advertisement.

We will be pleased to originate advertisements to advertisers' specifications. Details are available on request.

Appendix 7

Example of advertising rates, data and production information

EFFECTIVE CONSULTING ADVERTISING RATES AND DATA:

Full page – full out (ROM): 4-colour £1,200; Spot colour £800*;
 Mono £650; Premium position +25%; *A4 with 5mm bleeds each edge. (Type area 265 x 180mm)*
Inside front cover: 4-colour £1,400; *A4 full out with 5mm bleeds.*
Back cover: 4-colour £1,500; *A4 full out with 5mm bleeds.*
Inside back cover: 4-colour £1,350; *A4 full out with 5mm bleeds.*
Half page – landscape (ROM): Full colour £800; Spot colour £550*; Mono £500; Premium position +25%; *Type area 130 x 180mm.*
Half page – portrait (ROM): Full colour £800; Spot colour £550*; Mono £500; Premium position +25%; *Type area 265 x 85mm*
Quarter page (ROM): Full colour £500; Spot colour £350*;
 Mono £300; Premium position +25%. *Type area 130 x 85mm*
Display box (mono): £50; *Type area 50 x 58mm or 35 x 84mm*
Events Diary listing (mono): £8 per event listed
All prices exclusive of VAT

For all display ads,150#, pos film rred or 300 res PDF preferred.

* Please ask for details of the spot colour available.

Special features and inserts can be incorporated; please ask for full details.

If supplying text or photographs by email for us to use in articles of advertisements, they should be supplied as follows:

Text files: In your word processing programme, if possible, save and send as RTF (Rich Text Format). Graphics: Convert colour to 'Greyscale' and save as 300dpi TIF then convert to JPG for easy email. (Black & white 'bitmap' images should be saved and supplied at a minimum of 800dpi.) **Photographs:** If to be printed mono, convert colour image to 'Greyscale' and save as 300dpi TIF then convert to JPG format for easy email.
Note: When sending graphics or photographs by email, it saves a lot of telephone time (both yours and ours) if they are converted to JPEG (JPG) format first. All advertisements (including colour can be accepted as 300 dpi pre-press PDFs. If you have any queries regarding format, please contact us for advice and additional acceptable options.

If you do not have the appropriate software or human resources, we will be pleased to put together advertisements for you for a small charge. Please contact us so that we can discuss your requirements. In general, all we will need is a rough idea of your layout concept, your text, and copies of any logos or photographs that you intend to include.

Pentre Publications, Pentre House, Leighton, Welshpool, Powys SY21 8HL
Tel: 01938 553430; Fax: 01938 555355; Email: editor@effectiveconsulting.org.uk

Appendix 8

Setting Up a Website and Electronic Discussion Group

If you are running a magazine or newsletter, it can be very helpful to have a website. This will enable you to put part, or all, of your publication on the Internet, have additional information accompanying it, interact with your readers, take subscriptions, link to other organisations, and so forth.

Before deciding on what sort of website you need, you should think about what you are going to use it for – for example, to give information only, to supply goods and services, to use as an interactive communication medium, and so on. This will determine what kind of site you need and how complicated it needs to be.

If you only require a simple website, it can be very straightforward to set up and you can probably do it yourself; for more complex requirements you will almost certainly need a specialist to help you.

If you are doing it yourself, the first thing you need to do is to get a domain name (website name or URL). You can choose almost whatever name you like (there are a few exceptions), but may find that your chosen name is already taken, so it is worth having a few options in mind. Your ISP (Internet Service Provider) will be able to register a name for you or you can do it independently.

You will then need to have your site hosted on the Internet and, again, your ISP can arrange this. If your own ISP is not able to offer you the web hosting services you require at a price you can afford, you can check out computer magazines for lists of alternative suppliers – you do not have to have the same ISP for all your computer services. The range of services, and costs, for ISPs varies a good deal, so do research this effectively – and perhaps ask other acquaintances for their advice, before deciding on one.

You will then need to have your site registered on search engines (a kind of directory enquiry service for Internet suppliers). You can do this, or you can find someone who specialises in doing this for their clients. Various things affect the ease with which potential customers can find you on the Internet, and registering with several search engines, and having Internet links to several other organisations will help the process.

If you decide to have a specialist design and register a site for you, you can look in your local newspapers, the telephone directory or computer magazines for suitable people to do the job. *See the resources list for more on this (Appendix 2).*

Once you have your website, it will need to be maintained and updated regularly and, again, this is something you can do yourself or have a specialist do for you. If you have someone do it for you there will be a cost involved, which may be high if you choose to have lots of additions or alterations on a regular basis.

You may also wish to look into the possibility of taking Internet credit card payments for your magazine or newsletter, or associated products and services and this will also involve additional cost and site complexity.

Finally, you might wish to set up an Internet discussion group – probably as a readers' forum, where readers can exchange thoughts and ideas with each other and with you. To set up a discussion group you can use one of the free Internet services that specialise in this, or you can use specialist software to put a discussion forum up on your own site.

Appendix 9

Projects on Magazine Production – for Schools and Colleges

If you are involved with students and wish to give them an interesting and practical project to do, magazine production can be an ideal choice. This section will give you some ideas on how magazine production can be used as the basis for project work.

Objectives in using magazine production as a topic

In schools and colleges, a project on magazine production can achieve a range of purposes, for example:

- developing planning, research and project management skills
- developing financial skills
- developing questioning and listening skills
- developing presentation skills
- developing writing skills
- developing design and production skills
- developing editing, proof-reading and checking skills
- developing teamworking and collaborating skills
- developing objective setting and priority management skills
- developing time management skills
- developing publicity and marketing skills
- enhancing awareness of current issues and events
- exploring local community issues and activities
- Enhancing responsibility

Working on a magazine project will give students a range of experience and develop their general abilities to relate to others, to work as part of a team, to undertake defined roles, to produce a product to agreed time and standard criteria and to use a range of skills that are invaluable in business generally.

Activities involved in projects on magazine production

Some tasks which could be set to students are the following:

- agreeing roles in the project
- choosing a name for a publication
- deciding a format and size
- producing a budget
- researching specific issues
- selecting subjects for interview
- interviewing chosen subjects
- writing articles, news items, interviews, advertisements, etc.
- creating an advertising/PR campaign
- writing up learning from the project
- making presentations on the project

There will be many other possible activities and those above are intended simply as a guide.

Topics

Some examples of suitable topics for educational projects in this area are:

- a magazine for a school or college (for example, the students' own school or college)

- a magazine for a community (for example, the local community in the students' area)

- a magazine on a specific subject (for example, woodworking, geography, computers, sport)

- a magazine on a specific issue (for example, disability, drugs, how to get a job, relationships)

Your school or college may have its own preferred topics, or students may be invited to come up with a topic of their own.

How to get started

Here are a few suggestions for getting the project off the ground:

- **Have one adult as facilitator of the project.** This person will need skills in communications, teambuilding and facilitation; if they have magazine production skills too that could be an excellent asset, as long as they do not have a rigid or out-of-date approach to the topic.

■ **Have a professional advisor/mentor to the project.** This could be a journalist, an editor, a designer, a printer or someone similar. Having this kind of input is not essential, but could be an invaluable aid, particularly if the person facilitating the project has none of these skills personally.

■ **Provide basic information and materials.** Materials needed will depend on the scope of the project. If the project is a substantial one, as many of the following should be included as is possible:
  – a copy of this book
  – a computer with software for word processing, graphics, page design, spreadsheet facilities, financial planning, a scanner and a colour printer (some of these possibly donated by local firms as a sponsorship exercise)
  – photocopying facilities
  – a cassette recorder, microphone and tapes
  – a drawing board and large sheets of paper for layout design
  – a telephone
  – a dedicated room for the duration of the project where meetings and interviews can be conducted and work materials displayed
  – printing facilities (possibly donated by a local firm as a sponsorship deal).

■ **Arrange visits to organisations such as a commercial magazine producer, a printer, a graphic design studio, a telemarketing agency.** This will give students an insight into the working conditions, technology, activities and pressures involved in magazine production. It may be that different groups could visit different places and then compare notes as part of the total exercise.

■ **Get students to keep an ongoing 'log' of activities and progress.** This will help them manage their time, record their activities and act as a base for a final report or presentation on the project as a whole. The log can be kept manually or it can be held on a computer as part of a total project management process.

■ **Arrange an end of project event.** This will give students an opportunity to present their work and to get feedback on their results. The event can act as a motivating activity and, if possible, people involved in commercial magazine production can be asked to assess the students' performance and results.

Appendix 10

Sample Press Release

PRESS RELEASE
LAUNCH OF NEW MAGAZINE
FOR INDEPENDENT MANAGEMENT CONSULTANTS

March 2001 saw the launch of 'Effective Consulting', a magazine aimed at independent management consultants. The publication is also expected to have secondary readerships of people in larger consultancy practices, internal consultants and other sole traders.

The magazine has a lively, practical focus, aiming to enhance readers' effectiveness, bring an international perspective to their activities, provide a forum for exchange of ideas and practices, present new developments and research, encourage personal networking and promote interest in, and understanding of, consultancy in its many forms.

Published bi-monthly by Pentre Publications, the magazine contains regular columns, one-off articles and special feature sections. Elements include case studies, consultancy techniques, overseas working, performance coaching, financial advice, networking opportunities, course and conference listings and much more.

The first issue contains some fascinating articles, such as how to use 'horse whispering' in leadership development, Delphi study scenarios for the consulting market, how **not** to give a presentation, the tax implications of working from home, and the impact of environmental issues on management, as well as the special feature on health and fitness which incorporates advice on health screening, exercise, nutrition and stress management.

The magazine is available on subscription at £24 for six issues (seven if readers subscribe from Issue 1). Further details, and a subscription form, may be found on the magazine's website, or from the publishers, and the whole of the first issue is also available FREE on the website at: www.effectiveconsulting.org.uk

For more information contact the Editor (Carol Harris) at: Pentre Publications,
Tel: 01938 553430; Fax: 01938 555355, E-mail: editor@effectiveconsulting.org.uk

23 March 2001
ENDS

About the Author

Carol Harris has been involved in writing, editing and publishing for many years.

Some of the magazines she has edited are:

Rapport (The Association for Neuro-Linguistic Programming)
Image (Arts Council of Great Britain)
Afghan Review (Southern Afghan Club)
Brent Goose (Brent Health District)
The Cord (Hungarian Puli Club)

She is also the publisher and editor of *Effective Consulting* magazine.

As well as magazine production, Carol has written the following books:

The Elements of NLP
NLP: New Perspectives
NLP Made Easy
Think Yourself Slim (and the Super Slimming booklet, card and tape set)
Networking for Success
Consult Yourself – The NLP Guide to Being a Management Consultant
The Trainer's Cookbook
How to be your own Management Consultant (co-author)

She has also produced the 'Success in Mind' series of audiotapes, which include:

Active Job Seeking
Creating a Good Impression
Super Slimming (plus booklet and card set)
Super Self
Handling Social Situations

Apart from her publishing activities, Carol runs an independent training and consultancy practice – Management Magic – which provides consultancy, training, coaching, mentoring and facilitation for individuals and organisations, largely based on the application of NLP (Neuro-Linguistic Programming). Prior to establishing Management Magic, she was Director of Personnel and Administration for the Arts Council of Great Britain and, for four years, Chair of the Association for Neuro-Linguistic Programming.

For more information on Carol's publications, courses and other activities, see the following websites:
www.border.org.uk and www.effectiveconsultingmagazine.com or write to: Carol Harris, PO Box 47, Welshpool, Powys, SY21 7NX or email: editor@effectiveconsultingmagazine.com

Index

If you want to know how...

- To buy a home in the sun, and let it out
- To move overseas, and work well with the people who live there
- To get the job you want, in the career you like
- To plan a wedding, and make the Best Man's speech
- To build your own home, or manage a conversion
- To buy and sell houses, and make money from doing so
- To gain new skills and learning, at a later time in life
- To empower yourself, and improve your lifestyle
- To start your own business, and run it profitably
- To prepare for your retirement, and generate a pension
- To improve your English, or write a PhD
- To be a more effective manager, and a good communicator
- To write a book, and get it published

If you want to know how to do all these things and much, much more...

howtobooks

If you want to know how ... to write a report

'In this book you will learn how to write reports that will be read without unnecessary delay; understood without undue effort; accepted and, where applicable, acted upon. To achieve these aims you must do more than present all the relevant facts accurately, you must also communicate in a way that is both acceptable and intelligible to your readers.'

John Bowden

Writing a Report
John Bowden

'What is special about the text is that it is more than just how to "write reports"; it gives that extra really powerful information that can, and often does, make a difference. It is by far the most informative text covering report writing that I have seen ... This book would be a valuable resource to any practising manager' – Training Journal

ISBN 1 85703 810 X

If you want to know how ... to make an effective presentation

'Your ability to communicate is the single most important factor in your professional tool bag. People who make a difference, who inspire others, who get promoted, are usually excellent communicators. The people who have shaped the course of history were all excellent communicators. They could move audiences, win minds and hearts and get people to take action.

The need to communicate is even greater in today's fast-changing workplace. Of all the ways you communicate, the one that gives you the greatest chance to make a powerful impact is the presentation.

This book covers all you need to know about researching your material, structuring your message and designing your visual aids, it also shows you ways to develop confidence and gives tips on how to deliver. Whether you are a novice speaker or a seasoned pro, this book will give you tips and techniques that will take you to the next level.'

Shay McConnon

Presenting with Power
Captivate, motivate, inspire and persuade
Shay McConnon

'Shay's raw talent together with his passion for the audience and his material make for a magical experience.' – *Siemens*

'His engaging style of presentation captivates his audience whatever their background or current state of motivation.' – *Director, Walkers Snack Foods*

ISBN 1 85703 815 0